ICONIC POWER

Cultural Sociology

Series Editors: Jeffrey C. Alexander, Ron Eyerman, David Inglis, and Philip Smith

Cultural sociology is widely acknowledged as one of the most vibrant areas of inquiry in the social sciences across the world today. The Palgrave Macmillan Series in Cultural Sociology is dedicated to the proposition that deep meanings make a profound difference in social life. Culture is not simply the glue that holds society together, a crutch for the weak, or a mystifying ideology that conceals power. Nor is it just practical knowledge, dry schemas, or knowhow. The series demonstrates how shared and circulating patterns of meaning actively and inescapably penetrate the social. Through codes and myths, narratives and icons, rituals and representations, these culture structures drive human action, inspire social movements, direct and build institutions, and so come to shape history. The series takes its lead from the cultural turn in the humanities, but insists on rigorous social science methods and aims at empirical explanations. Contributions engage in thick interpretations but also account for behavioral outcomes. They develop cultural theory but also deploy middle-range tools to challenge reductionist understandings of how the world actually works. In so doing, the books in this series embody the spirit of cultural sociology as an intellectual enterprise.

Jeffrey C. Alexander is the Lillian Chavenson Saden Professor of Sociology and Co-Director of the Center for Cultural Sociology at Yale University. From 1995–2010, he edited (with Steven Seidman) the *Cambridge Series on Cultural Social Studies* and from 2004–2009 (with Julia Adams, Ron Eyerman, and Philip Gorsky) *Sociological Theory*. Among his recent books are *The Civil Sphere* and *The Performance of Politics: Obama's Victory and the Democratic Struggle for Power*.

Ron Eyerman is Professor of Sociology and Co-Director of the Center for Cultural Sociology at Yale University. His areas of research include social theory, trauma, and memory, and he has taught undergraduate and graduate courses on these topics. He is the author of *The Assassination of Theo van Gogh: From Social Drama to Cultural Trauma*.

David Inglis is Professor of Sociology at the University of Aberdeen. He is founding editor of the journal *Cultural Sociology*, published by Sage. His recent books include *The Globalization of Food* and *Cosmopolitanism*.

Philip Smith is Professor and Co-Director of the Yale Center for Cultural Sociology. His recent books include *Why War?*, *Punishment and Culture*, and *Incivility: The Rude Stranger in Everyday Life* (co-authored) among others.

Interpreting Clifford Geertz
Edited by Jeffrey C. Alexander, Philip Smith, and Matthew Norton

The Cultural Sociology of Political Assassination
Ron Eyerman

Constructing Irish National Identity
Anne Kane

Iconic Power
Edited by Jeffrey C. Alexander, Dominik Bartmański, and Bernhard Giesen

Seeking Authenticity in Place, Culture, and the Self
Nicholas Osbaldiston

Reinventing Evidence in Social Inquiry
Richard Biernacki

Central Bank Independence
Carlo Tognato

Liberal Barbarism
Erik Ringmar

ICONIC POWER

MATERIALITY AND MEANING IN SOCIAL LIFE

EDITED BY
JEFFREY C. ALEXANDER,
DOMINIK BARTMAŃSKI, AND BERNHARD GIESEN

ICONIC POWER

First published in 2012 by
PALGRAVE MACMILLAN®
in the United States—a division of St. Martin's Press LLC,
175 Fifth Avenue, New York, NY 10010.

Where this book is distributed in the UK, Europe and the rest of the world,
this is by Palgrave Macmillan, a division of Macmillan Publishers Limited,
registered in England, company number 785998, of Houndmills,
Basingstoke, Hampshire RG21 6XS.

Palgrave Macmillan is the global academic imprint of the above companies
and has companies and representatives throughout the world.

Palgrave® and Macmillan® are registered trademarks in the United States,
the United Kingdom, Europe and other countries.

ISBN: 978-1-137-37596-4

The Library of Congress has cataloged the hardcover edition as follows:

Iconic power : materiality and meaning in social life / edited by
Jeffrey C. Alexander, Dominik Bartmański, and Bernhard Giesen.
    p. cm. —(Cultural sociology)
    ISBN 978-0-230-34005-3
    1. Visual perception. 2. Visualization. 3. Branding (Marketing)—Social aspects.
4. Culture. I. Alexander, Jeffrey C., 1947– II. Bartmański, Dominik, 1978–
III. Giesen, Bernhard, 1948–

BF241.I26 2011
306.4—dc23   2011025833

A catalogue record of the book is available from the British Library.

Design by Newgen Knowledge Works (P) Ltd., Chennai, India.

First PALGRAVE MACMILLAN paperback edition: December 2013

10 9 8 7 6 5 4 3 2 1

CONTENTS

Part III

Part IV

FIGURES AND TABLES

FIGURES

TABLES

PREFACE

That there could be a sociological theory of iconic consciousness, which would extend a strongly cultural sociology to material culture, was an idea percolating in discussions and publications at the Yale Center for Cultural Sociology in the second half of the first decade of the new century. When Jeff Alexander and Bernhard Giesen discovered that much the same conversation was occurring in Konstanz—an overlapping that has often been the case during their decades of collaboration—this mutual project was launched.

It began with two seminars. There was an annual master class in July 2007 at Konstanz University in Germany devoted to "the iconic turn." Jeff Alexander, Gottfried Boehm, and Hans Belting delivered a series of lectures there. Some of the key ideas of the future book were discussed in the debates that ensued, in which Giesen and his students (Werner Binder, Slobodan Karamanić) and colleagues (Valentin Rauer, Daniel Šuber) played a central role. In December 2008, there followed another workshop in Konstanz on "the iconic turn," with talks by Boehm, Alexander, and Giesen as well as Piotr Sztompka and Philip Smith, among others.

After these initial events, the idea of a dedicated volume emerged. Dominik Bartmański, whose Yale thesis was already engaging iconicity and who had been present at both conferences, joined the editorial team. Subsequently, we invited the principal participants to prepare papers for a volume, and wrote to other sociologists whom we knew were involved in this new line of investigation.

We are grateful to Kaylan Connally at Palgrave for her assistance throughout the process of preparing this volume and to Nadine Amalfi, the senior administrator at the Center for Cultural Sociology at Yale, for her invaluable editorial guidance and organizational assistance.

MATERIALITY AND MEANING IN SOCIAL LIFE: TOWARD AN ICONIC TURN IN CULTURAL SOCIOLOGY

DOMINIK BARTMAŃSKI AND
JEFFREY C. ALEXANDER

With this volume, we push the study of culture into the material realm, not to make cultural sociology materialistic but to make the study of material life more cultural. We introduce the concept of iconicity, and alongside it the idea of iconic power. Objects become icons when they have not only material force but also symbolic power. Actors have iconic consciousness when they experience material objects, not only understanding them cognitively or evaluating them morally but also feeling their sensual, aesthetic force.

The concept of icon has endured across vast stretches of time and space. It represented the sacred for medieval churchgoers a millennium ago and remains central to the technical discourse of computer users today. This extraordinary continuity is not merely casual or linguistic, nor is it a response only to aesthetic need. It has to do, rather, with the cultural structure of iconicity and the kinds of social performances that icons allow to be projected and played.

Whether functioning aesthetically as a pictorial representation of a holy figure (transcendental intelligence) or as a broadly conceived visual interface of a virtual reality (artificial intelligence), icons fulfill the same social role, that of "passing on commandments which are encoded elsewhere to people who are ignorant of the code" (Heidenreich 1998: 85). Theologians and programmers alike are guardians of arcane scripts, codexes that contain intricate information that establishes meanings, directs how things should be run, and dictates which of the script's messages should be made into tangible and visible symbols that are publicly available to believers and users. Medieval Christians and contemporary computer users are equally "illiterate" (Heidenreich

1998: 82; Binder, this volume, pp. 101–102). They have neither invented nor can cognitively understand the scripts according to which the key ritual and strategic actions of their communities are performed. Yet, while they can hardly discuss these arcane meanings, let alone alter them, they can experience and make use of their aesthetic-material representation: iconic forms enable them to live not only an effective but a meaningful collective life.

Icons allow members of societies (1) to experience a sense of participation in something fundamental whose fuller meaning eludes their comprehension and (2) to enjoy the possibility for control despite being unable to access directly the script that lies beneath. Icons are cultural constructions that provide believer-friendly epiphanies and customer-friendly images. There is, then, a historical continuity of cultural orders. The icon has proven to be a powerful and resilient culture structure, and a container for sacred meanings, long after Friedrich Nietzsche announced the death of god.

There is a strong predilection for societies to naturalize their processes of cultural construction. This provides anxious human beings with a sense of ontological security and legitimates ongoing social arrangements, obscuring the arbitrary and constructed nature of social categories. Our aim in this volume is to reverse this process; we wish to denaturalize iconic power. While the contributions are variegated in message, subject, and disciplinary scope, they broadly agree on how iconic processes subtly work. Iconicity is about the interaction of surface and depth. What we experience phenomenologically is a sensible material *surface* that generates its own aesthetic power. This is what Gottfried Boehm, in reference to iconic images, calls the "iconic difference": the aesthetic power generated by the sensual surface of an icon cannot be reduced to what that iconic surface means in the representational sense. At the same time, however, for a material substance to become iconic, its aesthetic surface must, at one and the same time, stand for an invisible discursive *depth* (Alexander 2008). Icons are aesthetic/material representations, yes, but they are also signifiers of the ideationally and affectively intuited signified. In other words, their concrete materiality points beyond itself to the elusive but very real domains of feeling and thought.

It is, paradoxically, precisely because of this ideational duality that icons are practical. Icons provide an aesthetic contact with encoded meanings whose depth is beyond direct ratiocination. Iconicity consists in retrieving, activating, and articulating the depth of the signified by introducing it to the realm of immediate sensory experience, connecting discursive meaning with the perceptual and palpable. Such material conversion is a kind of reduction, or condensation (Alexander 2010b). In such an aesthetic and sensuous compression of meaning, a certain symbolic subtlety is surely lost, but something of great pragmatic import is definitely gained. Iconic compression allows meanings "portability," assuring their citational quality (Bartmański 2011). The semiotic durability of the icon distinguishes it vis-à-vis other cultural elements of social life.

Contemporary icons occupy a wide range of cultural registers. Conventionally, they are associated with visual emblems, from evocative sculptures, paintings, and architectural constructions to sublime scenes from nature, yet the sensuous surface effects of contemporary icons actually range much more widely, to popular songs, quintessential consumer products, brands and logos, celebrities, and perfumes that evoke lust. It is because they galvanize narratives that icons are not only aesthetic representations but also become full citizens of public discourse. In the iconosphere of society, the meanings of social life take on sensual form, whether by sight, hearing, touch, taste, or smell.

Iconic representations are intrinsic to the struggles of politics, war, and revolution (Binder, Bowler, and Bartmański, this volume), but also to the placid events of everyday life (Woodward and Ellison, Sonnevend, Rauer, this volume). The iPod, for example, is a domesticated icon that evokes latent myths and provides a powerful experience of immediacy in an increasingly mass mediated and seemingly mechanistic world (Bull 2007: 2). So was the Citroen car famously deconstructed by Roland Barthes (2001: 88–90). In the same manner, assembly-line automobiles can be turned into what Dick Hebdige (1987: 73) calls "beautiful one-offs." Describing his neighbor's intense attachment to a Ford Thunderbird, Hebdige wrote about "turning a sign into an icon." Such transformations of discursive into material reality occur all the time. Icons allow us to experience meaning sensuously, and to "control and manage" our experience at the same time (Bull 2007: 4).

The theory of iconicity provides a useful corrective to conventional understandings of capitalist commodification. Because social theory has preferred the trope of disenchantment over totemism, it has either disregarded or stigmatized the metaphorical and emotional power of economic objects. Regarding the relation of objects and humans, contemporary thinkers have become blind to powerful processes of iconicity or stigmatized them within Marxist cultural critique. Even when intellectuals choose to "reconsider" Walter Benjamin's insistence that capitalism eliminates sacrality, for example, they talk about "uniqueness without aura" (Virno 2008: 32). We suggest that it is sociologically more productive to document and theorize the reverse, namely how iconic aura continues to inhabit nonunique items, whether we like it or not.

Societies organize the empirical avalanche of facts into patterns, classes, and types to overcome cognitive saturation and effectively navigate reality. This is an inductive move from the atomistic to the general, from the empirical to the theoretical. Once constructed, however, these types must be exemplified and classified in turn. Iconic archetypes are one of the cultural bits that do this job, embodying meaning aesthetically and allowing a deductive move from the theoretical back to the empirical once again. This circling back and forth between the concrete and the theoretical, the mundane and the aesthetic, the fragment and the icon sits at the core of culture.

But icons exist not only in the *re-* mode—representing, reflecting, refracting. They are also actants, seeming to possess volitional qualities relative to human ways of being (see Kurasawa, Giesen, this volume; also Pels, Hetherington, and Vandenberghe 2002, and Latour 1993). Jean Baudrillard (2001) writes about the "seduction" of appearances, W. J. T. Mitchell (2005) about "what pictures want from us," Boehm about iconic difference. An iconic signifier does not just "communicate" the information of the signified; material surfaces do not simply represent hidden data. Communication as a cognitive conveyor belt is not privileged here. Icons transmit experience. They have their "social life" (Appadurai 1986) whereby they can accomplish anything from symbolizing "the eschatological hopes for salvation" (Alexander 2010a: 323) to "forging a communal sense of continuity" in the liquid times of late modern transformations (Bartmański 2011: 213). They inspire and invite us to interact with them. Iconic meaning emerges from embodied, sensual impressions, from emotional immersion in the sensual object that confronts us as a thing.

In the history of societies, iconicity in its visual form has often been fervently opposed by moralistic "iconoclasts" who denigrate vision and suppress images. But this has only served to confirm the icon's unique status. No matter how fiercely suppressed, for iconic power there is always an "eternal return."

In the history of social science, icons have not so much been opposed as simply ignored or downplayed. Celia Lury (1998) describes images as the "absent presence" of sociology, and Michael Emmison and Philip Smith (2000) refer to them as an "overlooked domain." The founders of critical social theory, from Karl Marx to Max Weber and Walter Benjamin, have insisted too much on disenchantment. We need to look much more to Émile Durkheim's notion of totemism if we are to capture the enduring parameters of material symbolism and the role materiality plays in social classification and boundary making. The French founder of cultural sociology insisted that "collective feelings become fully conscious of themselves *only* by settling upon external tangible objects" (1995: 421). With this volume, we build upon this classical insight, connect it with contemporary currents in cultural sociology and aesthetic philosophy (see Boehm, Belting, and Giesen, this volume), and demonstrate how a theory of iconic power can be put to work in an explanatory way. We suggest that iconicity allows us to see enchantment as a continuing presence despite tremendous historical change.

Iconic power stems from a mutually constitutive (horizontal), not a hierarchical (vertical) relationship between aesthetic surface and discursive depth. It emerges from their mutual contact, not as a causal sequence but as an intertwining. The logocentrism of modern Western culture (Jay 1994) has downplayed the visual surface, maintaining that it is preceded by depth and, therefore, merely reflects it. Postmodern theory inverts this thesis, downplaying discursive meaning and giving priority to the physicality of surface. Sheer presence (Moxey 2008) and appearance (Baudrillard 2001), the icon becomes an agent of seduction, a purely material actor capable of constituting social audiences on its own terms. If logocentrism unduly represses the surface, postmodern thinkers go too far the other way. Their stance runs the risk of being iconoclastic *à rebours*. Identifying meaning with discourse and reason, and presence with image and emotion, postmodern theory reproduces the old dualisms instead of reconfiguring them.

In this volume, we present iconic power as a bridging theory. Meanings can take nonverbal, nondiscursive forms, and when meanings attach themselves to these forms, they assume not only moral and cognitive but also affective and sensual effects. Meaning and presence, discourse and aesthetics, reason and affect are symbiotic, not mutually exclusive. As Richard Shusterman suggests, "surface and depth are essentially connected complementarities"; "reciprocal in function, they form the fullness of the aesthetic form" (2002: 3). Public discourses, for example, would not be the same without images (Lakoff and Johnson 2003). The enduring presence of visual metaphors in language attests to the fact that the seen profoundly affects the said. On the other hand, the very fact that we provide pictures with captions and try to verbalize even the most powerful iconic experiences—via such expressions as "ineffable"—underlines the irreducible efficacy of language in making experience intersubjective and thus truly social. It is the feedback between the two that matters (Bartmański, Šuber and Karamanić, Sonnevend, this volume). We need such investigations as the *Empire of Meaning* (Dosse 1999) but also such explorations as the *Empire of the Senses* (Howes 2005).

Barthes (1978: 36) suggests that the distinction between the symbolic carrier and the symbolized is "operational" rather than concrete, Claude Lévi-Strauss (1966: 20) that "intension and extension of some signs are not two distinct things." Analogically, sometimes an icon *is* what it stands for, even if it is also more besides. To speak of such entwinement is not to deny that iconic surfaces often appear to have power and meaning in themselves, and that aesthetic surfaces can, indeed, have independent, pragmatic, and material social effect. It is precisely this autonomy of the surface that relativizes the traditional dualism of signifier and signified. The Berlin Wall was a symbol of communist oppression, and also, by virtue of its purely physical form, a material vehicle for repression; it was a perfect material synecdoche of that divisive oppression (Bartmański, this volume). Yet, it would hardly be correct to suggest that, when the wall fell, the German Democratic Republic (GDR) collapsed too. Deep meanings and their material iconization are closely intertwined, but they are not the same. Che Guevara presents a related, if subtly different case. His material form not only symbolized revolution but also—as its powerful aesthetic embodiment—worked to bring it about. For this reason, killing the living person Che Guevara may have helped prevent the outbreak of revolution in a particular time and place. It did nothing, however, to inhibit the expansive iconic representation of revolution in "Che's" material form; in fact, it did everything to inspire it.

Boehm (1994, and this volume) first conceived iconicity in its philosophical form in the 1990s. Mitchell promoted "iconology" in the 1980s and has, for several decades, been attacking iconoclasm and pointing to an emerging "pictorial turn" (1986, 1995). These ambitious theoretical projects in the humanities strenuously evoke the idea of iconic power that does not just bring one more new object of sociological investigation into view. To appreciate the iconic, they suggest, is to think about social construction differently, broadening sociological epistemology in an aesthetic way. Two decades ago, David Hiley, James Bohman, and Shusterman (1991: 1) already observed that "it is now popular to mark shifts in philosophical method and preoccupation as 'turns,'" suggesting that dramatic intellectual shifts involve asking new sets of questions, adopting new research techniques, rescaling perspectives, and refocusing attention. The iconic turn in cultural sociology will involve all of these things.

THIS VOLUME

We organize the contributions that follow into four sections. This division is heuristic and does not mean to suggest a logical progression. It seeks, rather, to reveal the contexts and dimensions of iconological inquiry.

The two chapters in the first section make a series of programmatic statements. While each essay addresses empirical problems, the principal aim is to discuss the conceptual apparatus of iconology and to provide broad intellectual contexts within which iconological questions can be tackled. One of the opening questions that Boehm asks confronts squarely the issue of connections between the aesthetic and social aspects of iconicity: Does the power of images belong to a history of taste or to the sociology of audience? Boehm argues that in order to answer this question, one must return to the hard business of clarifying what "representation" is. It is not, according to Boehm, simply about restoring the absent it stands in for, but rather about intensifying it. Representation defines itself by its own boundaries, symbolic and tactile, introducing the "iconic difference," an idea that later appears in chapters by Werner Binder, Valentin Rauer, and Bernhard Giesen. Representation is a "performance of presentation," which not only marks space but introduces temporality. Boehm explains that the physical presence of images allows repeated performance; we can return to see them and thus be reminded of all the meanings with which they are associated. At once stable and portable, images look back at us, and in doing so shed light on the meaning of absence. The visible and the invisible, seen and imagined, constitute each other through endless feedback. In the end, Boehm argues, a science of the nexus of representation-presentation-presence is necessarily a science of performance and experience. This realization transcends traditional boundaries between disciplines and philosophical discourses.

The categories of performance and experience are central to Jeffrey C. Alexander's iconology as well. His main concern is to disclose the constructedness of iconic representations. He observes that the material, humanly molded elements of social life get routinely naturalized as self-evident "things," that is, they are taken for granted as mere objective, external "stuff." Economic efficiency may require and reward such objectification, but it conceals the cultural dimension of materiality. When we succumb to such a vision, we become victims of materialism. Alexander argues that even in its enlightened forms, such as Marxism, materialism severely circumscribes our sociological vision. It blinds us to the significance of the dialectic of sensual surface and intangible depth, reducing objects to mere commodities, and enchantment to fetishism. Instead of materialism, we need to embrace *materiality*, understanding it as a constitutive, symbolic part of sociability. Icons are central entry points to this empirical realm. While his theory of totemism provides an opening, Durkheim himself actually had precious little to say about the aesthetic dimension. By paying more attention to the formal qualities of aesthetic surfaces and to socially constructed circumstances of reception, Alexander shows why iconic objects do not matter equally and why a single object varies in its iconic power. Like Boehm, Alexander sees icons as agentic, relatively autonomous performers. As a sociologist, however, he expands the context of the production and reception of images beyond the question of their aesthetic power to their critical mediation by independent institutional and interpretive power.

Both theorists featured in the first part of the book see iconicity as an emergent quality associated with a series of invisible accretions, performative mediations, and particular temporal structures. The relations between these dimensions are unraveled in greater detail in the case studies gathered in parts 2 and 3.

The second part of the book begins its business where the first leaves off. The contributors look at bundles of visual and linguistic factors that seem to produce the emergent quality of iconicity. News icons rather than artistic creations are the center of attention here. But they are treated as portals to the relevant social processes, not as end points of iconological pilgrimage.

Interpretations of such images inevitably take us beyond the surface of *pictures* to the surfaces and depths of *events*, to singular bodies and powerful crowds, sights and sites, built structures, and symbolically constructed narratives. The subject matter the authors address might be old wine, but they provide new bottles constructed from iconic theory. It is precisely the new prism of iconicity through which the effects of shocking and euphoric events that seem well known can be explained in full. In each author's investigation, visuality figures directly in the creation and distribution of collective effervescence. If icons are indeed stars of the social universe, then sociological analysis provides lenses through which we can better see them. With the theory of iconic power, we can make use of the light of "social stars" to learn new things about the social universe as such.

In his chapter "Iconspicuous Revolution: Culture and Contingency in the Making of Political Icons," Dominik Bartmański revisits the European icons of the euphoric year of 1989 and asks what constitutes a powerful iconic fact. Specifically, he explains why the fall of the Berlin Wall emerged as the icon of 1989 and has retained this symbolic status ever since. The answer is not obvious. The year 1989 was full of epochal events and important figures busy making history. Especially the earlier, politically unprecedented changes in Hungary and Poland had opened up a revolutionary space in which such events like the fall of the wall became possible. And yet they have not attained the same lasting influence on the international audiences. To reconstruct this phenomenon is to tell a story about how the iconic can trump the political. By demonstrating what counts in public perception as "revolutionary," "political signal," and "beginning" and "end" of a social process, Bartmański shows the role that iconicity plays in constituting these key categories and thus in structuring our ability to notice, understand, and remember events. He argues that it is precisely the iconic power of events that turns them into "objective," temporal markers of history.

In the very different context of Russian famine in the early 1920s, Fuyuki Kurasawa continues the project of "denaturalizing what have become self-evident representational conventions." Focusing on the news images of that horrendous event, Kurasawa systematically explores what he terms "regimes of [visual] typification." He explains why certain images were powerful enough to constitute large sympathetic audiences, and how it was that viewers of these famine images initiated one of the first-ever global humanitarian actions. Connecting visual regimes to what Luc Boltanski and Laurent Thévenot call "orders of worth" (2006), Kurasawa demonstrates that these icons of famine are actants, hardly reducible to operations of institutional networks. It was the iconic evocation of collective sentiments rather than instrumental and normative arguments that were decisive in motivating subjects to move beyond a casual sense of pity. Kurasawa shows that, if visual images are sustained by performative work, icons of distant suffering make ignorance and lack of empathy a deeply moral problem, not just a cognitive or emotional issue.

Shocking occurrences can become foundational tragic events, to use Kurasawa's term, in various ways. Wendy Bowler takes up the most iconic tragedy of the last decade, the terrorist attack on New York's World Trade Center, and examines the role of iconic representations. Like Bartmański and Kurasawa, Bowler begins with high-profile visual media representations, viewing them as entry points to an event's tragic narration. Using the analytic grid of Nietzsche's philosophy, she examines how mass media representations of 9/11 seemed to lose the "feeling of reality." As iconic images of events became "detached from the underlying flow of narrative," viewers of the event experienced emptiness, a dark void captured by earlier classical paintings of religious apocalypse.

In the chapter following, Binder puts yet another spin on the iconic constitution of cultural and political shock. Interpreting the cultural structuring of the Abu Ghraib scandal, Binder formulates a formal criteria for the emergence of what he calls "secular icons." Here we approach the notion of icon as sacred text for the "illiterate." Binder argues that iconicity is increasingly significant in the multilingual, globalized, late-modern world, one that has ostensibly lost its grand (verbal) narratives. Not unlike Kurasawa, he demonstrates that iconic performances, and not only deliberative actions, can effectively constitute international communities of moral indignation and political outrage.

The third section further specifies and systematizes the parameters of iconicity. Here not only events and their primarily pictorial meanings are explored but also things and gestures. If iconicity unfolds between communication and experience, under what conditions do these modes of interaction remain powerful in actual social situations? Can there be one without the other? Do they constrain or enable each other?

In "Shifting Extremism," Daniel Šuber and Slobodan Karamanić investigate the communicative and experiential aspects of iconicity within the postsocialist mediascape of Serbia. Drawing on Régis Debray's mediology and on Michel Foucault, they delineate the complex relations between the visual and the political by reference to street art and graffiti. Here the definition of the pictorial is expanded to include gestures and visual performances in the public space of cities. Šuber and Karamanić demonstrate how aestheticization can increase state power, and how, in times of social crisis, iconic symbols attain an almost existential relevance. They also explain how, in the Serbian crisis, particular iconic constellations shifted from the peripheries of political culture to the national center.

In "Visualization of Uncertainty," Rauer continues to adjudicate between communication and experience. Just as icons can crystallize, concretize, and strengthen a sense of belief in certain values, they can also underline uncertainty. To the extent that imagined communities possess their own imagined material constructions, the threat to these icons can bring them face-to-face with what Rauer calls "imagined risks." Because the general public can neither gain direct access to, nor rationally comprehend complex diagnoses of social and natural crises, they need iconic shortcuts. Rauer asks how people perceive the social reality beyond formally and linguistically defined states of affairs. He interrogates visual representations of statistical data that form the body of popularly accessible sociological knowledge in Western media. In contemporary Western societies he finds that visuality continuously "interferes" with discursive rationality, and often in a productive and fruitful way.

Ian Woodward and David Ellison look at Australia's most famous wine brand, the Grange, in order to substantiate the claim that an icon is the "concretization" of complex culture structures. In contrast with the following chapter by Smith, however, Woodward and Ellison draw attention to the role of iconicity in creating consensus, whether in markets, culture, or politics. Iconic power makes it possible "to endure cultural changes and generate changing meanings across multiple cultural times and spaces." The Grange became an iconic product, not only of a specific industry but also of an imagined national community—the Australians. Woodward and Ellison suggest that Durkheim's totemism explains the meanings of such iconic commodities in a way that Marx's theories could not. Rather than the seeming irrationality and emptiness of commodity fetishism, commodities can "apotheosize" whole classes of aesthetic-cum-moral sensations and feelings.

The third part concludes with Smith's comparative investigation of how iconicity contributes to collective effervescence, if not euphoria, and its divisive capacity. In juxtaposing two very different music festivals, the American Woodstock and the German Bayreuth, Smith shows how the iconicity of both events is informed by charismatic myths and narratives. But the latter are only conditions of possibility. To achieve iconicity, each event also had to establish itself as controversial, not only discursively but visually, which meant dividing large audience communities into diametrically opposed camps of supporters and antagonists. According to Smith, an iconic event visualizes collective feelings via congregations of bodies and assemblies of images and discourses. Icons are cultural performers that, under propitious conditions, can define and crystallize cultural cleavages. As icons include, they may also exclude, which is why "the cultural trajectories of building bridges and building iconicity might at the end of the day be asymptotic."

The final part groups contributions that will return readers' attention to various conceptual rather than empirically delimited issues. It opens with a probing essay by Hans Belting that engages art historical understanding to illustrate the complexities of surface/depth relations. Understanding images not as passive reflections but as active performers that "reciprocate" our looks, Belting calls for a revision of the categorical distinction between the beholder and the beheld. Belting problematizes a series of traditional analytical divides, such as human look versus material image, mental/internal versus medium/external, deficient body versus powerful prosthetic media. Instead, we can profit from seeing images as constituted by acts of looking and bodies as sites of artificial images. Objects, such as masks, may intensify the performative actions of bodies. Both are performers. Body is a living medium, a living image, and also a repository of images.

In the wake of the German tradition exemplified by Belting's meditation, the essay by Giesen provides more general arguments for the claim that emerges independently out of several studies of this volume: iconic power is an "identity-forging power." Giesen suggests that the question of some collective identity is always at the core of the iconic image, engaging with artistic practices from Giorgio Vasari to Joseph Beuys, and from Sandro Boticelli to Max Ernst and René Magritte. Focusing on the cultural iconicity of actual works of art, Giesen describes paintings as entities capable of marking the transitory stage between the "natural presence" of immediate appearance and the artificiality of purely conventional links between signifying image and referent. He then interprets the figure of the artist him- or herself, that is, the body and mind of a creator, as an icon of heightened subjectivity. In this context, Giesen examines iconic representations of seduction. Iconicity is a mode of enchantment that, according to him, must be taken on its own terms if we are to understand how both early- and late-modern visual representations maintain social bonds.

Julia Sonnevend generalizes such instances of iconicity as visual seduction or commercial enchantment as a "ritual meeting with images." If Boehm and Belting are right that iconic pictorial "performers" look back at us, then encountering them is more like "meeting" than anything else. Moreover, if it is indeed the case that rituals continue to structure modern societies because these societies remain fundamentally committed to performative meaning making (Alexander 2004), then such a meeting with icons is amenable to ritualistic, not just strategic enactments and transformations. But while ritual is one possible outcome of iconic encounters, other less immediate, powerful, and all embracing reactions are also possible. Sonnevend insists that the encounter between actor and iconic image is actually highly mediated. She looks at the contingent effect of the construction of the iconic surface, of the spatial architecture that sets the scene for iconic encounters, of how the presence of others affects iconic contact, and of the ineffable "chemistry" that affects whether we experience an encounter as powerful right now.

Finally, Piotr Sztompka in his chapter "Visible Meanings" places icon and iconicity in the genealogy of related sociological metaphorics that have sparked the imagination of thinkers and societies alike. While Sztompka emphasizes communication more than experience, he evokes the "iconic imagination" as an important new concept for studying social life. He emphasizes that this visual imagination has been fueled by the epochal tool of photography, which has turned the cultural tables of the world. More than just a documenting device or an instrument of aestheticization, photography is a tool for the training of "visual imagination." It has allowed social actors to become gradually more conscious of their surroundings and more aware of the ways the surfaces and depths of social life are intertwined.

In concluding this review of the contributions, we must respectfully demur from our coeditor Bernhard Giesen (Afterword). We find that the contributors to this volume share a broad understanding about the nature of the iconic and how it sociologically works. They give attention both to aesthetic surface and discursive depth. The formal logic of aesthetic images and objects is a matter of continuous interest in virtually every contribution, even as the contributions attend to social conditions and discursive effects. The lay equation of icon with discursive preeminence is a mistake that the contributions to this volume rarely make; the iconic is almost always reserved for only those discursive meanings that also have aesthetic and sensual force.

This is not to suggest, however, that these pioneering contributions to a cultural sociology of iconicity have arrived at a thoroughgoing consensus. Until now, sociology has evidenced hardly any concern for iconicity. This volume marks what we hope will be the beginning of a conversation, and many questions remain. One point of disputation is, indeed, whether the iconic should be reserved for visual images or whether it can be expanded to the surface and depth intertwinements whose aesthetic impact relies on the other four senses as well. Another unresolved issue is whether the iconic theory applies to mundane material aesthetics or should be reserved for signs that declare themselves in a more decidedly auratic and ritualizing way. If icon does become an important idea in sociology, it will certainly remain a contested concept.

At this time, however, icon is most definitely not regarded as among the key concepts of social science. The nested ideas of icon, iconic power, iconosphere, and iconology have not only been neglected but also deeply misunderstood by the Western intellectual tradition. Part of this unfortunate story is that icons have been conceived as superficial, deceptive, and ultimately even as socially dangerous. Iconic power seems to have scared intellectuals, even as, most of the time, it inspired the ordinary masses of people. Ironically, those who first explicitly thematized the constitutive aspects of iconic power—as fetish, enchantment, and aura—predicted its downfall with modernity, preferring normative criticism to analytic exploration of epistemic cultures.

Our volume challenges this prediction, offering sociological models of strong and vibrant iconicity and showing how a theory of iconic power provides new explanations of taken-for-granted social facts. Marshall Sahlins (2000: 12) has warned that "all functionalizing arguments bargain away actual content for presumed effect, what culture is for what it does, thus giving up of what we know about it in order to understand it." Such a move "forecloses any serious interest in the *ways* different peoples have meaningfully constructed their existence" (italics ours). To explore the iconic way of constructing meaning is the aim of this volume.

REFERENCES

Alexander, J.C. 2004. "Cultural Pragmatics: Social Performance Between Ritual and Strategy." *Sociological Theory*, 22(4): 527–573.

———, 2008. "Iconic Experience in Art and Life: Surface/Depth Beginning with Giacometti's 'Standing Woman.'" *Theory, Culture and Society* 25 (5): 1–19.

———. 2010a. "The Celebrity-Icon." *Cultural Sociology* 4(3): 323–336.

———. 2010b. "Iconic Consciousness: The Material Feeling of Meaning." *Thesis Eleven* 103 (1): 10–25. (First published in *Environment and Planning* 2008, 26: 782–94).

Appadurai, A. ed. 1986. *The Social Life of Things: Commodities in Cultural Perspective.* Cambridge: Cambridge University Press.

Barthes, R. 2001. *Mythologies*. New York: Hill and Wang.

———. 1978. "Rhetoric of the Image." In: *Image, Music, Text.* Translated by Stephen Heath. New York: Hill and Wang.

Bartmański, D. 2011. "Successful Icons of Failed Time: Rethinking Post-communist Nostalgia." *Acta Sociologica*, 54(3): 213–231.

Baudrillard, J. 2001. *Selected Writings*. Stanford: Stanford University Press.

Boehm, G., ed. 1994. *Was ist ein Bild?* [What is an image] Munich: Wilhelm Fink Verlag.

Boltanski, L., and L. Thévenot. 2006. *On Justification: Economies of Worth.* Princeton, NJ: Princeton University Press.

Bull, M. 2007. *Sound Moves: iPod Culture and Urban Experience.* London and New York: Routledge.

Dosse, F. 1999. *Empire of Meaning: The Humanization of the Social Sciences.* Minneapolis and London: University of Minnesota Press.

Durkheim, É. 1995. *The Elementary Forms of Religious Life.* Translated by Karen E. Fields. New York: Free Press.

Emmison, M., and P. Smith. 2000. *Researching the Visual.* London: Sage.

Hebdige, D. 1987. "The Impossible Object: Towards a Sociology of the Sublime." *New Formations,* 1: 47–76.

Hiley, D. R., J. F. Bohman, and R. Shusterman, eds. 1991. *The Interpretive Turn: Philosophy, Science, Culture.* Ithaca: Cornell University Press.

Jay, M. 1994. *Downcast Eyes: The Denigration of Vision in Twentieth-Century French Thought.* Berkeley: The University of California Press.

Lakoff, G., and M. Johnson. 2003. *Metaphors We Live By.* Chicago: The University of Chicago Press.

Latour, B. 1993. *We Have Never Been Modern.* Cambridge: Harvard University Press.

Lury, C. 1998. *Prosthetic Culture: Photography, Memory and Identity.* London and New York: Routledge.

Mitchell, W. J. T. 1986. *Iconology. Image, Text, Ideology.* Chicago: The University of Chicago Press.

———. 1995. *Picture Theory: Essays on Verbal and Visual Representation.* Chicago: The University of Chicago Press.

———. 2005. *What Do Pictures Want? The Loves and Lives of Images.* Chicago: The University of Chicago Press.

Moxey, K. 2008. "Visual Studies and the Iconic Turn." *Journal of Visual Culture.* 7 (2): 131–46.

Pels, D., K. Hetherington, and F. Vandenberghe. 2002. "The Status of the Object. Performances, Mediations, and Techniques." *Theory, Culture and Society.* 19 (5/6): 1–21.

Sahlins, M. 2000. *Culture in Practice.* New York: Zone Books.

Shusterman, R. 2002. *Surface and Depth: Dialectics of Criticism and Culture.* Ithaca: Cornell University Press.

Virno, P. 2008. "Three Remarks Regarding the Multitude's Subjectivity and Its Aesthetic Component." In *Under Pressure. Pictures, Subjects, and the New Spirit of Capitalism,* edited by D. Birnbaum and I. Graw. Berlin: Sternberg Press.

PART I

CHAPTER 1

REPRESENTATION, PRESENTATION, PRESENCE: TRACING THE HOMO PICTOR

GOTTFRIED BOEHM

THE IMAGE AS FACT AND ACT

Cultural practices related to images have always been both about craftsmanship and about the domestication of powers assigned to images. We were concerned with the mysterious *effects* of images way before we started to celebrate the genius and glory of *artists*. This is supported by ethnological and archaeological findings as well the history of religion. Myths, fairy tales, and stories of living and punitive images also give way to the reconstruction of old assessments. If we take these sources literally, they seem to conceive of images in analogy to living beings: they attribute something like a "power spirit," emanation, and charisma to the physical body of the artifact. And, not least, they seem to endow images with the ability of a benevolent or vicious look. These kinds of images were respected, revered, or even feared.

The recurring iconoclastic attacks on images and the accompanying criticism of images were not able to render the discourse of the power of images obsolete. An enlightened audience will no longer permit itself to be frightened by living images, and it takes a Mozart to make the intervention of a stone guest appear acceptable. But the same audience is captivated by the magic of magnificent paintings and speaks about the paintings' unique, more-than-physical "presence" (German: *Präsenz*). The linguistic usage is vague, but "presence" seems to mean something else than mere physical "being-at-hand," (*Vorhandenheit*); it describes an enhanced presence (*Gegenwart*) of the image, which reaches beyond historical, referential, or documentary functions. It is certainly correct to assume that individuals have a psychological need for these kinds of attributions. The long history of art and taste gives an account of the swaying and even downfall of several types of assumptions about "presence." Does the power of images belong to a history of taste or to a sociology of public audiences? The fact that individuals endow images with living presence cannot shift the notion of presence away from our reflection about images. Even if we deem images not only as facts but also acts, as meaning-making objects, we will get back to the relationship between presence and representation. As Georges Didi-Huberman (1992) demonstrated, it is not just the finding of psychology but also of meta-psychology that something we look at, also looks back at us. When the viewer experiences the presence of the artwork, she is experiencing a being-there (*Dabeisein*) in an emphatic sense. This is beyond a subjective sentiment or a projection of mere preconceptions. Nothing constrains her experience of being completely taken in. The phenomenology of experiencing images provides us with many hints that it is "presence" that opens up the experience and not the mere decision of the person who absolutely *wants* to see. This holds true even more if we do not reduce images to a secondary status in which they merely repeat in visual or tangible form what was already expressed by cognitive means in a better and more verifiable way. Treating images as representations marks a factual and theoretical buffer zone (*Schonstufe*), which allows no one to approach the phenomenon of "presence." However, it always remains methodologically questionable to speak about *powers*, because we recognize powers only in *effects* that were triggered by the powers themselves.

PRESENCE/ABSENCE

Regardless of these complications, the relationship between presence and representation is deeply engraved into our reflections on images. Leon Battista Alberti is a typical and telling example of this, because he relates a lot of old rhetorical knowledge and thinking to distinctive humanistic and scientist intentions. He understands presence as a forceful power of active representation, which he illuminates with reference to the social phenomenon of friendship. Paintings contain a truly divine power, but this power differs from friendship, which makes people who are far away present to us. The power of images is even greater: paintings make the dead seem still alive after centuries. Thus, we repeatedly and joyfully look at the painting and admire the painter (Alberti 1972). The attendance of the absentee and the vanished is both the evidence and the biggest achievement of presence. This is, of course an altered presence: it is certainly not a palpable resurrection of the dead. The image is neither a ghost nor a double, and nobody confuses an image with the represented reality. But we allow ourselves to be taken in by that representation, and only this "representation" is able to show the liveliness of the absentee in a believable way. Alberti clearly distinguishes between two aspects. From the perspective of cultural history, there is a remembrance-related aspect and an artistic one. Using the concepts of image reflection, he connects the ability of representing the absentee to the self-presentation of art or image. The image displays something, and in doing so it displays itself. And as a result, the work of art addresses the viewer in a special way; it triggers pleasure and admiration in the viewer and mediates the experience of being taken in.

But how does re-presentation generate presence? What is the relationship between the various terms in the title of this text? If we take the perspective of Alberti, the prefix "re-" refers neither to mere repetition nor to reanimation. But what is then the meaning we assign to "re-"? The depiction certainly does not replace the thing it makes visible. Re-presenting is not about presenting something again. It is less and more at once. The depiction underbids what the depicted was or is, because it is completely confined to the possibilities of canvas and color, stone or bronze. The depiction also outbids the depicted, because it lends the enduring status of liveliness to the depicted, who long ago departed or crumbled into dust. The depicted becomes present only via the image: the image defines what the depicted is and can become. Thus, the prefix "re-" in "re-presentation" means *intensification*. This intensification adds a surplus to the existence of the depicted. According to this conception, the divine power—mentioned by Alberti—would be the ability to create existential growth (Gadamer 1986: 149). Presumably he thinks about the representational power of portraits. The enlivening of the dead is naturally emphasized in the sculptural gravestone, where indeed very different modalities of presence can appear: such as the *représentation au vif* and the *representation de la mort*, and it can also involve the dead as decayed (*transi*), the mourners (*gisant*), or a different type of depiction or a mixture of depictions (Panofsky 1964: 86f.). On the edges of sepulcher art we can still see actual representations: the skeleton of the saint, possibly attired in his own clothes, which—presented as an iconic enactment in a church—represents what it stands for, showing him, for instance, as an powerful and generous local patron of a community. The liveliness shifts from the artistic depiction to the invisible powers of grace. Because the representation refers to the physical materiality of the body of the absentee, the absentee becomes present in the presentation: one could almost say, he "is" the presentation.

Regardless of the particular content and the related religious, legal, and ethical interests and roles, this is about making the absentee present. By continually representing the body of the absentee—the body can be in any state: dignified, glamorous, or even putrescent. The representation withdraws the absentee from temporal succession and thereby gives him a place in the world. *Re-presentation* occurs as *presentation*. The presence owes its existence again to a special type of "showing." Therefore we can regard re-presentation as an *act of showing*, which has a particular temporal dimension at its disposal. Representation has the particular ability to present the represented that was originally subject to the passing of time, as if it were present. Thus it receives presence by the representation, and this presence possesses evidence or *enargeia* (Boehm 1995: 31ff.).

But what do we mean by "withdrawing the represented from temporal succession?" What exactly does the depiction do, when it gives presence to those who are dead or absent? Are the rules of entropy not applicable to iconic representations? Do representations that are themselves material not succumb to the order of materiality? Of course they do. It is thus not the avoidance of succession and decay that makes the representation outstanding from a temporal point of view. We always know that the represented person *has* lived. What actually makes representation temporally outstanding is related to the ability of showing: the representation prompts the viewer to return, and it presents the depicted at once as itself and continually as new and different than itself with all its memorable traits and exemplary characteristics.

The "divine power" of images to which Alberti refers and which is able to provide even the dead with presence is definitely not just about the mere power of depiction. We frequently even assign a legal rank, "legitimacy," to representations. The term *representatio* is deeply rooted in the legal sphere, apparently because of the idea to make the represented legally subsumable in the act of representation (Hofmann 1974). A weaker reflection of this legal status is the photo on our identification cards. It is the decisive touchstone, the thing we actually show others to prove a verbally asserted and modified identity and to effectively confer the established rights on the holder of the ID. The photographic portrait makes the person identical with herself—many have had to experience this at border crossings. In the history of photography, we can see how old models of representation can be kept alive and refined, such as the private "memorial photography," the family album, which is a genre, among others, that Roland Barthes extensively investigated (Barthes 1980).

THE BOUNDARIES OF REPRESENTATION

Representation ties itself to absence and death. It responds to and gains the gloss and power of its presence through the transparency of transience and void. This is all based on the binary code of presence/absence. The image is the dialectic reaction to the fascination and anonymity related to death. The most exquisite characteristic of the image is to give a face to the absentee and the departed and to even provide her name with a look and a presence. The European culture tends to expand the collection of images and thereby also the realm of presence. Initially, it was limited to simple monuments of stone, and later on it was monumentalized in pyramids or used ritually in temples. Then it appeared in peripatetic thinking spaces like the agora and the *museion*, even later in the chain of representation of sanctuaries, in cemeteries, and finally in museums. The boundaries of presence have been constantly extended. If we consider the current tendencies of image production, it seems that the space of presence will continue to grow, while we are going to repress the space of absence even more. In the brave new world of simulation, there is even an effort to abolish the space of absence entirely. The idea of presence possesses the features of a cultural utopia, which tries to realize itself with the help of all sorts of organs. If we were going to be able to reproduce the human genome in a proper way, the gap between the depiction and the depicted would be closed and people could become their own representations and their own lasting monuments.

But this myth of reclaiming a this-worldly Paradise at last makes clear that the relationship between presence and absence, representation and the nonrepresentable requires accurate definition. Presences constantly emerge and vanish. Presence has to be generated perpetually even in the most stable works that have been with us for thousands of years. For instance, we might award the role of witness to a mere—e.g., prehistoric—relic, but certainly not yet grant presence to it, because it is entirely identical with its material substance. But if we call the depiction an act that outbids this fact, which is its basis, then the verbal form "representing" is implied by the substantive "representation" as its actual driving power. Therefore the point is to uncover this inner motion. It has to do with temporality. The act of showing is temporally determined, even when it evokes outside-the-world or without-the-world eternity. Thereby it becomes again obvious that representation defines itself by its own boundaries. These boundaries are open on two sides. They exclude and include. Moreover, they also control the relationship between inside and outside. In other words: even in the representation itself, the absentee is not just present but also effective. The absentee accompanies, gives rhythm to, and structures the depiction just like shadow does to light.

The attentive viewer of images already knows something about this. For instance, by the fact that his gaze is always directed by the structure of an image, the viewer focuses—in a mode of sukzession—on this or that detail in order to know its literal meaning. But ultimately he returns to that decisive moment of seeing, when the image reveals itself as a whole, a simultaneity.

Undoubtedly, there are many pieces of information and insight, which we can get from particular signs, and these signs also satisfy our curiosity by their brightness, virtuosity, scrupulous accuracy, or the revealing of taboos. But we can speak of an image presence only if we can recognize the achievement of *presentation* in the successive signs on the image. Certainly the discrete views always enter the image at different focal points that are already within the horizon of the whole of the surface (German: *Horizont des Totums der Fläche*). However, we arrive at the image only when we force our attention in such a way that it becomes precise in relation to the *boundaries* of the representation and the entirety it includes. The switch from iconic facts to iconic power has to do with the changes in the order provided by the image. We discover in this and in that—the parataxis—first relations. Then the hypotaxis builds itself up on the parataxis and conveys its potential in the direction of a simultaneous overview, a real "syntax." It is an old insight that the in-between and the void and the unrepresentable—which the focusing gaze blocks out—are actually significant for an iconic presence.

There is always controversy around the experience of visual simultaneity, partly because it supposedly does not have any neuropsychologically measurable equivalent. On the other hand, one can argue that neuropsychology cannot get to a coherent image theory on this basis either. This is presumably a pointless conflict, which distracts us from the key phenomenon, namely the tension between viewpoints and a simultaneous view. When we look at the entirety, we "overlook" and disregard the abundance of details and "shift" to an inexpressible status. Conversely, when we gaze at the details, we "suppress" the capaciousness and the absorbing power of the image horizon. Two quite inevitable processes are in play here: the indelible blind spot in our perception and the inertia of our organs, which actually contains our iconic productivity. In other words, absence directs our attention, shades it, and conveys the essential adaptation. The eye participates in the process, but it is in a continuous movement. It follows the tracks of temporality that develop from the process of representation. It becomes evident here again that a third party of presentational performance, a deixis, is needed, if representation is to generate presences.

What the phenomenology of image perception elucidates has its equivalent in the history of design and in the related commentary. For instance, Giorgio Vasari makes a few remarks about the well-developed style of Titian that can be read as short theorems for his later painting. Vasari explicitly mentions Andromeda, who "was chained to rocks and Perseus rescues her from the sea monster," and also "Diana, who bathes with her nymphs and transforms Aktaeon into a stag." Moreover, Vasari mentions that Titian "also painted an Europa, who rode the bull across the sea." Based on these and other paintings Vasari makes an observation that differentiates these paintings from Titian's earlier work. Vasari praises him "for the liveliness he gave to the figures by color whereby they became almost vibrant and natural." This recognition of a particular type of presence is based on an approach that differs from the technique used in the early work. Titian "made his first works with a certain refinement and with incredible diligence with the aim that we can look at the paintings both from proximity and from a distance." But by now there is a difference between the close and the distant view, because the paintings "were painted without any presketches, the paint was broadly applied with bold strokes, so that you are not supposed to take a close look at the paintings as they appear in their entirety from a distant point of view" (Vasari 1996). These direct statements of Vasari are exceptionally salient when it comes to the relationship between representation and presence, especially, if we consider the role of the inexpressible in the image that we cannot decode precisely and that therefore keeps "absence" in play. It is due to this characteristic that Vasari gives priority to the entirety over the details in Titian's later work, which is adequate for the distant view, yet resists being focused. Vasari then emphasizes the role of the opaque—which he even places close to the ugly—in generating transparency scenes. Hence it is not Alberti's "open window" that Vasari had in mind: the completely transparent projection surface created by the method of geometrical perspective construction. It is, rather, the complete opacity of thick color that opens up the view in this case. Opacity establishes transparency for the imaginative mind. Titian artfully obfuscates the image window, thus creating his most significant artistic achievement. Vasari certainly pays a price for this, which he accepts in the case of Titian but not in the cases of his students and successors. The emergence of meaning is imperceptible from proximity. Presence holds itself momentarily up, but then with the help of this method it gains even more intensity by a distant view. This inhibition provided by iconic opacity also represents an inner reflexivity between the visual facture and the depicted scene of the painting. And finally, Titian—as characterized by Vasari—also attempted to enhance presence and liveliness. An increased presence-at-hand arises from the "thick and blotchy" layers of paint. This elevation is due to distance—as one would say, according to Walter Benjamin and his definition of aura—"however close it may be" (Benjamin 1961: 15).

In the depicted scene, the moment of namelessness will conceal itself and its vivid variety for those who open themselves to be captivated by the fascination of the living at a distant view. The facture of the painting will appear as a wall from a close proximity—as a complete absence of any meaning, simply the state of self-isolation and ugliness. But for a simultaneous distant view, the image opens its eyes and the meaning emerges in a magnificent way. The image exchanges glances with the viewer and responds to her questions. If we accept this process of generating a "relationship of looking" as a characteristic of an heightened presence, then it becomes obvious that this process requires an explicit *presentation*, a performance on the part of the image. Presentation negates all detailed pieces of information and lets the focusing eye go blind. On the other hand, this inexpressible is also the inevitable prerequisite for viewing an *image*. By this process the image gains the highest level of presence admired by Vasari and Philipp II. The art of painting is thus the mastery of the fruitful difference in which representation and the inexpressible interlock. Due to the specifics of its logic of presentation, representation incorporates the "inexpressible" in a way that allows for the shaded image to emerge, which is so typical of Titian's mature work.

THE LOGICS OF PRESENTATION

The act of showing—in which representation generates presence—comes more and more into the focus of our attention. It is also the special residuum of historical and interpretative analysis. But we have to investigate the act of showing a little further, as supported by two examples. These examples are the vertices of a wide spectrum by which we can show the range and the salience of the homo pictor.

The first example is that of a photograph of a piece of art from the Melanesian New Ireland Island, showing its inhabitants participating in obsequies. The photograph consists of a head that presumably belonged to a carved wooden figure. The head—and this is crucial—is actually the skull of the person who was commemorated in the ritual. It was formed with wax and chalk paste, and then moderately painted with ocher. The shells of turbo snails mark its eyes. This vivid composition through the use of body parts may seem less foreign to us if we remind ourselves of the already mentioned Christian presentational techniques of mummies and skeletons. After all: the signified serves here simultaneously as a signifier. This irritates our common expectation, which assumes a difference between the reality of the piece and its subject. Nevertheless, what we see is not a prepared corpse like the mummy of Vladimir Lenin in the mausoleum of the Kremlin, which is meant for long-term display. In this case, the skull gained a different type of liveliness through the techniques of figuration. This is not a static relationship in which the depiction "substitutes for" the depicted, but rather the evocation of a kind of liveliness that aspires to effect and credibility. The inclusion of the skull secures a spiritual power for the depiction. The depiction is shifted from the sphere of a natural relic to the artistic sphere by means of figuration; it was endowed with a face and, most notably, with an undirected and omnipresent look. The eye socket and the materiality of the cranial bone are filled with energy. We see here the intersection of two types of substance: the elevated presence of the deceased person. Provided that the deceased entered the world of the ancestors, who count as the creators of the world in this culture, the depiction is also about the anonymous presence of the cosmic creators who are at the same time experienced outside of the chains of generations in the abundance of time. The deceased person will not enter the realm of ordinary forgetting. The image makes her visible as the mental image of her ancestors, as the embodiment of their powers. This representation is based on a chiasm. The depiction lends its image value to the vanished who is depicted and makes it thereby present. And the archetype of the depicted also lends its power to the image. Hans-Georg Gadamer argued that the represented generates its being "essentially by self-presentation" (1986: 147) and that reality transgresses into the process of representation and becomes pictorial. It is the particular presentation logic that decides about the kind of presence. It does not leave the represented unaffected. There is not a real "thing" on the one side and its "image" on the other. Strong images provide the represented with a surplus, with an "increase in existence" (Gadamer 1986: 149; Boehm 1996: 95ff.)

It is highly probably that Alberto Giacometti saw the head from New Ireland in the Museum für Völkerkunde in Basel. In his 1947 sculpture *Head on a Pole* displayed in the Art Museum in Basel, he attempted to translate the piece with his own presentational strategies.

Due to the position of its neck, the head has been torn away from the dialogue with the viewer. Impaled on a stick, the head withdraws itself from the context of the living and its body. And yet there is still liveliness here: the liveliness of an unlocked mouth and of stiffness. Death turns an intense affect into a concealed trace of life. On the face, the trace was marked with ocher—the old color of life—expressing itself with horror. While this piece from New Ireland attempts to present death as a passage to the ancestors in order to use their powers of life, Giacometti's piece is about death. Giacometti emphasizes that, "in the perception…the continuity of life is suddenly interrupted" (Meyer 1998: 19). This performance of representation is about fear and scare. It is the threat of death, the vibrant presence of which hovers in front of us.

The presentational logic of Giacometti has a strong temporal dimension. Works like the *Le chariot* (1947), showing a woman on a "carriage," demonstrates his artistic technique. It is not the figure that drives: she is frontally driven in the direction of the viewer. Her celebratory, passive standing and the virtual movement of the vehicle seem absolutely unconnected. Presence is not a simple "being there" (*Dasein*) in this case but rather a kind of "making an appearance." Giacometti emphasized the illusion of a physical or thematic movement because he was interested in something quite different, namely in the emergence of a heightened presence, in representation in a *verbal* sense. Giacometti often gives his figures a certain epiphanic quality. Depiction achieves the transition from material presence-at-hand to appearance. This is performing the perpetual peace of the image.

Giacometti's logic of presentation has to do with the deforming of the human body. The body is stripped of its presence-at-hand and becomes a phenomenon (Boehm 1987: 39f.). When viewed from a distance, these bodies appear lively and intangible. The absentee participates in this process: nothing, or almost nothing, on the surface of the figures refers to corporeality. An effective yawning chasm between facts and presence causes the figure not to look like a body when we look at it. The facticity of the body comes across as a thick appearance. The gaze of the viewer responds to the eyeless "look energy" of the surface that has detached the act of viewing from the motif of the eye. The figures emerge in the act of viewing. The act of viewing allows itself to be taken in by the powers of presence. "Emergence means: not being emerged and being emerged." In this sentence, Jean-Luc Nancy subscribed to the phenomenon of presence, and he even added: thinking means "not yet thinking and already thinking."

The image process, which leads to presence, has a paradoxical structure. Therefore, we cannot mark the beginning and the end of the image process in time. A science of the inner nexus of representation, presentation, and presence is necessarily a science of performance and experience. The impulse of this science is to establish all the historical and analytical givens as a critical authority of perception and reflection. Such a scientific discourse fosters insight that images are bodies that are subject to historical determinants and effects as well as forces generating images and claiming recognition. If representations mainly want to find presences, then the sense of images fulfills itself in the act of perception. Images enable a copresence for the viewer: what we look at looks back at us, the look meets another look.

Translated by Julia Sonnevend and Dominik Bartmański, edited by B. Giesen

REFERENCES

Alberti, L. B. 1972. *On Painting and on Sculpture*. London: Phaidon.

Barthes, R. 1980. *La chambre claire: Note sur la photographie*. Paris: Seuil.

Benjamin, W. 1961. "Das Kunstwerk im Zeitalter seiner technischen Reproduzierbarkeit." In *Illuminationen: Ausgewählte Schriften*, vol. 1, Frankfurt am Main: Suhrkamp.

Boehm, G. 1987. "Das Problem der Form bei Alberto Giacometti." In *Louis Aragon mit anderen: Wege zu Giacometti*, edited by A. Matthes, 39–67. Munich: Seitz.

———. 1995. "Bildbeschreibung: Über die Grenzen von Bild und Sprache." In *Beschreibungskunst—Kunstbeschreibung: Die Ekphrasis von der Antike bis zur Gegenwart*, edited by G. Boehm and H. Pfotenhauer, 23–40. Munich: Fink.

———. 1996. "Zuwachs an Sein: Hermeneutische Reflexion und bildende Kunst." In *Die Moderne und die Grenze der Vergegenständlichung*, edited by H.-G. Gadamer, 95–125. Munich: Galerie Klueser.

Didi-Huberman, G. 1992. *Ce que nous voyons, ce qui nous regarde*. Paris: Editions de Minuit.

Gadamer, H.-G. 1986. "Wahrheit und Methode: Grundzüge einer philosophischen Hermeneutik." In *Gesammelte Werke*, vol. 1, Tübingen: Mohr Siebeck.

Hofmann, H. 1974. *Repräsentation: Studien zur Wort- und Begriffsgeschichte von der Antike bis ins 19. Jahrhundert*. Berlin: Dunker & Humblot.

Meyer, F. 1998. "Alberto Giacometti." In *Werke und Schriften*, edited by Alberto Giacometti, 13–24. Zurich: Artemis.

Panofsky, E. 1964. *Grabplastik: Vier Vorlesungen über ihren Bedeutungswandel von Alt-Ägypten bis Bernini*. Cologne: DuMont Schauberg.

Vasari, G. 1996. *Lives of the Painters, Sculptors and Architects*. London: Everyman's Library.

CHAPTER 2

ICONIC POWER AND PERFORMANCE: THE ROLE OF THE CRITIC

JEFFREY C. ALEXANDER

Materialism is a mundane mode of understanding, one that indulges the self-evident common sense of a rationalized, de-magicalized modernity. No doubt the most sophisticated manner in which the self-consciousness of modern mundanity has been applied to materiality is the commodity theory of Karl Marx ([1867] 2001). Energized morally by icono*clasm*, this radical critic of iconi*cism* produced a brilliant but deeply misleading empirical theory of modern social life. Marx believed that market processes strip material objects of their value—both use value (their practical or true value, as dictated by design, shape, and form) and moral value (their status as product of social labor). Insofar as material objects are so commodified, in Marx's perspective, they can be viewed only abstractly rather than in concrete terms; they are seen merely as exchange value and measured by money. Emptied of meaning, material objects become simply things. Any commodity is the same as any other commodity that can be traded at the same price, no matter how different they seem in their appearance.

At the opposite end of the modern social theory of material objects stands Émile Durkheim's late theory of the elementary, totemic forms of religious life. Durkheim ([1912] 1966) insists that material objects actually make tangible the moral values of society. Because moral values are specific and distinctive, totemic objects are concrete and distinctive in form. They are collective representations that carry social force, communicate sacred and profane meanings, and generate intense emotional identifications through ritualistic practices centering on their material form. Refining this originary understanding via structuralism and semiotics, such figures as Roland Barthes, Umberto Eco, and Rom Harré describe material objects that are referents, or signifieds, whose meanings are established not by themselves but by their relation to invisible signifiers. We do not see or experience an actual material object as such, but see it as sign, signifier, and signified combined.

Neither Marx (at all) nor Durkheim and the semioticians (only slightly) shed light on the artistic design of material objects, the formal properties of material surface that allow aesthetic experience. This feeling for form was first explained, in modern thinking, by eighteenth-century aesthetic philosophies of the beautiful and the sublime, and more recently by Heidegger-inspired writings about presence effects versus meaning effects, for example in the writing of Hans Ulrich Gumbrecht (2006).

My own contribution to this debate has been to suggest that, if there is to be a cultural sociology of material objects, then the aesthetic and the moral approaches to material stuff must be combined (Alexander 2008a, 2008b). The aesthetic can be thought of as surface form, the moral conceived as depth meaning. Surface and depth together create the basis for a modern theory of iconic consciousness. Constructing the material surface creates an aesthetic experience that works on the senses. The nature of this sense experience depends on the structure of form—in terms of visual sense, for example, on textures, colors, lines, curves. Sculpted and drawn forms are successful, according to the standards of classical aesthetic philosophy, if they are able to create sensations of the beautiful and the sublime. (Postmodern theory, à la Danto, would disagree, emphasizing the aesthetic significance of banality and ugliness, but that is another story.) Beneath the aesthetic surface there exists social meaning, the depth of material objects. The discursive and moral meaning of material objects comes not from aesthetic surface but from society, from somewhere outside the objects themselves.

The first thing that is remarkable about surface and depth is that they are invisible to ordinary lay consciousness. To everyday social actors, the world seems to be populated, not by aesthetically formed surfaces and culturally constructed depths, but simply by animate and inanimate things. The second remarkable fact is that, even when observers are aware of the aesthetic surface and moral depth, these two independently constructed and distinctive domains invariably seem to be thoroughly and completely intertwined. On the one hand, a particular aesthetic form seems to "be" the meaning of the material thing, to naturally and perfectly express it; on the other hand, some particular social meaning seems intrinsically to demand some specific articulation of the beautiful or the sublime. Everyday consciousness is reified; it seamlessly naturalizes arbitrary meaning structures even as it essentializes historically contingent aesthetic forms.

Let me give an example of how this works from Immanuel Kant's precritical *Observations on the Feeling of the Beautiful and Sublime*. Kant waxes eloquently about how women's moral qualities *allow* them to be "known by the mark of the beautiful"—"her figure in general *is* finer, her features more delicate and gentler, and her mien more engaging and more expressive" ([1764] 1960: 76, italics mine). Kant treats the aesthetic surfaces of women, in other words, as reflections of ingrained moral qualities; historically contingent judgments of gender appearance are naturalized as objective forms corresponding with social and moral difference. Women, he writes, naturally "prefer the beautiful to the useful." They are beautiful because from "very early they have a modest manner about themselves," knowing "how to give themselves a fine demeanor...at an age when our well-bred male youth is still unruly, clumsy, and confused." Affirming that "the moral composition makes itself discernible in the mien or facial features," Kant believes that a woman "whose features show qualities of beauty *is* agreeable," for "in her face she portrays a tender feeling and a benevolent heart" (87, italics in original). That women are thought to be beautiful is due neither to aesthetic convention nor social practice. They are beautiful, because they are, well, women!

PERFORMANCE AND ICONICITY

In this chapter, my interest is not *whether* iconic consciousness exists. For the sake of this discussion, I assume iconic objects can exert a powerful social force. My interest, rather, is *how* iconic power varies. Yes, material stuff matters, both morally (depth) and aesthetically (surface), but iconic objects do not matter equally. They vary in their impact, their power rising and falling in historical time and, within the same historical period, distributed differently not only across individuals but among the demographics of segmented and fragmented societies (see Bartmański, this volume).

I propose to understand this variation through the idea of performativity. One might think of an icon as a performer, sending off signals according to how it is designed. The effects of these signals, their signaling power, cannot be measured, however, simply by the intentions of an object's designer, even if it has one. There is the matter of reception, of audience impact. Between projected meanings and audience response are a series of mediations. In addition to its design, projecting iconic power depends, for example, on access to the means of symbolic production. You need a stage for the designed product, and lighting and photography to portray it. You need technical and artistic skills to put the iconic object "into the scene" (mise en scène). Iconicity also depends on power. These include the more obvious powers of production and distribution: you need a dealer, an agent, a gallery, a factory. But iconic effect is also mediated by "hermeneutical power," the understandings and evaluations offered by independent interpretation. Critics exercise interpretive power in a big way, getting in-between the designs of iconic objects and their reception.

Iconic objects produced by high art and popular culture send off potential meanings and experiences, often by design. Whether audiences—other designers and artists, or members of the lay public if connoisseur or commodity consumer—register these iconic impressions, indeed whether they are affected by these material performances at all, is an open question. The answer depends, to some significant degree, on how critics evaluate an object's aesthetic excellence and communicative success. In the research upon which I report very selectively here, I have collected from the pages of the *New York Times*—the most influential single popular medium in the United States—recent reviews of architecture, paintings, music, automobiles, dresses, and graphic logo designs. I analyze these reviews, not simply as *reflections* of iconic power but, more importantly, as *recipes* for understanding how iconic power comes about. My research explores the positive and negative mediation of popular criticism, illuminating how public rhetoricians and their putative audiences actually talk about an icon's surface and depth.

THE *NEW YORK TIMES* MEETS LOUIS KAHN

Sometimes critics distance their audience from an icon's potential power, negatively evaluating the designer, painter, or composer, proclaiming the icon a "false idol" whose aesthetic surface is ugly, stupid, boring, clichéd, or banal, or whose moral depth is confused, profane, polluted, or simply obfuscated by the aesthetic failures of the surface. Often, however, the opposite is the case. In this regard, let us consider the former architecture critic of the *New York Times*, Nicolai Ouroussoff. To examine Ouroussoff's reviews is to encounter an immensely influential critic who propels, undermines, explains, and explores iconic power. Occupying a relatively autonomous position in the performative production of iconicity, Ouroussoff mediates the performance process by which architectural icons are made, distributed, evaluated, received, and sometimes revitalized and enhanced.

Our type case for this discussion will be Ouroussoff's front page review in the Arts Section of the *Times* on December 11, 2006. Its headline is "Restoring Kahn's Gallery and Reclaiming a Corner of Architectural History, at Yale." In what follows, I will suggest that this review instructs us on how to become fused with the first great material sign that Louis Kahn—a revered American architect from mid-century— ever produced. Writing ostensibly from a critical distance, Ouroussoff closes the distance to become part of the process of creating iconic power. Fifty years after the building was designed and built, and long after Kahn himself has departed from this earth, Ouroussoff teams up with Kahn, revving up iconic consciousness for Yale's restoration of his earliest big project. Ouroussoff contributes to Kahn's performative success, even as he purports to provide a rational and objective appraisal.

Powerful icons combine the generic (they typify) and the unique (they singularize). Ouroussoff writes this combination into the surface of the Kahn building and also into its depth. "The restoration of the Yale Art Gallery," he announces, "reawakens one of America's great architectural beauties." It is "like the return of a long-lost friend." Ouroussoff communicates here a sense of archetype: the Kahn Gallery is an ur-example of "modern architecture." Yet, at the same time, the critic insists that Kahn's Gallery is special, its surface an idiosyncratic artistic object. Absolutely singular, Kahn single-handedly created a uniquely anti-Corbusier style. Ouroussoff's case for the singularity of the archetype's constructed surface is thickened by a continuous evocation of its "Yale" depth. The elite Ivy League university is everywhere visible in the background of this review, contributing its own cultural power as a singular yet simultaneously iconic archetype. The Kahn building is presented as just the kind of magnificent surface structure that a college as glorious as Yale would have.

Great icons salvage mundane material objects from the realm of mere banality, making them beautiful and sacred and counterposing them not only to the ugly but also to the morally profane. Ouroussoff continually frames the Art Gallery's aesthetic surface via the traditional criteria of beauty. He offers frank proclamations of aesthetic delight and evokes the philosophical criterion of beauty as the principal object of design.

These exclamations about the triumph of surface beauty are faithfully linked to an insistence on the Yale Art Gallery's sacred depth. It is because Kahn succeeds in producing an extraordinarily beautiful surface, Ouroussoff implies, that he has been able to create a deeply spiritual site for transcendental experience. References to divinity abound. Ouroussoff exclaims that the restoration allows Kahn to be "put back on the pedestal he so richly deserves." Sacred and great people and things— the critic freely dispenses with the adjective "great"—must be separated from the mundane, given higher and more elevated status. Kahn is not only great but also a "genius," which means that he is not only generically sacred but also unique. And just as totems procreate, producing other sacred objects, so Kahn possesses fecundity. He is said to have produced *many* "great masterpieces." Ouroussoff weaves Kahn a mythical narrative. A supernatural figure, Kahn is part of history, wrapped in folkloric stories, biographies, movies, and art books. Restoring his building's iconicity has a metaphysical quality. Telling this story about recovering a "long lost friend," Ouroussoff speaks of awakening "beauties from a slumber." So this is a story about discovering buried treasure, about bringing something dead back to life. Restoration has breathed life into a long "dead" relic of modernity. Ouroussoff narrates the past, present, and future of iconic temporality. Once great, his Art Gallery was abused and fell into oblivion, but it is now restored to its original glory. The icon's narrative arc takes on a teleological form. It becomes pivotal to the mythical story of modernity. The first great work of an architectural genius, its brilliance foreshadowed future landmarks, and its own beauty can now be discovered again.

The Art Gallery's surface is described in visual terms that reveal the "elements of genius." Ouroussoff writes fluidly and passionately about the "bold geometric forms, the sharp lines, the sensitive use of light, the tactile love of his materials." Revitalized, the Yale Art Gallery is "sleek," its sensuous surface fully possessing the aesthetic power to suck us in. Yet, even as the Gallery construction "stresses materials and surfaces," Ouroussoff reminds us that it reaches below mere surface, "projecting an air of mystery." Gallery surface draws us into a Gallery depth. "The project should also be understood," Ouroussoff instructs, "as part of a larger effort to reclaim a corner of the Yale campus." Architectural surface connects us to Yale sacred ground. Citing "the incorporation of an old rough-hewn stone retaining wall," Ouroussoff explains that Kahn used the wall "to frame his outdoor courtyard [and] to lock the building into its historic surroundings." The depth of the Gallery's aesthetic surface is linked to these historical surroundings, for Yale is not just a great university but also a historical container for the most sacred art of early modern and modern times. In this manner, the aesthetic power of Kahn's modernist building is intertwined with classical and romantic artistic forms: "Paintings [that] range from early Italian Renaissance to contemporary are displayed on partitions supported on steel legs that break the rooms down into a series of small informal spaces," and "paintings by Monet, Renoir and Pissaro hang in big gilded fames along the concrete-block wall that runs the length of the main façade."

Discussing the decades of obfuscating accretions to the Kahn building that now stand corrected, Ouroussoff condemns them as grossly insensitive, not only as ugly aesthetically but offensive morally. Here again the binary of sacred/banal is continually evoked. This is manifest first in Ouroussoff's mythical narrative about recovering spiritual depth. It is only because "years of callous alterations have been reversed" that the sacral elements of the iconic building can be restored "in all their glory." So also is this binary central to explaining the iconic power of the restored Gallery's surface form. Time and again light is evoked as a material representation of divine sacrality. It is central to the restoration of iconic surface, in part because it is visually alluring, in part because it evokes an ethereal sacred depth. Reporting that "the west façade has been rebuilt," Ouroussoff explains that "its glass and steel frame"—banal and mundane in itself—now "regains its original lightness." Pointing to another of Kahn's aesthetic innovations obscured by banal historical accretion— "a sunken exterior court that was senselessly roofed over"—Ouroussoff reports that this courtyard "has been restored, allowing light to spill down once more into the lower galleries." In reporting on the Art Gallery's interior court, Ouroussoff's narrative of aesthetic conversion is much the same: "The entire space is animated by [Kahn's] masterly handling of light…A narrow vertical slot of glass overlooking the entrance court…allows a stream of light to wash down a back wall."

The aesthetic power of the Gallery's surface, like the moral power of its depth, is sustained—we sense the ghost of Roman Jacobson nodding and smiling—by splitting meaning categories into sharp binaries. Ouroussoff sets light off against shadow, smooth against sharp, thick against thin, angle against curve. He reports, for example, that "the elegance of that west wall, gently set back from the street, contrasts with the forceful concrete-block façade of the main entrance, an opaque expressionless screen." Elegant is to concrete block as gentle is to forceful as transparent screen is to opaque—[Elegant:concrete-block::gentle:forceful:: screen:opaque]. We are drawn into the iconic power of the revitalized Gallery, the critic suggests, because "the stunning variety of the light and the tension between the forms and materials—the delicacy of the partitions…versus the brute weight of the concrete—keep us alert. Everything here is warmly alive." This creates iconic power: "Mysticism over purity. Obliqueness over transparency. Historical nuance over an abstract utopia."

Having explained the binary construction of the iconic power of the Gallery's exterior, Ouroussoff leads the reader inside the building, to the sensuously exalting contact with the sacred center, which is also rendered in a polarizing way. "Inside the building," the critic reports, the sense of restraint "gives way to an intoxicating blend of muscularity and delicacy." Surface sublimity leads powerfully to meaningful depth: "The deep triangulated beams of the ceilings, with their deep shadows, lend the room a mystical air; the stark silo-like concrete cylinder housing the staircase reaffirms the galleries' status as a sacred space." But "the true revelation occurs when you step into the galleries." Those who can take this step will experience objectification, and, as their subjectivity becomes concrete, they will experience transcendence as well: "The potent thrust of the concrete-beam ceiling draws you into them as if you were being lured into a sacred tomb. You gaze up in awe, and then turn to the paintings." Table 2.1 diagrams Ouroussoff's binaries, which he employs to describe, and bring into being for the reading audience, the restored Gallery's aesthetic and moral power.

Ouroussoff's passionate account of the Kahn renovation adumbrates another revelation, the imminent unveiling of the Paul Rudolph–designed Art and Architecture building just down the street. According to the *Times* critic, the Rudolph building, a controversial monument of "Brutalism," has also been polluted to the point of banality. Subjected to "physical abuse" and "gutted by fire," the 1960s building has

Table 2.1 The Binary Discourse of Iconic Power

Profane	Sacred
Kitsch	Art
Utilitarian	Aesthetic
Negative	Positive
Jumbled	Clear
Confused	Transparent
Muddy	Careful
Slipshod	Thoughtful
Heavy	Light
Clumsy	Fluid
Cringe-inducing	Epiphanic
Artificial	Authentic
Doctrinaire	Liberating
Engineered	Inspired
Efficient/hurried	Patient contemplation
Weak	Strong/bold
Cautious	Courageous
Parochial	Universal
Superficial	Deep
Banal	Lofty
Manipulative	Principled
Conformist	Creative
Reeking	Purity
Compromise	Conviction

endured "a series of unforgivable alterations" that have made its true sacrality invisible and, instead, suggested its profanation: "Skylights and windows were covered over, transforming the interiors into dark, cavelike spaces." The aesthetic-sacred has been defiled by mundane utilitarianism: "Additional studio floors were crammed, so that the towering vertical spaces that made up the core studios became cramped and gloomy." The result has been that the aesthetic "clarity" of Rudolph's original design has been lost.

The restoration undertaken by Charles Gwathmey, who was a student at Yale Architecture when Rudolph was dean, will allow the misunderstood Brutalist building's iconic power finally to shine through. In so doing, it will recreate a contagious interaction with the restored sacrality of the Kahn building next door. Rudolph had intended to create this concatenation but did not pull it off—at least in the minds of earlier critics and lay audiences. Restored, Rudolph's aesthetic surface will finally expose the building's daring and courageous moral depth, and connect it fluidly to the Kahn next door. "Its glass façade will regain its original transparency, echoing Kahn's glass façade across the street." The banal utilitarianism will be eliminated and Rudolph's sublimity restored: "The additional floors will be ripped out, opening up the old stark vertical spaces that lent the studios their grandeur." Sacred light will be let back in: "Light wells that were closed up will be replaced, allowing daylight to stream down the back of the library wall." The sensuous and meaningful will now be available, and iconic consciousness restored: "When finished, the building should feel as audacious as it did four decades ago, a delicious counterpart to Kahn's restrained elegance."

NATURALIZING ICONIC POWER:
THE DISAPPEARING CRITIC

In conclusion, let us return to iconic consciousness as reification. Iconic power depends on the seamless intertwining of surface aesthetic and depth meaning, such that an actor experiences sensuous surface and understands discursive meaning at the same time. Yet, in spite of an icon's social power, or more precisely because of it, social actors themselves are not reflexive about this process. As far as they are concerned, they feel themselves interacting with real, animate or inanimate, things.

My discussion of Ouroussoff's writings suggests how criticism can contribute to such naturalization of iconic consciousness. Critics report on architecture's aesthetic success, stating this objectively, as a truth. They employ the language of description: this façade works because it is beautiful, that one does not because it is ugly or banal. The critic's claim is that the plastic achievement—this column, that façade, this internal stairway—"is" good, that it functions aesthetically, in contrast to other plastic features that "are" bad, that "fail" the aesthetic test. Critics, in other words, do not own up to their subjectivity, much less to the interpretive power of their aesthetic judgment.

Whether this is modesty or false consciousness, critical performance not only creates interpretations of an icon for an audience but also creates an audience for the icon. Critics provide public judgments before lay members of the public, and even other artists have themselves been able to experience a work. The effect, in a large and complex society, is not just to offer an evaluation but also to create a context for its reception. Critics tell people what to look for and how to feel, and they often do so in a personal, not a distanced way. Far from being objective, and thus merely informative, Ouroussoff presents his review as an account of his personal experience. He describes the sensuous impact of the object on his own senses, and its depth of meaning for him. It is a breath-intaking record of an intimate encounter, an exhilarating first-person report on the critic's journey to the center of a sacred thing.

Through the critical text an audience first experiences the iconic power or weakness of an aesthetic object. The reader is primed; the critic instructs. The critic can distance the reader from a material form, defusing rather than re-fusing, by describing his own sense of being distant when encountering it himself. The critic can bring into being a hesitant and withholding audience, making it difficult for readers to give themselves over to the object, in the unlikely case they should now actually make the trip to encounter it face to face. Reading a critical review, we are wary and suspicious of the object; we are skeptical and raise our guard, most likely staying away. A glowing review has the opposite effect. We are halfway seduced already and waiting to fall in love. We want to be fused, to be taken by the experience, to fall into the object.

That Ouroussoff is constructing us as an audience, that he is instructing us so as to facilitate our fusion, is not at all explicit. It is not something that the critic would admit, and it is not something about which the reader, the person at the receiving end of this performative process, would be aware. This lack of awareness reflects the nature of iconic consciousness itself, and the success of the critic's role in causing an icon to perform powerfully enough to make it happen. The icon is absorptive. Feeding upon our need for transitional objects, it allows us to subjectify material reality and to materialize ourselves inside it in turn. As we read Ouroussoff's review, we are encouraged to imagine imminent experiences of absorption and projection, to participate vicariously in Ouroussoff's journey. We experience iconic consciousness at one remove, a second-order arousal. The review is presented as if it were communicating aesthetic judgments (which it is), yet these judgments are also simultaneously presented as immediate and personal reactions of a person to whose social power we, as interested readers, are inclined to submit.

THE CRITIC SPEAKS

In spring 2008, I invited Nicolai Ouroussoff to my undergraduate seminar on Iconic Consciousness in New Haven, and we engaged with Yale students in a spirited discussion of what it takes and what it means to be an architectural critic for the nation's most influential popular mass medium. Ouroussoff declares that the principal requirement is having a "feeling for the building as object," but, asked to reflect on how he employs this feeling in his capacity as influential critic, he betrays some confusion and concern. About the interpretive power he wields, he replies, "I don't think about it. It'd be a killer if I did," he explains, exclaiming, "I don't have power!" As evidence, he offers the fact that "I rarely can actually kill a project." When I respond that there are different kinds of power, and that I am asking him about power of an interpretive, not a material kind, Ouroussoff evokes the idea of objective aesthetic truth: "If you're getting closer to some kind of truth, then you [do] have power. If you're not, you don't have any."

Ouroussoff's reply illuminates something profound about just how hermeneutical power mediates performativity. To deny his power, the critic presents himself less as an interpreter than an accurate reader, an observer of objective form, a kind of scientist of the aesthetic life. On the one hand, he implicitly acknowledges possessing power, while on the other hand he denies it. He, as a subject, has no independent leverage. What actually possesses power is truth. Because aesthetic judgment is objective, it is truth that has power. One is a good reviewer, perhaps even a highly influential one, only to the degree that one's writing reveals objective truth. Ouroussoff asserts, in fact, that the nature of architectural truth has been discovered; it revolves around the nature of forms. We have a "growing understanding about how bodies move through space," he explains. Citing decades of architectural theory and psychology, he asserts that we now understand how people "experience their material environment." So, Ouroussoff does not see himself as guiding people to an opinion, but as educating them about the nature of aesthetic truth. If people actually go and see the building he has written about, they will agree with his review. Their reaction will be as influenced as his criticism by the revelation of an icon's objective power, or the lack of it.

This is so, not because of his influence, but because viewers will be able to confirm with their own eyes aesthetic truth. Faced with this assertion of aesthetic objectivity, I ask Ouroussoff why, then, are his reviews written with evocative language? Why bother to write so expressively, rather than simply suggest in an accurate manner the information at hand? At this point in the conversation, the critic confesses to being a writer and not only an author, in Barthes's sense. Reviews, for him, are about "feeling," not only about information. He wants to communicate the "experience" of "how you move through the space," of "how the narrative develops as you move through the building." He describes his review as a first-person narrative that aims to transmit the experience of seeing, making an analogy between his own literary creativity and the architect's plastic power: "You do through the writing what the architect has done through his building." Taking the reader through the building, you "use language to try to convey the sense of space, rhythm, motion." Just as today's architects "try to create an innocence" about forms and shapes, so Ouroussoff wants his readers to experience architectural objects in a fresh way. He offers an example. If one drives under one of the complex and curved overpasses of a Los Angeles freeway, one might experience it as ugly, filled with darkness, garbage, and potentially, crime. From the perspective of the architectural critic, "you need to get people to break through this 'learned reaction'"—"to see these spaces for what they are," to allow "emotional resonance." One needs words for that, not just pictures.

So the review is itself performative, a literary exercise that aims to recreate the feeling of plastic art. If Ouroussoff's own aesthetic performance succeeds, it will create fusion between his critical text and *Times*' readers and, at the same time, he will have drawn the reader's emotional-cum-symbolic identification toward the plastic object. He recalls for the assembled students a valuable piece of advice he himself received as a young critic. "Don't be afraid to fall in love" with a work of art, an older critic advised him, and he confesses that today, as an architecture reviewer, "I want to fall in love with the building" and "I feel a sense of tragic disappointment if I don't." What frustrates him most? "When I can't get people to see the things I see in a building. When they are blind."

CRITICISM AND THE DEFUSION OF ICONIC POWER

Iconic power is typically not mediated by critics in such an explicit manner. It often builds up by invisible accretions, without any relation to an organized social power that plans and engineers its production and distribution, or to interpretive powers that subject its success and worthiness to "review." Consider the iconic power of trees and sky and light, home furnishings, one's own hair, body, and clothing, or—for the most part—one's gender, race, and sexuality. That the presentation of an icon is not explicitly mediated by organized criticism, however, does not mean that its power is not subject to performative mediation. Iconicity is a process, not an objective fact, and it is subject to powerful social mediation. Iconicity has a temporal arc. To explore the "aura" of an icon is also to explore its half-life. Iconic power may continue to spiral and radiate long after critical mediation. Icons can perform without the apparent aid of other powers because, once launched, they have power independent of the processes that performatively produced them.

In traditional societies, iconic objects are tightly intertwined with sacred scripts, their producers with their consumers, and there are no critics. In complex and modern, and even more so in postmodern societies, the elements of iconic performance have become separated and defused. Thinking about them is often concentrated and separated. Production is in one place, design another, and display, advertising, and publicity are all somewhere else. Absorption by the viewer—which may be consumption, adulation, or appreciation, depending on the social arena—is so separated from these other elements that it is often not available for public scrutiny, and seems entirely contingent and arbitrary besides. It is because of this defusion that a fascinating new element has become central to iconic performance—the critic.

REFERENCES

Alexander, J. C. 2008a. "Iconic Consciousness in Art and Life: Beginning with Giacometti's 'Standing Woman,'" *Theory, Culture and Society* 25 (3): 1–19.

———. 2008b. "Iconic Consciousness: The Material Feeling of Meaning," *Environment and Planning D: Society and Space* 26 (5): 782–94.

Durkheim, É. (1912) 1966. *The Elementary Forms of Religious Life.* Translated by Joseph Ward Swain. New York: Free Press.

Gumbrecht, H. 2006. "Aesthetic Experience in Everyday Worlds: Reclaiming an Unredeemed Utopian Motif." *New Literary History* 37 (2): 299–318.

Kant, I. (1764) 1960. *Observation on the Feeling of the Beautiful and the Sublime.* Translated by John T. Goldthwaite. Berkeley: University of California Press.

Marx, K. (1867) 2001. "Commodities." In *Capital*, vol. 1, 1–53. London: BGR: ElecBook.

Ouroussoff, N. 2006. "Restoring Kahn's Gallery, and Reclaiming a Corner of Architectural History at Yale." *The New York Times*, Architecture Review, December 11.

PART II

Iconspicuous Revolutions of 1989: Culture and Contingency in the Making of Political Icons

Dominik Bartmański

> Among other things, the revolutions of 1989 were about visibility—making visible "the people."
>
> (Berdahl 2003: 9)

> In every society various techniques are developed intended to fix the floating chain of signifieds in such a way as to counter the terror of uncertain signs
>
> (Barthes 1978: 39)

INTRODUCTION

On the twentieth anniversary of the "fall of the Berlin Wall," the *New York Times* offered a richly illustrated and prominently displayed coverage of the event. The caption under the top slideshow read: "The Fall of the Berlin Wall signaled the beginning of the end of communism in Europe."[1] It is safe to assume that majority of the *New York Times*' audience found the message comprehensible, credible, and authentic. Coupled with iconic pictures, the news could hardly fail to confirm what older readers believed they knew well and to provide the young ones with a properly dramatic glimpse into recent history.

However, its legibility comes at a cost of elision typical of everyday speech. If we unpack this *linguistic signifier*, we will see that the act of signification and its referents are far more complicated than the implied message would suggest. By the same token, we will see that what both older and younger audiences can ascertain from it is only a *naturalized image* of the first "miraculous" link in the seemingly inevitable chain of revolutionary narrative. Interestingly enough, even some social scientists tend to settle for such unreconstructed linear accounts that make the "wall's fall" their favorite revolutionary big bang. Michael Kennedy captured it best when he wrote: "For many, a focus on 1989 is only a matter of commemoration, or anniversary for the year of miracles." He goes on, pointing out that the wall's fall came to be perceived as the biggest of the "miracles." Yet he provides an important caveat. "If we view 1989 with the image of the Berlin Wall's collapse, then perhaps historical inevitability would be the lesson. If the Round Table talks are our image, a very different value for contingency and negotiation emerges" (Kennedy 1999: 293, 301).

The present case study argues that no image allows thinking in terms of inevitability. Instead, it identifies parameters of cultural plausibility and emphasizes contingency. Its main question is how the iconic wall from Berlin eclipsed the iconic table from Warsaw. If this question is answered sociologically, we will be in a position to understand why the wall's fall could dominate the perception of the complex 1989 revolutions as it did. As Bruno Latour noted, "All dates are conventional, but 1989 is a little less so than some. For *everyone* today, the fall of the Berlin Wall symbolizes the fall of socialism" (Latour 1993: 8, italics mine).

I argue that the naturalized, universalized image of historical inevitability and political meaningfulness it conveys is exactly that—image. But it is not *just* an image. It is a powerful icon. As Kennedy noted, different imageries have serious epistemic consequences, both in lay and professional worlds. In what follows I delineate these consequences and link them to cultural conditions of iconic power. If only for this reason, an effort to study political icons would be warranted. But the value of the case inheres in its potential to yield generalized insights into a broader issue, namely how icons work in society. The analysis of the case in this respect begins with explaining what lies behind the aforementioned media "elision."

WHAT HAPPENED IN THE EPOCHAL YEAR OF 1989?

The historical depth of 1989 is of course greater than this project could ever hope to fathom. But it is sufficient for our purposes to outline the actual historical contours. First, what the *New York Times* means by "the Fall of the Berlin Wall" refers to the process of overcoming the wall on November 9, 1989, by the East Germans. It was spurred by the liberalization of its border regime announced in an apparently haphazard way at an official press conference that day. What ensued was the actual demolition of the wall, which occurred later during 1990. Thus the fall is semantically compressed here into one public event made possible both by the passive communist authorities and suddenly activated citizens.

Second, as far as the "end of communism in Europe" is concerned, the mass crossings of the wall on that euphoric night could stand for its beginning, first of all, in East Germany. For some other countries, it was not merely about signaling but confirming, and not of the historic "beginning" but rather of a symbolic "climax" of communism's erosion, the understanding shared by some Germans themselves (Wowereit, cited in Bahr 2005: 3).

Chronologically speaking, the November events in the communist German Democratic Republic (GDR) stemmed from rather than gave birth to the conviction that democratic revolution was an idea whose time had indeed come. Moreover, other East German cities such as Leipzig proved more rebellious than Berlin. As for the actual "signals of the beginning of communism's end" they had occurred elsewhere in Eastern Europe. They were epitomized by such figures as Mikhail Gorbachev or Lech Wałęsa, and such soundbites as Perestroika and Solidarność. While the dwindling power of the Soviet Union in the late 1980s was one of the key conditions of the possibility for change, there were at least two remarkable avant-garde processes in Central Europe that can be credited with directly triggering the 1989 revolutionary wave: (1) Hungary's political liberalization, and (2) Poland's Round Table talks.

The former was conducive to the loosening of Hungary's western border regime and the unprecedented breaching of the Iron Curtain there on May 2, 1989. On June 27, 1989, it was symbolically abolished when Austrian Foreign Minister Alois Mock and his Hungarian counterpart Gyula Horn traveled to the Austrian-Hungarian border "to send a signal that the division of postwar Europe was coming to an end" (Mayr 2009: 1). The thawing of the Cold War was in fact so swift that by June 27, 1989, not much of the Iron Curtain was left in Hungary. The Round Table in Poland resulted in the relegalizing of the 10-million-member Solidarność movement and the first, partially free democratic elections in the communist bloc that brought a landslide victory of Solidarność in June and delivered the first noncommunist prime minister in the region.

With these key anticommunist goals realized, the time of the *unprecedented* revolutionary signal in Central Europe simply expired. The temporal "beginning" of the so-called Autumn of Nations happened before autumn 1989, and the term would have to be used in the plural form to be adequate. The peaceful "fall" of the wall in the GDR in November and the Czechoslovakian Velvet Revolution in December could come across as such, because earlier Polish and Hungarian political experiments had significantly decreased the political risk of openly anticommunist actions in the region (Smolar 2009: 18). The same crucial but neglected point has also been made in Germany: "It is important not to forget that it was audacity and readiness to assume risk among Germany's neighbors that had laid foundations for revolutionary developments" (Perger 2009: 3). When asked about Wałęsa's and Poland's revolutionary merits, Klaus Wowereit, the mayor of Berlin, openly conceded "the indisputable achievements of Solidarność" (Wowereit 2009: 24). Other prominent German politicians like Helmut Kohl or Frank Steimeier publicly admitted this too on various occasions. Wałęsa felt entitled to go so far as to assert that "the opening of the German border was a decision that should have been made much earlier" (cited in Hildebrandt 2008: 117). Given the aforementioned rising tide of political transition, these words do not necessarily reflect his grumpy illusions but revolutionary realism.

IMAGE AND ICONIC PLAUSIBILITY

It is in this context that the role of the wall's "fall" as the historic marker of 1989 can be sociologically estranged and approached as iconic construct. This new perspective is useful because the occurrence has undergone the layered process of naturalization whereby the complex cultural conditions of its possibility and influence have ceased to be legible and are taken for granted or altogether ignored. The problem is compounded by the fact that the potentially helpful explanatory categories such as "cultural resonance" are more like sociological black boxes than transparent concepts. If we operationalize it systematically, we will see how it was possible that the Berlin-based icon eclipsed the earlier ones from Poland and Hungary despite the political advantages of the latter. In other words, a culturally sensitive, not just a purely political explanation is needed if we want to understand how the wall's fall became the superior emblem of 1989 (Kennedy 1999: 295), a "truly global event" (Drechsel 2010: 13). I argue that the iconological vocabulary allows an indispensable cultural interpretation in this respect. To adopt such an approach means, first of all, to take iconicity and contingency seriously and neutrally. Estranging the wall's fall instead of impugning the *New York Times'* credibility shifts this essay's engagement from political critique to the sociology of popular imagination.

As high-profile coverage of an important issue at an important time, the *New York Times'* material offers a propitious entry into the cultural reality of political iconicity. What makes it so is that it is formally typical as media representation and standard in terms of content as a voice on the wall's fall. First, it does not deviate from the basic mechanism of "covering" historical events in that, responsive to the nature of media reporting suggested by the English term itself, it conceals as it reveals, for images and discourses can never simply present "reality" but rather a "specific framing of it" (Bürgi and Fischer 2005: 6). Second, it does not deviate from the already established Western perception of 1989. Visually researching "1989" in the Internet and print media reveals the wall's fall to be "the symbolic date of the end of the Cold War" (Drechsel 2010: 18) or to signify "the return to Europe" of the Central European countries dominated by the Soviet Union (Kennedy 1999: 295).[2] In a book of the most iconic press photographs of the 1980s, the chapter tellingly entitled "All fall down" depicts the events of 1989 and contains twenty-five images. The GDR-related issues are featured in eight and Polish in four photographs. Two of the latter feature Wałęsa, and none the Round Table, whereas three of the former depict the wall (Yapp 2001: 104–30). There is no single image from Hungary.[3] Countless media representations of 1989 reproduced these visual proportions over years. Today the Hungarian revolutionaries are described as "secret," and those who truly breached the Iron Curtain for the first time as "quiet" heroes (Mayr 2009: 1).

Skeptics might, of course, argue that specific media reports do not constitute a representative sample. Yet the meanings of extensive coverage of a highly influential, respected paper can hardly be treated as idiosyncratic, let alone dismissed as inconsequential. Another skeptical objection might point to the fact that the groundbreaking revolutionary merits of Hungary and Poland are noted in different news outlets. For example, the BBC coverage on February 6, 2009, the day when the Round Table talks began, emphasized the unprecedented character of this political initiative and described its eventual results as "heralding the collapse of communism across the eastern half of Europe" (Lungescu 2009). The German *Spiegel* coverage on June 4, 2009, included a story about "a piece of furniture that made history" as a site of "sensational dialogue that turned out to begin the end of communism" (Mix 2009). But if such frames could relativize the interpretive consensus presumed by the *New York Times*, they would by the same token suggest the existence of interpretive confusion.

In reality, however, there is little evidence of such confusion. The acknowledgments of Polish or Hungarian revolutionary merits invariably read more like special reminders than an ongoing debate of their first-rate iconic significance. Most importantly for the present argument, they are mostly words about words, not images, and they are particularized rather than generalized. In the aforementioned BBC article, Nobel Peace Prize recipient Wałęsa is depicted as "an icon in Poland," whereby his celebrity status is explicitly circumscribed to a local context (Lungescu 2009). Even in his native country, Wałęsa's role is discussed mostly in political and moral terms, and its *meaning* as an icon remains unreconstructed (Rymkiewicz 2008: 271). An iconic view that visibly distinguished Poland in early 1989 was the economic bankruptcy of its communist system marked poignantly by the empty shelves of grocery stores (Mix 2009). That was an image of the decay of, not attack on the system. By contrast, the wall's fall "changed history" through an intensely visual performance whose revolutionary character was palpable and broadcast internationally. I argue that it is the stark visuality of the wall that makes its cultural image worthy of persistent commemoration, ritualization, discussions, and even commodification independent of any overtly political anniversaries. The wall's fall is rarely, if ever, presented only within the confines of the German context. It commands generalization as a visual, "deep" archetype.

Iconicity or the lack thereof is therefore one of the focal points of the issue. The main hypothesis regarding the meaning and validity of the *New York Times*' representation is that they hinge on the plausibility of the coverage as an "act of meaning" (see Bruner 2000: 108). Significance and validity are not predicated here upon the degree of representativeness or historical accuracy but upon meaningfulness undergirded by different aspects of iconic power encoded in the event and its media representations. It is a specific case of a general observation made by Jeffrey C. Alexander that "the iconic is about experience, not communication. To be iconically conscious is to understand without knowing.... It is to understand by feeling, by contact, by the 'evidence of the senses' rather than the mind" (Alexander 2008: 782).

The comparative story of the Berlin Wall, the Round Table, and other related political totems of 1989 in Eastern Europe provides a context in which we can understand how the iconically constituted plausibility trumps other important considerations, that is, how the mythical can and occasionally does override the political, or how the symbolic and the political may become virtually indistinguishable.[4] A systematic reconstruction of what and how count in the perception of this story as "beginning," "end," "signal," and "revolutionary" allows us to establish what we as societies tend to notice and how we construe, code, and associate events with each other.

One of the chief arguments is that, when combined with felicitous public exposure and lodged within propitious place-specific meaning structures, objects and events that evince various kinds of iconic power have a heightened chance of becoming conspicuous. When this occurs, they become "iconspicuous." I hypothesize that so conceived iconspicuity occasions the emergence of relatively consistent patterns of experiencing, remembering, forgetting, and symbolically connecting social occurrences. The experiential power of an iconspicuous thing is such that it is capable of relegating other, less or noniconic phenomena to the margins of collective consciousness.

In what follows, I show that it is precisely iconspicuous qualities of the wall, both as a thing and a cultural signifier, that have made it and its "fall" what it is today. It is the combination of the totemic, auratic, spectatorial, quotable, and archetypical properties that rendered the German upheaval "the signal of communism's end" despite its relative belatedness and the paucity of dissident intellectuals (Ladd 2009: 277). It is the iconic power of its pictorial representations that made the Berlin event the hierophany of 1989, even though beforehand, "the GDR's political backwardness and cultural stagnation compared with Poland and Hungary" had been visible (Stern 2007: 331–32).[5] Last but not least, it is the specific emplacement of the political event that increases its iconic potential, in that spatially located meanings have "their own logic" too (Löw 2008: 285). As a result, the cultivated absence of the iconic wall in the legendary numinous locale proves more meaningful to international audiences than the presence of new, conventional monuments in the less media exposed cities of Gdańsk, Leipzig, Warsaw, and Budapest.

I argue that it is precisely the deficits in those cultural parameters that contributed to making Poland's avant-garde role in the 1989 revolutions disproportionately underrepresented outside the country, for example, in average Americans' consciousness (Basara 2009:12). Needless to say, the material and financial deficits of Poland or Hungary as compared with Germany are not negligible, but to privilege them in a sociological analysis would mean to ignore their economies' responsiveness to cultural constraints and opportunities. One needs to attend to the workings of the latter in order to understand the capacity of the wall and its fall to eclipse other events and symbols of 1989. That this special attention is indeed needed is evidenced by the fact that even in domestic German affairs, the symbolic potency of the wall may obscure as much as it reveals. The wall's iconic surface seems to force its historical specificity to recede, whereby the unique complexities of the East German story are nearly superseded by more general meanings. Nowadays the majority of Germany's youth are unable to say exactly why the Wall was built and how it collapsed (Bonstein 2009: 2; Wowereit 2009: 24).

In other words, iconic power is a distinct kind of highly efficacious yet complex social force. In the context of 1989, the wall's visual agency is responsible for structuring the corresponding processes of attention and interpretation. Moreover, the power of iconicity is such that it can disguise contingency that is present at every stage of the historical process, elide social complexity, and eclipse noniconic occurrences. Kennedy's careful perspective cited above attests to this power, for he admits that the image of the wall's fall *may* convey a sense of historical inevitability. Conversely, the lack of this power means that symbolic reduction of complexity necessary for media communication is unattainable. Such a lack exposes social indeterminacy whereby the eventful potential of occurrences is diminished.

That iconic power can disguise contingency does not mean, of course, that it is not subject to it. One of the goals of this case study is to show how and with what effects cultural codes and contingent contexts intersect in society. Many kinds of iconic power as well as accidental circumstances have gone virtually unnoticed in the social sciences with regard to the Berlin Wall (Drechsel 2010: 4), let alone the Hungarian and Polish imageries. Thus, documenting and comparing them can reveal instructive points of contrast that accentuate the role of culture and contingency in the making of political icons.

POLITICAL ICONICITY IN ACTION

Unlike other 1989 events, the iconicity of the Wall was (1) significantly precoded by the accretion of pictorial capital in relation to a specific place, (2) "the fall" itself was a public, street-bound response to an unexpected liberalization of the wall's border regime whose carnivalesque effervescence was felicitously refracted through the available repertoires of political imagination, and (3) it was sustained via media performances, visual remembrance, spatial arrangements, and active commodification that squared with Berlin's reinvention of itself as an auratic "tourist city" (Richter 2010). While these cultural elements do not account for the entire story, they are neither sociologically peripheral nor epistemologically negligible for the case.

Such a research agenda entails examining the form and content of media coverage. However, I aim at revealing the cultural imperatives to which even powerful media respond. Thus, what follows is a Geertzian reconstruction. Clifford Geertz wrote: "The relevance of historical fact for sociological analysis does not rest on the proposition that there is nothing in the present but the past, which is not true. It rests on the perception that though both the structure and the expression of social life change, the inner necessities that animate it do not" (1983: 142–43). This study interrogates those "necessities" behind the making of a modern revolution. Putting the term in quotation marks signals that the present argument is also a Wittgensteinian reconstruction, for like Kennedy's work, it concedes that "the insidious thing about the causal point of view is that it leads us to say: 'of course, it had to happen like that,' whereas we ought to think: it may have happened like that—and also in many other ways" (Wittgenstein 1984: 37). The cultural sociology advocated here does not hold that specific social events can happen in *any* way. But it does argue that they are relatively open-ended. To specify the cultural probability of certain outcomes and the symbolic conditions of particular historical situations is one of its primary goals. Another is to account for contingency of social action. From this point of view, political iconicity should be approached as consistent potentiality rather than determinative actuality. It is realized via social performances that usually require a series of emplaced practices that are always enacted under changing circumstances and never in isolation from other icons.

ACCRETION OF ICONIC CAPITAL

First of all, each revolution more or less vehemently rejects what its agents see as an unbearable heaviness of being. Turning a cumbersome social order into an "ancien régime" often necessitates the destruction of its signs and tangible epitomes. The more visually compelling the destruction and the more symbolically charged the object of ritual destruction, the better for the revolution's conspicuity.

The German upheaval met these criteria to a high degree. The uprisings that preceded it did not. The German story had a rich and internationally recognized symbolic background. Importantly, it was in the legendary city of Berlin, where the West could easily and literally touch the communist reality's rough surface. The same could not be said about the Hungarian or Polish story. What we are talking about here is the possibility of the accretion of iconic capital constituted by a coalescence of visual, haptic, and discursive qualities connected to a particular place. These qualities operate in a state of reciprocal conditioning. They reinforce one another.

It is a commonplace that acts of radically reforming society need their Luthers, their indignant discourses, and new interpretations of old "sacred" sources. It is less remembered that each Luther needs a Cranach and a performative, public display of dissatisfaction. Likewise, few realize clearly that the actual meanings of revolutionary discourses emerge not merely "accompanied" by iconic images but crucially dependent on them. Images and discourses feed back into one another and remain in a mutually constitutive relation.

Perhaps nowhere was the significance of this fact more perspicuous than in Berlin. By 1989, the wall had come to be commonly perceived as "the central symbol" of communist oppression (Hertle 2007), and none of the truly avant-garde revolutionary societies, like the Hungarians, were in a position to erase it. The main duty rested solely with the Germans, and the key stage was Berlin, a historic capital poignantly divided by "the concrete monstrosity" (Friedrich 2005: 22) that marked it with a "sad *universal* notoriety during the Cold War era" (Haspel 2004: 8, italics mine).

The wall that brutally divided one population and caused death, innumerable damage and ordeals to those who supposedly were to be shielded by it was not merely a political but a human disaster. It was perceived as something "against nature, against man, against life" (Weizsäcker, quoted in Hildebrandt 1981: 44). The communist authorities who had built it to prevent the completion of the mass exodus of population to the West that occurred in the 1950s kept calling it "the antifascist protection wall." They used this name despite the glaring fact that the wall's death strip was on their side and that only their own citizens were being killed or arrested while violating its repressive rules. In return, the West German media, both tabloids and quality papers, referred to the wall as a "concentration camp wall" (Drechsel 2010: 11). Propagandist manipulation and journalistic overstatement only added to the wall's notoriety. That the wall constituted an "ugly thing" was acknowledged even by the highest echelons of Soviet political circles (see Khrushchev, quoted in Hildebrandt 1967: 80). The view of the wall as an "unnatural" barrier was widespread. This trope has been repeatedly invoked by

Western audiences (e.g., Kohl, in Hildebrandt 1989: 49; Harmel, in Hildebrandt 1967: 43). The wall became a totem of evil—"necessary" and thus justified for the communists, "unnatural" for their opponents.

In other words, the Wall became an object of intense debate and extreme experiences. This spawned the accretion of symbolic capital that meant a protracted process of endowing the wall with manifold iconic properties prior to its fall. So when, after the momentous night of November 9, 1989, the end of the wall's existence seemed inexorable, all those meanings could be and were activated. This is discernible in multiple accounts of "cultural significance" of the wall's fall that preceded the *New York Times*' coverage. The wall's fall has been "perceived as a signal event leading to further radical changes in the Eastern bloc and to the reordering of Europe" (Klausmeier and Schmidt 2004: 20). Referring to that famous night, the Swedish King Carl XVI said in December 1989: "The term Europe has received another meaning" (Carl XVI, quoted in Hildebrandt 2003: 116) and so has the term "freedom" too (Bahr 2005: 4). Gorbachev went even further in 1995 by saying that "not only did the Wall embody the division of Europe but of the whole world" (Gorbachev, quoted in Hildebrandt 2003: 97). Others stated that while "for Berliners the fall meant the long-awaited reunification with family and friends, for the rest of us it symbolized the end of the Cold War" (Fenech-Adami, quoted in Hildebrandt 2003: 128). Anita Gradin, the Swedish minister of foreign trade, captured the effervescent nature of the fall: "When the Wall fell the collective sigh of relief went through Europe" (Gradin, quoted in Hildebrandt 2003: 124). As a result, November 9 became "one of Europe's days of destiny," this being yet another piece of stark discursive evidence of the wall's "excessive aura of an icon" (Drechsel 2010: 17–18). This was hardly the case when the Round Table triumphed or the Hungarians cut their border fencing, although the political caliber of those events was similar and they were truly unprecedented in the broader scheme of the region's politics.

All these meanings were upheld by "a constant flow of pictures for prominent placement in the mass media" (Drechsel 2010: 13), many of them poignant and widely disseminated, carrying the human rather than the merely political aspect of the division: divided families, closed streets, corpses of escapees from the GDR, and defecting soldiers, as in the case of Peter Leibing's famous photograph of Conrad Schumann's escape over the rising wall. The picture was titled *Leap to Freedom*. From the uplifting image of Raisin Bombers that supported West Berlin during its blockade to the resolute speech of Ronald Reagan who four decades later demanded that Gorbachev "tear down the Wall," Berlin's division had been prominently present on the international media radar. All that had made the wall a highly quotable entity before it fell. In the West it offered a cognitive and emotional shortcut for knowing the communist East. Nearly three decades of the Wall's publicized postwar drama constituted a story of considerable depth, conveyed and confirmed by riveting, even if sinister imagery. The steadily accruing symbolic capital had created one of the key conditions for the iconic status of the East German upheaval in 1989. The divided German capital city and the rough instrument of its division became the symbol of the whole cold war reality because it could be a perfect visual synecdoche of another popular discursive trope, the Iron Curtain. As such a synecdoche, the wall seemed capable of blurring the distinction between the signifier and the signified—in the eyes of many it *was* a central element of the reality it symbolized as a sign.

It is probably not an exaggeration then to claim that any radical change within the parameters of Berlin's situation was likely to be conspicuous and capable of triggering even more far-reaching events. When "the ignominy of the Wall slicing the city in two" appeared to be suddenly discontinued (Reader 2004: 285), the outburst of mass euphoria could be coded as something at once very natural and very extraordinary. The breaching of the wall was "the pulsating sign of the epilogue of an absurd tragedy" (Ciampi, quoted in Hildebrandt 1999: 127). It was portrayed as constituting "not only a political story but also an intensely human story," as the *New York Times*' Berlin reporter in 1989 emphasized (Schmemann 2006: 12).

The stories of communism in Hungary and Poland did not yield similar icons of protracted oppression that could be "overcome." Of course, the Hungarian revolution of 1956 and the Polish upheaval of 1980–1981 sent significant images to the world whose long-term effects contributed to the eventual mobilization of revolutionary energies. However, they generated no archetypical image in 1989. The Hungarians came close to it when, on June 16, 1989, hundreds of thousands of them participated in the reburial of Imre Nagy, the charismatic leader of the 1956 uprising, in Budapest. It was a "cathartic" event that for the Hungarian participants signified the "symbolic burial of the entire post-1956 regime" (Kis 1998: 346). Yet the whole event could not be made equally and instantly legible for contemporary international audiences. It was associated with no generalizable images of an "intensely human story." The emergence of Poland's Solidarność movement in 1980 was quite spectacular, but at that time it failed to defeat the communist government. Also, the unique effervescence it generated then was not to be repeated in the more passive and apathetic atmosphere surrounding the Round Table talks (Tymowski 1993: 194; Mason, Nelson, and Szklarski 1991). There were few archetypical pictures that might fulfill an iconic role. Photographs like the one by Chris Niedenthal from Warsaw that shows a tank in front of a cinema called "Moscow," with a giant poster of Francis Ford Copolla's movie *Apocalypse Now*, became an enduring icon only in the local context. Such an image requires some discursive decoding and lacks an obviously "human" element, and since Solidarność was suppressed, it could only become an icon of a lost chance, not a triumph. If the lack of an archetypical capital or iconic pictures can be compensated for with other cultural assets, it is the cultural congruity of the spectacular event.

CULTURAL CONGRUITY—REVOLUTION AS GENRE

If a given social performance clearly matches popularly conceived parameters of the genre it is supposed to represent, it is likely to fulfill at least two of the elementary conditions of iconic power: the typification of an idea and the crystallization of feelings. The genre at stake is revolution.

Because the 1989 changes in Central Europe were embraced as "greatly surprising" (Gaddis 1998: 115), "miraculous" (Latour 1993: 8), or even "crazy" (Meiners 2009), rather than pragmatic, negotiated, and thus relatively expected, the media coded 1989 as a revolutionary year. This, in turn, would render certain expressions of it more congruent with the political genre than others, especially in retrospect. In this context, the events in Berlin worked very well since they took form of a palpable ritualistic effervescence enacted rapidly on the streets of the rather docile capital city. Most important, the eroding wall could again work perfectly as a distinguished pars pro toto of communism's general erosion, so that when it fell, the East European communist bloc could be seen as "collapsing" as well.

The Hungarian and Polish upheavals, on the other hand, may have been seen as ambivalent, paradoxical political breaks aptly dubbed "refolution" (Ash 1989), i.e., sharing the properties of both reform and revolution (Kis 1998: 301). Despite the people's deep discontent and desire for a "total political overhaul," they were so deliberative and gradual that Western left-leaning academics, for example Susan Buck-Morss (2002), do not regard these events as "revolutionary." Perhaps it could not have been otherwise given the limiting Marxist explanatory models they tend to adhere to (Chirot 1998: 385). But in Poland at least, the situation "on the ground" in 1989 reflected this objection—the word "revolution" did not dominate the Polish public discourse (Tymowski 1993: 175). No wonder, then, that international audiences may have perceived the Hungarian and Polish occurrences as quite anticlimatic, a mere installment of the protracted struggle for "socialism with a human face" (Žižek 2009). Even the members of Solidarność who sat at the Round Table felt that "the talks had no visible dramaturgy" (Smoleński 2009: 15). Surveys showed that despite extensive discursive press coverage of the Round Table talks in Poland, there was relatively little sense of truly radical change going on, no dramatic images conveying the huge revolutionary potential of the event or at least the collective belief in the possibility of communism's definitive end. Society talked about politics and change, but it did not directly engage in it, nor saw its leaders as performing change in a spectacular way (Nelson, Mason, Szklarski 1991: 206, 218). Rather, a "refolution" was being conducted by select groups of intellectuals and activists, and it initially aimed at incremental, negotiated even if potentially profound change. For this reason it could have even appeared to be top-down rather than popular despite the mass, clearly antigovernmental support the dissidents entertained. In sum, 1989 in Poland and Hungary was revolutionary in content but not in form, and only with the benefit of hindsight. The title of the *Spiegel* article "Die Herbeigeredete Revolution" [The revolution talked into existence] suggests correctly that the Round Table "changed history" through a discursive self-fulfilling prophecy whose revolutionary effects could be clearly discernible to all only in retrospect (Mix 2009). The Round Table talks, first exercised in Poland and later replicated in Hungary, could be a better synecdoche of reconciliation than revolution. The talks did prove that "the language of the government and of the opposition was constitutive of meaning rather than reflective of it" (Holc 1992: 122), but they featured little specifically iconic agency. Due to this performative difference between the German *Wende* [turn] and the Polish/Hungarian "transformation," it was much easier in the former case to *see* that the *people* were indeed against the *state*.

For example, although prompted by mass demonstrations in March 1989, the Hungarian Round Table talks involved a "small number of elite organizations, whose grassroots links were poorly developed and whose very existence stemmed in part from the collaboration of key Communist reformers" (Bartlett 1997:143).

In Poland, the political confrontation was at least very clear—Solidarność versus the communist government. However, the Round Table meant *talks* that lasted two months and were carried out at a high level, often behind closed doors. It has been noted that "if the Round Table negotiations had lasted several days instead of several weeks, they would have attracted everybody's attention" (Smoleński 2009: 15). The trilateral character of the Hungarian Round Table talks that lasted even longer severely diminished the potential of typical revolutionary binarization. These actions, *transitional* rather than revolutionary, had no well-defined climax, were considerably stretched out over time, and at least partially possessed the character of *arcanum*. Putting them together with another Central European case, that of Czechoslovakia, into the category of the Velvet Revolution made perfect sense. Yet the image of the upheaval might have appeared not exactly groundbreaking at the time. After all, although the Velvet Revolution may be something morally highly desirable, it is politically and culturally as confusing as any oxymoron can be. Employing and popularizing the term "velvet" was more than a regular qualification of the genre of political action; it enabled the application of the genre in the Western media at all. As such, it points to an emotional desire and a cultural utility for viewing 1989 in dramatic terms, not only to its "velvetness." As one observer concluded, "'Revolution' conveys the drama and epochal measure of the times; 'transition' focuses on the dispassionate management" (Tymowski 1993: 169).

Because the changes in Hungary or Poland deviated in these crucial respects from a conventional revolutionary script, they were culturally less congruent, and their chances of becoming iconic accordingly decreased. The Hungarian tearing of the Iron Curtain had dismantled an important, concrete object, but it appeared neither as spontaneous nor rapid, nor was it humanly poignant and enacted within the "sacred" streetscapes of the society. Above all, the object itself had no special iconic, historically constituted symbolic capital. It was not a quotable, auratic entity, and thus could hardly serve as a cognitive shortcut or spectatorial element of the central social landscape. The Polish transition may have seemed similarly incremental and bereft of visual drama. It was also synecdochic in an imperfect key. At the end of the 1980s, despite their avant-garde and their mass resistance, neither the Poles nor the Hungarians carried out sustained social performances of a public repudiation of internationally recognized, nontrivial totemic signs of communist oppression.

There were many reasons not to do this. As truly avant-garde dissidents, they ran a much greater risk. Political prudence and uncertainty favored a low-key "refolution." Such a decidedly pragmatic approach to political change precluded spectacular gestures of a heroic or, worse, a martyrological kind. Burdened by the heavy historical legacy of such moves, "the shadow of Brezhnev's doctrine," and by social unrest stemming from the profound economic demise of the 1980s, the Polish dissidents were particularly wary of the ramifications that any "revolutionary philosophy" could have had (see Michnik 2009: 13). Rather, they sought to cultivate the spirit of communication following the script of civil disobedience (strikes) and dialogue (negotiations). Neither yielded iconic images. The idea was, first of all, to exert pressure on the communist government without alienating it from reformist programs or prompting the type of military violence it had unleashed in 1981. Hungary treaded a similar path since it had been the first country ever to taste the ruthless implications of open anticommunist uprising. Although Gorbachev was apparently gentler than his predecessors, the wound of 1956 had not been healed.

In general, if both countries had strong anticommunist traditions, potentially significant civil resources, and hosted some unprecedented political occurrences, they did not deliver performatively fused, iconic events that would provide a kind of international symbolic catharsis to communist traumas. In the key year of 1989, their struggle was not particularly photogenic, their "revolutions" were piecemeal, and the main events not perfectly congruent with the genre at stake. Although well covered by the media and skillfully negotiated, the "revolution" in Warsaw consisted of a protracted elite *communication* carried out *indoors*, while in Berlin it was a tangible *experience* enacted *outdoors* and televised. Thus the latter was fully "iconspicuous," while the former lacked totemic, auratic, spectatorial, and striking pictorial qualities. In the context of Alexander's aforementioned understanding of iconicity that emphasizes experience versus communication, this difference between the two becomes particularly significant. What the Poles and the Hungarians jointly achieved in the first half of 1989 was politically pivotal but culturally incongruent (the former) or performatively illegible (the latter). The material did not unequivocally translate into the symbolic, and the political did not quite match the revolutionary, at least as far as the mainstream of the Western tradition is concerned. It was precisely the effervescent drama of violating the iconic wall that made the East German *Wende* cross the threshold of a profound national revolution and become something more than a socialist reformation triggered by the earlier Leipzig demonstrations (Walser Smith 1991). The Polish and Hungarian "revolutions" lacked that effervescence and produced no strong images. That is why they ultimately failed to iconize 1989 globally, even though they also contained strong national and universal moral sentiments.

William Shakespeare's notion that something might give "more light than heat" provides a useful construct to capture this difference, but it is one that demands an adaptation in this context. Here the Polish and Hungarian revolutionary processes could have been perceived as developments that gave more heat than light. In this inverted form the Shakespearean notion indicates the cultural implausibility of political trailblazing that does not begin with a big fire. It might indicate the existence of a certain incredulity on the part of the producers and consumers of news alike towards rites of passage without apparent effervescence or the renunciation of the totems of an "ancien régime."

By contrast, the bottom-up, massive, sudden, unexpected, and carnivalesque character of the German *Wende* lent revolutionary authenticity to its appearance. Crucially, it was performed on the streets of the society's numinous center (Walser Smith 1991: 236). Like in Poland, the *contingently uttered words*, especially on the part of the government, were significant—a fact to which I will return. But unlike in Poland, *visibly performed deeds* followed too. To use Richard Sennett's language, on November 9, the *Wende*'s binary script could easily be exemplified with the flesh of the society in conflict with the stone of the state right in the middle of its capital city. Moreover, it stood in stark contrast to the words of the GDR's leader, Erich Honecker, who on January 19, 1989, pronounced that "the Wall will remain in fifty and in a hundred years," and who still in August of that year maintained that "the masses' unity with the party has never been as strong as today" (Honecker, quoted in Hildebrandt 2008: 87). The lay international audiences that followed such enunciations could imagine desperate people rebelling against the regime's cynical or unhinged leader. In this respect, the situation in the GDR efficiently typified "a comic feature of all the 1989 revolutions, namely that the communists, at each stage of their descent to powerlessness, deceived themselves into thinking they could break the fall before they reached the bottom" (Hawkes 1990: 5). Perhaps they deceived themselves that they could continue to fool the people this way. In any case, "this was the price they paid for exercising power in isolation" (5).

On the other hand, East Germans trained to read between the lines of communist propaganda could feel that perhaps something new was in the air. They were likely to remember that the building of the wall had followed solemn proclamations by Walter Ulbricht that there was "no intention to build any wall." Still, many of them, even those who happened to be part of the massive anticommunist manifestations were deeply surprised by themselves, and this fact added to the experience of revolutionary emotions such as exasperation, exhilaration, elation, shock. As a young witness to that sense of disbelief recalled, "even the grown-ups seemed confused... The GDR couldn't disappear. Not in a million years" (Hensel 2004: 3). Those who actually crossed the wall on the miraculous night of November 9, 1989, for example Eckard Löhde, reported that "it definitely felt like a festival at Brandenburg Gate" (quoted in Bahr 2005: 33). After the wall had been breached, the East German civil rights campaigner Bärbel Bohley described the situation tersely: "The government is crazy, and the people have gone crazy too" (quoted in Hildebrandt 2003: 95).

The "craziness" of this unusual street performance was crucially underscored by the visibly festive attitude of the shocked and yet extremely exuberant, massive crowd that showed up at the iconic checkpoints and landmarks as if it were a giant, Internet-era flashmob suddenly disregarding any, even the strictest, rules of public conduct. The sense of unexpected craziness and incomprehensible celebration (Meiners 2009: 8), a kind of "carnival of freedom" as it was called in the Poland of 1980 but where it was extinct by 1989, was instant, overwhelming, palpable, and visually arresting. Because of these performative qualities, the event of November 9 could be coded and represented as "a revolutionary fall of the Wall," even though its actual demolition started in spring 1990 and lasted several months (Sälter 2007: 11–12). As was the case with the Hungarian border fence, the proper dismantling of Berlin's border system had to take some time because, by 1989, it was in fact a very complex structure that rendered the wall itself "a simplification of everyday speech" (Friedrich 2005: 21). However, this very discursive simplification contributed to the successful construction of the November 9 social performance as something decisive—once thousands of people sitting on top of some concrete parts of the border were seen celebrating, journalists could conclude that "the nightmare has ended and a dream has come true" (Bahr 2005: 31). One linguistic simplification enabled and indeed invited the usage of others connected to it. The revolution assumed an undeniable reality through immediacy and the enchanting aura it apparently exuded.

The fact that the mass crossing of the wall was the first event to resemble a classic revolutionary situation at various levels is one of the cultural reasons for which it now can be remembered and imagined as "signaling the beginning" of communism's rapid "collapse" in Europe. Because the coverage of the German event could draw on classical scripts and myths of popular uprising, it assumed legibility and importance as enthralling political reportage, a properly rebellious cover story, and a real example of revolutionary spirit. In fact, "the 'fall' of the Wall was often compared to the French Revolution of 1789" (Drechsel 2010: 13), an interpretation uncannily warranted by a coincidence that it happened exactly two hundred years after the start of the iconic French event of similar national and European significance.

Simply put, the German revolution was a paradigmatic social performance of its own kind. It had a clearly defined address (stage), a transfixing typical plot (script), numerous participants (social actors), a totemic symbol (prop), a spontaneous carnivalesque style (authentic mise-en-scène), and last but not least, it was perfectly public, not arcane. Thus it could easily be turned into a kind of generalizable cathartic ritual emphasizing the meaning of that strange revolution, velvet but swift, peaceful but sweeping, spontaneous but consequential, unexpected but legible. As the German writer Martin Walser put it, "The Germans in the GDR created a revolution which is really new: the gentle revolution" (quoted in Hildebrandt 2003: 55). One could perhaps amend his comment and say: the Germans did not create it, but they instantiated it iconically and thus powerfully crystallized its meanings and feelings.

From the perspective of the international audiences, a combination of the need for cognitive abbreviation and emotional dramatization made the so enacted and narrated overcoming of the wall the representational shortcut of choice. The only violent uprising in 1989 occurred more than a month after the mass German demonstrations in various cities of distant Romania. Most importantly, its brutal character made it an outlier to the widely praised specificity of 1989. It was the exception that underlined Berlin's peacefulness as the rule (Banac 1992: 5). If Poland, Hungary, and Czechoslovakia were very or even too gentle, Romania was too radical, or so it may have seemed at the closing of 1989 when the year's historic mythology was sealed by Václav Havel's velvet success. Berlin had poised itself perfectly in the emergent cultural and political landscapes by discernibly meeting the criteria of a *genus proximum* (mass "crazy" revolt) and a *differentia specifica* (peaceful "velvet" execution).

AFTER THE BATTLE—HISTORY AS MEMORY AND IMAGINED COMMODITY

Thus far, I have analyzed the factors within two distinct temporal dimensions, namely, the relatively long period preceding the revolutions and the relatively short period of the upheavals proper. The third dimension in which the iconicity of the revolutions should be assessed belongs to the time that came afterwards, i.e., to the transitional period launched by the revolutions. The questions of what happened to the revolutionary icons and how they have since been acted upon are crucial here. In order to understand the power and durability of icons, it is not enough to unravel the contexts that occasioned their emergence; one needs to reconstruct the subsequent uses of these icons too.

Although the transitional time in all the Central European countries meant some version of capitalist "shock therapy," the respective social trajectories were quite distinct. In Berlin, it meant, literally, instant, full contact with the West, prompt reunification of the partitioned country, and a profound, very fast-paced process of stitching the two Germanys together. Only during the 1990s and only according to the official, rather conservative statistics did the German government acknowledge that it had spent $330 billion for the reconstruction projects that followed the formal reunification in 1990. As John Reader remarks, "even for Europe's largest and most robust capitalist economy, taking over and assimilating its former socialist neighbor was proving to be 'a heavy lunch'" (Reader 2004: 291).

Heavy, no doubt, it has been, but for precisely this reason it was marveled at internationally. The very heaviness of the whole enterprise meant extraordinary attention paid to the German story of unification and transition. It was a natural social laboratory in which new things were constantly happening as observers spoke. This special attention meant that the media exposure of the Wall was considerable. Berlin found itself in the thick of the postcommunist metamorphosis business. The postwall reconstruction frenzy in the city resembled the immediate post–World War II efforts, not only in terms of the scale of the infrastructural investment but the symbolic one as well. In fact, the latter gained astonishing momentum that could be perceived by outsiders as a symbolic extension of revolutionary thrust. Still, to quite a few Western observers the revolutionary break posed uneasy questions. "Declaring Berlin the capital of the country seemed more of an idealistic gesture than a sensible pragmatic reaction to the collapse of communist East Germany" (Reader 2004: 292). It even seems that not all Germans themselves found the symbolism of the center absolutely worthy of this gesture because the required parliamentary voting brought only a narrow majority. Yet the numinous aura prevailed. Once taken, the decision to acknowledge and fully restore Berlin's numinous status was set in stone, figuratively and literally. As the capital of the freshly united and thus biggest European society, Berlin was back in the historical spotlight. Consequently, so was the wall, or rather its vestigial presence and vexing cultural legacy. Solving the practical problems of reconnecting the two Berlins also meant solving the issue of the wall. As the public discussions about its physical and symbolic fate went on, the wall's presence endured, even if only as a spectral, fragmented entity looked at by the increasing waves of voyeuristic tourists.

The "big Western brother" was there neither for Poland nor for Hungary. This circumstance meant at once relatively less transitional dynamism but also more internal, volatile struggle over the meaning of the revolution. It also took fifteen years for the two countries to join the European Union (EU), which was brought to life by the Maastricht Treaty in 1992 and enlarged by the Central European countries in 2004. During these years, the postcommunist transformation in Warsaw and Budapest simply did not match that of Berlin. The so-called "decommunization process" in these countries meant a gradual decomposition, not a consolidation of whatever was left from the revolutionary mythology. Twenty years after the Round Table, its myth has many contentious versions in Poland (Derkaczew 2009), each with its own *votum separatum* regarding the revolutionary history. A deep division over the meaning of 1989 strips that year of its symbolic power.

The difference between Germany and Poland is informative in this respect. It lies above all in the literal and figurative packaging and promoting of the 1989 icons. While Berlin and the Germans in general seem to have done a lot to pursue the perfect public relations to the maximum, Warsaw and the Poles appear to have settled for a curatorial minimum. As separate, imagined communities in possession of two different iconic entities, these nations constructed two different imagined commodities of their "revolutionary" history. This divergence has to do not only with the contrast between a pronounced martyrological, "postcolonial" self-understanding of Polish society (Thompson 2006; Janion 2007) and an ostensibly more liberal, post-imperial and progressive national narrative of the Germans, but also with the sheer tangible properties of the revolutionary icons that have had considerable bearing on how their artistic and commercial afterlives could be and have been enacted.

First of all, the ring of the wall was made of 45,000 concrete segments, each weighing 2.75 tons, a circumstance that made it potentially more accessible during the cold war only from the West and later, from both sides. This facilitated, for example, the emergence of the wall as a "unique collective artwork" featuring a huge array of visually arresting and politically engaged graffiti (Kuzdas 1998: 5). Some of these works of art became famous and won prizes in competitions, like the one entitled *Overcoming the Wall by Painting on the Wall*. Today, they are reproduced on Berlin souvenir postcards, and constitute a pattern to follow for artists like Banksy who graphically subvert other border walls, for example, the one in Palestine.

Following the wall's demolition, 360 segments were sold, partly for the graffiti artwork. Other sections were publicly displayed, and the entirety of its image "domesticated" by layers of aesthetic interventions, the activity of so-called "Wall-peckers," and co-optation by the tourist industry. These actions have translated into the wall's lasting as a cultural symbol beyond the temporal limits of its being at the center of revolutionary attention. Thus, "Berlin's longest structure refuses to die" (Bahr 2005: 41). By contrast, due to its history and material properties, the Hungarian border fence hardly possessed a comparable cultural potential. Similarly, the ring of the table was much smaller and less conspicuous, and its tangibility reduced by making it a regular, indivisible "museum item." It remains in the Presidential Palace in Warsaw where it was originally placed. Thus it is permanently removed from the direct public gaze.

The potential of the wall as an object that could inspire not only dread but also future curiosity was discerned immediately after its creation. Hugh Gaitskell, Chairman of the British Labour Party, noted in 1962: "What an exceptional phenomenon this miles-long prison wall is! It could attract tourists. It would not surprise me if visitors would come by the hundreds or thousands to see it" (quoted in Hildebrandt 2003: 39). Following the wall's collapse, visitors by the millions were coming to Berlin indeed. Reflecting on this phenomenon, Dubravka Ugrešić wrote that the wall became the "biggest souvenir in the world" (1996). Although the only remnants of the actual wall that could be seen after reunification in 1990 were scattered segments and sections, the media images, artistic interventions, and political debates persisted. Moreover, the official physical "traces" were engraved on the surfaces of the city's sidewalks and streets. The 1.3 kilometer-long section near the Ostbahnhof, now with graffiti art on both sides, was left intact and turned into an open-air museum called the East Side Gallery. Memorial centers at Bernauer Strasse and Checkpoint Charlie have been established. Especially the latter excels in full-scale commercialization of the wall's legacy. Solitary segments covered by graffiti are scattered around public spaces of Berlin, from big plazas to side-street restaurant gardens. Perhaps most interesting, little chunks of the wall are being sold as souvenirs in different locations of the city, some of them with the slightly sardonic caption "certified by West." Two decades after the fall, one can still buy postcards with small plastic bubbles attached to them containing alleged shards of the wall. Through the conduits of the tourist industry, the political and material body of the communist wall began to steadily dissolve into the most mundane capitalist entertainment market. The chunks of concrete could cheaply enter millions of households as auratic "shards of history" and "private political fetishes" (Feversham and Schmidt 1999: 126). There was also an upscale version of this phenomenon. Soon after the momentous events in November 1989, eighty-one wall segments were sold at high-profile auctions, for example in Monte Carlo in June 1990 (Sälter 2007: 19; Flemming 2006: 74–75).

It is noteworthy that nothing of comparable scale and inventiveness has occurred in Poland or Hungary. Neither Warsaw nor Budapest has promoted their original symbols so dynamically. Representational practices related to the local icons of 1989 that would target, first of all, uninitiated visitors have been relatively scarce there. Budapest's tourist program, the "Tipsy Lenin Tour," is a remarkable exception, but it is parasitical on the cosmopolitan, generic pop communism rather than genuinely Hungarian. Especially the decade of the 1990s, when the memory of the revolution was still fresh and the myth-driven curiosity about the "new Europe" and authentic "wild East" was high, did not witness the cultivation and celebration of icons on the scale sustained in Berlin. On the contrary, Poland saw the bitter breakup of Solidarność that meant the irrevocable loss of revolutionary solidarity.

Some of the consequences of this were clearly visible when it came to the celebration of the twentieth anniversary of the revolution. The events in Poland were marred by acrimonious political conflicts, and the urban locus of the festive efforts was contested up to the last moment. Just as Leipzig could claim to be Germany's real cradle of the revolutionary movement, so could and did Gdańsk vis-à-vis Warsaw, diffusing the iconic power of the latter. Consequently, the country failed to deliver an iconspicuous anniversary celebration. Twenty years after the epochal changes, Poland seemed to lack not only the sufficient "light" but also proper "heat."

The problem of the internal inefficiency of public communication and symbolic chaos was compounded by the international underrepresentation of the merits of the Polish revolution. The Poles have justifiable reasons to complain that their historic contributions have not been duly appreciated or have even been ignored in Germany and other Western countries (Perger 2009; von Salzen 2009).[6] Yet for their part, they could have done more, and what they eventually did hardly matched the consistency and thoroughness of Germany's own efforts.[7]

If German society may be perceived as somewhat reluctant to fully acknowledge its political debt to its eastern neighbors, it can be credited with setting standards for the effective realization of its iconic potential. The festive celebration on November 9, 2009, in the capital of Germany skillfully used the iconicity of the wall. The notorious barrier was imaginatively reinstalled in the center of the city as a giant domino row whose visually impressive falling effect symbolized not only the very collapse of the structure but also the chain reaction of separate national upheavals in the region. Wałęsa's iconic stature was acknowledged by an invitation to him to set the whole thing in motion. Yet it could also symbolize the individual's modesty compared with the spectacle's grandeur underlined by the decisively festive atmosphere. Berlin itself once again lived up to its reputation as a fun capital, if not the European capital of fun.

Could those culturally and materially conditioned contrasts be at least mitigated, if not altered, by different patterns of display and narration? Various counterfactual considerations might be taken into account to heuristically simulate an alternative, more conspicuous system of symbolic representation. For one thing, Poland and Hungary did not sufficiently circulate and ritualize the iconic capital they did possess. For instance, had Poland creatively recycled its reputation as "the merriest barrack of the communist camp," its message could have achieved more touristic exposure. Nowadays, liberal observers in Warsaw suggest that if the Poles had retained the united spirit of contestation and a future-oriented attitude, they might have secured better perspectives of cultural appeal (Środa 2009). They suggest that if Polish icons had been packaged attractively, they could have had more international impact.

With regard to the two specific iconic entities discussed here, one may elaborate on this point by saying that if the Round Table had been more exposed and more interactively displayed, it could have assumed a more dynamic cultural biography. A more systematic visual cultivation could have strengthened its citational and experiential qualities. For example, if it had been built into the cityscape of Warsaw, the way Theodor Adorno's desk was in Frankfurt, its public visibility and hence iconic biography could have been more robust. Ensconcing the historical piece of furniture in a transparent cube at one of the capital city's plazas with historic, personalized artifacts still laying there could have sparked the imagination of the locals and visitors alike. Instead, the authorities maintained the status of this Polish icon as an indoor artifact. Moreover, political groups emerged that openly coded it as the defunct site of a bad "compromise," not the sign of a clear-cut "victory." This domestic political struggle over the meaning of the key material icon may have lent additional credence to the international perception of the Round Table as an ambiguous, not a well-defined symbol. Consequently, it may have indirectly enabled the relevant debates in countries like Germany to be couched in the language of "ownership of revolutionary victory over communism" (Schuller 2009: 5). In Germany itself, on the other hand, the meanings of the wall and its fall remain by and large incontrovertible. In Berlin, the wall's chunks are still being sold, and its graffiti icons from the East Side Gallery have recently been repainted despite organizational difficulties (Woś 2009). The parts of the wall are still treated as an iconic currency of the city.[8]

To be sure, not all Germans have been entirely happy about the ways the wall's cultural heritage has been used. The process of demolition and even the very fall happened to be debated (Flemming 2006: 76; Haspel 2004: 21). There were also international voices that raised an issue of the wall's special architectural value (Koolhaas 2006: 84). However, these arguments and sentiments were idiosyncratic or elite rather than mainstream; they had the status of radical opinion or professional and academic speculation rather than popular representation. Iconic potential can be realized despite such voices, or perhaps be even fueled by them, but it can hardly flourish when the ambiguity of the key props permeates the myth at stake.

CHANGE AND CHANCE

Iconic capital, cultural congruity, and remembrance patterns are three dimensions that contribute to structuring public attention and interpretive tendencies in the long run. However, the cultural resonance is shaped not only by these partly controllable elements but also by sheer chance. Contingent iconic events beyond the actors' control can either amplify or reduce the impact of an event, and they can shape the context of reception.

When Solidarność won the elections on June 4, 1989, it became clear that the first noncommunist government in the communist bloc would soon become a fact. However, before even that news could be confirmed and its results materialized, another groundbreaking event from within the communist world riveted international attention. On the same day, a democratic, student-led protest was crushed in Tiananmen Square in Beijing. Moreover, the picture taken there by Jeff Widener, showing a solitary human figure in front of a row of tanks, became an international icon of society's vulnerability vis-à-vis the totalitarian state. In the aforementioned book of the iconic images of the 1980s, the blowup of this picture is printed on two neighboring pages (Yapp 2001: 108–09).

It was only two months after the landslide victory of Solidarność that the noncommunist government of Poland was finally formed on August 19, 1989. Moreover, that was an important day for Hungary and Germany, too, in that the former enacted at the exact same moment the Pan-European Picnic near the Austrian border. The historic exodus of East Germans to Austria began. As a result, "the Polish changes were overshadowed as tens of thousands of people started escaping to West Germany via Hungary. When Hungary permitted the East German plastic Trabants to drive on to Austria, it broke the fundamental convention of the bloc—that states cooperate in restricting each other's refugees" (Banac 1992: 3). Interestingly enough, as far as international publicity was concerned, the situation benefited the Germans more than the Hungarians who made it possible. As for Poland, it took more than a year before more high-profile political news from the country would emerge. It was only on December 9, 1990, when Wałęsa became the President of Poland. On that day, Slobodan Milošević fatefully assumed the same position in his own country, Serbia.

In order to emphasize the great importance of timing as well as the ramifications of cultural and physical accessibility, it is instructive to put this issue in a still broader international context. Considered together by the Western observers, the East European revolutions had occupied a more central political position than the similar emancipatory democratic changes in sub-Saharan Africa that occurred simultaneously. As a result, the latter went largely unnoticed in the West, which remained transfixed by the former. As one *New York Times* reporter, Howard W. French observed, "The misfortune of Africa's newly pluralistic countries like Congo-Brazzaville, Benin, Zambia and Niger was to have had their democratic moment at the very same time that communism was collapsing in Eastern Europe. Timing is everything" (French 2004: 158).

In the contingent context of 1989, Poland's anticommunist iconicity faced a kind of formidable symbolic "competition." The legibility of the German revolution consisted in its being not only one event centered around one symbol and located in a numinous location but also in its occurrence in a different news context. Due to the very proximity of West Berlin, it also featured a different structure of journalistic accessibility. Moreover, as popular romantic narrative had it, it was aided by a fortunate accident. The epochal opening of the border with West Berlin was somewhat reluctantly announced at an evening press conference on November 9, 1989, that was broadcast live on GDR television. The announcement was made in response to an apparently serendipitous question about travel to the West. "History has never been made quite so casually," reads one description of the moment when the spokesman of the East German communist party, Günter Schabowski, said that free movement across the border to West Germany was possible "immediately" (Flemming 2006: 66). A seemingly unplanned pronouncement happened to trigger a euphoric social reaction both due to its unexpectedness and its instant media availability. This caused some to assert that "the fall of the Wall was the first event in world history to attain reality because the media had announced it" (Hertle 2007:150), thus making it all the more cinematographic and amenable to pop-cultural citation. One could say, contradicting Gil Scott-Heron's famous lyrics, that the revolution did happen to be televised. A casual, apparently random and broadcast introduction to something truly extraordinary can hardly fail to be compelling. And so it was. This narrative sank in and remained an official myth, an urban legend of the revolution even though, in reality, it is most probably just a myth in the negative sense of the term.[9]

The proximity of the event to New Year's Eve enabled euphoric Germans to celebrate the new year as a truly fresh chapter of their country's history. The international audiences did not fail to realize this, either. Many foreigners, with such iconic photographers as Richard Avedon among them, joined the celebration. *Wahnsinn* (craziness) was still the key word (Kuzdas 1998: 8). According to the then-mayor of West Berlin, Walter Momper, "The Germans were the happiest people on earth" (quoted in Hildebrandt 2003: 51). And the earth witnessed this. The exuberant mood gained momentum as the reunification negotiations were promptly carried out. In summer 1990, West Germany won the Soccer World Cup, accentuating symbolically the new chapter of German history and the prowess of the society's Western part. The celebration of this victory felt like a continuation of the festive national mood that had commenced in November. It provided the newly reunified country with publicity that was unheard of in Poland or Hungary.

That was the atmosphere in which the Central European countries entered the transitional period of the 1990s. The brief but fast-paced liminal time meant to many the triumph of democracy and capitalist aspirations. But as such, it was iconically finished by another "simple and well-defined symbolic collapse"

(Bowler, this volume). The terrorist attack on the World Trade Center could be and was seen as the end of an era (Schlögel 2008). The eerily symmetrical dates of the two epochal falls, 11/9—9/11 may be perceived as iconic brackets of a special period of Western history. Through such contingent patterning, the wall's fall could assume yet another valence of its iconic power.

As a closed historical time, the 1989 revolution became a well-entrenched event of the past. Thus the details recede in collective memory faster than in individual minds directly connected to it. What remains is the particular iconosphere. In a social reality saturated by the news media, icons are recognizable tips of informational icebergs. In the visual and discursive sea full of free-floating signifiers, only "iconspicuous" stories firmly inhere in the public imagination. Audiences may be empirically incorrect if they judge the weight of presented events solely by the surface value. But often that is all they can and want to digest, and there is a chance that they can be symbolically right. At the time when "the terror of uncertain signs" seems more palpable than ever before, the iconic fixing of the floating chain of signifieds amounts to a cultural imperative. The media are among key "fixers." Roland Barthes's cultural diagnosis sounds prophetic here, for it is the propitiously emplaced, culturally legible icon that carries the day rather than the historically unprecedented but ambiguous one.

When combined, different kinds of iconic power can effectively override other types of social authority. The historic events are not simply born and told, but shown. They never speak for themselves. They have specific visual, material, spatial, and performative properties that can be framed in particular ways under specific circumstances and therefore lend themselves more to certain representational and experiential patterns than to others. Their social impact does not depend solely on what facts "say," but crucially on how they can be performed, how they look, and on the dynamics of interplay between the seen and the said. A political "signal" needs not only to be discursively but also iconically valid to be remembered and to work as a temporal marker. The factual, strictly *political* strength of events may be necessary, but it is not a sufficient condition of their *cultural* power. When "reality becomes an increasingly symbolic order under the dominion of iconic pictures" (Bürgi and Fischer 2005: 6), the political strength is not neatly separable from the cultural one. In order for events to be treated as historic or groundbreaking, it is often enough if they are "iconspicuous." Such power of icons consists in "the empirical giving way to the symbolic" (Bowler, this volume).

Strong iconic entities derive cultural power from their unique sensuous properties and place-specific meanings. At the same time, the nondiscursive, experiential qualities rarely if ever exert this power independently from the narratives and myths that comprise the cultural landscape of a given time and place. This study sought to demonstrate that while relatively autonomous, the surface and depth remain in mutually constitutive relation to each other. When the former seems to perfectly crystallize the latter and the latter effectively anchors the former, we witness the emergence of a consequential iconic process. At least three analytically distinct dimensions conditioned this process with regard to the political iconicity of 1989: (1) symbolic resources (icon's gestation), (2) genre adequacy (icon's parturition), and (3) remembrance patterns (icon's biography). The fulfillment of their combined potential is not automatic, but hinges on other, place-specific and contingently performed icons of a given time.

The wall felicitously met all of these criteria. The specific visual qualities and infelicitous contingencies of the Polish and Hungarian revolutions meant that neither the egalitarian image of the Round Table nor the unprecedented breach of the Iron Curtain was in a position to decisively iconize the democratic turn of history's wheel. When it came to making and representing an anticommunist revolution, the cultural logic of iconicity favored an anonymous but conspicuous crowd, not a hero-led, avant-garde group of dissidents plotting in the nooks and crannies of an eroding system. When it comes to a democratic political ritual, the *publicum* trumps the *arcanum*, as was already shown elsewhere (Alexander and Smith 1993). This logic favored the community that seemed to "openly" overcome the symbolically charged barrier at one time, not the "quiet heroes" who "secretly" dismantled the mundane one in increments. The former, not the latter, is more culturally convincing and lends itself more easily to the media dramatization craved by media-saturated late modern audiences. It is the vigorous physicality and directly graspable human aspect of a crushing concrete symbol in a famous location, not the pragmatic deliberations and unprecedented votes cast to discontinue a whole "system" in culturally under-exposed locales that prevail in media. It is not just the *factuality of first occurrences* but the *iconicity of well-placed events* that indicates what counts as the "beginning," "end," "signal," and "revolution." Temporal, political markers arise contingently out of iconic emplacement.

The cultural production related to the 1989 revolution incessantly delivers evidence to support anew these claims. One of the most recent ones comes from the cinema. In February 2010, a Polish documentary was nominated for an Oscar. *Rabbit à la Berlin,* created by Konopka and Rosolowski in 2009, depicts the strange life of the rabbits that inhabited the wall's death strip. In the movie, the rabbits allegorize people and domesticate what Rem Koolhaas called "the areas of nothingness." The isolation meant both impoverished conditions conducive to apathy and protection from the hard reality of competition. The abrupt disappearance of the wall put this way of life to an end. The decidedly Aesopian form points to a more generalizable denouement. Nevertheless, the title explicitly reveals the story's specific reference, showing that it is the Berlin Wall that is really worth bringing to the table when it comes to imagining communism and its end. Once again, its image seems sufficient, indeed perfectly potent to allegorize the key meanings of the oppressive system and the odd, grand revolution of 1989 that discontinued it.

NOTES

1. See: http://topics.nytimes.com/topics/reference/timestopics/subjects/b/berlin_wall /index.html
2. For example, the Wikipedia entry "1989" features the breached wall as the first and only image.

3. Similarly, no picture of any Hungarian event from 1989 is reproduced in the popular Wikipedia entry "The Revolutions of 1989." See: http://en.wikipedia.org/wiki/Revolutions_of_1989#Hungary.

4. An insightful empirical discussion of "the ascendancy of myth over interests" can be found in Tim Snyder's "National Myths and International Relations: Poland and Lithuania 1989–1994" (Snyder 1995). The present project aims to show that myths are a regular part of the interest structure of social actors.

5. Recalling the difference between the GDR and Hungary, Fritz Stern wrote that upon arrival in Budapest, he "sensed at once that this was a different, freer atmosphere," imbued with the mood of resistance and perceptible cultivation of liberty he had never observed in the GDR (Stern 2007: 331). Yet shortly after the dissolution of communism, those differences themselves dissolved into the Berlin-dominated images of a postcommunist transition.

6. The problem is compounded by the corresponding discourse that intends to designate unequivocal national "victors" of the anticommunist revolution instead of fostering a civil sense of European "we" (see Schuller 2009).

7. Perhaps having understood the dwindling iconic capital and subsequent relative international neglect of the Round Table, Poland displayed in Berlin in 2009 a giant poster of it with the caption "It began in Gdansk" and a list of other key revolutionary East European cities. It was hung on one of the buildings in the center of Berlin in the vicinity of the Russian Embassy. Alas, such a singular visual intervention could hardly alter the already deeply entrenched public imagination of 1989.

8. For example, when a high-profile opportunity to give someone an award in Berlin presents itself, a segment of the fallen wall is offered as a gift. This was the case at the World Championships in Athletics in Berlin in 2009, when Usain Bolt received a piece to honor his breaking of the world record.

9. The press conference event may have been staged by the embattled communist government of the GDR in order to announce a new border regime as mundanely as possible. Riccardo Ehrman, an Italian journalist who asked the question, had been urged to do so by the director of the East German Press Agency prior to the conference. Thus Schabowski probably did not reply to an accidental question (Wielinski 2009). However, he could have phrased his answer differently, in which case his words may not have triggered a revolutionary situation. Instead, a kind of rebellion ensued. Because Ehrman revealed the secret only in 2009, the narrative of a confused slip conducive to an outburst of anticommunist effervescence could be disseminated for two decades and sank in, to this day shaping the discourse in Germany and beyond.

REFERENCES

Alexander, J. 2008. "Iconic Consciousness. The Material Feeling of Meaning." *Environment and Planning D: Society and Space*. 26: 782–94.

Alexander, J., and P. Smith. 1993. "The Discourse of American Civil Society: A New Proposal for Cultural Studies." *Theory and Society*. 22 (2): 151–207.

Bahr, C. 2005. *Divided City. The Berlin Wall: Photos and Facts, Personal Accounts, Traces Today*. Berlin: Jaron Verlag.

Banac, I., ed. 1992. *Eastern Europe in Revolution*. Ithaca and London: Cornell University Press.

Barthes, R. 1978. *Image—Music—Text*. New York: Hill and Wang.

Bartlett, D. L. 1997. *The Political Economy of Dual Transformations.* Ann Arbor: University of Michigan Press.

Basara, Z. 2009. "Rewolucja w pigułce" [Revolution condensed]. *Gazeta Wyborcza,* November 5, 12.

Berdahl, D. 2003. "Introduction: An Anthropology of Postsocialism." In *Altering States. Ethnographies of Transition in Eastern Europe and the Former Soviet Union,* edited by D. Berdahl, M. Bunzl, and M. Lampland. Arbor: University of Michigan Press.

Bonstein, J. 2009. "Homesick for a Dictatorship. Majority of Eastern Germans Feel Life Better Under Communism," *Spiegel Online,* July 3, http://www.spiegel.de/international /germany/0,1518, druck-634122,00.html.

Bowler, W. forthcoming. "Seeing Tragedy in the News Images of September 11." In *Iconic Power: Materiality and Meaning in Social Life,* edited by J. Alexander, D. Bartmański, and B. Giesen. London: Palgrave Macmillan.

Bruner, J. 2000. *Acts of Meaning.* Cambridge, MA: Harvard University Press.

Buck-Morss, S. 2002. *Dreamworld and Catastrophe: The Passing of Mass Utopia in East and West.* Cambridge, MA: MIT Press.

Bürgi, B., and H. Fischer. 2005. *Covering the Real: Kunst und Pressebild von Warhol bis Tillmans* [Art and the press picture, from Warhol to Tillmans]. Basel: Kunstmuseum Basel.

Chirot, D. 1998. "The Lessons of 1989: Comments on Janos Kis." *East European Politics and Societies* 12 (2): 384–89.

Derkaczew, J. 2009. "Mity Okrągłego Stołu i 1989 Roku" [Myths of the Round Table and the year 1989]. *Gazeta Wyborcza,* May 23–24, 13.

Drechsel, B. 2010. "The Berlin Wall From a Visual Perspective: Comments on the Construction of a Political Media Icon." *Visual Communication.* 9 (3): 3–24.

Feversham, P., and L. Schmidt. 1999. *The Berlin Wall Today.* Berlin: Bauwesen Verlag.

Flemming, T. 2006. *The Berlin Wall: Division of a City.* Berlin: be.bra Verlag.

French, H. W. 2004. *A Continent for the Taking: The Tragedy and Hope of Africa.* New York: Alfred A. Knopf.

Friedrich, T. 2005. *Where the Wall Stood.* Berlin: Nicolai Verlag.

Gaddis, J. L. 1998. *We Now Know: Rethinking Cold War History.* Oxford: Oxford University Press.

Geertz, C. 1983. *Local Knowledge: Further Essays in Interpretive Anthropology.* New York: Basic Books.

Haspel, J. 2004. Foreword. In *Wall Remnants–Wall Traces: The Comprehensive Guide to the Berlin Wall,* edited by A. Klausmeier, and L. Schmidt, 8–9. Berlin: Westkreuz Verlag.

Hawkes, N., ed. 1990. *Tearing Down the Curtain: The People's Revolution in Eastern Europe by a Team from 'The Observer.'* London: Hodder & Stoughton.

Heidenreich, S. 1998. "Icons: Pictures for Users and Idiots." *Localizer.* 1 (3): 82–86.

Hensel, J. 2004. *After the Wall: Confessions from an East German Childhood and the Life that Came Next.* New York: PublicAffairs.

Hertle, H.-H. 2007. *The Berlin Wall: Monument of the Cold War.* Berlin: Ch. Links.

Hildebrandt, A. 2003. *Citations on the German Division, the Wall and the Reunification.* Berlin: Verlag Haus am Checkpoint Charlie.

———. 2008. *The Wall: Figures, Facts.* Berlin: Verlag Haus am Checkpoint Charlie.

Holc, J. P. 1992. "Solidarity and the Polish State: Competing Discursive Strategies on the Road to Power." *East European Politics and Societies.* 6 (2): 121–40.

Janion, M. 2007. *Niesamowita słowiańszczyzna: Fantazmaty literatury* [Amazing Slavicness: phantasms of literature]. Cracow: Wydawnictwo Literackie.

Kennedy, M. 1999. "Contingencies and the Alternatives of 1989: Toward a Theory and Practice of Negotiating Revolution." *East European Politics and Societies*. 13 (2): 293–302.

Kis, J. 1998. "Between Reform and Revolution." *East European Politics and Societies* 12 (2): 300–83.

Klausmeier, A., and L. Schmidt, eds. 2004. *Wall Remnants–Wall Traces: The Comprehensive Guide to the Berlin Wall.* Berlin: Westkreuz Verlag.

Koolhaas, R. 2006. *Conversation with Hans Ulrich Obrist.* Cologne: Verlag der Buchhandlung Walther König.

Kuzdas, H. J. 1998. *Berlin Wall Art.* Berlin: Espresso Verlag.

Ladd, B. 2009. "Local Responses in Berlin to Urban Decay and the Demise of the GDR." In *Cities After the Fall of Communism: Reshaping Cultural Landscapes and European Identity,* edited by J. J. Czaplicka, N. Gelazis, and B. A. Ruble, Baltimore: The Johns Hopkins University Press.

Latour, B. 1993. *We Have Never Been Modern.* Cambridge, MA: Harvard University Press.

Löw, M. 2008. "A City's Own Logic. The Perspective of Spatial Sociology on Urban Theory." In *Urban Potentials: Ideas and Practice,* edited by J. Bielanska and T. Birne, 280–86. Berlin: Jovis.

Lungescu, O. 2009. "Poland Reflects on Communism's Fall." *The BBC Online News,* February 6, http://news.bbc.co.uk/2/hi/europe/7873613.stm.

Mason, D. S., D. N. Nelson, and B. M. Szklarski. 1991. "Apathy and the Birth of Democracy: The Polish Struggle." *East European Politics and Societies.* 5 (2): 205–33.

Mayr, W. 2009. "Hungary's Peaceful Revolution: Cutting the Fence and Changing History." *Spiegel Online,* May 29, http://www.spiegel.de/international/europe/0,1518,druck 627632,00.html.

Meiners, A. 2009. *Berlin 1989: Eine Chronik in Bildern* [Berlin 1989: a pictorial chronicle]. Berlin: Nicolai.

Michnik, A. 2009. "Nasz stół" [Our table: an interview with Adam Michnik and Helena Łuczywo]. In: Smoleński, P. 2009. *Gazeta Wyborcza,* February 7–8, 13–15.

Mix, A. 2009. "20 Jahre Runder Tisch. Die Herbeigeredete Revolution" [20 years of the Round Table. The revolution talked into existence]. *Spiegel Online,* June 4, http://einestages.spiegel.de/static/topicalbumbackground/3626/die_herbeigeredete_revolution.html.

Perger, W. A. 2009. "Mehr Respekt vor den Polen" [More respect for the Poles]. *Zeit Online.* May 27, http://www.zeit.de/online/2009/22/polen-deutsche-einheit.

Reader, J. 2004. *Cities.* New York: Atlantic Monthly Press.

Richter, J. 2010. *The Tourist City Berlin: Tourism and Architecture.* Salenstein: Braun.

Rymkiewicz, W. 2008. "Czy Peerel jest czescia historii Polski?" [Is the People's Republic of Poland a part of Polish history?] *Kronos* 4: 259–73.

Sälter, G. 2007. *Mauerreste in Berlin–Relics of the Berlin Wall.* Berlin: Verein Berliner Mauer–Gedenkstätte und Dokumentationszentrum.

Salzen, C. von. 2009. "Polen ärgern sich über EU-Video zum Mauerfall" [The Poles get upset over the EU-video on the fall of the wall]. *Zeit Online (Tagesspiegel),* May 22, http://www.zeit.de/online/2009/22/polen-mauerfall-einheit.

Schlögel, K. 2008. *Die Mitte Liegt Ostwärts: Europa im Übergang* [The middle is located eastwards: Europe in transition]. Frankfurt am Main: Fischer Verlag.

Schmemann, S. 2006. *When the Wall Came Down: The Berlin Wall and the Fall of Soviet Communism.* London: Kingfisher.

Schuller, K. 2009. "Wem gehört der Sieg über den Kommunismus?" [To whom does the victory over Communism belong?] *Frankfurter Allgemeine Zeitung,* June 5, 5.

Smolar, A. 2009. "Okrągłostołowy happy end" [The Round Table happy end]. *Gazeta Wyborcza.* February 7–8, 17–19.

Smoleński, Paweł. 2009. "Nasz stół" [Our table: an interview with Adam Michnik and Helena Łuczywo]. *Gazeta Wyborcza,* February 7–8, 13–15.

Snyder, T. 1995. "National Myths and International Relations: Poland and Lithuania 1989–1994." *East European Politics and Societies.* 9 (2): 317–343.

Środa, M. 2009. "Niech Mury Runą" [Let the walls fall]. *Gazeta Wyborcza,* November 13, http://wyborcza.pl/1,80322,7250187,Niech_mury_runa___.html

Stern, F. 2007. *Five Germanys I Have Known.* New York: Farrar, Straus & Giroux.

Thompson, E. 2006. "O naturze polskich resentymentów" [On the nature of Polish resentments]. *Europa,* 46.

Tymowski, A. 1993. "The Unwanted Social Revolution: Poland in 1989." *East European Politics and Societies.* 7 (2:) 169–202.

Ugrešić, D. 1996. "The Confiscation of Memory." *New Left Review,* I/218, http://www.newleftreview.org/?view=1861

Walser Smith, H. 1991. "Socialism and Nationalism in the East German Revolution, 1989–1990." *East European Politics and Societies.* 5 (2): 234–46.

Wieliński, B. T. 2009. "Słowo burzy mur berliński" [A word destroys the Berlin Wall]. *Gazeta Wyborcza,* November 9, 9.

Wittgenstein, L. 1984. *Culture and Value.* Chicago: University of Chicago Press.

Woś, R. 2009. "Artystyczny renesans muru berlińskiego" [Artistic renaissance of the Berlin Wall]. *Dziennik,* April 25.

Wowereit, K. 2009. "Berlin–Warszawa wspólna sprawa" [Berlin–Warsaw, a common matter]. *Gazeta Wyborcza,* January 15, 24.

Yapp, N. 2001. *Getty Images 1980s: Decades of the 20th Century.* London: Könemann and Getty Images.

Žižek, S. 2009. "20 Years of Collapse." *The New York Times.* November 9.

CHAPTER 4

THE MAKING OF HUMANITARIAN VISUAL ICONS: ON THE 1921–1923 RUSSIAN FAMINE AS FOUNDATIONAL EVENT

FUYUKI KURASAWA

INTRODUCTION

In the summer of 1921, the specter of famine stalked the territory of Soviet Russia. A combination of sociopolitical and economic factors—the aftermaths of the First World War and the Russian Revolution, civil war between Red and White forces, and the Bolshevik policies of forces collectivization of agricultural lands—formed an unholy alliance with natural causes (principally, a severe drought in the Volga River Valley) to bring parts of Southern Russia and Ukraine to their knees. Agricultural production was decimated, leading to mass starvation and the consequent migration of several hundreds of thousands of peasants flooding into Russian cities. The famine had the potential to seriously destabilize the Bolshevik regime, which already had its hands full fighting a Western-backed, antirevolutionary enemy. Thus, on June 26, 1921, via the pages of *Pravda*, the Soviet government could do little but to officially confirm the famine's existence to the rest of world (Cosandey 1998: 3). This admission was followed, shortly thereafter, by dramatic appeals from two of Russia's towering figures—appeals that captured the tension between the two incipient ethicopolitical logics of humanitarianism: Maxim Gorky's "To All Honest People" ("Soviet Accepts" 1921) evoked the highest liberal humanist ideals of dignity of the person and the overcoming of ideological differences between peoples, whereas Vladimir Lenin's "Appeal to the International Proletariat"[1] called upon international working-class solidarity to protect the accomplishments of the Russian Revolution.

In the wake of these appeals, during the last half of 1921 and the first half of 1922, the public in North America and Western Europe was frequently exposed to news stories about the famine, whether through newspaper articles or cinematic news-reels. In addition, readers of British newspapers were bombarded with full-page or half-page advertisements from one non-governmental organization (NGO), the Save the Children Fund (SCF), which peppered its fundraising entreaties with scream-ing, attention-grabbing, and guilt-inducing headlines. One oft-reproduced version of this advertisement, which highlighted an illustrated drawing of a starving family, began with a quotation from David Lloyd George about the famine: "The Most Terrible Devastation That Has Afflicted the World for Centuries." Accompanying it were declarations such as: "Piteous Appeal for the Succour of Russia's Little Ones/ Their Utter Helplessness Claims First Consideration/Every Minute is Precious—So Send **All** You Can **Now**!/Children Are Dying Agonising Deaths While **You** Read and Hesitate."[2] Such publicity campaigns drew their rhetorical and visual tech-niques from the nascent science of modern commercial advertising in order to grab the attention of Euro-American subjects who, like citizens via-à-vis the society of mass consumption, needed to be constituted as sympathizers and supporters of the work of humanitarian organizations in Russia.

Although hyperbolic in both tone and substance, these kinds of advertisements demonstrated the unprecedented character of the Russian famine: in the summer of 1922, at the height of the famine, up to 30 million people were undernourished in the Volga district, and by the time the famine subsided nearly a year later, it had caused between 2.5 and 5 million deaths across the region. In response, it engendered what was, by far, the largest international humanitarian aid campaign in history and one of the humanitarian movement's defining events. On August 15, 1921, in Geneva, a joint committee of the International Committee of the Red Cross (ICRC) and the League of Red Cross Societies hastily convened a conference involving rep-resentatives of various governments, national Red Cross societies, and other NGOs (the American Relief Administration, the Society of Friends, the Union internation-ale de secours aux enfants, etc.) to organize rescue efforts to the affected populations on Soviet territory. Out of this conference emerged the International Committee for Russian Relief (ICRR), headed by Fridtjof Nansen, which coordinated most European efforts (Durand 1978: 175–76; Breen 1994: 223–24).[3] Three other enti-ties of the humanitarian movement were involved in Russian relief operations: the American Relief Administration (ARA), headed by Herbert Hoover (which chose not to join the ICRR and to operate apart from it); the various Comintern-affiliated organizations (such as the Internationale Arbeiter-Hilfe and the Friends of Soviet Russia [FSR]); and independent socialist parties and labor unions (the Belgian Workers' Party, the International Ladies' Garment Workers' Union, etc.) (Curti 1963: 288). The Russian famine occupied such a prominent place in the Euro-American public sphere that both the Vatican and the Church of England, via Pope Benedict XV and the Archbishop of Canterbury, became active supporters of the relief cam-paign. Soon, a vast network of feeding centers was set up in Russia: the ARA fed a total of 10.5 million people throughout the famine, and the ICRR was providing food for 2 million persons per day (with the SCF feeding 300,000 children and 250,000 adults in the city of Saratov alone) (Weindling 1994: 206).

Yet beyond the sheer scale of the famine and the rescue campaign, it was an inter-vention by Anatole France, the French writer and winner of the 1921 Nobel Prize for Literature, which encapsulates the mutually constitutive relationship between the iconicity of distant suffering and humanitarianism that interests us here. Inserted in a fundraising pamphlet published by the Comité français de secours aux enfants (the French SCF) on the occasion of a public lecture about the Russian famine that Nansen delivered at the Trocadéro in Paris on February 17, 1922—a lecture that Nansen copiously illustrated with photographs and film footage of the famine—France wrote the following:

> Rescue the Russian Children!/They are children, innocents, and they are dying; they are children and they are starving./If they are not rescued, five million of them will die. You have seen them, these children, as they are represented by this merciless photography: bony, inert, deaf, imploring a mouthful of food with a gaze that is almost extinguished./If you do not rescue these poor little ones, this image that you have seen will pursue you like a remorse for the whole of the rest of your life and you will ponder: I saw him agonizing and I turned away from him, and he is dead. ("L'homme" 1922)[4]

His words concisely give voice to several themes animating this chapter: the pivotal role of visual representation in the creation of icons of distant suffering; the iconic power of images for the humanitarian movement; and the social construction of victimhood through visual means. More precisely, France implicitly suggests that icons are actants, stalking the conscience of subjects who, through the very process of seeing images of suffering, are constituted as moral audiences upon which is thrust the burden of responsibility to alleviate it; the act of viewing depictions of starving children collapses the normative and experiential boundaries between Euro-American publics and Russian victims, who become part of the same moral community. This mechanism of collapse of ethical, sociocultural, and geographical distance through iconicity is precisely that upon which humanitarianism relies, for once iconic images of distant suffering circulate widely and ordinary citizens are exposed to them, publics lose their innocence. They can no longer claim ignorance by denying knowledge of an unfolding humanitarian crisis, becoming culpable of crass indifference if they decide not to act. As presented in France's sentimentalist appeal, humanitarian iconicity implicates its audiences in either saving starving populations or, conversely, letting them die.

Accordingly, the following pages examine what I would term the visual economy of humanitarian iconicity, which results from a complex triangulation of prominent objects of study in the human sciences today, namely, distant suffering, humanitarianism, and visuality—a triangulation that is explored, at least partly, in several recent works (Campbell 2003; Rancière 2003; Sontag 2003; Mirzoeff 2005; Boltanski 1999; Campbell 2007; Azoulay 2008; Barnett and Weiss 2008; Calhoun 2008; Rancière 2008; Butler 2009; Wilson and Brown 2009). This chapter proposes to intervene in the midst of these debates by studying the central yet hitherto underrecognized role of iconography, notably by asking the question of how iconic images of humanitarian situations are made (and thereby constitutive of such situations). Responding to this query requires, in the first place, a process of historicization in order to understand how the contemporary iconography of distant suffering in the Euro-American world has been established over time by humanitarian NGOs. In other words, I want to denaturalize what have become self-evident representational conventions in this iconographic system by analyzing their historical creation in and through the humanitarian movement.

Secondly, answering the question demands an attempt to reconcile seemingly incommensurable paradigms of cultural analysis of visual icons. On the one hand, a version of Bourdieusian field theory formulated in historical sociology (Steinmetz 2007; Go 2008) is useful in its foregrounding of the principle of hierarchical differentiation, which enables me to posit the existence of a visual field of humanitarianism in which social actors relationally struggle and compete against each other to establish certain images as iconic and to attach certain meanings to these images. On the other hand, my argument benefits from a semiotics of the image that analyzes the latter's underlying symbolic system, the patterned relations of signs that structure an image and give it meaning (Barthes 1977; Barthes 1981; Metz 2003). Hence, semiotic formalism can assist in the identification of symbolic regimes in the visual economy of humanitarian iconography, that is to say, iconographic conventions or regimes of typifications (shared representational repertoires and regularized arrangements of signs) found in images of distant suffering created or framed by humanitarian organizations. As we will discuss below, two defining iconographic typifications to represent humanitarian crises were either invented or consolidated during the Russian famine: personification (via the representation of an individualized victim), and massification (via the portrayal of an undifferentiated mass of victims).

Combining field theory and semiotics produces a theoretical framework that retains the strengths of each paradigm, while dispensing with the flaws that affect one when not calibrated by the other. Therefore, only the interplay of these two approaches can account for how humanitarian iconography takes shape out of both the institutional relations between the social actors producing it and the symbolic conventions that define it.[5]

Before tackling the substance of this chapter, I want to underline the fact that the visual economy of humanitarian iconicity is inserted into, and contributes to the formation and reproduction of, three moral grammars of humanitarianism, that is, three discursive "orders of worth" (Boltanski and Thévenot 2006) through which humanitarian NGOs understand their own functioning and justify it to exogenous actors, including governmental and civil society critics as well as Euro-American public opinion. The first of these can be termed instrumental, in that it draws upon principles of organizational efficiency and scientificity through the use of rational-calculative logic. Hence, these NGOs legitimate their activities, at one level, by documenting and supplying evidence of a given emergency situation in which they are intervening. As an attribute of humanitarianism that rapidly developed during and in the aftermath of the First World War, professionalism is a key component of this instrumental moral grammar—aid work being transformed from a noble yet vague ethos of benevolence toward the less fortunate (the good samaritan) to a specialized, professional occupation requiring technical knowledge and expertise (the heroic and skilled nurse) as well as sound fiscal management.

The second moral grammar is explicitly normative, appealing to conceptions of the good that articulate various ethical worldviews underpinning humanitarian universalism—that is, the principle of providing relief on the basis of "need alone," regardless of a person's affiliation or community of belonging.[6] Over the course of Euro-American humanitarianism's history, at least three such normative frameworks have come into use: a Christian affirmation that all human beings are "god's children" or inhabited by the divine[7]; a liberal conception of human dignity grounded in natural law, whereby all members of humankind are posited as morally equal and endowed with intrinsic rights[8]; and a socialist perspective based on transnational working-class solidarity and socioeconomic equality[9][10]. Furthermore, a fourth normative discourse, which was ancillary to the others and grafted onto them (rather than functioning autonomously), understood humanitarianism as an instrument of a Western civilizing mission, for the provision of aid to distant populations could become a means through which European values and norms could be diffused to the rest of the world.[11]

Humanitarianism has also operated through a third, sentimental moral grammar, which seeks to nurture or trigger a multiplicity of emotional responses from Euro-American publics and thus prompt action on the part of these publics (primarily through financial donations and political support). Although the justificatory discourses of humanitarian NGOs have tended to foreground instrumental and normative arguments, the implicit evocation and generation of collective sentiments have greatly contributed to bolstering these NGOs' appeals. Indeed, humanitarianism has sought to induce a repertoire of at least five emotional responses from Western public opinion. Most widespread among these are compassion, a sympathetic mode of concern for the suffering of other human beings in situations of distress; and pity, a sense of sorrow vis-à-vis these same persons and situations that is frequently constructed through rhetorical or visual means. Closely related to the latter sentiment is guilt, cultivated in discourses that juxtapose the living conditions of victims of humanitarian crises to those of ordinary citizens in Euro-American societies, or those that underscore the grave consequences of inaction and bystanding (e.g., the deaths of innocent victims). Lastly, aid organizations have resorted to two particularly visceral reactions: shock, that is, revulsion or horror due to being confronted with the magnitude and gravity of a particular emergency (e.g., through graphic photographs or news footage); and outrage, a sentiment of revolt toward injustices underlying humanitarian crises, or of condemnation of perpetrators and structural causes of these crises (mainly used by the Left and socialist NGOs).

ICONIC PORTRAITS OF THE RUSSIAN FAMINE

Let us now consider the iconographic analysis of certain images of the Russian famine, the selection of which is based on two factors contributing to their iconicity: their representativeness as conventional or typified portrayals of the famine; and their recurrence, being among the most widely circulated and reproduced images of the famine in Euro-American public spheres. The sources of these images are both endogenous to the humanitarian movement because they are located in documents produced by NGOs themselves (via pamphlets, journals, posters, postcards, and documentary film), as well as exogenous to it because they are published in newspapers and cinematic newsreels.[12] Furthermore, the semiotic model of the visual economy of humanitarian iconicity that I am proposing here is organized around the structural relations between two categories of visual signs: situational symbols, which construct the roles of subjects in relation to the situation being portrayed (i.e., the famine itself); and compositional symbols, which construct the roles of subjects in relation to each other (e.g., distinguishing aid workers from victims). And as mentioned above, personification and massification were two iconographic typifications of the visual representation of humanitarian crises that came into being or were reproduced during the Russian Revolution. Personification is a representational genre that singles out a specific person's condition as a figurative and literal embodiment of the gravity or intensity of the suffering caused by a humanitarian crisis. It is created by a close-up shot of a single victim (or, occasionally, a small group of victims) who is portrayed in a state of raw, existential pain, often in isolation from others and in a manner that is stripped of any contextual information. Personified images tend to be framed in an expressionist aesthetic style, which emphasizes the capture of unfiltered, powerful emotions in the victim's facial traits; the trope of the suffering child is pervasive here, conveying his or her innocence vis-à-vis the relevant disaster so that—not being responsible for the condition within which he or she finds herself—the victim can be presented as "deserving" of the receipt of humanitarian aid.[13]

One of the most iconic personifications of the Russian famine came in the form of a photograph of a starving young girl leaning against the doorframe of a stone house.[14] In late 1921 and early 1922, the image acquired a presence in the Western European and North American public spheres due to its publication in newspapers[15] and use by humanitarian NGOs holding a variety of ideological stances: it appeared on the cover of a bulletin published by the American Friends Service Committee (AFSC), entitled "Do You Know the Reality of the Russian Famine?" (AFSC 1921), was made into a postcard issued by the Union internationale de secours aux enfants (UISE)[16], as well as reproduced in an aforementioned FSR pamphlet on the famine (FSR 1921 [?]: 29). The picture's situational symbols operate in a manner that constructs the young girl as a victim, with her skeletal body, distended stomach and thin limbs existing as corporeally marked signs of starvation. In case the point was missed, the image's caption in the FSR pamphlet stated: "A little famine victim at Samara wasted away to a skeleton" (29). Several other situational symbols contribute to the constitution of the girl's condition of victimhood. Her nakedness, straggly hair, and grimy body stand as signifiers of extreme deprivation, her gaze and posture (supporting herself with an outside wall and doorframe) suggest frailty, whereas the angle of the shot—she is photographed sideways, looking away from the camera yet with her face and eyes being visible— implies helplessness. Textual signs strengthen these situationally symbolic intentions, the girl as an emblem of grave suffering and vulnerability; in the UISE postcard, she is described as a "poor little one," whereas the caption under her image in the February 18, 1922, issue of L'illustration (Cosandey 1998: 30) reads "[a]t the final limits of exhaustion." Much like the first example of personification discussed above, this photograph is framed through compositional symbols that buttress the subject's state of situationally acute vulnerability, for she is portrayed as a socially isolated and generic child by removing the larger social context within which she is situated, including the details of her location and existence. The aforementioned UISE postcard is telling in this regard, with its existential-sounding title of "Alone in the World!" that laments her facing the famine without kin or caregiver.

The figure of the child (and more precisely, the female child) and her body are essential signifiers of humanitarianism's instrumental moral grammar. The picture performs an evidentiary role regarding the famine's corporeal ravages, while simultaneously becoming itself a tool to solicit donations and make a case for the urgency of emergency aid.[17] Normatively, what is evoked is the liberal humanist ethos according to which we have a universal duty to protect children, who share a condition of innocence and vulnerability, as well as to rescue them from starvation regardless of where they live and who they are. Nevertheless, it is the moral grammar of sentimentalism that is most powerfully deployed in this image's framing, since it solicits pity about the girl's fate ("poor little one"), and just as meaningfully, a sense of care or protectiveness towards her; appearing to be alone or abandoned, she cannot be left to starve to death. And as a quotation appearing as a caption to this photograph on the cover of the AFSC bulletin makes clear, the consequences of callousness are grave: "Famine will bring more than one-half of the children of the famine-area to this condition unless foreign aid arrives" (AFSC 1921: 1).

The second typification in the visual economy of humanitarian iconicity consists of massification, that is to say, the depiction of an undifferentiated mass of victims meant to convey the magnitude of a disaster. Generally, images of massification regroup a large number of corpses or surviving victims, who quantifiably signify the scale of suffering and desolation wrought by a humanitarian crisis. One of these to emerge out of the Russian famine is composed of between seventy and eighty unburied corpses, piled up in a mound on the snowy grounds of a cemetery, with gravesite crosses in the background. Several versions of this scene exist, its two most frequent variants being a tightly framed close-up shot of the pile of corpses or a more panoramic one taken from a greater distance.[18] According to a 2003 article from the Swiss newspaper *Le temps* commemorating the ICRC's rescue activities during the Russian famine, the various iterations of the image circulated around the world (Haller 2003)[19], through the means of newspaper articles[20] and documentary film footage. Indeed, commenting upon the scene in a report about the film *Famine: The Russian Famine of 1921*, which was produced by the SCF and screened widely in Britain in the winter of 1922, the *Manchester Guardian* described it thusly:

> In Buzuluk, in Samara province, there is a graveyard to which the dead are brought in cartloads, stripped naked, because the living cannot afford to bury clothes.... The snow is falling, and mercifully covers the ghastly forms, which look the more horrible for a remaining semblance of humanity. They lie in piles for a time, and then a communal grave is dug they are piled in. ("Nansen on Russia" 1922)

In its different iterations, the image appears to have been a mainstay of fundraising campaigns by humanitarian agencies. In fact, the aforementioned pamphlet from the Comité français de secours aux enfants (the French SCF), in which appeared the quotation from Anatole France cited above, featured the photograph prominently[21], and postcards of it were also produced.[22] Even today, it remains one of the defining portrayals of the Russian famine, having been selected by the ICRC to appear on its Web page dedicated to documenting the organization's relief efforts during the emergency.[23]

The image's iconic power stems, in part, from its semiotic structure. By depicting an indiscriminate mound of bodies, it contains situational symbols designed to illustrate the magnitude and devastating consequences of the disaster—symbols that are metonymic signifiers of the suffering of the Russian people in the face of the famine. Furthermore, due to its explicit representation of death on a mass scale, the photograph was unprecedented in the history of the visual economy of humanitarian iconicity. The corpses themselves function as a sign of the millions of victims who perished and thus could not be rescued, vividly contrasting with the conventional imagery of survivors requiring, and potentially saved by, humanitarian aid work. Yet the picture's compositional symbols also bolster its "massifying" effects for the viewer, stripping the corpses of dignity by virtue of their positions in relation to one another and their general appearance; dead bodies are randomly piled atop each other, with entangled limbs and in various states of undress (some are naked, others are fully or partially clothed). Compositionally, they form a heap of generic corpses, the deceased losing the individuality and sense of personhood that are so significant in modern Euro-American social life. And the pile of corpses relates to the landscape incongruously, the cemetery overflowing with unburied and unidentified bodies that are juxtaposed with the gravesite crosses surrounding them.

This photograph of massification is inserted into humanitarianism's three moral grammars. From an instrumental perspective, it provided graphic evidence of the scale of the ravages and deaths caused by the Russian famine, thus confirming that existing eyewitness accounts hardly captured the full extent of the horror that had been unfolding since the summer of 1921. Normatively, the graphic nature of the image itself made it such that its publication did not require framing through the three competing humanitarian political ideologies (Christian, liberal, and socialist). Nevertheless, the reality captured in the picture did violate key normative principles that cut across these ideologies, foremost by affronting the notion of human dignity accorded to the dead in Judeo-Christian sociocultural traditions that sacralize the disposal of bodies (through, inter alia, rituals of concealment and individualized, underground burial). The second humanitarian norm undermined by the scene depicted in this image is the duty to assist those in need and the possibility of saving them; it exposed the failure to do so in a timely and sufficient manner, leading to the preventable deaths of millions. But it is perhaps at the level of sentimental moral grammars that the photograph is most effective, since it generated revulsion and horror among Euro-American viewers. As demonstrated in the description from the *Manchester Guardian* cited above, the scene was considered gruesome not merely because of its unadorned display of corpses, but also because of their sheer number and manner of disposing of them. Indeed, the situation was viscerally shocking due to its illustrating massive corporeal desecration, with the dehumanization and objectification of the famine's victims—whose bodies are discarded like objects or dead animals, placed in a scrap heap before being tossed into a communal grave. Another emotion strongly evoked by the picture is guilt, since its viewing serves as a severe indictment of indifference and inaction by exhibiting that to which these attitudes lead for those affected by the famine. Implicitly, then, the image functions to indicate that it is the inevitable fate that awaits many other victims if Euro-American publics do not respond to the calls for humanitarian assistance.

THE CONTEST OF ICONOGRAPHIC MEANING[24]

The question that I would like to ponder now is that of understanding how iconicity operates in the public sphere. Conventional art-historical explanations of iconography are grounded in Kantian aesthetic formalism, according to which an image's iconic status is determined by its degree of correspondence to universal criteria of beauty (symmetry of form, harmony of color, etc.). However, as mentioned at the beginning of this chapter, the iconographic theory proposed here seeks to articulate a semiotic hermeneuticism, via the sort of interpretation of the meaning of sign systems employed in the previous section, to a structuralist field theory in order to bypass formalist internalism. To do so requires introducing the concept of the visual field, which allows us to map out the visual economy of humanitarian iconicity as a sociopolitical sphere structured by a principle of hierarchical differentiation. Accordingly, the visual field takes shape out of the varying positions occupied by institutional actors producing and circulating images of the Russian famine (i.e., humanitarian NGOs and the media) as well as the competing discourses about the meaning of specific images within Euro-American public arenas. In a departure from the structuralist determinism of Bourdieusian field theory, however, this model of the visual field centrally incorporates an interpretive component in that the positions across its axes are established by the symbolic meanings attributed to images—which cannot be determined a priori by the distribution of capital among social actors.

Reiterating the argument that visuality is a complex ensemble of relations between spoken, textual and pictorial signs, I want to suggest that the visual field is organized along two axes corresponding to fundamental points of distinction in the visual economy of humanitarian iconicity: ideological coding and representational style. The first of these concerns the political stance that particular Western institutions adopted vis-à-vis Soviet Russia and its Bolshevik government, which impacted such institutions' framing of images of the Russian famine; all of the NGOs and newspapers consulted for this chapter were sympathetic to the plights of the famine's victims, yet they held widely differing explanations of the causes of the famine. Within the visual field, Bolshevism generated three basic ideological positions. Comintern-affiliated and independent socialist organizations developed a stance of solidarity with Russian workers and the Soviet state, thereby tending to attribute the famine to natural factors (i.e., drought) or to the Western economic blockade and interventionism (by supporting the White armies in the Russian Civil War). At the opposite end of the ideological spectrum, conservative anticommunist and nationalist newspapers were outright hostile toward Bolshevism, the famine being explained with reference to the failures of an intrinsically flawed socioeconomic system and the Soviet authorities' coercive policies of agricultural collectivization; some populist and nativist British newspapers went so far as to question the gravity and magnitude of the famine itself. Due to their liberalism and adherence to the principle of political neutrality, most humanitarian NGOs were located somewhere in the middle of this ideological spectrum and, as a result, depoliticized the famine by foregrounding both its natural causes and the suffering of victims (e.g., through the creation of a sentimentalized condition of universal, vulnerable childhood).

The second axis structuring the visual field consists of the representational style adopted in the selection and presentation of photographs of the Russian famine, which lies at the intersection of aesthetic and journalistic standards. On the one hand, NGOs and newspapers followed an expressionist or subjectivist mode of representation, which favored explicit portrayals of the suffering of the famine's victims in order to visually capture the latter's emotional states or spiritual condition. Edvard Munch and Käthe Kollwitz[25] are among the best-known representatives of expressionism in the visual arts, which is exemplified through the iconic image of personification analyzed above (that of the starving girl). In journalistic terms, expressionism is characterized by the subjective statement of opinions in and through the reporting of news, which, in the case of the Russian famine, could take the form of sensationalist and emotionally laden or ideologically driven commentary. On the other hand, a realist or objectivist style was equally influential as a representational ideal type, privileging a more visually and textually restrained, factually based observation and documentation of the living conditions and circumstances of the Russian people subjected to the famine. Although largely discarded today, realism has been the dominant tradition of portraiture in Western aesthetics; William-Adolphe Bouguereau's *Charity* (1878) is a manifestation of it that also captures humanitarian ideals, as is the photograph of a group of Russian children analyzed above. Journalistic realism is defined by its striving toward objective, impartial reporting of events that prefers a dispassionate and analytical perspective underpinned by a sober tone of analysis ("letting the facts speak for themselves").

Applying the axes of ideological coding and representational style to structure the Russian famine's visual field produces the following results (see Figure 4.1):

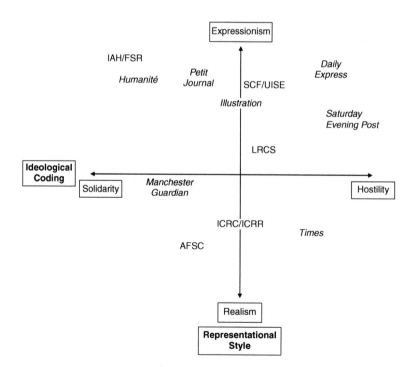

Figure 4.1.   The Russian famine's visual field.

HUMANITARIAN NGOS AND SOURCE DOCUMENTS

AFSC: American Friends Service Committee (USA), *Bulletin*

IAH/FSR: Internationale Arbeiter-Hilfe (Germany)/Friends of Soviet Russia (USA); *Soviet Russia* and (FSR 1921 [?])

ICRC/ICRR: International Committee of the Red Cross (Switzerland)/International Committee for Russian Relief (Switzerland), various publications and *Famine* (film)

LRCS: League of Red Cross Societies, *Bulletin*

SCF/UISE: Save the Children Fund (UK)/ Union internationale de secours aux enfants (Switzerland); *The Record, Famine* (film), postcards, and posters

Although an exhaustive description of the various facets of this figure would take us outside the scope of this chapter, a few brief remarks should be made. The visual field is characterized by a struggle between institutional actors (namely, humanitarian NGOs and newspapers [see table 4.1]) over the meanings and interpretive framings of iconic images of the Russian famine. Each institutional actor strives to establish its own representational and interpretive position about a specific visual icon as socially authoritative or hegemonic, by having such a position publicly recognized and, in semiotic terms, by attempting to naturalize its preferred visual and textual coding of such a visual icon—that is to say, stabilizing its signifying chains by attaching particular signifieds to signifiers within the image. In other words, the dominance of an organization's mode of framing within the Russian famine's visual field can be explained through a process of semiotic naturalization, which in turn enables this mode of framing to gain public legitimacy (e.g., that the starvation of children, as depicted in an image, is caused by drought or, on the contrary, by Bolshevism). Hence, what is actually an arbitrary relation between the signifier and the signified appears self-evident or necessary to most viewers, who consequently take for granted the meanings attributed to such an image by an institutional actor (as opposed to that advanced by a competing actor in the visual field).

What this means is that images do not contain discrete meanings, strictly generated out of their symbolic structures. Iconic pictures do not speak for themselves, nor are humanitarian NGOs passive conduits for the dissemination of such pictures

Table 4.1   Newspapers[26]

Title	Location	Issue
The Daily Express	London, UK	multiple (1921–1922)
The Manchester Guardian	Manchester, UK	multiple (1921–1922)
The Times	London, UK	September 15, 1921, p. 10
		September 16, 1921, p. 10
L'humanité	Paris, France	multiple (1921–1922)
L'illustration	Paris, France	multiple (1921–1922)
Le petit journal	Paris, France	February 6, 1922, p. 1
The Saturday Evening Post	Philadelphia, USA	June 24, 1922, pp. 10–11
		July 1, 1922, p. 15
		July 29, 1922, p. 23

via different exogenous forms of media (e.g., newspapers and newsreels). On the contrary, these NGOs perform sustained work to create and reproduce certain significations, intervening in public spaces to influence popular perceptions of a humanitarian crisis and promote their own symbolic coding of it as the most credible, both by producing images themselves, selecting those to be released, editing them, and developing endogenous institutional networks of circulation of them (via bulletins, posters, postcards, public lectures, and film screenings). Thus, for the humanitarian movement, the existence of icons of distant suffering and the contest over their meaning perform the function of shaping Euro-American public opinion, making persons and groups more favorably inclined toward NGOs (as the actors entrusted to relieve such suffering) and thereby more likely to support the latter both financially and politically.

CONCLUSION: ON ICONS AS ACTANTS

I would like to conclude by advancing the claim that the iconicity of pictures of distant suffering is also what constitutes them as actants. Whereas actor-network theory has coined this term to attribute a strong capacity for agency to human and nonhuman components of social assemblages (Law 1992; Latour 2006), I employ the notion of "actant" to refer to the weaker yet nevertheless significant agentic capacities of visual icons; indeed, they are not simply inert objects through which meaning is transmitted to human actors or to which can be attached any meaning, nor are they reducible to the effects of the operations of the institutional networks through which they circulate and the visual fields in which they are situated.

Visual icons of the Russian famine perform as actants to the extent that their presence altered public discourse and social imaginaries about human suffering. The event marked the first time that the humanitarian movement sought to expose Western European and North American viewers to gruesome still and moving images of a famine of such gravity and magnitude (starving children, mounds of corpses, etc.)—pictures that were widely disseminated through a variety of technologies of circulation.[27] Their publication sparked considerable public debate regarding the ethics of representation. Was it necessary, and legitimate, for NGOs and media organizations to depict suffering victims or the scale of death and devastation wrought by the famine, or conversely, did such depictions veer into a lurid sensationalism and crass exploitation of the suffering of these victims (for fundraising purposes or newspaper sales)? What were the "limits of the tolerable" (Cosandey 1998: 6), the thresholds of the representable to which Western audiences should and could be exposed?[28] Was an allegorical or a literal mode of visual portrayal of distant suffering more appropriate or effective?

At the same time, the visual icons of the Russian famine functioned as actants in and through their capacity to interpellate or address members of Euro-American publics, constituting them into receptive audiences that were cognitively, normatively, and emotionally involved in the catastrophe. The circulation of visual material about the Russian famine by humanitarian NGOs and news organizations socialized persons and groups to become spectators of distant suffering, who had to acquire practices of viewing and making sense of images of such situations. Rather than being given or self-evident, these practices of viewership and interpretation had to be gradually fostered through a visual economy of humanitarian iconicity that directly addressed subjects, or textually or orally exhorted them, to not merely glimpse at pictures of victims of the Russian famine, but to carefully observe them and reflect upon their moral implications. The cultivation of these kinds of viewing and interpretive perspectives was most blatant in the expressionist mode of representation, whereby printed material contained captions appealing to normative or sentimental grounds; it was also striking in the words and music used during Nansen's public lectures about the famine, as well as during public screenings of the documentary film *Famine*.

Accordingly, viewers were urged to cognitively think through the representations of the famine, to examine with their own eyes the visible evidence of starvation seen through its ravages etched on the bodies of victims. Implicitly, icons were framed in ways that generated a phenomenological thickening of their experiential dimensions, in a manner that counters their objectification (that is, their phenomenological "flattening" or loss of affective depth) so as to preserve and amplify their status as affectively evocative actants that trigger viewers' moral imaginations and sentimental dispositions (Jameson 1991). By encouraging acts of transposition, whereby spectators put themselves or their own kin in the place of the represented subjects in distress, or attempt to temporarily enter into the experiential lifeworlds of these subjects, iconicity could push for a widening or questioning of the "commonsensical" boundaries of Euro-American populations' moral communities. In other words, it could expand the circles of those for whom these populations cared and toward whom they felt responsible; once transposed into the position of the victims of the Russian famine, audience members could grasp the duty to assist them through humanitarian means. Moreover, visual icons operated through an unstated "civil contract of photography" (Azoulay 2008) with audiences, which was built into Anatole France's aforementioned appeal: once they bore witness to the suffering captured visually, publics were ethically bound to the fate of victims and had a responsibility to participate in their rescue. To remain a bystander, to be guilty of indifference or passivity in the face of disaster, then, appeared as nothing less than a moral failing. Emotionally, iconicity drew persons into participating in collective rituals of viewing images that provoked shock and revulsion which, in turn, could create feelings of pity and empathy—yet, simultaneously, voyeuristic curiosity toward seeing the pain of others and sensationalistic titillation.

Lastly, let us mention the standing of icons of distant suffering as catalysts to action. During the Russian famine, the humanitarian movement's contextual framing of such visual icons insisted on the fact that bearing witness to the crisis and responding emotionally to pictures of it was neither sufficient nor adequate in themselves; instead, for NGOs, the social act of seeing images of the famine's victims was but a vehicle that would prompt moral and political engagement on the part of members of Euro-American civil societies, via public support and financial donations. However, as much as humanitarianism drew upon the iconic power of the images of the Russian famine to mobilize public opinion, it was also playing with fire by potentially unleashing forces beyond its control. Exposure to these images could have unpredictable and unintended consequences, notably by causing concerned spectators to experience a sense of despondency or hopelessness when confronted with a catastrophe of such magnitude and intensity. Because these spectators could not directly intervene to help victims of the famine, the humanitarian movement faced the delicate task of harnessing their aroused sense of moral disquiet and strong emotional reactions toward appropriate outlets; Western publics had to be persuaded that donations represented suitable proxies for in-person assistance, and that aid workers were both effective and benevolent proxies for engaged members of these publics. Iconicity had to be tamed, for unless such surrogates were widely accepted, its symbolic power could easily turn against the humanitarian movement that had nurtured it. If unable to demonstrate their capacity to rescue victims of the Russian famine, humanitarian agencies left themselves vulnerable to the prospect of a vigorous public backlash that reinterpreted their use of visual icons as propagandist and self-serving manipulation of collective sentiments and morality. In turn, this would undermine humanitarianism's very raison d'être, its campaigns being perceived as an instrumentalization of victims (particularly those depicted in visual material) in order to advance endogenous organizational ends—that is to say, the claim of rescuing persons in distress being a mere pretext to achieve institutional growth and amass funds for private gain. It is a peril that continues to haunt the humanitarian movement to this day, and the reason for which the iconic power of images of distant suffering has had to be channeled and controlled with great care lest it destroy the social actors who play with it.

NOTES

The research and writing of this chapter were made possible by a Standard Research Grant from the Social Sciences and Humanities Research Council of Canada. For their invaluable research assistance, I would like to thank Michael Christensen, Marcia Oliver, Philip Steinersen, and Stephen Tasson. Thanks are also due to Carl Emil Vogt (Research Fellow, Department of Archeology, Conservation and History, University of Oslo), Guro Tangvald (Curator of the Picture Collection at the National Library of Norway), and Natalia Lavrova (Art Director of the ArtUkraine. com website).

1. The text of Lenin's address is reproduced at: <http://www.marxists.org/archive /lenin/works/1921/aug/02.htm> (accessed November 10, 2009).
2. *Daily Express* (hereafter DE), August 25, 1921, 7 (italics in original). For variants on this advertisement, see, inter alia: DE, August 30, 1921, 8; *Daily Mirror* (hereafter DM), August 25, 1921, 8; DM, August 30, 1921, 6; *Manchester Guardian* (hereafter MG), August 26, 1921, 4; MG, August 31, 1921, 3; MG, December 15, 1921, 3.
3. Nansen was a Norwegian adventurer and one of the most important figures of the humanitarian movement in the early twentieth century. He won the Nobel Peace Prize in 1922, in part for his work on behalf of Russian famine victims and European war refugees.
4. The translation is my own. France's statement is reproduced in two other sources: Cosandey 1998: 12, and http://www.histoire-image.org/site/oeuvre/analyse.php?i =574&d=401 (accessed November 11, 2009>.
5. I understand an iconic image to be less a strictly visual entity than one whose meaning is created out of the ensemble of relations between text, speech, and sight

(Mitchell 2005). Thus, the captions or intertitles that frame an image (published in a newspaper or screened in a newsreel) and the context of its presentation (during a public lecture, in a pamphlet, etc.) greatly contribute to its meanings for audiences.

6. See "The Code of Conduct for the International Red Cross and Red Crescent Movements and NGOs in Disaster Relief," http://www.icrc.org/web/eng/siteeng0 .nsf/htmlall/code-of-conduct-290296 (accessed January 10, 2010).

7. This Christian logic was articulated by the Save the Children Fund and the Quakers' Society of Friends (in Great Britain) and the American Friends Service Committee (in the United States).

8. The International Committee of the Red Cross was, and remains, the best-known representative of humanitarian liberalism.

9. Socialist humanitarianism was most strongly found within the ranks of Comintern-affiliated organizations, such as the Internationale Arbeiter-Hilfe and the Friends of Soviet Russia.

10. Within humanitarian NGOs, there has been considerable overlap between the three frameworks, notably between Christian and liberal ones. For instance, the SCF forged its organizational philosophy out of an amalgam of these two ideologies, with a gradual shift from a religious to a more secular order of worth.

11. This civilizational logic was held by Gustave Moynier, one of the ICRC's founders, among others (Boissier 1978: 365–67).

12. It should be noted, however, that the two kinds of sources were not independent of each other; in particular, newspapers tended to rely on photographs and film stills distributed by NGOs to illustrate news stories about the famine.

13. This logic of "deserving," and by implication "undeserving," victims is derived from the Victorian moralization of charity towards the poor.

14. The image is republished in the Nansen Electronic Photographic Archive (file 6a053): http://nabo.nb.no/trip?_t=0&_b=NANSEN_ENG&_r=1072&_s=E&_n=0 &_q=10&_l=www_eng_l (accessed November 12, 2009). It was taken in the town of Buguruslan in the fall of 1921

15. For instance, see L'illustration (a Paris-based illustrated weekly newspaper), February 18, 1922, 160, republished in Cosandey 1998: 30.

16. One version of the postcard was issued by the Mouvement de la jeunesse suisse romande affilié au Comité suisse et à l'Union internationale de secours aux enfants (Lausanne, Switzerland). It was the ninth of a series of postcards published by UISE and distributed by UISE itself in Geneva and its national branches in Switzerland and France, with the theme "La famine en Russie." See <http://www.artukraine .com/famineart/famine10.htm> (accessed November 8, 2009). Such postcards are found in the UISE archives, which are housed in the Archives d'Etat de Genève (item Archives privées 92.31.7) in Geneva, Switzerland.

17. The text of the UISE postcard reads: "An upsetting image of childhood misery! Let us hurry to rescue thousands upon thousands of children just like this poor little one." The translation is my own.

18. The photographs were taken in the city of Buzuluk in December 1921. See the Nansen Electronic Photo Archive (files 6a047 and 6a043) <http://nabo.nb.no/trip? _t=0&_b=NANSEN_ENG&_r=1091&_s=E&_n=0&_q=10&_l=www_eng_l> and <http://nabo.nb.no/trip?_t=0&_b=NANSEN_ENG&_r=1099&_s=E&_n=0& _q=10&_l=www_eng_l> (accessed November 8, 2009).

19. The article is republished on the ICRC's website: <http://www.icrc.org/web/fre /sitefre0.nsf/html/5QKJLH> (accessed October 25, 2009).

20. For instance, the image was printed with another photo of a single corpse to accompany an article entitled "The Tragedy of Russia" in the April 20, 1922, issue of the *Manchester Guardian* (on p. 5) and in the February 11, 1922, issue of *L'illustration* (on p. 135), reprinted in Cosandey 1998: 6.

21. According to Jean-Claude Panne, from the "L'histoire par l'image" Web site <http://www.histoire-image.org/site/oeuvre/analyse.php?i=574&d=401> (accessed November 12, 2009), the pamphlet was produced in collaboration with the Red Cross and contained twenty-five graphic images of the Russian famine.

22. One postcard was published by a Brussels-based Belgian organization devoted to Russian famine relief. See <http://www.artukraine.com/old/famineart/famine10.htm> (accessed November 12, 2009).

23. See <http://www.icrc.org/web/fre/sitefre0.nsf/html/5QKJLH> (accessed October 25, 2009).

24. On the notion of "the contest of meaning" in the history of photography, and the consequent social constructivist reinterpretation of images, see Bolton 1989.

25. It should be noted that Kollwitz drew a portrait of Russian famine victims, "Help Russia" (1921), in order to support the Internationale Arbeiter-Hilfe and its fundraising efforts to respond to the crisis.

26. Two major newspapers are missing from this table, namely the *New York Times* (New York, USA) and *Le Figaro* (Paris, France). In both instances, the archives of these newspapers were searched and numerous articles on the Russian famine were found and analyzed. However, because none of these articles were accompanied by photographs of the famine itself, the newspapers were not included in Figure 4.1.

27. Photographs of various nineteenth-century Indian famines did precede those of the Russian famine, but their distribution in Europe and North America appears to have been limited and they were not part of a humanitarian campaign.

28. For instance, the editors of the French illustrated newspaper *L'illustration* defended their publication of ghastly photographs of piles of corpses in the Buzuluk cemetery and scenes of cannibalism among Russian peasants by asserting their journalistic duty to reflect the truth about the horrors of the Russian famine, while also claiming that they used relative restraint in the selection of which images were published; readers were assured that far more gruesome images, portraying states of "human butchery," were left off the newspaper's pages (Cosandey 1998: 6).

REFERENCES

American Friends Service Committee (AFSC). 1921. "Do You Know the Reality of the Russian Famine?" *Bulletin* 44 (December 1). Philadelphia: American Friends Service Committee.

Azoulay, A. 2008. *The Civil Contract of Photography.* New York: Zone Books.

Barnett, M., and T. G. Weiss, eds. 2008. *Humanitarianism in Question: Politics, Power, Ethics.* Ithaca, NY: Cornell University Press.

Barthes, R. 1977. "The Third Meaning: Research Notes on Some Eisenstein Stills." In *Image Music Text.* Translated by S. Heath, 52–68. New York: Fontana Press.

———. 1981. *Camera Lucida: Reflections on Photography.* Translated by R. Howard. New York: Hill and Wang.

Boissier, P. 1978. *Histoire du Comité international de la Croix-Rouge: De Solférino à Tsoushima* [History of the International Committee of the Red Cross: from Solferino to Tsushima]. Geneva: Institut Henry-Dunant.

Boltanski, L. 1999. *Distant Suffering: Morality, Media and Politics*. Cambridge, UK: Cambridge University Press.

Boltanski, L., and L. Thévenot. 2006. *On Justification: Economies of Worth*. Princeton, NJ: Princeton University Press.

Bolton, R., ed. 1989. *The Contest of Meaning: Critical Histories of Photography*. Cambridge, MA: MIT Press.

Breen, R. 1994. "Saving Enemy Children: Save the Children's Russian Relief Operation, 1921–23." *Disasters* 18 (3): 221–37.

Butler, J. 2009. *Frames of War: When Is Life Grievable?* London and New York: Verso.

Calhoun, C. 2008. "Altruistic Work: Humanitarian Assistance as Ethics, Politics, and Profession." Paper presented at the American Sociological Association Annual Conference, Boston, MA, August 3.

Campbell, D. 2003. "Salgado and the Sahel: Documentary Photography and the Imaging of Famine." In *Rituals of Mediation: International Politics and Social Meaning*, edited by F. Debrix and C. Weber, 69–96. Minneapolis: University of Minnesota Press.

———. 2007. "Geopolitics and Visuality: Sighting the Darfur Conflict." *Political Geography* 26: 357–82.

Cosandey, R. 1998. "Eloquence du visible: La famine en Russie 1921–1923, Une filmographie documentée" [The eloquence of the visible: the 1921–1923 famine in Russia]. *Archives (Institut Jean Vigo)* 75/76.

Curti, M. 1963. *American Philanthropy Abroad: A History*. New Brunswick, NJ: Rutgers University Press.

Durand, A. 1978. *Histoire du Comité international de la Croix-Rouge: De Sarajevo à Hiroshima* [History of the International Committee of the Red Cross: from Sarajevo to Hiroshima]. Genève: Institut Henry-Dunant.

Friends of Soviet Russia (FSR). 1921 [?]. "The Russian Famine: Pictures, Appeals." *Russian Famine Pamphlet No. 1*. New York: Friends of Soviet Russia.

Go, J. 2008. "Global Fields and Imperial Forms: Field Theory and the British and American Empires." *Sociological Theory* 26 (3): 201–29.

Haller, F. 2003. "Secours en temps de paix: la famine en Russie" [Rescue in peacetime: the famine in Russia]. *Le temps*, August 12.

"L'Homme qui veut vaincre la famine: Hier, Nansen, acclamé par 6.000 Parisiens, a évoqué la grande détresse des affamés de Russie" [The man who wants to conquer famine: yesterday, Nansen, acclaimed by 6,000 Parisians, evoked the great distress of the starving people of Russia]. 1922. *L'humanité*, February 18, 1.

Jameson, F. 1991. *Postmodernism, or, The Cultural Logic of Late Capitalism*. Durham, NC: Duke University Press.

Latour, B. 2006. *Changer de société, refaire de la sociologie* [*Changing society, remaking sociology*]. Paris: La Découverte.

Law, J. 1992. "Notes on the Theory of the Actor Network: Ordering, Strategy and Heterogeneity." Lancaster, UK: Centre for Science Studies, Lancaster University, http://www.lancs.ac.uk/fass/sociology/papers/law-notes-on-ant.pdf.

Metz, C. 2003. *Essais sur la signification au cinéma* [*Essays on signification in film*]. Paris: Klincksieck.

Mirzoeff, N. 2005. *Watching Babylon: The War in Iraq and Global Visual Culture*. New York and London: Routledge.

Mitchell, W. J. T. 2005. *What Do Pictures Want? The Lives and Loves of Images*. Chicago: University of Chicago Press.

"Nansen on Russia: 'The Most Appalling Famine in Recorded History.'" 1922. *Manchester Guardian*, February 7, 6.

Rancière, J. 2003. *Le destin des images* [*The destiny of images*] Paris: La Fabrique.

———. 2008. *Le spectateur émancipé* [*The emancipated spectator*]. Paris: La Fabrique.

Sontag, S. 2003. *Regarding the Pain of Others*. New York: Farrar, Straus and Giroux.

"Soviet Accepts Hoover's Terms for Famine Relief." 1921. *New York Times*, July 31, 1.

Steinmetz, G. 2007. *The Devil's Handwriting: Precoloniality and the German Colonial State in Qingdao, Samoa, and Southwest Africa*. Chicago: University of Chicago Press.

Weindling, P. 1994. "From Sentiment to Science: Children's Relief Organisations and the Problem of Malnutrition in Inter-War Europe." *Disasters* 18 (3): 203–12.

Wilson, R. A., and R. D. Brown, eds. 2009. *Humanitarianism and Suffering: The Mobilization of Empathy*. New York: Cambridge University Press.

CHAPTER 5

SEEING TRAGEDY IN THE NEWS IMAGES OF SEPTEMBER 11

WENDY BOWLER

> Let us now imagine the great Cyclops eye of Socrates—that eye that had never
> glowed with the sweet madness of artistic inspiration – turned upon tragedy.
> —Friedrich Nietzsche (*The Birth of Tragedy:* 67)

> It is immersion into an aesthetic object that makes it into an icon.
> —Jeffrey C. Alexander (2008b: 6)

September 11, 2001, New York City: the day terrorism impresses a powerful sequence
of pictures on television viewers worldwide. Leading the image assault are depictions
of the World Trade Center's (WTC) Twin Towers at the moment a ball of fire erupts
from one of the buildings. News reports name it a "tragedy," and it looks like one,
the day's events causing suffering, death, and loss on a scarcely conceivable scale. On
the newspaper front pages of September 11 and 12, what we might call the "moment
of attack" appears as the dominant news picture-type, commonly at the expense
of all written reportage apart from an evocative headline, sometimes only a single
word.[1] It is as a poster telegraphing a news-drama with many of Aristotle's components of tragedy: magnitude and gravity, completed action, an ordered sequence of
events (strong plot) and spectacular effects. The fundament of tragedy in Friedrich
Nietzsche's *The Birth of Tragedy*—Dionysian destruction, a terrible depth beneath
the sphere of Apollonian surfaces, images and beauty—may also be seen to appear
in the shape of the giant flames and ominous smoke.

   Sleek, silver towers; bright orange fireball; pillar of grey-black smoke: "simple"
and "well-defined" visual symbols that have turned this type of image into a ready
emblem of "9/11" and the global phenomenon of terrorism, of ours being an age of

terror (Durkheim, quoted in Alexander 2008a). It is a photo- or news icon in the commonly held sense of providing an "instant and effortless connection to some deeply meaningful moment in history" (Goldberg 1993: 135). Within a week of the events, the UK *Guardian,* for instance, is writing in terms of "the now iconic images of planes crashing into the World Trade Center towers" (Hodgson 2001: 9). But the question is, besides being a historical marker, can the 9/11 attack-image be seen as an icon of tragedy? May it stand as an icon in this deeper sense, providing for and allowing "immersion," as Jeffrey C. Alexander has called it (2008b), which I relate to that sense of being able to see as from the inside and outside of a scene almost simultaneously, similar to the double viewpoint of the Nietzschean tragic spectator? May it "light up with remembering" in the manner of an icon, prompting reflection, pathos, and even tragic vision (Carroll 2001: 5, 9)? Roland Barthes thought newspaper images could "shock" but not really "wound" (2000: 41). The September 11 imagery has probably lost even this capacity, given the celebrity of these pictures and viewers' growing remove from the time of the events. The planes, the towers, the fireball, the palls of smoke: after the news media's deluge, what is there left to see, feel, and say?

Amid the continuous flow of images on television, the Internet, and in the daily newspapers, magazine editors and designers had to decide their own response, particularly how to use their covers to reflect the mood. The attack-image, and thus a strong note of terror, continued to dominate the American news weeklies, but the choice of cover image was more difficult for the monthly magazines, with many of these in the process of closing-off issues (dated November 2001) as the hijacked planes flew in. What image-word combination could they employ that might still be relevant to readers in around four weeks' time?

The Manhattan-based *Esquire,* a men's general-interest magazine, was unusual in its decision to depict the moment of attack, yet it was given a twist in the cover design.[2] Instead of appearing as an oversized image, the burning towers are seen in miniature—like model buildings—as a photo-within-a photo of a big human eye. The terror image is put at a distance. What is foregrounded is the concept of the 9/11 viewer; the viewer's experience of seeing September 11 as a "tragedy" that came close, an idea helped by the two cover lines set top and bottom of the eye: "What They Saw"/"stories from Inside an American Tragedy." In other words, the *Esquire* Eye might be viewed as an effective image through which to reflect upon the process of seeing September 11 as a tragedy.[3] It can be used as an entry point to the complete visual narrative, I suggest. In this chapter, however, the 9/11 news icon will be the focus, followed by a counterview from the end of the story, an image of the "ground zero" ruins.

ESQUIRE'S COOL, DRY EYE

When he conceived of the cover the day after the events, the then-design editor of *Esquire* magazine, John Korpics, knew of his editor's idea to run material with the eventual title "Emails from Hell," first-person accounts of what people had seen. Korpics' instinct was to use the "greatest picture" of the events of the day, yet he was concerned that an image of the burning towers would be "generic" by the time the next issue went on sale in mid-October.

Speaking one year later, Korpics reflected on the depressing experience of reviewing the September 11 imagery: "I could hardly get up in the morning, because you were coming to work and there'd be another 200 pictures for you to look at, of people jumping out of the windows."[4] All told, he guessed he had reviewed a thousand images on top of the continuous television coverage switched on at home. Interestingly, his intention with the *Esquire* cover was to avoid a picture that was depressing or horrific. He wanted to "downplay... the actual image of the towers exploding" and show events from the "point of view of the people who saw it," using the eyeball as a motif.

As things turned out, sales of this issue were disappointing, according to Korpics, who supposed readers must have already wearied of the widespread coverage. Nevertheless, to a reviewer curious about the process of generating tragic icons—as a form of cultural and personal recovery work—this is a timeless cover. The irony of the Eye (and the reason it has captured my own) is that it establishes an aesthetic distance between the moment of viewing and the icon of 9/11, while also promising to reveal the "inside" of a tragedy.

The *Esquire* Eye is wide open as if all-seeing yet blank, impervious, or unaffected. It is a dry eye, suggesting no emotion despite the violent image it is directing us to see. It is like the mechanical eye of a camera at the point of fixing its object, caught between the photographic instant and the human response, and also between a past event and a current viewing. The photographic image being what it is, the Eye is fixed on the moment of attack. I, the viewer, on the other hand, am looking back from a position of having seen the rest of the visual news story: a plane flying in; victims jumping to their deaths; firefighters moving towards the site bearing enormous loads; the total collapse of both buildings; and the ruins of Ground Zero. Knowing the ending, there is pathos in coming back to the opening image of September 11; pathos and fatigue.

The *Esquire* cover is playing on the idea that we viewers will have seen a complete sequence of news images—probably repeatedly—and will have some of these stored in our memory, as "interior" images founded on the media's "exterior visualisation" (Baxandall 1974: 45). To borrow John Shearman's ideas on Renaissance art and spectatorship, "by exploiting the spectator's familiarity with image types," the moment of attack is able to articulate "sequence, or the passage through moments" in a whole narrative (1988: 82). There is a "genealogy of the moment" operating through the core image: we know it belongs with other pictures not illustrated here and is iconic of a whole story of terrible events.

The *Esquire* 9/11 Eye is a blue eye in a darkened face. It is like a black-and-white cover—helping to put historical distance between the viewer and the events—to which color is applied. The red of the *Esquire* logo, the blue of the eye's iris, and the white of the eyeball and headline words convey an American patriotic theme. It is an enlarged, right eye detached from a face and body, so it is "arty" in the surrealist sense of being a part object. The technique of magnification brings the image close to the viewing space; it is an Eye that is "in your face." The tight frame created by the cover lines makes the Eye look bigger still. Interestingly, the "What They Saw" and "stories From Inside an American Tragedy" have a grip on my eye almost equal to the picture. The strong sense of frame helps to keep the terror of the core image at bay. Conversely, the words capture my attention and encourage me to see a certain depth in the image. The "What" adheres to the "9/11" that is so emphatically conveyed by the icon in the eye (the text does not need to name the events). The "They" sets up a tacit "we" and creates the impression of a divide in the spectatorship, while also speaking to this as a collective or public tragedy. "Insiders" are signified as participants in the events, who are opposed to us the viewers who saw from "outside" (another silent word) via the media. Theirs is a privileged perspective, for "They Saw...Inside" what the cover proceeds to name "an American Tragedy," the implication being that it is a perspective hitherto missed.

We cannot seem to get this mediating eye out of the picture, which is true of the way most of us saw the events. Even eyewitnesses spoke of the blurring of the mental pictures of their own direct experience with the stream of media images.[5] The 9/11 Eye might thus be seen to occupy an ambiguous but assertive space between participants and viewers, similar to a Greek chorus mediating between the elevated stage-world and the *theatron* proper. "Tragedy" is given the final word, not as a theoretical term but a common word of journalism, one that connotes a sorrowful story of sudden and inexplicable human loss and, in this case, mass death. It signals that we can expect to be moved besides being informed. Similar to the photo icon of the core image, "Tragedy" is a quick news label that requires minimum effort to read. I flick my eye between the components to arrive at "9/11 Tragedy," followed by "Inside" this tragedy—and the realization that this issue of *Esquire* is naming the terms of my inquiry. A tragic perspective on the events, my own, finds a powerful cue and emblem in the cover image. But can such a seemingly dry and objective news eye (a journalistic ideal type that was challenged on September 11) lead its viewer to see a tragedy? Can journalistic fact-finding and empirical evidence prepare the ground for tragic vision? Interestingly, Korpics's own response to the cover months later was that it seemed "flat and unemotional": "I think I was so concerned with avoiding the horrific imagery I knew was going to be out there, that I went the other way. It doesn't convey any real emotion. *It's too detached*" (Korpics, quoted in Spiker 2003; italics mine).

There is a deep contradiction in the cover image, then, between the drive to uncover surface facts (the news impulse) and the desire to create and review a story of tragedy. The nature of tragic spectatorship is to see as from two positions simultaneously; it is dual in nature, stereoscopic. In Nietzsche's conception of the structure of vision in tragedy (via his writerly image of the Greek theatron), the spectator sees "actually" from the raked seating in the theatron proper and "virtually" as one with the Dionysian chorus in the circular *orchestra* (see Shapiro 2003: 140–42)—the latter viewpoint the key for engagement, enchantment, and tragic participation. The view from the theatron implies a distant, self-conscious, Apollonian perspective; the virtual view, as if seeing through the eyes of the chorus, a Dionysian loss of self. It was Nietzsche's reading that the cultural capacity or sensibility for tragedy, with its Dionysian source and soaring metaphysical effect, had been swamped by Socratic thinking, what we might call the scientific-rational response. Thus, a critical question prompted by the *Esquire* Eye is whether the kind of cool, dry, detached (modern?) viewer it appears to symbolize is capable of seeing "inside" tragedy? Can the news icon of 9/11 be viewed as a *tragic* icon?

This *ekphrasis* has so far taken account only of the outer image, the core picture being instantly read as "9/11." The iris of the eye, like a frame for the inside image, is reminiscent of the clear blue sky over New York on the morning of the events. Its fine lines lead to a tightly cropped photograph of the Twin Towers, which instead of being seen against the blue are set in a circle of black. A faint line rises from the top of the exploding tower on the left into the blue of the eye, presumably the telecommunications mast that sat on top of one of the buildings, distinguishing it from its otherwise identical twin. But to which tower did the mast belong? Which was the building first hit? These were questions that Korpics asked himself a year after the events; it was hard to remember.

In fact the North Tower, the building supporting the mast, was the first to be struck. The Eye is directing us to remember the initial explosion, but is what we see in the image how we actually saw the events? The exploding-tower image in the *New York Times* the next day suggests not: the North Tower is on the right, already on fire and sending a pall of thick black smoke up and over its blazing twin. The image seared on the *Esquire* Eye now appears *not* to be the icon of 9/11. We are either being provided with a rare still of the first attack or this is a digitally manipulated image. It is hard to conceive that a design editor with a thousand news pictures before his eyes should choose to create his own, but this is what Korpics told me he did do: "This isn't an actual image, it's a composite image. [The photo illustrator] took an image that he had of the trade towers, just a regular image before the explosion, and then he superimposed an explosion on to it. So this is not really a picture of the event.... There was no picture of somebody hitting the first tower because people weren't training their cameras at that point. And because it was a reaction to the event itself, I wanted it to be the moment—the first moment—with people saying, 'Oh, my God, what was that?'"

But why the seeming disregard for what Susan Sontag has called the "truth-telling" function of photography? Why show the first attack when the "decisive moment," in a news sense, was the crash of the second plane into the South Tower: the moment when shock turned to terror. The point for Korpics was to show "What They Saw" (and what we missed): the "first moment" of September 11. The result is an image that appeals to photography's ulterior function as art, using the techniques of digital photo manipulation, photo montage, and object magnification. The Eye only *refers* to the icon of 9/11.

The trick in the Eye, the fact of it being a manipulated photo illustration, points to an inherent tension in the story, between 9/11 as hard news and high tragedy; between being a testimony of the terrible realism of actual life and the drive towards a tragic-artistic representation as an attempt to recover meaning—of events that went beyond our comprehension and language. Journalistically, it has overstepped a line in not being true to the visual facts: it is a "false mirror," to apply the title of the surrealist painting by René Magritte (an antecedent eye image Korpics could well have had in mind).[6] Yet the *Esquire* Eye is useful to a project on tragedy through its attempt to marry the realism of the news with an imaginative, artistic response. It speaks to the limit of the powers of Socratic detection in a drive towards art, and also to what Sontag calls "the dual powers of photography—to generate documents and to create works of visual art" (2003: 76). Inadvertently, it also speaks to, of, and for the iconicity of the image that it fails to show. We can now appreciate not only how fixed in visual memory is the shape of the image of the exploding second tower, but also how sacrosanct, to the point that an illustration merely approximating what actually happened can offend or affront us.

The most striking aspect of the Eye, when I stand back as the viewer, is its disproportionate size in relation to the object of regard: 9/11 as a deeply embedded picture. It is an overblown eye, as if the experience of viewing the events had been so overpowering that this had become the story: the "where I was when it happened" kind of account, familiar from earlier big news events, such as the assassination of President Kennedy and the death of Princess Diana. Besides asserting the role of the viewer—the *beholder's share* of an image, as E. H. Gombrich has called it (1972: 155)—the enormous eye may be read in Freudian terms as a negation of the felt response of impotence in the face of the visual might of September 11.

But let us follow the cues of our framing image and try to see further, by turning to some news pictures of the dramatic opening of the events, notably the icon of 9/11 on the front page of the *New York Times*.

9/11, MOMENT OF TERROR

"It's 8:52 here in New York and I'm Bryant Gumbel. We understand that there has been a plane crash on the southern tip of Manhattan…we understand that a plane has crashed into the World Trade Center…."[7]

Six minutes after the first plane hits the WTC's North Tower—at the precisely recorded time of 8:46:40 on the morning of September 11, 2001—CBS breaks into its morning programming with a "live" news report from New York. The viewer is briefly taken to Gumbel in the studios before the network switches to the first pictures of the 110-storey Twin Towers, looking south from a viewpoint in midtown Manhattan. The focus is the thick, dark smoke rising out of the building.

As Gumbel does his first phone interview with an eyewitness, who said he saw a plane and then a "huge ball of fire on top of the building," the live camera closes in on the ragged gash in the top of the smoking tower. Fire can be seen through a hole in the wall just above the gash. Smoke is pouring out of the highest floors and blowing over the top of the Twin Towers towards the southeast. In this change of camera angle, the picture has gone from a background sky of "severe clear" in pilot parlance to an atmosphere of murky yellow. Five minutes later, Gumbel is receiving the calm and articulate phone report of a woman, Theresa Renaud, who has had a clear view of the North Tower explosion from her office window: "Approximately 10 minutes ago there was a major explosion from about the 80th floor—looks like it affected probably four to eight floors. Major flames are coming out of the north side and also the east side of the building. It was a very large explosion, followed by flames, and it looks like the building is still on fire on the inside."

Much more arresting than this description, however, is the discontinuity between what is on the screen and what is being articulated. The approach of the second plane can be spotted. In the space of a single second of replayed videotape, what I know to be United Airlines Flight 175 has moved into the top of the picture and disappeared behind the black smoke blowing across the roof of its target: the South Tower. After further unenlightened commentary, I see, before Gumbel and his guest see it, a fireball invading the lower picture. Only a portion of the flames is in the frame, however, owing to the most recent change of camera angle: we are now being shown a tight shot of the hole in the North Tower, which suggests the CBS producer has also missed the second plane. Besides the restrictive camera angle, the rising flames are also obscured by the headlines running across the bottom of the screen: "CBS News Live Coverage/Plane Crashes Into World Trade Center," words that are already behind the news. They are signed-off with the CBS logo: a single eye.[8]

Finally, the second attack upon the World Trade Center, and the first thought of terrorism, registers in language:

Renaud: Oh, there's another one—another plane just hit…Oh, my God! Another plane has just hit—it hit another building, flew right into the middle of it. My God, it's right in the middle of the building.

Gumbel: This one into [Tower 2]?

Renaud: Yes, yes, right into the middle of the building…. That was definitely…on purpose.

Gumbel: Why do you say that was definitely on purpose?

Renaud: Because it just flew straight into it. (CBS 2002)

Several seconds later, the spectacular fireball turns to a pillar of grey-black smoke. Renaud is gasping, and Gumbel is struggling for the right words: the images, whether direct to the eye (for her) or mediated by TV pictures (for him), have flowed too fast for their eyes to see, partly because they are "unthinkable," "inconceivable," as people would later remark. They are living through these events as minor participants, not unlike heralds bearing ominous news in a Greek tragedy; they cannot give them a perspective because theirs is too close. The media story that begins with reflections by the journalist of how strange it feels to be a participant in the news—almost as an apology for the loss of professional objectivity—would become a phenomenon of the 9/11 reportage. Gumbel and his guest are here part of the news. It will be 2004 before one of the official descriptions of the events unfolding before their eyes is published: "At 9:03:11 on September 11, 2001, United Airlines Flight 175 hit 2 WTC (the South Tower) from the south, crashing through the 77th to 85th floors" (*9/11 Commission Report* 2004: 293).

About two minutes later, less than ten minutes into the CBS special report, the network broadcasts the first of many replays of the opening images of September 11, and Gumbel says: "Now, Theresa, hang on one second, we're going to re-rack [*sic*] the tape of when we were talking to you to see if we can tell…um…we can't see anything; we can't see a second plane in the picture. There, we see the explosion!" (CBS 2002).

But the plane *is* on the tape. Gumbel has missed it again. This time a wider picture of Lower Manhattan is selected, taken from midtown, with the Empire State Building in the foreground of the picture. The plane, coming from the right, appears to cross the narrow gap of blue sky between the skyscraper that used to be the city's tallest and its usurpers, the WTC towers. Then it disappears behind the thick smoke of the North Tower. Seconds later, the fire from the explosion of the plane mushrooms out of the second tower's southeast corner. Although it will take a bit longer for CBS and the other American networks to confirm this, the fact of the image is that a second plane has flown into the South Tower and blown up inside it.[9] This is a turn of events, the moment of a dramatic shift in meaning: what began as a report of a possible aviation accident now, instinctively, feels like terrorism. The image that has just registered with Gumbel will rapidly become one of the most famous in the world.

Before morphing into a poster image on the front of newspapers and magazines worldwide, the terror image is shown in an endless loop of television replays married to the other hard news images of the morning: both towers totally collapsing; scenes of people running ahead of huge balls of dust; damage to the Pentagon after the impact of the third hijacked plane; and the scene of the crash of a fourth plane in a field in Pennsylvania. They are like television's version of the punctum: the images with the greatest capacity to "pierce" or "wound" the eye (Barthes 2000: 27). Through constant repetition, the television replay will have the effect of slowing the story down. No story needed this device more. The "re-racked tape" becomes a sign of the speed of events: the plane coming in too fast for the unknowing eye to see.

Now, of course, as reviewers of the images who know the story, beginning, middle and end, we can take a position of retrospective detachment. The eye has the benefit of hindsight, a power of omniscience; the reverse side is, because aesthetic rather than immediate, a weaker emotional response (Fry 1956: 18–20). We are the beneficiaries of a reduced, less "numbing" pathos. We do not need to anchor a live television program of "unthinkable" events, duck to miss falling debris, or run from the ball of dust that came coursing through the streets of Manhattan like a Hollywood tidal wave. The retrospective viewer is able to "see the event much more clearly" and notice the pathos as it arises (18). Roger Fry speaks of the "artistic attitude of pure vision abstracted from necessity," and observes that the "need for responsive action hurries us along and prevents us from ever realizing fully what the emotion is that we feel. . . . In the imaginative life, on the contrary, we can both feel the emotion and watch it" (27). "Pure vision" is suggested by the *Esquire* cover, an Eye as absorbed in its own visual process as in the picture of 9/11. This is a highly Apollonian eye, in Nietzsche's terms.

In this spirit I can choose the slowest form of the 9/11 news spectacular, the still image, to encourage a similar stillness in my spectatorship and to counter the maelstrom of events depicted. It is a method that happens to converge with A. D. Nuttall's idea of tragedy requiring a "peculiar stillness in the watcher together with strenuous activity in that watcher's sympathetic imagination" (1996: 78). Conversely, when a still image loses its feeling of reality, as an icon can tend to do, through becoming too detached from the underlying flow of the narrative, video sequences have the capacity to restore something of the emotions associated with the raw viewing.

My method is to *still* the 9/11 telemovie (as if the television tapes are replaying in a mental cinema) through a review of images selected as punctum pictures or "impression points" (Dilthey) of the visual story, like *tableau vivants*. These hold the rapid movement of events at the points of greatest tension, suspense and pathos, allowing the eye to return with what Barthes has called pensiveness: a quality of returning with both thought and feeling. It is a method that aims for a clarity of vision through a retrospective detachment and engagement—what I call *detached re-engagement*—and which compensates for the viewing eye's spatial and (growing) temporal remove from the events and the original act of viewing. It is a method that also engages with photography's "pathos of distance," like an encounter with tragic time. The referents of the photos are from the past, while the material images and act of viewing belong to the present. This is what Barthes and Sontag meant by the photograph having an inherent pathos, reminding me of the inescapable fact of time having passed; I am holding these towers in my hands, and can change nothing. Yet, as Barthes tells us, photography also has "something to do with resurrection" (2000: 81).

* * *

How does the 9/11 reviewer "preserve intact the incredible incandescence of the images" of the exploding World Trade Center tower (Baudrillard 2002: 4)? It might be similar to asking an art historian to see afresh the *Mona Lisa* or *The Scream* (Elkins 2004: 77). There are two apparent contradictions as we approach a reading of a single photograph of the moment of terror. The first is how to properly see it, not only as a news icon detached from a wider visual narrative but also as a photo document with a literal surface. Does such a celebrated image prove its iconicity through its resistance to being seen and interpreted—it just *is* the picture of 9/11— and through the intimidation that I, the viewer, feel when faced with the magnitude of events it is directing me to see? It may be that my eye is being thrown straight to the rhetoric of the image. So familiar and emphatic are its visual elements—the Twin Towers, a brilliant fireball shooting out of one and a heavy column of smoke arising from the other—that the viewer sees "9/11" and thinks of terrorism. It is as though the elevation of this photo object as an icon of the news, an icon that comes culturally supplied, would thwart my own attempt to really see it, as with fresh eyes. But I suggest that a symbolic, that is to say, *tragic*, interpretation really must unfold from, first, an ekphrasis of the literal surface of the picture: simply, to say what the eye can see and create an honest response in words. But there is a problem with finding words for an image this famous, particularly when the things I am called to describe include built structures. The response does not require empathy with the emotional states of human figures, but rather the development of an "aesthetic relationship" with a pair of modernist towers. As Eric Darton has written: "You know they are office buildings, yet their design makes it nearly impossible to imagine they are full of people. It is at this point... that you realize the trade towers disappear as sites of human habitation and reassert their power at the level of an aesthetic relationship" (1999: 118).

The second problem, as encountered with the core picture of the *Esquire* Eye, is how to, if not get rid of the image seared on the eye (since my aim is to preserve it), see through or move beyond this moment by recognition of its "genealogy": the special capacity of this one image to articulate the passage through a sequence of charged moments in time. My idea is that to see past the decisive moment of September 11 means, first of all, to really see and describe it.

By 9:03 a.m., the time of the second crash, a small army of professional and amateur camera operators and photographers were training their lenses on the burning North Tower, so they could not help but capture the explosion from the second plane flying into its twin. It was as if the perpetrators had designed events with media viewers completely in mind, appropriating the idea of the television replay;[10] the second attack was the photo opportunity primed by the first. In contrast to the rare shots of the first plane crash, there are so many versions of the exploding South Tower that the 9/11 news icon cannot be regarded as one image (as Nick Ut's photo of the napalmed girl running down the road became iconic of the Vietnam war, for example) but an image-type, shown typically from the east side and putting the fireball on the left of the picture. The views are always wide enough to show the North Tower and its pall of smoke, blowing back across both towers and marring the blue sky. In the most successful images, the smoke does not obscure the North Tower's communications mast, for this becomes as important a marker for the 9/11 reviewer as for the pedestrian.

If the visual narrative has so far been slowed with the viewing of the CBS video, then it might now be stilled through allowing our eyes to come to rest on a single shot. My choice is the punctum of the *New York Times* (by Steve Ludlum, September 12, 2001). This was the lead of a package of four front-page photographs, claiming three columns of space and the depth of the page below the headlines ("U.S. ATTACKED" and "Hijacked jets destroy Twin Towers and hit Pentagon in day of terror"), an extraordinary visual display in context of the relatively restrained design of the *Times*.[11]

The top half of this strongly vertical picture is dominated by giant flames and ominous smoke. The viewpoint is from across the East River, looking over the Brooklyn Bridge and one of its two elegant masonry towers, the one marking the Manhattan side. The towers are set at a slight angle, allowing a glimpse of their north sides besides a full view of the east walls, whose silver "skins" are shining in the bright morning sun. The famous fireball is, in this view, more of a wildfire blowing out of the second tower, its flames forming giant swirls that cover the view of the twin. At the farthest edges, the bright orange mass is edged with the same sort of charcoal-grey smoke being belched out by the North Tower. Another way of describing the explosion is as a body of flames throwing out two extensions. One, sweeping across to the North Tower, is a giant lick of bright orange flames and thick smoke; the other a finer curl of orange reaching around to the south wall and merging with a giant dust cloud that (I know from seeing other images) is blowing out of the second plane's entry hole. The still image has the dust cloud, a sign of the "pulverized contents" of the floors of impact, suspended over the blackish box of the Deutsche Bank building.

In an opposite movement to the powerful upswirl of fire and smoke, a shower of thousands of pieces of debris is coming down on the surrounding buildings and, in this view, unseen streets. Many of the larger chunks are falling like lethal torches, accompanied by a finer shower of what must be broken aluminum and glass, and paper the size of confetti. On the left side, debris is cascading down the South

Tower's southern face, presumably from the hole made by the plane. On the far right, against the North Tower, a few burning pieces are falling against a strip of blue sky. I catch myself wondering if one might be a human figure, for people were seen jumping around this time, but my eye cannot distinguish any people in this picture. The earlier explosion in the North Tower has blown a rectangular "window" in the east wall facing me. This and the entry hole of the first plane, around the corner, are feeding the mass of black smoke. I can still see, though, a part of the communications mast, my security marker. Light winds are directing the smoke across the top of the exploding building and out of the frame.

In the lower part of the photo stand the dual arches of the Brooklyn Bridge before an array of lower-rise buildings. Like the towers above it, the bridge is a landmark of New York City and an engineering feat of its day, including through its use of both masonry and steel. Some photographs in the September 11 Digital Archive show tourists using the Great Bridge of 1883 as a staging point for photos of themselves with the Twin Towers in the background. The structures are here functioning as ordinary icons for tourists, who may be seen as borrowing the magnitude and notoriety of their architecture for photos of themselves "being there," helping them to make an event of this time in their lives. The view of both bridge and skyline is not half so impressive when one sees images with the towers removed, unless the point is to see them as "after images" marking the presence of an unthinkable absence.

THE SUBLIME RUIN

Having said what I can see in the image of 9/11, I must reflect on what I cannot: the people in this tragedy. As the anchorman Aaron Brown observed: "This isn't about planes and towers...it's a people story" (CNN 2003), as if, looking back on the spectacular imagery, we were forced to remind ourselves of the need to recover the human scale. Strangely, the news icon is exterior to the pathos of events; it is outside the core tragedy (or countless personal tragedies) occurring inside the planes and towers, and on the streets far below. We have got inside the *Esquire* Eye, in a sense, with our slow reading of this lead image of the *Times*, yet are still remote from the human tragedy, when surely tragedy is a human thing. This predicament is signed in the dryness of the ekphrasis: language that for all its careful description of the photo's literal surface is without emotional depth. As Korpics's wide eye prefigured, the spectacular images of September 11 put the viewer at a distance, partly because they are skyline or architectural views in which the teeming metropolis cannot help but be made invisible. Consequently, I am left with both a *flat* feeling and a nagging doubt about the adequacy of the celebrated news image as an icon of the 9/11 tragedy.

Images of the exploding, imploding towers may be as a covering for the human tragedy, shielding us from reaching an inside drama that does not bear thinking about. Barbie Zelizer's interpretation is similar: the towers "took the place of depictions of people about to die" (2004:176), the spectacle of them being what we have preferred or needed or been obliged to see. However, rather than consider the 9/11 news icon a block to the viewing, I am again encouraged to see this image as an entry point to the whole drama; an exterior visualization linked to a sequence of interior images, owing to the process of the "re-racked tape," a literal thing also pointing to the workings of memory. The images come flooding back: a blurred firefighter climbing the stairs of the North Tower beside a queue of workers filing down; trapped people leaning out of the highest windows and standing on ledges; a lone woman spotted standing, incredulously, in the gaping hole made by the first plane and *waving*; and the famous "falling man," a photo in which the sleek verticality of the grey towers forms a chilling background for a man's death, surely the story's real moment of terror. These are the hard-core pathos images that the 9/11 news spectacular, as suggested by the *Esquire* cover, both entices us to view and keeps us from really seeing. But, then, is not the process of aesthetic distancing and magnetizing part of the nature—the enchantment—of tragedy, at least of the archetype of tragedy of which Nietzsche writes? And is it not when a kind of centered perspective, equilibrium, or *sophrosyne* is attained, however fleeting the still vision, that we know we are in the presence of tragedy and can think of ourselves as *bearing witness* to tragedy?

Finally, there is an image from the end of the breaking news story that I call the sublime ruin (by Gary Miller, *NYPost*/Rex in *The New Yorker*, September 24, 2001: 75), a counter to the lead icon in more ways than one, owing to its capacity to break the drought of feeling. As Nuttall reminds us: "Of all the literary genres, tragedy is the one which lays the heaviest emphasis on ending, and the ending is a mimesis of a death. In so far as we sympathise, we experience the dying, but of course we do not die. The hypothesis dies instead" (1996: 78).

This lesser-known image of the events, although just as much a part of the photo-documentary record as the *Times'* 9/11, strikes me as a more personal icon because of what it has allowed me to see. In T. S. Eliot's terms, it is a more successful "objective correlative" of the 9/11 tragedy,[12] a truer icon, following Alexander, owing to my deeper "fall" into the photo object. Its "presence effects" are of the terrible absence of human life for which the ruined tower is here standing. Again, there are no people in this image, yet the sense of them as "missing" (the title of so many posters made by loved ones) is palpable. It is through this end image that I am able to re-rack the tapes of terror and see the Twin Towers as tragic towers.

In this final scene, in the *still* moment of the just fallen, we approach the edge of a site beyond recognition. An ashen backlight, strangely violet in hue, is streaking the dust and smoke. As the ground has been shaken, so has the aesthetic. From seeing whole towers glistening like sculptures against the skyline—the picture postcard angle before September 11—the view is of metal wrecks and smaller shards leaning out of a jagged, smoking, cavernous ground. No longer do we have to crane our necks to see, for the towers have been brought near to the ground. We have also gone from fast-moving objects needing to be seen in film and photographic sequences to still images of fixed objects. The fires have gone underground and the air is sour. What is beyond our sight is worse. Further, all that glorious design, technology, engineering, and construction work—all that creative human endeavor—has been reduced to a chaotic heap of steel, aluminum, and pulverized concrete.

There do not seem to be words in the language to describe the effect of what I see and feel. There is no longer a World Trade Center but a "ground zero" and then a "hole," "pile," or "pit," the bald words of a revised vernacular (when this scene is calling for poetry). I look into Miller's photograph and have the sense of passing through a dim, narrow side street as in the chiaroscuro of a Caravaggio painting. A news photograph here displayed as the final, full-page image of *The New Yorker's* 9/11 essay, it inhabits that border zone between the realism of hard news and the sublimity of tragic art. Directly ahead, in place of the density of the WTC buildings, stands a pyramidal piece from the South Tower with the suggestion of empty space behind. This is a tower that had "not just collapsed. It had apparently disappeared" (Glanz and Lipton 2003: 274). All that remains is a fragment of "exoskeleton" from the Twin Towers' "hollow tube" design of load-bearing steel walls (Robins 1987: 46). An engineering marvel of its time has been reduced to a "ruin," a fragment of skyscraper facade sheathed in the language of pathos.

Despite the absence of a human figure, or perhaps because of it, I get the sense of there being a "positioned viewer" at the end of the alley happening upon the ruin not long after the fall. This is the photographer in actual terms, whose window onto the desolate site is shared by the viewer. Before long I am counting floors since the horizontal lines are, for the first time, as visible as the vertical. There are fewer than a dozen, out of a structure of 110. As the eye traces the pattern of crossed lines and dusty sky, empirical vision seems to give way to a more symbolic ("inside") view of the tragedy. The spaces represent window openings: "points of impression" that are pathos points to my eye, knowing that they marked the limits of human beings on the day of September 11. With the row of slender arches at the base, the whole effect is of seeing the misty ruin of a vaguely Gothic cathedral, as in a Friedrich painting. "General Motors gothic" was how one architecture writer summed up the effect of seeing dainty arches at the top and bottom of what were, at the time, the world's tallest buildings. Such ornamentation was part of their designer Minoru Yamasaki's reaction against the "coldness" of modernist architecture (Goldberger 2005: 24) and a gesture to the problem of how to design with a "human scale." It was a contradiction in terms, this ideal of a humane architecture welded to the commercial demand for ten million square feet of office space. Yet there is a sharded, cathedral-like humanity suggested by the image of the ruin.

As a desecrated monument just holding to the life of the vertical, a terrible beauty born of an even more terrible urge for destruction, this fragment of tower ironically redeems its architect's failed vision: of buildings in relationship to which there would not be a "diminution of the soul" but a "soaring feeling" (Yamasaki 1979: 114).[13] The photograph of the ruin refers the eye to the might of the events and magnitude of our loss, simply, to the tragedy of it all.[14] To be still with it and struggle to realize, through language, the photo's potential as a *tragic icon* shows what art can do, especially once I have taken my beholder's share and reached for (however imperfectly) an artistry in the response.

NOTES

1. From an informal survey of U.S. newspapers by Phil Nesbitt, in the American Press Institute's *Crisis Journalism: A Handbook for Media Response* of October 2001: 19–22. The shot of the exploding tower also appeared on the front pages of all the U.K. national newspapers of September 12 except the *Financial Times*, which published a wrap-around image from the stage of collapse.

2. *Esquire,* November 2001 edition.

3. As I discovered when reviewing and interpreting a select sequence of September 11 images for a doctoral project on the "tragedy" in the media's story, undertaken within the Sociology Program of La Trobe University, Melbourne, under the principal supervision of Professor John Carroll.

4. In conversation with me at the magazine's offices in Manhattan on September 10, 2002.

5. Craig Calhoun, for example, who was a few hundred meters from the World Trade Center at the time of the events, said some of the television images were "as indelible as those formed while I was close enough for the smoke to sting my eyes" (Calhoun 2002: 1). Meanwhile, Jay McInerney wrote: "I'm not quite sure whether I was looking at the TV screen or at the window when the second plane hit a few minutes after I'd returned to my bedroom. I've seen the replay so many times now...." (McInerney 2001: 1–2).

6. *The False Mirror,* 1928, Museum of Modern Art, New York.

7. Transcriptions of Bryant Gumbel's introduction and the interview with Theresa Renaud (to follow) are from the DVD included with CBS's commemorative book, *What We Saw: The Events of September 11, 2001—In Words, Pictures and Video.*

8. A graphic design version, as it happens, of Magritte's *The False Mirror* (Lansing 1985: 83).

9. Writing about the reporting of the ABC network, James Carey noted that it took until 11:00 a.m. (just over two hours after the first plane hit) for the basic details of the morning's events to be known and confirmed. "Slowly the magnitude of the events dawned on reporters" (Zelizer and Allan 2002: 72). This was also the sense of the subsidiary headline "A Creeping Horror" on the *New York Times'* front page next day (September 12, 2001).

10. An observation from the Digital Cultures Project, "After 9/11: Wiring Networks for Security and Liberty".

11. The *Times* published over fifty photos related to the 9/11 events in its front section the next day, compared to its usual twenty or so (Zelizer and Allan 2002: 55).

12. "The only way of expressing emotion in the form of art is by finding an 'objective correlative'; in other words, a set of objects, a situation, a chain of events which shall be the formula of that *particular* emotion: such that when the external facts, which must terminate in sensory experience, are given, the emotion is immediately evoked" (Eliot 1972: 145; italics mine).

13. Thank you to Dr. Chris Eipper, co-supervisor of my thesis project, for helping to find the words for this response to the photo of the ruin.

14. The fact that these too have disappeared adds to the iconicity of the photographs and the tragedy of the towers as monuments of memory.

REFERENCES

Alexander, J. C. 2008a. "Iconic Consciousness: The Material Feeling of Meaning." *Environment and Planning D: Society and Space* 26: 782–94.

———. 2008b. "Iconic Experience in Art and Life: Surface/Depth Beginning with Giacometti's *Standing Woman.*" *Theory, Culture and Society* 25 (5): 1–19.

Barthes, R. 2000. *Camera Lucida: Reflections on Photography.* Translated by R. Howard. London: Vintage.

Baudrillard, J. 2002. *The Spirit of Terrorism: And Requiem for the Twin Towers.* New York: Verso.

Baxandall, M. 1974. *Painting and Experience in Fifteenth-Century Italy: A Primer in the Social History of Pictorial Style.* Oxford: Oxford University Press.

Calhoun, C. 2002. "Introduction," first section. *Understanding September 11*, edited by C. Calhoun, P. Price, and A. Timmer: 1-2. New York: New Press.

Carroll, J. 2001. *The Western Dreaming: The Western World Is Dying for Want of a Story.* Sydney: HarperCollins.

CBS. 2002. *What We Saw: The Events of September 11, 2001—In Words, Pictures and Video.* DVD. New York: Simon & Schuster.

CNN. 2003. *America Remembers: The Events of September 11 and America's Response* (television documentary). Time Inc. Home Entertainment.

Darton, E. 1999. *Divided We Stand: A Biography of New York's World Trade Center.* New York: Basic Books,

The Digital Cultures Project. 2002. "After 9/11: Wiring Networks for Security and Liberty." Last modified February 27, http://dc-mrg.english.ucsb.edu/committee/warner/911.html.

Eliot, T. S. 1972. "Hamlet." *Selected Essays*, 3rd ed. London: Faber and Faber.

Elkins, J. 2004. *Pictures & Tears: A History of People Who Have Cried in Front of Paintings.* New York: Routledge.

Fry, R. 1956. *Vision and Design.* New York: Meridian Books.

Glanz, J., and E. Lipton. 2003. *City in the Sky: The Rise and Fall of The World Trade Center.* New York: Times Books, Henry Holt.

Goldberg, V. 1993. *The Power of Photography: How Photographs Changed Our Lives.* New York: Abbeville.

Goldberger, P. 2005. *Up from Zero: Politics, Architecture, and the Rebuilding of New York.* New York: Random House Trade Paperbacks.

Gombrich, E. H. 1972. *Art and Illusion: A Study in the Psychology of Pictorial Representation,* 4th ed. London: Phaidon Press.

Hodgson, J. 2001. "Only One Story in Town." *The Guardian*, MediaGuardian section, September 17.

Lansing, G. L. 1985. "René Magritte's *The False Mirror*: Image versus Reality." *Source: Notes in the History of Art* IV(2/3): 83–88.

McInerney, J. 2001. "Brightness Falls." *The Guardian,* Saturday section, September 15.

Nietzsche, F. 1993. *The Birth of Tragedy.* Translated by S. Whiteside. New York: Penguin.

The 9/11 Commission Report: Final Report of the National Commission on Terrorist Attacks Upon the United States. 2004. New York: W. W. Norton.

Nuttall, A. D. 1996. *Why Does Tragedy Give Pleasure?* Oxford: Clarendon Press.

Robins, A. 1987. *Classics of American Architecture: The World Trade Center.* Englewood: Pineapple Press, and Fort Lauderdale: Omnigraphics.

The September 11 Digital Archive. View at http://911digitalarchive.org.

Shapiro, G. 2003. *Archaeologies of Vision: Foucault and Nietzsche on Seeing and Saying.* Chicago: University of Chicago Press.

Shearman, J. 1988. *Only Connect: Art and the Spectator in the Italian Renaissance.* Princeton: Princeton University Press.

Sontag, S. 2003. *Regarding the Pain of Others.* New York: Farrar, Straus and Giroux.

Spiker, T. 2003. "Cover Coverage: How U.S. Magazine Covers Captured the Emotions of the September 11 Attacks: And How Editors and Art Directors Decided on Those Themes." *Journal of Magazine and New Media Research* 5 (2), Spring, http://aejmcmagazine.bsu.edu/journal/archive/Spring_2003/Spiker.htm.

Yamasaki, M. 1979. *A Life in Architecture.* New York: John Weatherhill.

Zelizer, B. 2004. "The Voice of the Visual in Memory." *Framing Public Memory*, edited by K. R. Phillips: 157–186. Tuscaloosa: University of Alabama Press.

Zelizer, B., and S. Allan, eds. 2002. *Journalism after September 11.* New York: Routledge.

CHAPTER 6

The Emergence of Iconic Depth: Secular Icons in a Comparative Perspective

Werner Binder

INTRODUCTION

In recent years, the concept of the "secular icon" has become more and more popular in the field of visual studies. Secular icons are widely regarded as images of extraordinary symbolic power and as carriers of collective emotions and meanings. The following contribution offers a theoretical elaboration and a comparative case study of secular icons. Before entering the discussion on secular icons, I will address a more general problem: What is an "icon" and what does "iconic" mean? The answer to this question allows us to deal with secular icons in a broader cultural sociological perspective. In the English language, the word "iconic" has a double meaning. First of all, "iconic" is used for objects of visual experience, for example images and pictures.[1] The second meaning of "iconic" refers to a certain type of collective symbols in the center of modern rituals, "cultural icons" such as famous wines or pop stars.

This double meaning of "icon" is by no means accidental, but grounded in the history of the concept. "Icon" is derived from the Greek word for picture (*eikon*). In Orthodox Christianity, this word is used for holy paintings that are part of the religious cult. In the past, the worship of those pictures was often controversial. During the seventh and eighth centuries, the Byzantine Empire was shaken by conflicts between the iconoclasts and the idolaters. The idolaters triumphed, and therefore icons are still an important part of the religious practice in Orthodox churches from Russia to Greece. The Roman Catholic Church opposed the worship of icons from the very beginning, though it is said that Pope Gregory I valued those paintings as texts for the illiterate (Bevan 1979: 126). In the religious icon, the double meaning of iconicity—visuality and sacredness—is still fused. I will argue that the same holds true for secular icons. Secular icons, as the name already indicates, are no longer religious in the strict sense of the term. Nevertheless, they have structural similarities to religious icons. Secular icons, due to their specific visual surface, create an iconic depth that allows them to become symbols in modern rituals. To be sure, it is always the properly socialized spectator and the civil discourses that endow an image with deeper public meanings. However, the emergence of iconic depth is never completely arbitrary, but rather tied to the iconic properties of the surface.

I will first discuss the role of visuality in social life and the relation of image and text. The second part of this study focuses on the sacred in sociology and modern society in order to clarify in what sense secular icons can be regarded as sacred. Third, I will develop a catalogue of formal criteria for secular icons that can also be viewed as dimensions of iconicity. The fourth part applies this model to the Abu Ghraib photographs, in particular to the image that became the icon of the scandal. The fifth part introduces a comparative case, the most iconic photographs of the Vietnam War. Finally, my conclusion offers a résumé, a short discussion of two problematic cases and some reflections on the growing importance of secular icons in a globalizing civil sphere.

VISUALITY, IMAGE, TEXT

Visuality plays a growing role in contemporary society. Nevertheless, sociology neglected its importance for a long time. Though Western culture valued seeing above all other senses, it disregarded the nonverbal channels of meaning in comparison to the logos of the spoken or written word. This already problematic tendency was radicalized by the "linguistic turn" in humanities and social sciences (e.g., Rorty 1967). Other "turns" followed to make up for this one-sidedness, for example by emphasizing the cultural, performative, and iconic aspects of social life.

In 1994, the German art historian Gottfried Boehm published a collection of essays by various authors addressing the question: what is an image? Boehm interpreted these essays as markers of an "iconic turn," as steps towards a recognition of the autonomy of the visual and against the hegemony of the logos (1994). Drawing on different approaches, he developed the concept of "iconic difference." Iconic difference is not only a categorical difference between image and text; it also designates the constitutive distinction between the picture and its visual environment, best exemplified by the frame of a painting. Furthermore, iconic difference separates the visual surface of an image from its emerging visual depth. Boehm offers valuable insights into the nature of visuality and pictures, but his insistence on the strict categorical difference between images and texts remains somewhat problematic: whatever the image reveals can never be grasped by spoken or written words. The early Ludwig Wittgenstein faced a similar problem in his discussion of the limits of language (1984: 82–85): the unspeakable can only reveal itself and thus attain a mystic quality. But if we were doomed to remain silent about images, this would mean the end of any scientific approach to the visual. A metaphor borrowed from Wittgenstein is in this context more appealing to me (1984: 301): iconology, understood as the science (or logos) of the image, is constantly struggling with the borders of our language and running up against the walls of the visual. Though images can never be completely translated into language, we are able to talk about images and share our experiences with them. The scientific necessity to speak and write about images seems at first rather trivial—Boehm has to use words to discuss the nature of images too—but forces us to recognize the complex relationships between image and text.

In order to actually say something about images, we can approach them from a "hermeneutical" point of view. Sigmund Freud (2005), Paul Ricœur (1970, 1973), and Clifford Geertz (2006) argued that dreams, symbolic action, and cultural performances among all other meaningful products of human activity should be understood after the model of the text. The art historian Erwin Panofsky conceptualized iconology as such a hermeneutics of the visual (1955). His iconology is basically a three-step method of interpretation that allows us to decipher images like texts. Panofsky showed that even the first step, the preiconographic description of the object level, is always an act of interpretation. As spectators, we need a particular knowledge of artistic styles to transform the flat visual surface of a painting into a three-dimensional scene. Panofsky's next step is an iconographical analysis that focuses on pictorial motifs, as every image stands in an intertextual relation with other images. The third and final step is Panofsky's genuine contribution to art history, the iconological interpretation of the image in a very specific sense. He invites us to treat pictures as "manifestations of underlying principles" or "cultural symptoms." A good example is Michel Foucault's interpretation (1973) of *Las Meninas*: Velasquez's painting is not only representing the classical concept of representation, but is also symptomatic for the episteme of a whole epoch.[2] Such findings suggest certain structural similarities between images and texts, as well as the existence of a common cultural logic underlying them. Panofsky's iconological method can be of great value for cultural sociologists because it allows the reconstruction of deep cultural structures. Still, there are two major problems with Panofsky's method. First of all, it culminates in a definitive interpretation and authoritative reading. Second, iconology loses sight of the autonomy of the recipients and the historical discourses informing them. The knowledge of styles, motifs, and epochs is part of an art historical discourse that enables and shapes the act of interpretation. Both problems are connected to each other because they result from Panofsky's exclusive interest in the relation between producer and product, between the artist and his painting. Panofsky remains blind to his own role as individual interpreter and ignores the potential meanings that paintings might hold for other recipients. For a full picture, the relation between product and recipient, between visual surface and the spectator also has to be taken into account.

A good starting point for bringing the spectator back in is Jeffrey C. Alexander's model of "iconic experience" (2008). He conceptualizes the interaction of visual object and recipient as an immersion into aesthetic forms, as a movement from the iconic surface to moral depth. This model not only allows us to understand the social significance of family photos, advertisements, and celebrities (2008: 7ff.), but is also crucial for an adequate understanding of secular icons. In Alexander's model, visual textures and the cultural text of social life are inseparably linked.[3] My conclusion is that the relation between discourse and image needs to be rethought. Images are interpreted by discourses, but remain nevertheless relatively autonomous. In return, images are often used by discourses to make claims or even to constitute themselves. In this respect, secular icons are a good example. They are not only an essential part of our cultural memory, but play a vital role in the public discourses of civil society. In order to understand their specific role, we have to develop a Durkheimian understanding of the sacred in modern society.

THE SACRED AND THE IMAGE

For a deeper sociological understanding of the sacred in archaic and modern societies, Émile Durkheim's *Elementary Forms of Religious Life* is still an invaluable book ([1912] 1995). Durkheim claims that there are no objective criteria for the sacred, except for its radical otherness and its separation from the profane. Instead, the distinction between sacred and profane is drawn by beliefs and rituals. These rituals and beliefs are accompanied by collective feelings that constitute the experience of the sacred. Durkheim argues further that these collective feelings would only have an ephemeral and precarious existence, if it were not for material objects called symbols. Symbols store collectively shared emotions and provide a focus for subsequent rituals; they embody the sacred. Religious icons are perfect examples of collective symbols in the Durkheimian sense. They attract the adoration and love of worshipers, but they can also arouse the contempt and hatred of iconoclasts. Religious icons are part of individual and collective rituals: individual believers often pray to icons and even kiss them; whole communities of believers make processions and carry them around in town. Furthermore, there are shared beliefs about religious icons, for example about their divine origin and miracles performed by them.

Durkheim noted the importance of shared feelings and societal community in his early work on the *Division of Labor* ([1893] 1965: 85-105). Back then, he argued that these integrative factors become less important to the same degree that a society becomes more differentiated and individualized. As individuals become more and more dissimilar from each other, the sacred core of society shrinks to a last common denominator—the "cult of the individual" ([1893] 1965: 172). At that time, Durkheim is still convinced that this cult is unable to produce any solidarity. During the Dreyfus affair, when Durkheim became a founding member of the Ligue des droits de l'homme, he changed his mind. In a public intervention, Durkheim distinguishes between a utilitarian and a normative understanding of individualism ([1898] 1969). He argues that the normative cult of the individual, embodied by the declaration of universal human rights, has the structure and integrative force of a religious belief system. Facing a national crisis, Durkheim declares that human rights are the "only system of beliefs which can ensure the moral unity of the country" ([1898] 1969: 25). Today, we witness the emergence of human rights as a global system of common beliefs, norms, and institutions bridging political, ethnic, or religious divisions. Durkheim offers a functional definition of sacredness and religion. I propose to conceptualize secular icons in a similar way. Secular icons are sacred images in their functions as symbols in a shared system of beliefs and convictions. Not only their function, also their experience seems often to resemble religious experience. Susan Sontag, for example, uses a religious register to describe her first encounter with photographs from the Nazi concentration camps as a "negative epiphany" and "modern revelation" (1977: 19).

Every cultural icon has its ritual or cult community. A pop star is celebrated by a fans, and an iconic wine is supported by a group of connoisseurs. But what distinguishes secular icons from fan posters? Quantitatively, the community of believers in universal human rights seems to be bigger than any single fan community. Qualitatively, the emotions in response to human rights violations are more collective and intense than the effervescence at a pop concert. We are outraged if someone denies the existence of the Holocaust or mocks its victims, but we tolerate someone who dislikes a certain type of music. Still, there is another crucial difference between the religion of the old days and the fan clubs of today on the one hand, and the modern religion of human rights on the other hand. We can describe this difference as a shift from a positive to a negative form of transcendence (Giesen 2005). Human rights and human dignity only become visible through their violation. The modern cult of the individual is first of all a "cult of victims" (Giesen 2004). Secular icons are therefore almost exclusively images that show human rights violations and war crimes. Like religious icons, these "emblems of suffering" require an "equivalent of a sacred or meditative space in which to look at them" (Sontag 2003: 119), such as the civil sphere as a sacred or meditative space of modern societies (Alexander 2006). Only in a public space created by mass media and discourses, interactions and institutions, do secular icons emerge as carriers of collective emotions and cultural memory.

The term "secular icon" entered the debate on visual culture for the first time in a dialogue on photography by Patrick Maynard (1983). By comparing photography with the famous shroud of Turin he identifies two different sources of photographic authenticity: material connection and visual similarity. Maynard's insights into the double nature of photography resemble very much Charles Peirce's distinction between indexical and iconic signs (1998: 5f.). An index is a sign caused by its referent, for example the symptom of a disease or the footprint of an animal on the ground, whereas an icon is based on similarity. Peirce's paradigmatic example for indexicality is the photographic image, though it is crucial that the photograph is also an icon. According to Maynard, the causal and mechanical quality of photography bears resemblance to the Orthodox icons: the latter are not man-made, but are divine manifestations of the sacred (1983: 165). Maynard concludes that the photographic image as such also has to be understood as a "manifestation picture."

According to Maynard, every photograph is a manifestation picture and a secular icon. A more specific understanding of secular icons can be found in Vicky Goldberg's book on the *Power of Photography* (1991). She uses the term exclusively for photographs that made history. Still, the criteria for symbolic and historical impact need to be elaborated further. Drawing on Maynard and Goldberg, Cornelia Brink tries to specify the term "secular icon" in a strict analogy to religious icons (2000). She lists four criteria of iconicity: authenticity, symbolization, canonization, and a dialectic of veiling and showing. The authenticity of religious icons is derived from their resemblance to an original painting or archetype ascribed to inspired artists or even angels. Copies of medieval icons that showed more power with regard to miracles than their respective originals were supposed to be more similar to the archetype and therefore considered to be more authentic. According to Brink, this quasi-causal relationship between archetype and image is imitated by photography. Symbolization, the condensation of meaning in one image, is another common feature of both religious and secular icons. Brink further points out that the canonization of religious and secular icons has to be understood in a double sense. On the one hand icons draw upon religious imagery and an iconographic canon; on the other hand they become themselves canonic for future pictorial representations. Last but not least, Brink argues that the pictorial wall in an Orthodox church hides the altar in the same way that secular icons both show something and also stand between us and the unmediated reality. The following chapter will take up these suggestions in order to develop a more substantial and formal model of iconicity.

FOUR DIMENSIONS OF ICONICITY

Drawing on Alexander's distinction between "iconic surface" and "iconic depth" (2008), I will introduce four criteria of iconicity that are crucial for becoming a secular icon. Each of these dimensions of iconicity characterizes a specific relation between visual surface and iconic depth. My concept of *reference* has some similarities to Peirce's "indexicality" and Brink's "authenticity." By virtue of being a fusion of an index and an icon, a "mechanical analogue of reality" (Barthes 1977: 18), the photographic image, despite its susceptibility to manipulation, unfolds its own "rhetoric" of "authenticity." However, not every photograph is regarded as equally authentic. Take for example the "Shock Photos" in Roland Barthes's *Mythologies* (1979: 71–74): their rhetorical power is weak, because they appear too artificial. We must not think of authenticity purely in terms of causality or as a general property of the photographic medium. Authenticity has to be regarded as the outcome of a pictorial performance. Performances can fail, but only a successful reference turns the image into an "emanation of the referent" or an "emanation of a past reality" (Barthes 1981), and shocking photos into gateways to the sacred and terrible pain of others. Or in the words of Maynard: a successful reference appears as a "manifestation" of the referent.

Secular icons are never only manifestations of a referent but also of something transcendent. Drawing on Kenneth Burke's theory of the substitutability and translatability of symbols (1966: 3–9), I will call this dimension of iconicity "transcendence." Also Ricœur, in his theory of iconicity as "aesthetic augmentation," characterized iconicity as "the revelation of a real more real than ordinary reality" (1976: 42). A secular icon transcends not only the event or person indicated by it but also its immediate context. Typical examples of this iconic transcendence are allegories and personifications from the eighteenth and nineteenth centuries, for example the pictorial representation of liberty, reason, and the Supreme Being in the Declaration of Rights of Man and Citizen (1789), although these icons usually lack the power of reference. By fusing reference and transcendence, modern secular icons render abstract notions like human dignity visible and concrete. However, with regard to their generalizable transcendent meaning, secular icons remain substitutable by other symbols.

The third and the fourth dimensions of secular icons are constituted by the syntagmatic and paradigmatic openness of images. The syntagmatic structure of a text (or an image) is the relation among its elements, whereas the paradigmatic structure refers to the substitutability of these elements (see Lotman 1977, Michel 2006). *Syntagmatic openness* refers to a breach in the visual surface of the image, a tension between pictorial elements that encourages the spectator to explore its iconic depth. The image becomes a puzzle and an ambiguous object, quite similar to the ambiguity of the symbol highlighted by Ricœur (1970) in his interpretation of Freud. A good example of dealing with syntagmatic openness is Freud's essay on Michelangelo's *Moses*, a composition with a strong tension among its sculptural elements. Freud tries to achieve syntagmatic closure by reconstructing its dynamics ([1914] 1955). The last dimension of iconicity is the *paradigmatic openness* of an image. Whereas the syntagmatic openness is characterized by structural underdetermination or ambiguity, the paradigmatic openness leads to symbolic overdetermination or polysemy. On a paradigmatic level, pictorial elements refer to other images and contexts as motifs. Therefore, pictorial elements often have multiple readings. Closure is only achieved by the interpretative exhaustion of all possible motifs. I argue that secular icons resist closure on a syntagmatic as well as on a paradigmatic level. The puzzling aspects of those photographs call for narratives that explain them, and their symbolic overdetermination creates a multitude of competing and coexisting interpretations.

Reference and transcendence, as well as syntagmatic and paradigmatic openness invite the spectator to immerse him- or herself into the visual surface of an icon in order to discover its *iconic depth*. The prerequisite of iconic depth is of course the iconic difference. Only because the image has the power to reveal something else is the emergence of an iconic depth possible. The four dimensions of iconicity open a space for an engagement with the image. Thus the depth of a secular icon is created by an interaction of spectator and material surface, by the dialectic of "immersion" and "materialization," informed but not determined by discourses.

THE ICON OF THE ABU GHRAIB SCANDAL

On April 28, 2004, the American news program *60 Minutes II* (CBS) broadcast several shocking photographs documenting the inhumane and humiliating treatment of Iraqi detainees by American soldiers.[4] Ironically, the site of the crime happened to be the Abu Ghraib prison, where Saddam Hussein had once tortured the enemies and victims of his regime. The photos were taken by the perpetrators themselves and circulated among the soldiers until one of them informed his superiors. The New Yorker and the notoriously well-informed investigative journalist Seymour Hersh published even more photographs and a series of articles based on classified documents shortly after.[5] No later than three weeks after their initial publication, some of these images became iconic visual symbols of a global prison scandal. A second wave of photographs rekindled the scandal in 2006,[6] but up until today hundreds of images and videos have been held back from publication by the U.S. government.

Figure 6.1   Abu Ghraib prisoner image.
Photo courtesy of U.S. military personnel on active duty.

The most famous of these photographs, which W. J. T. Mitchell called "the icon of the scandal" (2004), appeared first as a frozen picture of a recorded video at *60 Minutes II,* and also later in a nearly identical photographic version in *The New Yorker.* The preiconographic description of the visual surface shows us a hooded human figure in a black cape, standing on a box with outstretched arms and wires attached to its hands. Why has this photograph above all other become a "secular icon"? First of all, the image has a clear reference. There is a real person behind the hood, the action all happened at Abu Ghraib, and the authenticity of the image is beyond doubt as even the U.S. Army confirmed. Still, on the syntagmatic level, the picture poses several puzzles: Who is the person hidden behind the hood? Why is he standing on a box? What are the wires there for? And what about the macabre costume of the prisoner?

The person behind the iconic image was from the very beginning the center of interest. On March 11, 2006, the *New York Times* proclaimed it had finally uncovered the identity of the "Symbol of Abu Ghraib." Unfortunately, after a week, the former Abu Ghraib prisoner, Ali Shalal Qaissi, turned out to be the wrong man after all.[7] The spectator of the image is further informed by military reports and newspaper articles that the prisoner was threatened with electrocution if he fell off the box, though the army claimed that the wires were never connected to electricity. Those familiar with modern torture will recognize an interrogation technique out of the textbook, a stress position that leads to self-inflicted pain. Of all the Abu Ghraib images, the icon of the scandal ironically complies with most standard operating procedures and therefore played no decisive role in the trial against the perpetrators. Not the actual deed depicted but rather its symbolic surplus turned the photograph into a secular icon. The visual surface contains a syntagmatic and paradigmatic openness that begs for closure and interpretation. The bizarre arrangement in the photo requires and inspires an imaginative reading by the spectator. Slavoj Žižek, for example, mistook the image at first for "a piece of performance art" (2004). He uses this rather loose connotation as a starting point to achieve syntagmatic disambiguation by providing a disputable interpretation of the Abu Ghraib photos as manifestations of the obscene side of American culture. Let us now take a look at various connotations of the image and the way they were used to attain syntagmatic closure.

The image of the hooded prisoner is a paradigmatic example of a symbolically overdetermined picture. As early as April 30, 2004, blogger Jeff Sharlet described the scene in the photograph as the Crucifixion, but focused in his analysis on another motif, the Inquisition (2004). He compared the hooded figure with some drawings and paintings of the Spanish artist Francisco Goya depicting the humiliation and interrogation of alleged heretics, mostly Jews and Muslims, during the Spanish Inquisition. In these pictures, the accused often wear big pointed hats that resemble the hood in our photograph. In both cases, the costume identifies and defines the victim; it is used to ridicule and humiliate him. This connotation allows Sharlet to close the ambiguity of the image by arguing that the image expresses the religious fervor and missionary zeal of the war on terror. As a consequence, the image transcends itself as a symbol of the war on terror.[8]

Another visual connotation of hood and cloak appeared in a wall painting in Baghdad by the Iraqi caricaturist Salah Edine Sallat. A photograph of his street art was taken by Ali Jasmin and first published in the *New York Times* on June 13, 2004. The image soon became widespread among international newspapers and magazines. The mural depicts the Statue of Liberty, a symbol of the United States, which is covered by a white Ku Klux Klan hood and which is also electrocuting a black-hooded prisoner. Being a reverse image of a Ku Klux Klan member, almost like a photographic negative, the prisoner is portrayed as a victim of American racial supremacy. Accordingly, the icon of the scandal has to be read as a collective symbol of racism. A similar iconological reading was proposed by those who viewed the icon and other images from Abu Ghraib in the tradition of American lynching photography (see for example, Sontag 2004).

The electric wires that were used to simulate the electrocution constitute another important visual element of the photograph. In his book on the cultural logic of punishment, Philip Smith points out that the "eerily hooded, Inquisition-like figure standing on a box holding electric cables" in "the most notorious" photograph of the Abu Ghraib prison scandal has the connotation of the *electric chair* (2008: 200). The electric chair, as Smith shows, started its career like the guillotine as a humane exercise of the death sentence, but soon became a polluted symbol for which lethal injection was finally substituted. Smith argues that this polluted message of the electric chair was also "repeated in the Abu Ghraib prison scandal." The motif of the electric chair in conjunction with the Abu Ghraib abuses appears also in the American television series *Prison Break* about an innocent man convicted to die by the electric chair. In the retrospective sixteenth episode of the first season, there is a scene at an Iraqi prison, where a hooded prisoner is tortured in a wooden chair by electroshock. Here we can clearly see the fusion of the electric chair and the Abu Ghraib motif, but also the resonance of our secular icon in the American popular culture.

Let us return to the motif of *christomimesis* mentioned by Sharlet. Mitchell argues that, though the other abuse photographs were more shocking and even sometimes pornographic, the "dominant icon has been reserved for a quieter and more modest image" which is "a figure from the Passion plays, the staging of the humiliation and torture of Jesus" (2004). This connotation turns the hooded figure into a sacred victim, an exemplification of the modern cult of the victim.[9] In Christian art, the Crucifixion posed to painters the difficult task of visualizing the dignity of the savior being humiliated (Spaemann 1987: 299). It seems that our photograph profits from centuries of artistic work. Christian iconography enables us to see the inherent sacredness of human beings in the face of their profanization and dehumanization. This christomimetic aspect was also repeated by the artist Matt Mahurin in his cover painting for *Time Magazine* of May 17, 2004, who depicted an emaciated man, hooded and handcuffed, resembling Jesus in the *Mocking of Christ* by the medieval painter Matthias Grünewald. The respective headline brings the puzzle, which the Abu Ghraib photographs still pose, —their syntagmatic openness— to the point: "How did it come to this?"

Many of the Abu Ghraib photographs—not only the icon of the scandal—work on all four dimensions of iconicity. They not only refer to specific events and concrete persons, but also became manifestations of the thitherto hidden suffering of innocent victims in the war on terror. These photographs raise questions and resonate within a broader cultural reservoir of images, including religious imagery, tourist photography, and pornography. The images of the human pyramid in the Abu Ghraib prison resembled an orgy (or even cheerleaders), but they shocked as well due to the syntagmatic breach: American soldiers bluntly posing for the camera, smiling, and giving a thumbs up. The photograph of a female soldier holding a prisoner on a leash recalls the dominatrix motif. The image appeared as a mural in Tehran, where it was regarded as a manifestation of the humiliation of the Islamic world by the West. Barbara Ehrenreich, a female commentator in the West, interpreted the same image as the end of feminist assumptions about the moral superiority of women (2004).

The discourse on the Abu Ghraib images never really achieved a paradigmatic or syntagmatic closure. The symbolic overdetermination of the images intrigues us, and the abuses depicted remain a mystery. When officials concluded that these acts were abuses committed by a "few bad apples," a counterdiscourse emerged interpreting those images as evidence of systematic torture (Hersh 2004), as a predictable outcome of the social dynamics in a terrible situation (Zimbardo 2007), or as cultural symptoms of societal decay (Sontag 2004). The photographs and the abuses also became the subject of art and popular culture. They inspired theater plays and movies, including the Academy Award-winning documentary *Taxi to the Dark Side* (2007), and Errol Morris's *Standard Operating Procedure* (2008). The photographs of Abu Ghraib were able to transcend their particular contexts and became collective representations of emancipation and sexism, of racism and imperialism, of torture and the war on terror. But above all, they are emblems of radical evil and human dignity.

SECULAR ICONS OF THE VIETNAM WAR

A discussion of secular icons from the Vietnam War is helpful in order to put the Abu Ghraib images in a broader comparative perspective. The Vietnam War started in 1965, when American forces entered the military conflict between North and South Vietnam. The conflict turned into a proxy war, typical for the cold war period after World War II. The Vietnam War is one of the best documented wars, partly due to advances in media technologies, partly because of the government's liberal policy concerning censorship and media regulation. There are many important photographs from Vietnam, though only a few became part of a transnational collective memory.

Seymour Hersh's Pulitzer Prize-winning report on the My Lai massacre would have never been successful without the photographs of Ronald L. Haeberle, which played an important role for the opposition against the war (Sontag 2003: 90f.). Nevertheless, these images of dead bodies, mostly women and children, never became secular icons in the strict sense. Their visual surfaces lack the syntagmatic and paradigmatic openness necessary to engage the spectator with the image. Though the photographs had a clear reference, the dead bodies remained too faceless to encourage identification with them. Last but not least, the images lacked the visual qualities to become a collective representation transcending the My Lai massacre, whose generalizability was disputed. Unable to develop an iconic depth, the images simply remained photographic documents of the atrocities committed by an American infantry brigade—nothing more but also nothing less. However, there were two photographs of the Vietnam War that undoubtedly attained the status of secular icons. One picture shows a Viet Cong being shot by a South Vietnamese general, the other depicts a naked girl running away from a napalm attack.

Let me start with Eddie Adams's photo from 1968 showing the execution of a man by an American ally. What is so fascinating and shattering about this particular image? On a preiconographic level, the photograph literally shows a man being shot. The executioner holds a pistol to the victim's head, and it seems that he already has pulled the trigger. The victim is still standing on his own feet, but his head leans violently away from the weapon: whether this is due to the fear of being shot, the acoustic shock of the weapon, or the impact of the projectile is hard for the spectator to decide. Either way, the victim is literally—or better—visually between life and death. In terms of iconography and canonical reference, this snapshot recalls the iconic photograph of Robert Capa from the Spanish Civil War.[10] The moment of being shot is the "punctum" (see Barthes 1981) of both images that connects them to universal and existential questions of life and death. Both photographs are, to use a term of Barbie Zelizer, "about-to-die" images. Zelizer argues that contemporary mass media institutions have a general "preference of the about-to-die photo over photos of people who are already dead" (2005: 33). She adds critically that "the visual trope of people about to die" encourages identification with the depicted victims and a emotional reaction towards the image, instead of triggering a cognitive process that might lead to "a reasoned responsive action" (2005: 33). However, this is not a problem for their status as secular icons. To the contrary, the symbolic value of secular icons always supersedes their documentary value. The about-to-die moment captured by the photo of Adams is not the only syntagmatic breach in the structure of the image. There is also a tension between the casual execution on the open street and its dire consequences that makes us shudder. An execution in a backyard, after a fake trial and with a proper gun at a distance, would not have had the same effect on the spectator. Only due to its particular composition did this image become an emblem of cruelty that not only raised doubts about the American allies in Vietnam but also timeless questions about war and death.

The photograph of the running and screaming children was taken by the Vietnamese photographer "Nick" (Huynh Cong) Ut on June 8, 1972. It already appeared the day after it was shot on the front page of the *New York Times;* a year later it was awarded the Pulitzer Prize. The original unpublished picture shows another photographer on the right side. This photographer was cut out in order to make the image look more authentic and condensed. In the center of the image is a naked girl, Kim Phuc Phan Ti. The other children wear clothes. Why is she naked? This question designates a syntagmatic breach on the visual surface. There is also a visual tension between the children in the foreground and the smoking cloud in the background. Furthermore, there are four men with equipment in the background of the photograph who look like soldiers, though we know they were merely journalists and photographers. The screaming children and the naked girl constitute the image as ambiguous, calling for a narrative to make sense of it: the children were fleeing from a napalm attack, and the girl had to tear off her clothes because of the napalm burning her. Now a grown woman, she still suffers from the aftermath of the attack. After her immigration to Canada in 1992, she became an object of public interest, the subject of books (for example, Chong 2000), and a UNESCO ambassador. Myths and legends emerged around the alleged involvement of American troops in the bombing, which was actually flown by the South Vietnamese, though the Americans provided the napalm for it.[11] On a paradigmatic and iconographic plane, the screaming children draw on Edvard Munch's *The Scream*. The horror of a mute scream on a visual surface should not be underestimated with regard to the impact of this particular image. Furthermore, the silent scream lures the spectator behind the surface of the image and forces him to use his imagination. The naked and screaming girl is a visual personification of helplessness, vulnerability, and victimhood. It is no surprise that the picture acquired a transcendent meaning as an emblem of the suffering of the innocent in wartime.

CONCLUDING REMARKS AND OPEN QUESTIONS

In order to understand the emergence of secular icons, we have to account for the specific relation between visual surface and iconic depth. My comparison of secular icons suggests that all four dimensions, reference, transcendence, syntagmatic, and paradigmatic openness, play a crucial role in this dialectic of surface and depth. Furthermore, the structure of the icon is partly defined by its relations to other images, discourses, and historical events, partly by its internal ambiguity and non-closure. Once a secular icon achieves closure, it can be filed away; it becomes part of an archive and no longer takes part in the living cultural memory.

As we have seen in our discussion of the Vietnam War photography, not all documents of human suffering have the iconic qualities to become secular icons in the strong sense. Rather controversial in this respect is the status of Holocaust photographs. Brink argues that the photographs from the concentration camps are secular icons par excellence (2000). On the other hand, "there is no one signature picture of the Nazi death camps" (Sontag 2003: 86). Our model of iconicity might be able to shed some light on this discrepancy. On the dimension of reference, Holocaust photography poses a problem, as most of the photographs were taken during the liberation of the death camps. With regard to transcendence, there seems to be a huge disproportion between the individual images and the cultural trauma of the Holocaust. Furthermore, most photographs lack ambiguity and symbolic overdetermination. Instead of creating an iconic depth, these images make us, as Brink has rightly remarked, silent. Rather than fostering identification with the victims, the mass of photographs reflects the anonymity of the genocide. The research literature suggests that photography was at best secondary for the construction of the Holocaust as a cultural trauma compared to the narrative testimonies of the survivors and their dramatic re-enactments (see Alexander 2009).

Though the model of iconicity proposed here draws primarily on theories concerned with photography, it might also be applicable to paintings and other forms of visual media. For instance, is Pablo Picasso's *Guernica*, which one of its biographers calls a "twentieth-century icon" (van Hensbergen 2004), a secular icon in our sense? The picture itself is a powerful black-and-white composition with silent screams and twisted bodies in a cubist style. It draws on Christian iconography, but also uses different motifs of Picasso's oeuvre. However, the reference of this picture is solemnly established by its title, Guernica, a Basque town destroyed by a German aircraft fleet during the Spanish Civil War. Nevertheless, the iconic status of the painting was powerfully demonstrated at the United Nations Security Council, when the U.S. government feared its antiwar rhetoric and demanded that the picture be covered. Picasso's *Guernica* might very well be the only painting that ever attained the status of a modern secular icon.

It is now up to other researchers to apply this model of iconicity to these and other cases, to revise or discard it. Let me conclude for now with some remarks on the role of secular icons in a globalizing world. In the beginning, I referred to Pope Gregory's dictum that religious icons are texts for the illiterate. In our multilingual world society, secular icons seem to fulfill a similar function by providing common points of reference for a global civil discourse. This seemed to have happened to *Guernica* and Abu Ghraib, images that are widely recognized and remembered outside their national contexts. The cultivation of images as secular icons allows for social imaginations of good and evil, even in postmodern times, when grand narratives have lost their plausibility. However, images are far from being a universal language. Their meaning depends on cultural contexts and is always open for interpretation. The misunderstanding of images as well as the disagreement about their meaning can cause global conflicts, as we saw in 2005, when the Mohammed cartoons were published in Denmark. Surprisingly, these drawings have caused much more outrage in the Arab world than the Abu Ghraib photographs. Nevertheless, the icon of the Abu Ghraib scandal remains part of the global cultural memory.

NOTES

1. Sometimes icons are even defined as objects with visual-like qualities. Take for example Peirce's definition of the "icon" as a sign based on similarity, in contrast to arbitrary "symbols" or "indexical signs" (1998). The visual-like criterion of similarity refers also to nonvisual objects like onomatopoetic words.

2. The early Foucault most likely would have disagreed with my interpretation of his picture analysis. He would have insisted that paintings and discourses have to be treated as monuments to be uncovered by an archaeology of knowledge, not as documents of a social reality (1980).

3. Also W. J. T. Mitchell's pictorial turn seems to acknowledge the complex relation between words and images (1987, 1994). He even claims "that the interaction of pictures and texts is constitutive of representation as such" (1994: 5). However, it is not clear from his work, how to conceptualize this relation. In my view, Boehm's iconic turn, though maybe one-sided, is more important for our understanding of visuality in modern society.

4. The original show is still available on the website of the broadcasting company: http://www.cbsnews.com/stories/2004/04/27/60II/main614063.shtml, last accessed December 12, 2009.

5. The first article was published online on April 30 in *The New Yorker* magazine (Hersh 2004), the additional images in the print edition of May 3.

6. A total of 279 photographs and 19 videos along with the those images published earlier can be seen at http://www.salon.com/news/abu_ghraib/2006/03/14/introduction/index.html, last accessed December 12, 2009.

7. *New York Times,* March 18, 2006. Bad luck for Mr. Qaissi, who "had even emblazoned the silhouette of that image on business cards."

8. This reading was of course not uncontested. The art historian Stephen F. Eisenman criticized the iconographic reference to Goya as misleading (2007: 19f.) and argued for a reading of the images of Abu Ghraib in the Western tradition of the "pathos formula" as outlined by Aby Warburg (2000).

9. This christomimetic representation and reception of suffering is not an entirely new phenomenon; take for example the framing of the Armenian genocide in the American media at the beginning of the twentieth century (Torchin 2006).

10. The authenticity of Capa's snapshot is frequently questioned (see Marsh 2009).

11. For the myth of the girl and the fraud behind it, please consult the following writings of Ronal N. Timberlake: http://www.gratitude.org/myth_of_the_girl_in_the_photo.htm; http://www.ndqsa.com/myth.html; last accessed December 12, 2009.

REFERENCES

Alexander, J. C. 2006. *The Civil Sphere*. Oxford; New York: Oxford University Press.

———. 2008. "Iconic Experience in Art and Life: Surface/Depth Beginning with Giacometti's Standing Woman." *Theory Culture Society*, 25 (5): 1–19.

———. 2009. "The Social Construction of Moral Universals." In *Remembering the Holocaust: A Debate*, edited by J. C. Alexander, 3–102. Oxford; New York: Oxford University Press.

Barthes, R. 1977. *Image—Music—Text. Selected and translated by S. Heath*. New York: Noonday Press.

———. 1979. *The Eiffel Tower and Other Mythologies*. Translated by R. Howard. New York: Hill and Wang.

———. 1981. *Camera Lucida: Reflections on Photography*. Translated by R. Howard. New York: Hill and Wang.

Bevan, E. R. 1979. *Holy Images: An Inquiry into Idolatry and Image-Worship in Ancient Paganism and in Christianity*. New York: AMS Press.

Boehm, G. 1994. "Die Wiederkehr der Bilder" [The return of the images]. In *Was ist ein Bild?* [What is an image?], Edited by G. Boehm, 11–38. Munich: Fink.

Brink, C. 2000. "Secular Icons. Looking at Photographs from Nazi Concentration Camps." *History & Memory* 12 (1): 135–50.

Burke, K. 1966. *Language as Symbolic Action: Essays on Life, Literature and Method*. Berkeley; Los Angeles: University of California Press.

Chong, D. 2000. *The Girl in the Picture. The Story of Kim Phuc, the Photograph, and the Vietnam War*. New York: Viking.

Durkheim, É. (1893) 1965. *The Division of Labor in Society*. Translated by G. Simpson. New York: Free Press.

———. (1898) 1969. "Individualism and the Intellectuals." Translated by S. and J. Lukes. *Political Studies* 17: 14–30.

———. (1912) 1995. *The Elementary Forms of the Religious Life*. Translated by J. W. Swain. New York: Free Press.

Ehrenreich, B. 2004. "Feminism's Assumptions Upended." In *Abu Ghraib: The Politics of Torture*, edited by M. Benvenisti, 65–70. Berkeley: North Atlantic Books.

Eisenman, S. F. 2007. *The Abu Ghraib Effect*. London: Reaktion Books.

Foucault, M. 1973. *The Order of Things: An Archaeology of the Human Sciences*. New York: Vintage Books.

———. 1980. *The Archaeology of Knowledge*. Translated by A. M. Sheridan Smith. New York: Harper & Row.

Geertz, C. 2006. *The Interpretation of Culture: Selected Essays*. New York: Basic Books.

Giesen, B. 2004. *Triumph and Trauma*. Boulder: Paradigm.

———. 2005. "Tales of Transcendence." In *Religion and Politics: Cultural Perspectives*, edited by B. Giesen and D. Suber, 93–137. Leiden: Brill.

Goldberg, V. 1991. *The Power of Photography: How Photographs Changed our Lives*. New York: Abbeville Press.

Hensbergen, G. van. 2004. *Guernica: The Biography of a Twentieth-Century Icon*. London: Bloomsbury.

Hersh, S. M. 2004: "Torture at Abu Ghraib. American Soldiers Brutalized Iraqis. How Far up Does the Responsibility Go?" *The New Yorker*, May 10. http://www.newyorker.com/archive/2004/05/10/040510fa_fact

Lotman, Y. M. 1977. *The Structure of the Artistic Text*. Ann Arbor: University of Michigan Press.

Marsh, B. 2009. "Faked Photographs: Look, and Then Look Again." *New York Times,* August 23.

Maynard, P. 1983. "The Secular Icon: Photography and the Function of Images." *The Journal of Art and Criticism* 42 (2): 155–69.

Michel, B. 2006. *Bild und Habitus: Sinnbildungsprozesse bei der Rezeption von Fotografien* [Image and habitus: processes of sense-making in the reception of photographs]. Wiesbaden: VS Verlag für Sozialwissenschaften.

Mitchell, W. J. T. 1987. *Iconology: Image, Text, Ideology.* Chicago: University of Chicago Press.

———. 1994. "The Pictorial Turn." In *Picture Theory: Essays on Verbal and Visual Representation,* 11–34. Chicago: University of Chicago Press.

———. 2004. "Echoes of a Christian Symbol: Photo Reverberates with the Raw Power of Christ on Cross." *Chicago Tribune,* June 27.

Panofsky, E. 1955. *Meaning in the Visual Arts: Papers in and on Art History.* Garden City: Doubleday.

Peirce, C. S. 1998. "What Is a Sign?" In *Selected Writings (1893–1913),* 4–10. Bloomington: Indiana University Press.

Ricœur, P. 1970. *Freud and Philosophy: An Essay on Interpretation.* New Haven: Yale University Press.

———. 1973. "The Model of the Text: Meaningful Action Considered as a Text." *New Literary History* 5 (1): 91–117.

———. 1976. *Interpretation Theory: Discourse and the Surplus of Meaning.* Fort Worth: Texas Christian University Press.

Rorty, R. M., ed. 1967. *The Linguistic Turn: Essays in Philosophical Method.* Chicago: Chicago University Press.

Sharlet, J. 2004. "Pictures from an Inquisition." *The Revealer,* http://www.therevealer.org/archives/revealing_000355.php.

Smith, P. 2008. *Punishment and Culture.* Chicago: University of Chicago Press.

Sontag, S. 1977. *On Photography.* New York: Farrar, Straus and Giroux.

———. 2003. *Regarding the Pain of Others.* New York: Farrar, Straus and Giroux.

———. 2004. "Regarding the Torture of Others." *New York Times,* May 23.

Spaemann, R. 1987. "Über den Begriff der Menschenwürde" [On the concept of human dignity]. In: *Menschenrechte und Menschenwürde: Historische Voraussetzungen— säkulare Gestalt—christliches Verständnis* [Human rights and human dignity: historical presuppositions—secular form—Christian understanding], edited by E.-W. Böckenförde and R. Spaemann, 295–313. Stuttgart: Klett-Cotta.

Torchin, L. 2006. "Ravished Armenia: Visual Media, Humanitarian Advocacy, and the Formation of Witnessing Publics." *American Anthropologist* 108 (1): 214–20.

Warburg, A. 2000. *Der Bilderatlas Mnemosyne* [The atlas of images Mnemosyne]. Berlin: Akademie-Verlag.

Wittgenstein, L. 1984. "Tractatus logico-philosophicus." In *Tractatus logico-philosophicus: Werkausgabe,* vol. 1: *Tractatus. Tagebücher 1914–1916. Philosophische Untersuchungen* [Tractatus. Diaries 1914–1916. Philosophical investigations], 9–85. Frankfurt am Main: Suhrkamp.

Zelizer, B. 2005. "Death in Wartime: Photographs and the 'Other War' in Afghanistan." *Harvard International Journal of Press/Politics* 10 (3): 26–55.

Zimbardo, P. G. 2007. *The Lucifer Effect: How Good People Turn Evil.* London: Rider.

Žižek, S. 2004. "Between Two Deaths: The Culture of Torture." *London Review of Books,* June 3.

PART III

CHAPTER 7

SHIFTING EXTREMISMS: ON THE POLITICAL ICONOLOGY IN CONTEMPORARY SERBIA

DANIEL ŠUBER AND SLOBODAN KARAMANIĆ

> The administration of signs and images has effects and stakes that are tangible, constraining, and at times violent.
>
> —Régis Debray

What the founder of "mediology" captured in this citation is generally held as true with respect to the sociopolitical context, which shall be the subject of our analysis. Serbia is not only depicted as the main culprit of the recent Balkan Wars, but also as a paradigm case of a modern society that is (still) imbued with a mythically distorted perception of the past and the present. In his acclaimed work on *The Politics of Symbol in Serbia*, the Serbian anthropologist Ivan Čolović detailed the ways in which the (re)presentation of politics in Serbia draws on epical storytelling and narrative genres (2002: 5–12). However, it is quite remarkable that Čolović's anthropological account does not deliver any analytically derived information about how exactly the complex transmission of political meaning is actually managed and achieved within the specific context of the area.[1] The aim of this contribution is to provide initial steps towards the difficult task of tracing the "peculiar logic which mediates the pictorial and the political" (Müller 2004: 335) in Serbia. What this task entails is not self-evident since two decades after the announcement of the "iconic turn" "an overarching visual approach that unites all social sciences is missing so far" (Müller 2008: 102). Therefore, we deem it appropriate to clarify the theoretical foundations and conceptual tools with regard to our empirical case in the first section. In the rest of the essay, we will introduce an empirical study of street-art and graffiti production in Serbia undertaken from 2008 until 2010 (section 2), and provide an iconological analysis of the most visible political icons of the contemporary Serbian visual landscape (section 3). In the concluding section, we shall reflect on our results on a more theoretical level by discussing the conceptual inventions of Michel Foucault.

TOWARDS AN ICONOLOGY OF THE (POST-)YUGOSLAV MEDIASCAPE

Régis Debray designed "mediology" as an independent social scientific subdiscipline to examine the "black box of meaning's production" (2000: 7). The urgency of rethinking the role of the visual as the key for understanding the shaping of individual as well as collective perceptions can be exemplified by our empirical point of focus. The features that render the Serbian case most compelling for the testing of some of the most essential hypotheses of the "iconic turn" are reflected in varied scientific observations on the subject itself. First, if there are points of agreement among the vast and heterogeneous field of Balkan Studies for the explanation of Yugoslavia's disintegration at all, the central role of the media for the incitement of ethnic prejudice and feeling of threat would surely be one of the top candidates on the list. Observers from all disciplinary areas were taken by surprise at how a supposedly modern nation so promptly and entirely succumbed to the nationalist narratives of certain groups. A second point that social scientists observed a long time ago is the centrality of the oral tradition in the process of "transmitting culture" (Debray) in the Balkans.[2] Finally, we may hint at another characterization of the Yugoslav mediascape that is particularly relevant to our endeavor. It has been occasionally noted that the semiotic regime in the Balkans was "diametrically opposed to the Western one and produced within a different semiotic regimen" (Vlaisavljević 2002: 194). That specific regimen, according to some, was shaped by the experiences of war (196–99). It is not our purpose here to question the substance of these arguments, but to shed a different light on such presumptions by providing systematic empirical analysis.

To begin, we must mention three variations on the theme of mediation in the literature on the recent Yugoslav wars. The first and second types of transmission theories rest on the conventional division between sender and audience. Most widespread is the line of reasoning that asserts that the Milošević regime, which had gained control over the Serbian media since the late 1980s, was fully successful in coaxing the Serbian people towards the wars against their neighboring republics. In this perspective, it goes unquestioned that the absolute majority of Serbian citizens supported the war policies conducted by Slobodan Milošević since the early 1990s. In the style of how the German population reputedly offered unambiguous support for Hitler, we denote this hypothesis as the *seduction model*.

The second line of argumentation shares a similar logic with the former, but it runs in the reverse direction, from *bottom-up* instead of *top-down*. It is best expressed in the sentence by the renowned Croatian writer Dubravka Ugrešić who, alluding to the Croatian case, stated that "Tudjman was our puppet." We may hint at critical observers such as Boris Buden (1997) and Zoran Terzic (2005: 197), who seem to suggest that the nationalist and malicious policies undertaken by the political leaders in Serbia, Croatia, and Slovenia must be viewed as authentic expressions of the collective will of the respective populations. Consequently, these political leaders ought to be seen as puppets manipulated by the strings of a uniformly shaped mass.

In both extreme manifestations, the *seduction* and the *puppet* model, a unilinear direction of manipulation is presumed. Yet, we should not pass over a third alternative that also occurs frequently in the literature. It differs from the aforementioned models in that it cedes the question of mediation in the first place. Any discrimination between sender and audience is obviated in this version. Instead, the Serbian nation is portrayed as a closed and undivided "container," which, to be more precise, was unified in the sharing of mythological beliefs and nostalgic reminiscences of an allegedly glorious medieval past.

We deem these accounts sociologically untenable for reasons that will become more apparent during the course of our empirical analysis in the subsequent sections. For a different source of mediation concepts, we will therefore turn to Foucault's inventive discourse theory, which is based on presumptions that explicitly avoid unilinearity and monocausality. In the concluding section, we shall recapitulate our findings in the light of Foucault's mediological premises.

Our actual interpretation, though, is guided by methodological principles derived from *iconology*. Its founder, Erwin Panofsky, as well as his contemporary heir, W. J. T. Mitchell, have insisted that visual data must not be treated in isolation from other manifestations of visual culture. Hence, our interpretation in the next section will depart from graffiti and immediately turn to billboards, public advertisements, media presentations, the Internet, and state iconography. Furthermore, we have accounted for the norm of *transmediality* in our interpretation by couching it in evidence we gathered from informants with whom we conducted focus group interviews as well as a standardized questionnaire evaluation. This additional methodological step was meant to control and (re)direct hypotheses we derived from merely *looking* at the visual materials.

Finally, we want to stir up Mitchell's general conviction that any valid knowledge about how images represent cannot be achieved through abstract theory, but rather only on the basis of concrete observation of actual practices and histories of representation: "the best terms for describing representations, artistic or otherwise, are to be found in the immanent vernaculars of representational practices themselves" (1994: 14–15). Since the question of mediology in the sense delineated here has rarely been addressed within the vast field of Yugoslav Studies and because the existent models lack sophistication to meet with the actual dynamics on the empirical plane, we attribute to this study a preliminary status.

INTRODUCING THE GRAFFITI SAMPLE:
CONTENT AND CONTEXT

Every visitor to Serbian cities and towns could easily testify that graffiti is an omnipresent and obtrusive phenomenon. Although graffiti had not been unfamiliar in the socialist context (see Lalić, Leborić, and Bulat 1991), these street media gained vital political significance only in the hands of anti-Milošević campaigners and student movements in the early 1990s, in 1996–97, and 2000. The *recapture of the streets* names one of the main strategies of these campaigns designed at liberating the public space from the vile political propaganda spread by the regime. On this note, local observers have concluded that "graffiti here carry a true message of revolt and resistance, subversive in substance and with much longer durability than in western societies" (Dragićević-Šešić 2001: 83). This belief accords with the sociological reflection on the social function of graffiti. Since the 1970s, when graffiti analysis was introduced as a social scientific tool, the dominant view has taken the idea as axiomatic that "the majority of graffiti...are satirical" (D'Angelo 1974: 173–74). To be more concrete, "they attack worn out beliefs, political and social stereo-types, false pride, conventional respectabilities, hypocrisy, and sham" (180). Proponents of the Birmingham School of Cultural Studies celebrated the new "signifying practice" as "the triumph of process over fixity, disruption over unity, 'collision' over 'linkage'" (Hebdige 1979: 119). Whether such a positive view on the role of street art and graffiti as an outstanding means of political subversion can be sustained in the contemporary Serbian context will be one of the challenging questions to answer in the following discussion.

The empirical basis of this study is a survey of Serbian graffiti production conducted between March 2008 and April 2010. We attempted to cover, at least approximately, all geographical regions of Serbia (excluding the Kosovo region). Also, we strove to include rural areas that were frequently omitted from prior studies due to the prejudice that graffiti and street art are considered strictly urban phenomena. Of the total volume of our sample, only a limited quantity was selected for this study. Leaving out a considerable amount of soccer-related, subcultural, and adolescence-related drawings, we focused on images that openly displayed political content. For the sake of representing our findings, we used the techniques of content analysis and tabulation.

The political taxonomy we employed in the coding process was informed by public opinion, displayed in domestic media sources and political debates. According to widespread perception, articulated not only in Western but also in Serbian media portrayals, there is an ideological rift between the Serbian population that divides the pro-European, democratically oriented part from the nationalist and retrograde part. As an illustration, we quote a leading political scientist: "In Serbia one is dealing not only with a sharply polarized society—roughly half favoring Europeanization...and half opposing it—but also with a society in which, for much of its history, there has been 'a collective consensus that the status quo is untenable'" (Ramet 2010: 18).

In our approach we refrain from taking these stances at face value. Still, they can serve as an initial indicator of ideological structures, political configurations, and public moods. Especially when dealing with political graffiti, such sources become significant. With "political graffiti," we reach out for such writings that are directed at mobilizing the Serbian citizens for particular political sentiments. Different from other approaches towards this medium (cf. Antonijević and Hristić 2006, Radošević 2008), we do not attempt to *individualize* our data, i.e., to trace their meanings back to subjective beliefs and individual attitudes. We also shy away from any pretension to present our findings as representative for the Serbian population. Rather, we focus our investigation on comparing official political campaigning by state and

Table 7.1 Political Content of Graffiti Sample

Political Content	n=1031	Percentage
Nationalist	445	43.20%
Antinationalist	209	20.30%
Philosophical[3]	121	11.70%
anti- NATO/EU/DOS/LDP/B92	74	7.20%
fascist/racist	62	6.00%
Nostalgic	58	5.60%
Anticommunist	10	0.97%
anti-Muslim	9	0.87%
Liberal	7	0.67%
pro-homosexual	5	0.48%
anti-Roma	5	0.48%
pro-Russian	4	0.39%
anti-Croat	3	0.29%
anti-Serb	2	0.19%
Other	16	1.55%

party institutions on the one hand, with street campaigning agencies such as civil societal organizations or individuals on the other.

For a start, we seem to get a surprisingly lucid picture from the condensed representation of our sample. If we focus on the results of the political contents (see Table 7.1) we find, by and large, a structure analogous to the cleavage portrayal rendered by the media. Since we started our investigation in the beginning of 2008, right after the declaration of the independence of Kosovo by the Provisional Institutions of Self-Government Assembly of Kosovo (February 17), we quite expected an abundance of patriotic-nationalist outpourings on the walls, considering that the question of the Kosovo status had become a dominant political issue in the preceding months. While "nationalist" and "antidemocratic" statements together prevail with more than 50 percent, "antinationalist" and "philosophical" (which are generally directed against the mobilized mainstream) messages make up more than 30 percent of our data. These observations may tempt us to make facile conclusions such as that street politics does not, at least in content, differ much from official politics, or that the Serbian wall writings lack any subversive intelligence and power per se, or finally, that the many voices that attribute a low democratic potential to the Serbian citizens, due to their allegedly inherited authoritarianism, are supported by these numbers. In line with these accounts, citizens would numbly absorb the manifestos of the public media. Thus, mediation would actually come down to mimicry. That the situation is much more intricate will be elaborated in the following section.

OF FISTS AND FINGERS: SERBIA BETWEEN CHANGE AND CONTINUITY

As we indicated in our conceptual consideration above, the task of laying the groundwork for a mediology of the post-Yugoslav space can only be achieved by means of empirical scrutiny. Consequently, we decided to focus on one particular but cardinal instance that displays characteristic features of the contemporary Serbian political discourse. As will become clear from the next chronicle, the interplay between the various political ideologies and groups, the public and the private realm, the past and the present, is complicated to such an extent that it renders the picture presented in the last section ludicrously simplistic.

A closer look at the political dynamics taking place at the time we launched our research in spring 2008 provides the basis for a sociological interpretation of the aforementioned results. A peculiar feature of the Serbian public discourse, barely recognized by public media renderings and journalists, is rendered by the observation that the great majority of nationalist slogans and graffiti have been designed, branded, and disseminated by a number of right-wing organizations like the Fatherland Movement "Dignity" (Otačastveni Pokret Obraz [Obraz]), the Serbian People's Movement 1389 (Srpski narodni pokret 1389 [SNP 1389]), or Association Ours (Udruženje Naši [Naši]). These political movements[4] began to take shape in the wake of the so-called Serbian October Revolution in 2000, which ousted the Milošević regime from power. Not only were they opposed to the replacement of Serbian values with more Western ones, which they sensed in the policies of the new government led by the democratic coalition, but they were likewise suspicious of the prior "red" regime of Milošević. Their common ideological agenda mentions the protection of *Serbianness*, family values, the Cyrillic alphabet, the Orthodox faith, and national statehood. Yet, they do not perceive themselves as ultrarightist and extremist, but rather as legitimate defenders of patriotic values and normality, struggling against (post)modern and deviant forms of behavior (sects, drug addiction, the gay movement, organized crime, and corruption). As has been noted by a few scientific observers (Sundhaussen 2008: 45–47, Wiesinger 2008, Bakić 2009), their influence in shaping the political climate in Serbia grew steadily during the course of the decade. This did not happen by chance. Their activities follow a certain premeditated visual strategy. The marking of street walls with their signatures or slogans, often both at once, is only part of a larger campaign project and representational tactic. The latter is probably best expressed in the Web presentation of the Russian fraction of Obraz: "Obraz is not a gang, a PR agency or a political party. We are everything taken together."[5] In addition to graffiti, these groups also use such media platforms as street- and Web art, (pseudo-) intellectual journals such as *Serbian Gateways* [*Dveri srpske*], *Serbian Organic Studies* [*Srpske organske studije*], *New Spark* [*Nova iskra*] or *Outlooks* [*Pogledi*], billboards, T-Shirts, and political actions. To cite just the most recent example of the effectiveness of their activity, we can hint at the occurrences around the organization of the second gay parade in Belgrade, which was supposed to take place on September 20, 2009. The event had to be cancelled the day before, however, since the Head of Police announced it could not guarantee safety to the participants. The preceding months had seen the spreading of unambiguous and aggressive threats to the protagonists of the Belgrade Pride event, such as "Gay parade—we're waiting for you" and "Death to faggots," on the walls of Belgrade. In the end, the SNP 1389 group celebrated "a great victory for the normal Serbia" and a defeat for the "infidels and Satanists."[6]

What seems paramount about their ideological stance and what at the same time sets them apart from their Central European sister organizations is their self-positioning in the center of the societal spectrum. In their public appearance, groups like Obraz entirely renounce any specified visual code (dress codes, etc.) that would separate them from their fellow citizens, while their Central European counterparts display many features prototypical of subcultures. To draw an initial conclusion, the argument that the high number of nationalist slogans and messages apparent in our survey represent the mere expressions of spontaneous or "banal nationalism" (Billig) cannot be sustained.

THE RISE OF THE "THREE-FINGER" SYMBOL

Along with the nationalist groups' growing hold over the Serbian public sphere came the proliferation of a particular symbol, that of the "three fingers" (see Figure 7.1, right).

Figure 7.1   Left: Otpor's Fist; Right: Three-Finger symbol.

Originating in the late 1980s, this political icon is now virtually omnipresent. Servicemen and politicians use it, and pop stars and famous athletes flash it to greet their fans. It seems to be universal in the sense that it is not instantly aligned with any particular political worldview. In our opinion survey, we asked our interviewees about the ideological roots of the finger icon, giving them a few alternatives to chose from. They came up with the following picture (see Tables 7.2 and 7.3):

Table 7.2   Responses: Ideological Roots of Three-Finger Symbol

What is the ideological root of the three-finger symbol?	%
a) religious sign alluding to the Holy Trinity	40.4
b) related to the military (as a sign for Serbian victory)	5.5
c) Serbian version of the international symbol for piece (V sign)	21.2
d) connected to Serbian history	14.6
e) other/undecided	18.3

(n=106).

Table 7.3   Responses: Political Meaning of "Three Finger" Symbol

What is the political meaning that this symbol conveys?	%
a) nationalist	63
b) prodemocratic/pro-European	4.9
c) conservative	9.6
d) liberal	0.9
e) socialist	0.9
f) politically neutral	15
g) other/undecided	5.7

(n=106).

These numbers and the responses voiced during the focus group sessions indicate a paradoxical pattern: the respondents acknowledge that they do not know the actual origins of the icon; however, they nonetheless attribute a "nationalist" meaning to it. According to many of our focus group participants, the tendency to attribute a religious interpretation to the three-finger sign is inspired by the orthodox rule of crossing oneself, which is done with three closed fingers. On the other hand, this narrative may have been incited by a curious incident occurring during the opening ceremony of the 2008 Summer Olympic Games in Beijing that received considerable attention from the Serbian media. When the Serbian president, Boris Tadić, greeted the arriving Serbian team with the finger gesture, he was reportedly asked by then U.S. president George W. Bush, sitting a few rows below him, about its meaning. Tadić explained his response to Bush in a television interview: "It's the Holy Trinity, didn't you know that? He found it interesting that we adopted it as part of our identity. I explained that's what we are fighting for, this is our idea."[7]

In contrast to its contemporary use, it was most probably invented in a quite distinct ideological context, by Vuk Drašković, a then royalist-nationalist writer and key figure of the Serbian political opposition to Milošević and the foreign minister between 2004 and 2007. According to Drašković's own testimony, he first promoted this salute in the Serbian Literary Club in 1986.[8] It was only in 1990, however, that it entered the public realm, when Drašković waved it to the attendees of a mass rally against a media blockade imposed by the Milošević regime. From this context, it inherited its association with resistance against the communist oppression of freedom of speech and, what is more, a certain sense of national pride. As our survey results conveyed, the fingers sign has retained this connotation to the present day. As we will demonstrate, it is moreover a means for effectuating the normalization, harmonization, and reconciliation of a certain worldview with the societal mainstream.

Our working hypothesis stems from what Seymour Lispet called "extremism of the center" (1960: 127–79). Analyzing the rise of German fascism, Lipset identified a third kind of extremism, one located at the political center as opposed to those versions typically associated with the far left and far right. Dramatic moves from peacetime to a crisis, Lipset observed, can create a dramatic shifting of support structures. We are not arguing that fascism is currently dominating in the Serbian case, rather we argue that a particular representational complex consisting of a particular ideology and carrier group (the above-quoted "normal Serbs") had over the last few years moved from the periphery into the societal center. Again, we emphasize that this symbolic complex cannot be reduced to an established ideological program. As can be proven with the history of the rise of the three-finger icon, many different political factions have indeed contributed to its contemporary profile.

NEGLECTED AFFINITIES: FROM "FIST" TO "FINGERS"

To chronicle the rise of the three-finger sign, we begin by referencing its iconological counterpart, the "clenched fist," which was invented and effectively proliferated by the anti-Milošević movement Otpor (Resistance) at the end of the 1990s. Probably quite familiar to the reader, the clenched fist (see Figure 7.1, left) almost instantly gained iconic status and soon came to represent the "other Serbia," which would be "democratic" and "pro-Western" oriented. The clenched fist symbol has been adopted by democratic movements against authoritarian regimes in other parts of the world such as Georgia, Ukraine, Belarus, Albania, Russia, Kyrgyzstan, Uzbekistan, Lebanon, Venezuela, and Kenya, and thus it became Serbia's most successful symbolic export for at least the first decade of the new century.

Neither literature on the clenched fist and three-finger symbols nor the people we interviewed in our focus groups make reference to a direct connection between the two hand signs. This is surprising, considering the apparent correspondence between both symbols and their being part of the broader genre of "hand" symbols that include the peace "V," the forward-thrust-fist, and the clasped hands. An initial and indirect approach to establish a link could start from the modes of their proliferation.

Starting chronologically with the "fist," it was invented and designed by a small group of students active in the student organization that became Otpor.[9] One of the group's main figures, Aleksandar Marić, reported that the founding group consisted of about fifteen activists.[10] In contrast to their public image of being nonhierarchical and loosely organized,[11] they were actually quite structured and stable in their internal makeup.[12] Likewise, the symbol of the black-white colored fist was the result of a meticulously planned out marketing strategy invented by the group leaders. Ivan Marović disclosed the motives behind their choice of the symbol: "Our inspiration came from multinational companies and things like Coca-Cola or Levi's. What we needed was a simple message. What we needed was a simple logo, so people could recognize it after one second. So that's why we picked the name Otpor—which means 'resistance,' and also we picked a clenched fist."[13] On another occasion, he extrapolated what the icon in his view would symbolically indicate: "The symbol of the clenched fist is the symbol of unity, because every finger is individual and different, but put together, they stand for a real resistance against aggression and repression. One of my friends once said that when the fist is lifted, it resembles an antenna which connects us with God."[14] The tension between a mere *pragmatic* reference to the icon as a means of communication on the one hand, and the *transcendental* allusion on the other will concern us later. For now, it shall be stressed that the fist was originally devised as a branding strategy to reach a wider public and that, obviously, any iconological reference to prior historical applications of the sign[15] were intended.

Another criterion that influenced its selection was its noticeable demarcation against the symbolic order established by the (allegedly) socialist regime of Milošević. The student movements of 1996–97 had aspired to—symbolically—recapture the public sphere that they perceived as being polluted by the regime propaganda. Their strategic "carnivalization of the city" (Dragićević-Šešić 2001: 75) (of Belgrade) employed playful visual and sonic methods to satirize the means the regime itself had used to homogenize and nationalize the public sphere. Typically, the young protesters waved the national flags from any country available to them for the sake of mocking the hyperbolic display of the Serbian flag that nobody could actually relate to.[16] In a similar direction, the Serbian national slogan "Only unity can serve the Serb," abbreviated with the four Cyrillic S's in the coat of arms, was restated as "Only walking can serve the Serb" (Jansen 2001: 39). The four months of protests were organized around the general theme of "walking," thereby indicating a specific mode of approaching and rediscovering the public space, which stood against the solemn "marching" and "rallying" of the mass demonstrations the Milošević regime had staged between 1987 and 1989 to legitimate a so-called "anti-bureaucratic revolution." Milena Dragićević-Šešić adequately summarized the visual approach of the latter as the reproduction of "iconographic stereotypes—same slogans, same photos, same typestyles, same colours, with even the frames of the banners stressing the seriousness of the participants" (2001: 85–86). To show their disgust with politics in general, the young protesters held their noses when passing government buildings during their walks or, most effectively, used noise as a weapon to drown the political information the regime communicated through the wires. It soon became a ritual to gather on the streets at the time the evening news was broadcast on television and to join together in deafening noise.

As compared to the carnivalization strategy of the 1996–97 protests, which in the end were unsuccessful in overthrowing the regime (cf. Bieber 2003), the 2000 resistance movements headed by the Otpor group appeared more mature and thoughtful. The Otpor strategy to unify a heterogeneous mix of opposing groups under the umbrella of an unambiguous icon and slogan was certainly stimulated by the experiences of the "winter of discontent" (Lazić). Even the choice to stick to black-white patterns must be seen as a means to deflate the extensive exposition of most varied multicolored ideological symbols. In this sense, the protagonists of Otpor perceived the contemporary political opposition movement in Serbia as "grey," i.e., ideologically disoriented and wavering (Ilić 2001). While this pragmatic strategy proved immensely successful in achieving the primary goal of ousting the Milošević regime, it too contained the germ of its failure in the ensuing period. Formally, the movement imploded soon after its leaders decided to transform into a political party in 2001 and failed to climb the five-percent hurdle in the following year's elections.[17] However, we do not follow suit with such interpretations that argue that this outcome was fated because Otpor merely consisted of its slogan. Rather, we find it appropriate to pay heed to the political program of the Otpor movement, laid down in documents such as the so-called Memorandum[18] or the Declaration. It has been noted that Otpor's—literally speaking—black-and-white drawing of the political alternatives in Serbia could easily be picked up by the general public but barely by any other alternative movement, since any genuine political communication on the basis of such "radical binary oppositions" gets blocked in the first place. This strategy is, for instance, manifest in Otpor's Memorandum, in which the authors contrast an "Asiatic mentality" inherited from the five hundred years of Ottoman occupation with a "European root" embodied in the Reformation visions of St. Sava and Dositej Obradović. The latter vision, accordingly, was governed by the "the laws of personal motivation and the free market in all the spheres of active life; both material and spiritual" (Memorandum, quoted in Marković 2001). From the quoted passage we can extract (1) a reproduction of an *orientalist* and dichotomizing discourse that displays similarities to Huntington's Clash of Civilization thesis or, as some argue, even a *cultural* form of "racism" (Marković 2001).[19] (2) With similar aggression, the Memorandum advocates what today may be called an uncritical neoliberal ideology, uncritical since it has no concept of counterbalancing the side effects of a capitalist market economy such as welfare systems or mechanisms securing social justice. (3) Finally, we deem the reference to St. Sava, the founder of the Serbian Orthodox Church (SOC) in the thirteenth century, to be revealing in several respects. While this connection may appear odd to the reader unfamiliar with the Serbian context and especially to those readers who recall the role of the SOC in boosting the Kosovo issue in the early 1980s, we can recount the fact that already the student protesters of 1996–97 walked, again in the literal sense, hand in hand with the Patriarch (Pavle) of the SOC. The joint celebration of the Mass even became the "highlight" of the student actions (Stefanov 2008: 248). Also, an opinion survey on the political attitudes of Otpor activists conducted in 2000 conveyed the surprising finding that, asked to identify the most important personalities of Serbian history, most votes were cast for St. Sava. Directly asked whether the Church should take a more active part in society, about one-third of the respondents expressed a favorable standpoint (Ilić 2001).

To drive home the point, a closer look at the political attitudes behind the public scenes of Otpor exposed a militant anticollectivism and hostility against

any political content associated with the "Reds." Their pragmatism" is most manifest in their adoption of virtually any ideological stream they depict as enemies
of the old regime, be it (a crude variant of) neoliberalism or religious orthodoxy.
In practice, this ideological pragmatism amounted to arbitrariness. Not only did
Otpor seek support from the most influential domestic opposition parties[20] and
non-governmental organizations, but they also went to Athens, Greece, to approach
the former Yugoslav dynasty represented by Aleksandar Karadjordjević, the heir
to the throne, who declared his support publicly. Moreover, they strove for support from politically dubious institutions such as, besides the SOC, the Serbian
Academy of Sciences and Arts (SANU), the Association of Dramatic Artists, and
the Philosophical Society, some of which must be clearly judged as prime movers
of the nationalist dogmas that not only licensed Milošević's seizure of power in
1987 but likewise, in the long run, spurred the tensions that led to the breakup of
Yugoslavia. Yet, this absurdity came to a head when the activists even appealed to
the (in)famous author and short-time former Yugoslav president, Dobrica Ćosić, to
sign a membership application form, which the latter even agreed to. Typically, this
step was defended by Marović's hilarious statement that he was glad that Otpor had
been joined by "a tried and true antifascist" or by simply admitting: "We admit to
the movement everybody who is against the Milošević regime" (Ilić 2001).

Our portrayal is not meant to ridicule the matter at all. Rather, we tend to assume
that Otpor's ideological confusion in fact bespeaks the often-quoted "pragmatism"
of the late prime minister and "symbol for a European Serbia" (Ivanji 2008: 161),
Zoran Djindjić, who is often also depicted as the main force behind Otpor and the
factual defeater of Milošević. Barely installed in office, one of his first political activities was to lead a delegation to a meeting with Bill Gates in Redmond, Washington,
thus becoming the first head of state to pay an official visit to Microsoft. Together
they laid down a strategy for the modernization of Serbian public services and
agreed upon a strategic partnership. In turn, Belgrade was to become Microsoft's
main residence in Southeastern Europe. Simultaneously, Djindjić undertook two
measures in promotion of the SOC and the public role of religion, namely the passing of a new law on religious education in state schools and the founding of a con-
sortium for the reconstruction of St. Sava Church in Belgrade, often hailed as the
biggest Orthodox Church in the world. In the eyes of interpreters such as Nenad
Stefanov, the democratic movement thus paved the way for the one institution that
had inherited the destructive tendencies of the prewar socialist regime and currently
functioned as the safeguard and placeholder for "conformism," "ethnonationalism,"
and "escapism" (2008: 251–52). These specified indications must suffice to disclose an apparent paradoxical constellation that we already encountered in Otpor's
programmatic outfit. Marković's depiction of Otpor as a steady and long-lasting
influence on Serbian politics and even a "'hegemonic force' [Gramsci] within the
civil society" (2001) does not seem exaggerated given the preceding observations
and the following considerations. As we shall sketch out now in the final subsec-
tion of this chapter, Otpor left a marked imprint on even such civil organizations
that were strongly opposing the democratic coalition, the Democratic Opposition
of Serbia (Demokratska opozicija Srbije; DOS), ensuing from the Serbian October
Revolution. This continuity is already suggested by some findings of the interview

Table 7.4   Responses: Symbolic Meaning of Otpor

What meaning do you ascribe to the Otpor icon today?	%
a) Symbol for *victory*	18.6
b) *revolutionary* symbol	20.4
c) Symbol for *future* and *prosperity*	7.4
d) Symbol for national *pride* and *defiance*	32.3
e) other/undecided	21.3

(n=106).

survey to which we referred above. In addition to asking our interviewees about the meaning of the finger icon, we included a question about how they would relate to the Otpor fist, which is still surprisingly present on the street (see Table 7.4).[21]

We were surprised to find almost one-third of the votes for "national pride and defiance," because, as already delineated above, such would be the same meaning attributed to the three-finger icon. This case neatly captures the logic of the transmission of meaning in a sociocultural context in which the "discourse about politics and the nation...today is largely confined to story-telling" (Čolović 2002: 6). The Serbian "semiosphere"—to adopt a term by Lotman (1977)—is characterized by semantic density, not only in terms of quantity but also in terms of quality. To conclude the semiotic history of the fist and finger symbol, they originated from opposite ideological contexts but, through an intricate process of transmission of meaning, both ended up reflecting and spurring national pride. The remainder of this chapter is devoted to bringing more light to this finding.

THE RESURGENCE OF THE SERBIAN FAR RIGHT AND ITS VISUAL STRATEGIES

Many analysts were surprised by the steady increase in far right parties' electoral successes in the wake of the fundamental changes in 2000, particularly in light of the tragedies that Serbia had suffered under the coalition regime of Milošević and the Serbian Radical Party (SRS) (Stefanović 2008: 1196).[22] Not even three years after the democrats' victory over the old regime, the SRS emerged as the largest single party from the December 2003 parliamentary elections, thus becoming "the most successful far right party in post-communist Eastern Europe" (1195). However, the reaction of bewilderment is only reasonable from a perspective that conceives of a public civil sphere as partitioned into separate and clearly discernible ideological segments in the first place.[23] How such a view is betrayed by the facts in the Serbian case shall be demonstrated. Hereby, our main argument is delivered by demonstrating how the tactical visual inventions of the democratization movement were directly adopted and instrumentalized by their self-declared opponents, such as the organizations mentioned at the outset of this chapter.

The far right groups in Serbia are not aiming at preserving an existence on the periphery of Serbian society (as do subcultures in general) but at bringing forth *normalization* of the motherland, which in their eyes means leading a life according to "Serbian values." "In these times," as reads Obraz's home page, "being Serb is harder than ever before."[24] If we leave aside the dimension of violence that pervades some of their actions and street messages, their branding campaign pretends to express the alleged views of the "normal Serb." The most characteristic visualization of this frame of mind is represented in a widely reproduced poster that proclaims that it is "in" to be a Serb.[25],

It is impossible to ignore that groups like SNP 1389 and Obraz follow upon the well-tried dissemination tactics introduced by Otpor, that is, they make extensive use of the Internet, Web logs, and, most prolifically, street and public space. Similar to Otpor, they created easily recognizable logos that are very often tagged on walls without any further additional comment. Basically, their icons merge nationalist symbols (a double-headed eagle referring to the Serbian medieval Nemanjić dynasty, the four S's symbolizing the Kosovo covenant, or the red and blue colors going back to the earliest Serbian flags) with traditional Christian iconography.[26] To reach their main target group they use stickers, buttons, posters, graffiti, stencils, and billboards.

Yet, it is not only the forms that these groups took over from their ideological opponents. Another mode of adaptation of democratic icons can be termed *persiflage*. Here, the symbolic expressions that the Otporaši invented to mock or mobilize against Milošević are turned against their designer. For instance, nationalist groups redirected Otpor's legendary slogan *Gotov je* (He's finished) simply against the Democrats' leader and current president Boris Tadić.[27] On the walls, we have also registered several ironic annotations to Otpor slogans such as *Džaba ste šarali!* (You have achieved nothing!) or *Otpor—je horor*! (*Otpor—is horror*!).

It is also worth mentioning that the communicative genre (Luckmann 1989) in which the public gets reminded about "Serbian values" is not at all times as violent or forceful as one would probably expect. Hence we cannot close this section without explicitly avoiding the impression that the current visual scene and atmosphere on the Serbian streets is merely caused by the aggressiveness of these youth and student organizations. Occasionally, the message to love your motherland (Kosovo) is packed into a corresponding neat symbolical form. This representational strategy most manifestly appears in stickers and buttons that display the geography of Kosovo in the form of a heart that is broken, thereby adopting a symbolical language typical of adolescent communication genres. Another interesting form of adaptation of styles and motives can typically be found on walls in the backyards of the typical suburban apartment building that serve the adolescent population for expressing their views. Here we came across many colorful and carefully crafted imitations of state iconography.[28] It is through the aestheticization of state iconography and the mimicry of slogans spread by the state and other (nationalist) agents that *normalization* and the shifting of collective consciousness is effected and effective.

Another related typical instance of the mechanism for which we want to apply the term "everyday Hegelianism"[29] is exemplified in a remarkable poster action by SNP 1389. The tourists coming to Belgrade from Germany, the United States, China, and so forth were informed in their respective tongues that "Kosovo has always been and will always remain Serbian." However, this strategy of *internationalizing* or even *universalizing* the Kosovo issue was at the same time also adopted by the (democratic) government. More precisely, the central slogan "Kosovo is Serbia" has neither emerged in the Serbian public space entirely spontaneously nor as the sole invention of far-rightist groups supposedly residing on the societal margins. Rather, it was a campaign by the Serbian government, hence the political center of Serbia. To be more concrete, the Ministry for Kosovo and Metohija engaged in the promotion of this vital political message in 2007. The campaign was announced under the same slogan as an "expression of the democratic Serbia to preserve those values which the West accepted long time ago."[30]

Among the predominant media the Ministry resorted to were video clips broadcast on public television stations and billboards all over Serbia. It also approached many Serbian public celebrities (athletes, actors, directors, writers, etc.) to take part in the campaign. Even legendary Western politicians (Willy Brandt, Winston Churchill, Charles de Gaulle, John F. Kennedy, Abraham Lincoln, George Washington) were resurrected for the campaign and appeared on well-crafted billboards that were displayed on the side of highways. The figures were presented behind their respective national flags and a famous quote of their own. The Ministry public relations explained the use of the quotes in the following way: "The selected quotes are telling how we should orient ourselves towards the national interest. Those are people, statesmen, great politicians, from whom we have learnt, and whom we now quote in order to continue working on the basis of their experiences."[31]

The presumed message of the billboard campaign is suggestive of the motif to equate the defense of Serbian integrity with that of universal democratic principles. What is more, in contrast to the widespread assumption of the Serbs being entirely entrapped in their closed worldview that is imbued with mythical thinking, the branding strategies of the state agents in fact made heavy reference to the international discourse of international law and peaceful conflict solution.

Taking these impressions together, we can conclude that in form and content a clear distinction between the visual creation pertaining to different social domains such as the state, civil societal organizations, and the sphere of everyday life cannot be maintained. Hence, any concept of mediation premised on a bottom-up or top-down relation between separate sectors of society would be misleading from the complexities given in the Serbian case. In our concluding remarks a more refined theoretical conceptualization of mediation dynamics shall be outlined.

CONCLUSION

Rather than summarizing our arguments again, we will integrate them within a theoretical framework offered by Foucault. To be clear, by the reference to this magisterial figure, who has probably inspired the *visual turn* more than any other single author has, it is not our intention to hold up the assorted implications generally attributed to a Foucaultian approach. However, in his classical analysis *The History of Sexuality*, he formulates four "rules" that are not to be viewed as "methodological imperatives" but as "cautionary prescriptions" (1990: 98). They portray a picture of sociocultural dynamics that suits the empirical case studied here better than any model outlined in the first section.

From Foucault's first "rule of immanence" (98), we can derive a suitable approach towards the sociological problem of agency. As Foucault describes it, the different social domains would not relate to each other in a mode "exteriority" (98).

The Serbian case demonstrated vividly that a clear demarcation between the state ministries, civil organizations, and graffiti-sprayers with regard to the reproduction of nationalist slogans and iconography did not apply. In this fused constellation we may finally see the effect of the implementation of the *extremism of the center*. Consequently, any attempt to trace this effect back to any single source seems pointless.

The second "rule" marked out in Foucault's book maintains that power relations in modern societies are decentered in the sense that they constantly change with the shifting of positions among the participants of the discourse. This feature was so obvious in our case that any further remarks would be redundant. Our empirical study has brought to the fore that the political dynamics since the Serbian October Revolution in 2000 predominated over various ideological factions and constellations. With this study we tried to cast some light on the complex relations between political parties and civil organizations by focusing on visual culture. Foucault's advice to conceive of power as a fleeting and constantly changing relation between different agents is underscored by our inquiry.

Thirdly, the "rule of double conditioning" (99) suggests that the interrelations between the varied discursive spheres must not be reduced to any crude model, be it homogeneity or dis-continuity. As we might illustrate by hinting again at the intricate cross-references between the fist and the finger symbols, the constitutive elements of a discourse encroach upon one another and stand in a relationship of *mutual conditioning*. In consequence, the meaning of either one particular discursive constituent, let alone the discourse as a whole, cannot be grasped without taking these interlocutions into account.

Finally and most importantly, we turn to the "rule of tactical polyvalence" (100). Accordingly, discourses would be polyvalent because they could be "both an instrument and an effect of power, but also a hindrance, a stumbling block, a point of resistance and a starting point for an opposing strategy. Discourse transmits and produces power" (101). Sociology has delivered good evidence about the intricate ways in which the perception of an ambiguous and confusing cultural sphere can, under certain circumstances, foster potentially destructive phenomena such as widespread apathy, passivity, criminality, and violence. The anthropologist Mary Douglas, drawing on Émile Durkheim's classical study on suicide, laid out such an approach towards collective actions. Recently, this line of argument had been revitalized and applied towards explaining the (cultural) logic of collective violence (Malkki 1995; Appadurai 2005).[32] We make special reference to this aspect here because it helps us to comprehend the significance of the *visual turn* for sociological analysis from another angle.

Ivana Spasić, a Serbian sociologist, has hinted at the fact that the Milošević regime deliberately took advantage of the production of "symbolic confusion" for the sake of remaining in power (1999: 117), thus leaving the citizens without any ideological orientation and unable to define any concrete culprit for their country's misfortune. By spreading symbolic messages and images that neither distanced themselves unmistakably from the Yugoslav communist iconography of the late regime nor indicated any hallmark of a new worldview, the regime provided for itself the comfortable situation of being able to decide at the last minute. Taking into account that it is during times of trouble in particular that, as Maja Brkljačić and Holm Sundhaussen emphasized, symbols attain an "almost existential relevance" (2003: 934), the importance of this point becomes clarified.

To sum up these impressions and our story about the shifting of "extremism" into the "center" of present-day Serbian society, we can return to Debray's truthful statement at the opening of this essay and add that the effects of signs and images are, in fact, only mediated through multifarious social and cultural mechanisms.

NOTES

1. Another publication is devoted to presenting more evidence on the role of the visual in the Balkans. See Šuber and Karamanić (2011).

2. Just be reminded that Milman Parry and Albert B. Lord validated the *Oral Formulaic Hypothesis* empirically on behalf of their famous studies of the Yugoslav (Bosnian) regions.

3. This term, introduced in the graffiti study by Antonijević and Hristić (2006: 287), does not denote a certain political ideology, but refers to "efforts to create individual ideology and personal needs. They do not refer to daily political issues, though they can be thought of as a response to current circumstances faced by their authors." Unsurprisingly, the majority of these expressions display a critical attitude vis-à-vis the state of Serbian society.

4. The homepage of '1389' lists fifty-eight connected groups and associations. See http://1389.rs/veze.html.

5. See http://www.rus-obraz.net/en.

6. *Neue Zürcher Zeitung*, September 21, 2009, 4.

7. See the video on YouTube: http://www.youtube.com/watch?v=AbHffYh5MTI.

8. As Drašković reported, he was inspired by Paja Jovanović's famous painting depicting the Serbian prince Miloš Obrenović greeting Serbian rebels during the Second Serbian Uprising against the Ottomans 1815. In this invocation, one may instantly grasp the role of the visual in the contemporary perception of politics.

9. Otpor was originally meant as a protest movement against the implementation of a particular university law at Belgrade University. Soon after, however, it redirected its target against Milošević.

10. The following information is taken from an interview from the Internet magazine *Nero*, April 1, 2004. See http://www.neon.de/kat/sehen/gesellschaft/protest/5814 .html.

11. They were following up on the (Western European) model of a nonhierarchical principle of organization developed in the 1980s. See Marković (2001).

12. See the carefully researched portrayal by the Serbian sociologist Vladimir Ilić (pdc.ceu.hu/archive/00005016/01/Files05.doc).

13. Quote taken from: http://www.onthemedia.org/yore/transcripts/transcripts_120304 _revolution.html.

14. See the documentary "Otpor: The Fight to Save Serbia," issued in 2001.

15. See Cushing's "brief history of the 'clenched fist' image," http://www.docspopuli .org/articles/Fist.html.

16. Be reminded that officially and symbolically the Federal Republic of Yugoslavia, constituted in 1992, and consisting of the (former) Socialist Republics of Serbia and Montenegro, succeeded the former Socialist Federal Republic of Yugoslavia. Hence, just the socialist "star" was removed from the former Yugoslav flag. On the occasion

of international sport competitions, the audience increasingly showed a negative attitude towards the state iconography. For example, they ritualistically turned their
backs towards the playing field during the playing of the national anthem.

17. In the aftermath of the fiasco, most of the leaders joined the Democratic Party (DS)
of Zoran Djindjić. Still today, some of the former leading Otporaši retain important
functions within the state apparatus.

18. This designation obviously alludes to the infamous Memorandum of the Serbian
Academy of Sciences and Arts that was formulated around 1986 and is widely
perceived as containing the cornerstone of the Serbian nationalist program.

19. Marković traced this pattern of perception back to some of Otpor's political
actions.

20. Otpor established contacts with the opposition parties soon after its founding in
December 1998. However, actual cooperation only developed after the formation of
the DOS (Democratic Opposition of Serbia) alliance. Otpor activists were regular
attendees at the DOS meetings and even participated in its election campaigns.

21. To be sure, the presence of the fist is not due to recent activity, but is a relic from the
year 2000.

22. It was from 1992–93 during the height of the Bosnian War, as well as 1998–2000
during the Kosovo conflicts that the SRS formed the coalition government with
Milošević's Socialist Party (SPS).

23. Symptomatically, Stefanović's (2008) explanation of the "Resurgence of the Serbian
Far Right" does not make any reference to the democratic movements.

24. See http://www.obraz.rs/index1.htm.

25. The poster is reprinted in Šuber (2009: 153).

26. Compare the logos of the Serbian National Movement Naši 1389 (http://www
.snp1389.rs) or Dveri Srpske (http://www.dverisrpske.com/).

27. See http://www.kosovoimetohija.org/lat/uhapsen-zbog-lepljenja-plakata-gotov-je-.

28. For example, we took from Novi Sad (the second largest city of Serbia). See Šuber
(2009: 153).

29. Thus alluding to G. W. F. Hegel's much debated sentence: "That which is reasonable is real, and that which is real is reasonable." The underlying dialectic betrays the
logic of reconciliation of state and society.

30. http://www.slobodnaevropa.org/content/article/1049257.html.

31. "Kampanja 'Kosovo je Srbija', opet" [The Campaign 'Kosovo is Serbia,' again].
December 6, 2007, B92. http://www.b92.net/info/vesti/index.php?yyyy=2007&mm
=12&dd=06&nav_category=11&nav_id=275339

32. For an overview and discussion of this approach with regard to the case of the
breakup of Yugoslavia, see Šuber (forthcoming).

REFERENCES

Antonijević, D., and L. Hristić. 2006. "Belgrade Graffiti: Anthropological Insights into
Anonymous Public Expression of 'World-view.'" *Ethnologia Balkanica* (10): 279–90.

Appadurai, A. (2005). *Modernity at Large. Cultural Dimensions of Globalization*. Minneapolis:
University of Minnesota Press.

Bakić, J. 2009. "Extreme-Right Ideology, Practice and Supporters: Case Study of the Serbian
Radical Party." *Journal of Contemporary European Studies* 17 (2): 193–207.

Bieber, F. 2003. "The Serbian Opposition and Civil Society Roots of the Delayed Transition
in Serbia." *International Journal of Politics, Culture, and Society* 17 (1): 73–90.

Brkljačić, M., and H. Sundhaussen. 2003. "Symbolwandel und symbolischer Wandel: Kroatiens Erinnerungskulturen" [Change of symbols and symbolic change: culture of memory in Croatia]. *Osteuropa: Zeitschrift für Gegenwartsfragen des Ostens* [Eastern Europe: Journal for Contemporary Questions of the East] 53 (7): 933–48.

Buden, B. 1997. "Mission Impossible." *ARKzin,* Zagreb, Croatia, Issue 83, January 31.

Čolović, I. 2002. *The Politics of Symbol in Serbia: Essays on Political Anthropology.* London: Hurst.

D'Angelo, F. J. 1974. "Sacred Cows Make Great Hamburgers: The Rhetoric of Graffiti." *College Composition and Communication* 25 (2): 173–80.

Debray, R. 2000. *Transmitting Culture.* New York: Columbia University Press.

Dragićević-Šešić, M. 2001. "The Street as Political Space: Walking as Protest, Graffiti, and the Student Carnivalization of Belgrade." *New Theatre Quarterly* 17 (1): 74–86.

Foucault, M. 1990. *The History of Sexuality.* vol 1. Translated by Robert Hurley. New York: Vintage Books.

Hebdige, D. 1979. *Subculture: The Meaning of Style.* New York: Routledge.

Ilić, V. 2001. "The Popular Movement Otpor—Between Europe and Re-traditionalization." *Central European University Files,* pdc.ceu.hu/archive/00005016/01/Files05.doc.

Ivanji, A. 2008. "Wie eine Parteienlandschaft entstand" [How a party landscape emerged]. In *Serbien nach den Kriegen* [Serbia after the wars], edited by J. Becker and A. Engelberg, 141–79. Frankfurt am Main: Suhrkamp.

Jansen, S. 2001. "The Streets of Beograd. Urban Space and Protest Identities in Serbia." *Political Geography* (20): 35–55.

Lalić, D., A. Leburič, and B. Nenad. 1991. *Grafiti i subkultura* [Graffiti and subculture]. Zagreb: Alinea.

Lipset, S. M. 1960. *Political Man: The Social Bases of Politics.* Garden City, NY: Doubleday.

Lotman, J. 1977. "Myth—Name—Culture." In *Soviet Semiotics: An Anthology,* edited by D. P. Lucid, 233–52. Baltimore: Johns Hopkins University Press.

Luckmann, T. 1989. "Prolegomena to a Social Theory of Communicative Genres." *Slovene Studies* 11 (1-2): 159–66.

Malkki, L. (1995). *Purity and Exile: Violence, Memory, and National Cosmology among Hutu Refugees in Tanzania.* Chicago: University of Chicago Press.

Marković, V. 2001. "'The Other Serbia' in Discrepancy. The Elements of Neoliberal and Orientalist Ideologies Incorporated in the Process of the Development of a Civil Society in the Balkans." *Diskrepancija* 2, 3. http://diskrepancija.org/casopis/index.php?id=116,0,0,1,0,0.

Mitchell, W. J. T. 1994. *Picture Theory. Essays on Verbal and Visual Representation.* Chicago: University of Chicago Press.

Müller, M. G. 2004. "Politologie und Ikonologie: Visuelle Interpretation als politologisches Verfahren" [Political science and iconology: visual interpretation as method for the political sciences]. In *Politikwissenschaft als Kulturwissenschaft. Theorien, Methoden, Problemstellungen* [Political science as cultural science: theories, methods, problems], edited by B. Schwelling, 335–49. Wiesbaden: VS.

———. 2008. "Visual Competence: A New Paradigm for Studying Visuals in the Social Sciences." *Visual Studies* 23 (2): 101–12.

Radošević, L. 2008. "'Nevidna' energija beograjskih ulic" ['Invisible' energy of the streets of Belgrade] *Časopis za kritiko znanosti* [Journal for the critique of science] 36 (231–32): 291–306.

Ramet, S. P. 2010. "Serbia since July 2008: At the Doorstep of the EU." *Südosteuropa: Zeitschrift für Politik und Gesellschaft* [Southeastern Europe: journal for politics and society] 58 (1): 15–40.

Spasić, I. 1999. "Identity Void: Structural Confusion and Everyday Life in Today's Serbia." In *Models of Identities in Post-Communist Societies*, edited by Z. Golubović and G. McLean, 109–24. Washington, DC: Council for the Research in Values and Philosophy.

Stefanov, N. 2008. "Serbische Kontinuitäten" [Serbian continuities]. In *Serbien nach den Kriegen* [Serbia after the wars], edited by J. Becker and A. Engelberg, 233–56. Frankfurt am Main: Suhrkamp.

Stefanović, D. 2008. "The Path to Weimar Serbia? Explaining the Resurgence of the Serbian Far Right after the Fall of Milosevic." *Ethnic and Racial Studies* 31 (7): 1195–221.

Šuber, D. 2009. "Semiotische Kämpfe im Nachkriegs-Serbien: Zur politischen Ikonographie der Straße anhand von Graffiti und Street-Art" [Semiotic fights in postwar Serbia: a political iconography of the street on the basis of graffiti and street-art] In *Erinnerung in Kultur und Kunst: Reflexionen über Krieg, Flucht und Vertreibung in Europa* [Memory in culture and art: reflexions on war, flight, and displacement], edited by A. von Oswald, A. Schmelz, and T. Lenuweit, 141-62. Bielefeld: Transcript.

———. forthcoming. "Collective Violence between Rationality and Incommensurability: Lessons from the Serbian Case." In *Southeast Europe—Comparison, Entanglement, Transfer*, edited by S. Rutar, Münster: LIT.

Šuber, D., and S. Karamanić, eds. 2012. *Retracing Images: Visual Culture after Yugoslavia*. Leiden: Brill Publishers.

Sundhaussen, H. 2008. "Serbiens extremes Zeitalter" [Serbia's extreme age]. In *Serbien nach den Kriegen* [Serbia after the wars], edited by J. Becker, and A. Engelberg, 28–56. Frankfurt am Main: Suhrkamp.

Terzic, Z. 2005. "Von Phantomkulturen und nationalen Logiken: Vier Thesen zur postjugo-slawischen Befindlichkeit" [On phantom cultures and nationalistic logics: four theses on the post-Yugoslav condition]. In *Bilanz Balkan* [Balkan accounts], edited by M. Daxner, 189–218. Wien: Verlag für Geschichte und Politik.

Vlaisavljević, U. 2002. "South Slav Identity and the Ultimate War Reality." In *Balkan as Metaphor: Between Globalization and Fragmentation*, edited by D. Bjelić, I. Dušan, and O. Savić, Obrad, 191–207. Cambridge, MA: MIT Press.

Wiesinger, B. N. 2008. "The Continuing Presence of the Extreme Right in Post-Milošević Serbia." *Balkanologie* 11 (1-2). http://balkanologie.revues.org/index1363.html.

CHAPTER 8

THE VISUALIZATION OF UNCERTAINTY: HIV STATISTICS IN PUBLIC MEDIA

VALENTIN RAUER

INTRODUCTION

Cultural historians have identified two different modes of how societies perceive their history: a circular and a linear mode of time. In circular time, the future just repeats the past, such as in the recurrence of different climate seasons each year. Linear time implies a future that will differ from the past (Koselleck 1979, Pierson 2004). How much it will differ, whether a slow and small aberration or a rapid fundamental rupture, remains uncertain. Societies that have replaced the idea of circular time with the idea of linearity and progress create a vision of the future that lacks predictability and security. By giving up the idea of circularity, modern societies face problematic questions of how to act under conditions of "uncertainty" (Bauman 2007).

Sociology has reacted to the modern challenge of the future with the concept of "risk" (Beck 1992). However, as often criticized, the concept of risk reduces social action to rationalistic techniques of calculation and probabilities (Bonss 1995). The rational calculation of probability is only one strategy among many that deals with an "unknown" future. Instead, as political scientists argue, modern states have to deal with both, the risk as "known unknowns" as well as the uncertainties of "unknown unknowns" (Daase and Kessler 2007: 413). Beyond risk calculation, various cultural forms have been developed in order to show how societies cope with unknown futures (Douglas 1992; Alexander and Smith 1996; Nowottny 2005; Daase 2010). These cultural aspects are still disregarded by risk sociology. This omission might be due to the methodological reduction of sociology to numerical and textual data. Public imagination of future scenarios refers to images, not to numbers—a visual form of public communication. Unfortunately, the sociological expertise to identify these visual data adequately is quite underdeveloped. This essay attempts to provide one step toward a more refined approach to the study of the iconicity of uncertainty.

To avoid misunderstandings, this argument is not at all meant to downplay the significance of numerical statistics and calculable risks. The rise of statistics and the attempt to transform uncertainty into a calculable probability demonstrates the high impact this field has had in modern and postmodern societies. Statistical probability enables political actors to decide on the means by which to calculate a situation that will show its effects in the future. The invention of statistics initiated what Michel Foucault called the "biopolitics" of modern states (Foucault 2007). Risk calculation is a major tool to define and deal with collective dangers and to legitimize political actions and decisions. The societal impact of the statistical technique should not in any way be underrated. However, the efforts of risk calculation will never eradicate the problem of uncertainty. If we focus only on risk, we ignore the powerful role that such uncertainties have, since Westernized cultures have replaced a circular time with a linear time.

Risk statistics are a technique based on a numerical epistemology of recurrence and frequencies. When communicated to a broader public, these data are usually illustrated with graphics or pictorial elements, ranging from simple curves to sophisticated icons or even whole sets of pictures. By visually representing numerical data, mathematical probabilities are combined with nonlinguistic artifacts. This combination of numerical logic with visual logic produces new iconic meanings. Thus, with their realization as illustration, calculations of probabilities alter their proposition.

The quest for a method by which to make statistical knowledge visual to a non-scientific audience without obliterating the probabilistic logic was already raised at the beginning of the last century by Otto Neurath (1991), a social philosopher from Vienna. Neurath developed the so called "isotype," an acronym for an International System Of Typographic Picture Education (Hartmann and Bauer 2002: 65). The main idea behind this system was to combine neutral data with an appealing illustration to disseminate sociological knowledge to a broader audience (Leonard 1999; Nikolow 2007). Neurath lived at a time when sociology's unwavering trust in its statistical data and social rules was still unbroken. The conviction was not widely accepted, that each single data has to be interpreted within a culturally bound frame. The methodological challenge is to revise Neurath's concepts with regard to current cultural approaches in sociology.

The following essay presents the results of a study on the iconic meaning of statistical illustrations—isotypes—in public media. The results demonstrate that many such graphs combine two logics: risk calculations and the imagination of uncertainty. These results are interpreted in reference to a concept called "iconic difference" coined by the German art historian Gottfried Boehm (1994, 2004). With his concept of iconic difference, the difference between the logic of spoken language and the logic of visualized images can be systematically outlined.

The argumentation unfolds in three parts: the first part briefly summarizes the theoretical assumptions of the current visual sociology. The second part presents the results of a study that analyzed the iconic means of HIV infection rates in the public media. The last part concludes with the impact of this study in overcoming the rationalistic reduction of risk research with a strong program of visual sociology.

TOWARD A STRONG APPROACH OF VISUAL SOCIOLOGY

By initiating and defining the "cultural turn" in the social sciences, Jeffrey C. Alexander differentiated cultural sociology into either weak or strong approaches (Alexander 2000). The weak program reduces culture to a product of social structures or social practices. Correspondingly, they criticize the functional reduction of culture, whenever culture is treated as a subsystem among others, such as economics, law, or social welfare. Instead, the strong program of culture defines culture as a network of meanings, to which every interpreter of single acts has to refer (Geertz 1972; Reckwitz 2006). There exist no "meaningful" social acts beyond culture. Culture is the collective dimension of individual sense. In other words: culture is a more or less a shared network of meaning to which people refer when they try to make sense of a situation, a social action, or an object. Networks of meaning are relatively autonomous because they are represented in collective infrastructures such as public media, rituals, images, symbols, and so forth. Cultural meaning systems have their own material and medial logics and have to be studied with specific sets of methodological instruments. Hence, the cultural turn initiated a set of new methods such as performativity (Alexander, Giesen, and Mast 2006), actor-network theory (Latour 1988; Guggenheim and Potthast 2011), or currently and still in the making: iconicity and visuality.

However, concerning current approaches to an emerging visual sociology (Rose 2001; Raab 2008; Burri 2008), similar cleavages between weak and strong research programs can be identified. The weak approach takes visuality and iconicity mainly as an outcome of social practices. Whether a material artifact is taken as a picture or as an icon depends foremost on the actor's presuppositions and framings based on the situational context. A picture becomes only a "picture," if the actor thinks, due to the situational context, that the artifact "is a picture." This approach can be traced back to Erving Goffman's well-known framing concept (1974) or even to the definition of social reality by the famous Thomas Theorem: "if men define situations as real, they are real in their consequences" (Thomas and Thomas 1928: 572). Applied to visual sociology, the phrase would go: "if people define artifacts as images, they are images in their consequences." The weak approach does not differentiate between the heterogeneous ability of the spoken word, texts, or images to store or represent meaning. Meaning is just seen as a result of defining actions. Pictures and images are nothing more than, for instance, a "variable product of socio-technical practices" (Burri 2008: 247). This approach has methodological consequences: if iconicity derives solely from social practices, it must be studied in the practices of producing or consuming visual artifacts. The pictures themselves, their forms and aesthetic structures, can be neglected. Such a weak approach, of course, is not entirely wrong, but it does mislead by overemphasizing the role of the practices and by underestimating the epistemological power of images. The weak approach leaves the simple question unanswered: why do people refer to or produce images instead of words or texts?

In contrast to the weak approach, there exists a "strong approach" that raises these questions and claims different methodological techniques. The strong approach argues that pictures and icons have their own logic that cannot be reduced to an outcome of social practices or linguistically produced meaning. This argument was developed most strongly by Boehm (1994, 2004), who became famous with a concept that he calls the "iconic difference." The concept presumes that, "Images have their own logic that is solely related to pictures. By logic we understand the consistent production of genuine sense of pictorial means.... This logic is nonpredicative; it is not formed on the model of the sentence or other linguistic forms" (Boehm 2004: 28–29, my translation)[1]

A linguistically produced logic is based on constative speech acts (Austin 1967; Rauer 2006) and conclusions, as for instance: "A is different from B; C equals A, thus C differs from B." Linguistic logic is built on words and abstract signs as "A" or "B" that enable the speaker to claim true-or-false distinctions. Iconic logic presents different perspectives, not true-or-false-distinctions. In iconic logic, the referent "A" never appears as a true "A," but as a certain perspective "A_1, A_2 or A_n." In other words: the iconic differentiation refers to different visualizations, not truths. That is the reason why, as Boehm argues, images are not "spoken," but "realized by perceiving" (Boehm 2004: 29, my translation)[2]. If we hear or read a sentence "A," we understand the meaning by cognition; if we see an image of "A," we realize the meaning of "A" by perceiving the perspective "A_n." The linguistic cognition refers to definitions; the act of perceiving refers to sights.

This difference between cognitive understanding and visual perception can explain the reason why, for instance, some pictures of 9/11—the falling people— are almost entirely banned in the public space (cf. Bowler, this volume). It is not the linguistic sentences and words that inform about these horrible incidents that are taboo, but their images. In our current public culture it is accepted to "know" cognitively about such horrors, but not to "show" them. Thus the concept of iconic difference draws sociological analyses to the question of how people perceive the social world beyond cognitive definitions of situations.[3]

Furthermore, approaches of the strong program argue that images contain a certain ambiguity and an associative suggestibility (cf. the contributions in Knieper and Müller 2005). Images provide "multiple meanings" and "surprising synthesis" (Boehm 1994: 28, my translation).[4] To give an example: the "icon of Abu Ghraib," the infamous "hooded man on the box," is associated with attributes of the "Ku Klux Klan" or the "hood of the hangman," and might be therefore associated with "American Racism" (all quotations Soussloff 2007: 172). Others associate the man on the box with the "passion and crucifixion of Christ" (Holloway 2008: 148; cf. Binder, this volume). As this example shows, the meaning of images is always multiple; it cannot be reduced to linguistic either-or definitions.

Finally, Boehm argues that images produce meaning by an act of iconoclastic negation. Images are not the perfect imitation of reality, but set off a certain difference. Images obtain their meaning by covering a surface with colors. The act of painting a surface produces in-transparency. Only by such an act of "de-visualization" may a different meaning that has no material referent be visualized. The act of making something invisible creates a new, specific iconic visibility.[5] For instance, "uncertainty" consists of no material corporeality, it is just a linguistic cognitive abstract concept. However, as will be shown in the following section, uncertainty can be perceived and realized by visualization.

THE ISOTYPE

As mentioned in the introduction, the isotype visualizes sociological data to disseminate knowledge. Neurath was not interested in questions of iconicity or visual sociology as such. Instead, his normative intention was the democratization of expert knowledge. He developed the concept in order to reduce the complexity of statistical knowledge and to "humanize every careful [statistical] argument" (Neurath 1991: 594, my translation). The illustration of sociology should familiarize its knowledge without losing its scientific adequacy.

However, despite his educational intentions, Neurath foreshadowed the theoretical implication of the difference between linguistic and iconic logics. For instance, one among his definitions of the isotype is particularly revealing: isotypes "show connections between facts instead of discussing facts. [Isotypes] serve not only as illustration or eye-catcher; they are even part of the explanations" (Neurath 1991: 450, my translation). This definition corresponds with Boehm's concept of iconic difference. Isotypes consist of visual means that enable people to realize sociological knowledge by perceiving, not by cognitively translating scientific concepts into their own language (cf. further Leonhard 1999). In this respect, the famous "population pyramid" might be a paradigmatic example. The isotype visually shows black figures that refer to the sexes "man and woman." Each single black figure denotes a numerical quantity of individuals. The figures combine a numeric rationale (e.g., one figure stands for N=1 Mill.) with a visually realized form of pyramid.

Isotypes are positioned in-between a linguistic and a pictorial way of presentation, which enables them to combine neutral abstraction with emotive concreteness without merging this difference: "In our word-language, we can mix up emotional elements with [rational] arguments much more than in the isotype language. [The latter] is much more 'neutral' than our everyday language. If one made such neutral and sober statements in our word-language like it is possible to make with an isotype visualization, these statements would become quite weak and boring" (Neurath 1991: 595, my translation).[6]

Neurath was not naïve; he saw the danger of the suggesting effects of isotypes. For him, nothing seemed more "dangerous than a sign that for some [observers] says more than one actually wanted to express" (Nikolow 2007: 257, my translation). Unfortunately, he himself did not develop a concept to focus on the systematic connotation of these additional meanings.

To give a simple example: the famous "population pyramid" depicts figures (isotypes) of the age cohorts of "man" on the left and figures (isotypes) of the age cohorts of "woman" on the right. Such a population pyramid could also be read as an icon for a biologically caused binary order of gender relations. The isotype represents gendered differences both in numbers and in pictorial figures. The "man" and the "woman" as ordered triangle connote an aesthetic meaning, which goes beyond the pure numerical data of birth and mortality rates of generational cohorts. The population could even be perceived as a symmetrical body and a natural collective organism. The pyramid combines numerical logic with pictorial figures by presenting age and gender differences as corporeality. It imagines a community as a symmetrically gendered and aged complete entity.

In conclusion: isotypes are not immune to metaphorical reading. Indeed, Neurath's isotypes appear amazingly neutral at first, but they nevertheless can suggest more meaning than originally intended.

HIV STATISTICS IN PUBLIC MEDIA

The data presented in this section are based on the cover stories of two weekly periodicals that covered acquired immunodeficiency syndrome (AIDS) or the human immunodeficiency virus (HIV), the German weekly *Der Spiegel* and the American weekly *Time Magazine*. [7]

The selected period was 1983 to 2004. The entire pictorial elements—pictures, graphics, drawings, comics, cartoons, and so forth—were sampled and archived (N=504). All elements were selected for coding.

The coding was methodologically oriented on the classical iconological method that includes three steps of analyses and interpretation and was developed by Erwin Panofsky (1962): first, to identify the subject matter of the picture, for instance, the image depicts a "patient with HIV"; second is the iconographic context, which includes the concrete conventions of symbols and images with which the picture was produced, perceived, and understood; and third is the iconological meaning, which includes cultural and social interpretations, for example, why and how an AIDS patient is arranged in a visual image like a "suffering Jesus" (Gilman 1988). In this last step many approaches can be used. Among others, narrative methods (Cerulo 1998; Giesen 2004) help to organize the interpretation systematically and more precisely.

In the coding process, elements of classical content analysis were also used to classify the different types of categories (Rose 2001). An additional methodological technique was to analyze a series of categories across a certain time span. The underlying assumption is that comparisons help to diachronically disclose structures of iconic forms that would otherwise remain unnoticed. As result of the coding process, the three most frequent pictorial motives were identified: first, "individuals with HIV/AIDS," second, "scientists and experts," and third, pictures, graphs and isotypes of the virus and its aftereffects.[8]

The following analysis refers only to the third category: the statistics and isotypes used by the media.[9]

In 1987, *Der Spiegel* published a graph to show the cumulative development of AIDS cases in the United States (left curve) and the Federal Republic of Germany (right curve) (Figure 8.1). This graph was among the first to illustrate numerical

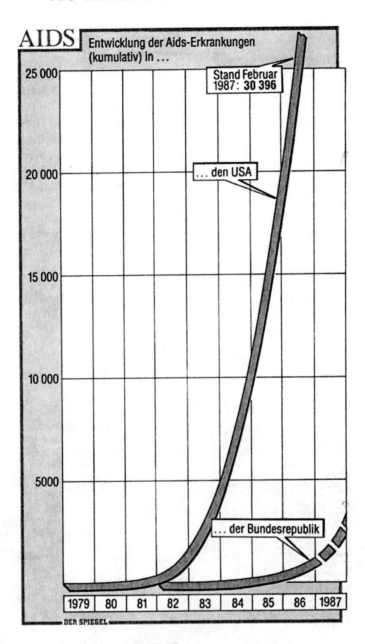

Figure 8.1   (© *Der Spiegel*, February 7, 1987, 37).

knowledge about the disease. The graph resembles an "E-Function" mathematically. By means of the logic of the E-Function, one could calculate precisely when the last inhabitant on earth would die of AIDS. The graph contains an interesting detail; the left curve exceeds the numerical scale and the visual frame of the table.

The table ends with the number twenty-five thousand. One could have also chosen thirty thousand without any further ado. What kind of meaning derives from that visually expressed spillover?

The curve transgresses the limits of numerical measurements visually, not numerically. The iconic performance of the curve suggests a threatening future scenario. It assumes an alarming collapse of measurable capabilities to deal with the situation. The disease might exceed all limits of hitherto known "normal" pandemics. In addition, the transgression marks the limits of medical probability. The track of the curve differentiates visually between a field of probability and a field of uncertainty. Numerical and visual meaning fuses to an ambiguous form of an uncertain future.

Another graph in *Der Spiegel* dates from the year 1991 (Figure 8.2). At this time, it became more and more evident that human biology does not follow the logic of an E-Function. The curve flattens out and shows up and downs rather than an accumulative increase. Nevertheless, a visual transgression between numerical knowledge and uncertainty can be found here as well. The graph presents the numbers of registered AIDS patients per year in West Germany. In addition, the graph is embedded in an isotypical illustration of a so-called "defense-cell," a lymphocyte. The lymphocytes represent the immune system, which is targeted and destroyed by

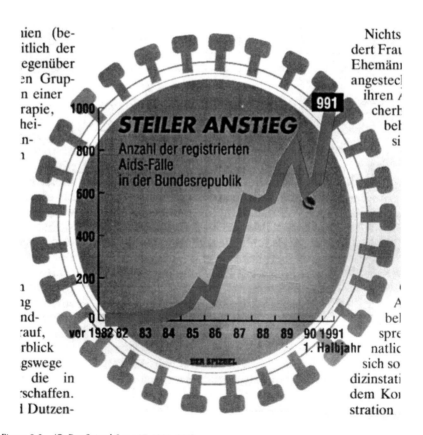

Figure 8.2   (© *Der Spiegel*, June 17, 1991, 293).

the HI-virus. The peak of the curve reaches numerically the amount of N=991 and does not cross the upper limit of the scale that is N=1000.

However, graphically the curve crosses the cell border of the lymphocyte. Again, numerical and visual logic produce in their combination an iconic meaning. The meaning derives from the combination of numerical knowledge about infected persons on the one hand and a curve that cuts across a cell border on the other. The graph tells us about possible dangers of AIDS not by providing terrifying numbers of infection rates, but with graphical lines that irregularly transgress a cell border. Thus, possible danger is not constructed with words, but with visual means.

Another example uses the associative logic of iconicity. *Der Spiegel* published a cartoon that shows Mister Death, alias AIDS, and *how he causes* an accumulative domino effect with his finger (Figure 8.3). In visual terms, the image of the domino pyramid appears quite similar to Neurath's famous population pyramid. Obviously in a linguistic-based logic, the domino game has nothing at all in common with Neurath's population pyramid. The target group of AIDS is neither, as the cartoon suggests, the elder generation, nor is a pandemic caused by the oldest person of that society. The suggested meaning is "AIDS might cause a coming apocalypse, because its spreads like an E-Function" (cf. Figure 8.1). If formulated as linguistic proposition, it could be falsified. Presented with iconic means, the audience perceives a "pandemic threat" without realizing that they are accepting an epidemiologically contradictory hypothesis.

Figure 8.3   (© *Der Spiegel*, June 17, 1991, 294).

The logic of presenting scientific knowledge as "known unknowns" in combination with "unknown unknowns" can be observed in many examples in the years that followed. Just the visualized target groups changed according to the changing assumptions about the "cause" of HIV and AIDS. Figure 8.4 dates from 1992. At that time, HIV and AIDS were no longer seen to be "caused" by members of gay communities exclusively. Instead, in the public perception, HIV increasingly threatened "ordinary heterosexuals" as well (Gilman 1988). However, this change in the public perception did not lead to a different iconic logic, as Figure 8.4 shows. The graph illustrates the increasing numbers of infected heterosexuals. The meaning is represented with the figurative heterosexual couple. The numbers of infected heterosexuals, presented by read bars and letters, literally grows above their heads. Moreover, the iconic intemperance is substantiated by the typographic enlargement of the letters from the left to the right. Usually, the big letter stands at the beginning of a word and not at the end. With the inversion of typographical order and accumulation, the threat effect results from the difference between numerical and typographic components.

Another revealing example dates from 1991 (Figure 8.5). In contrast to the prior images, this graph combines temporal accumulations with spatial transgressions. In this case, the threat to the "ordinary population" is expressed by the increasing rate of infected women. The "threat" is visualized by the "masses" of infected women in Africa. Their pure appearance as marching people visually overruns the spatial scale, the geography of the continental shores and borders. The African women "march" beyond the continental order of the world. They even appear in a more aggressive red color (not in a black-and-white reproduction). This effect of a more aggressive appearance of the "African women" is realized purely by means of isotypical

Figure 8.4   (© *Der Spiegel*, September 28, 1992, 89).

Figure 8.5   (*Der Spiegel*, June 17, 1991, 285).

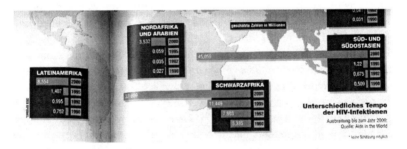

Figure 8.6   (© *Der Spiegel*, May 3, 1993, 172–73).

logic. The "non-African women" are drawn in a plain mode, in a two-dimensional aesthetic form. In contrast to this plain mode, the "African women" appear almost as as three-dimensional figures (cf. Figure 8.5). This example shows that, by using isotypes there are multiple ways of suggesting counterfactual difference with pure aesthetic means.

The African isotypes consequently appear more active, while the remaining isotypes appear more passive. Although it is not stated linguistically, the graph suggests the message that the threat to the world is located in Africa. From Africa, AIDS might cut across national and continental borders and infect the rest of the world. Formulated within the linguistic logic of propositions, such a threat would seem to be unlikely. However, if realized as a visualization, it just seems to illustrate an epidemiological law.

Another comparable variation of spatial transgression on a global scale is shown in Figure 8.6. While the infection rates in North Africa, Middle East, Latin America, and Europe (in this reproduction not printed) remain within the limits of the black box, in Africa and Southeast Asia, the sheer number of infections seems to stretch beyond the scales of "normality." The red columns exceed the volume of the black boxes, which guarantee the social order symbolically. Concerning their isotypical presentations, Southeast Asia and Africa are bursting at the seams.

In similar ways, a spatially and globally varied situation of uncertainty is represented in the year 1995 (Figure 8.7). In this case, only Asia exceeds the limits of measurability. The scale of the table ends with the value of 1.2. The visual limit functions as a limit of probability: beyond 1.2 million infections, the iconic sphere of uncertainty begins. The limit of scale marks the limits of "known unknowns." Uncertainty is not linguistically proposed, but is realized by means of iconicity.

In 1997, *Der Spiegel* printed a combination of graphical elements that included the entire range of iconic forms discussed so far (Figure 8.8).[10] The images consist of both the temporal and spatial forms of visual transgression. The temporal chronology is positioned in the center, surrounded by concentric circles of geographically exceeding clouds of red spots (not in this black-and-white reproduction). The clouds of red spots are neither canalized by national borders (white lines), nor do their dissemination halt at the shores of continental coastlines. The clouds repeatedly transgress natural and national boundaries. The epidemiology of AIDS is illustrated with both: temporal and spatial thresholds. The temporal mechanism of accumulation in terms of the devastating E-Function is visually paralleled with spatial diffusions. The difference between probability and uncertainty is depicted both in chronological and topological forms.

Finally, in order to compare the results found in *Der Spiegel*, the same analyses were applied to the American *Time Magazine*. Unfortunately, copyright regulations do not allow the reprinting the graphs here. However, Internet access to the archive of *Time Magazine* might present the opportunity to cross-check the arguments of the following analysis. The first table in *Time Magazine* dates from August 12, 1985. This graph still represents the infection rates in a numerical form and includes no isotypical elements. However, during the following years *Time Magazine* uses a couple of transgressing forms comparable to *Der Spiegel*. For instance, one graph published on February 16, 1987, shows a cloud that originates from a mass of

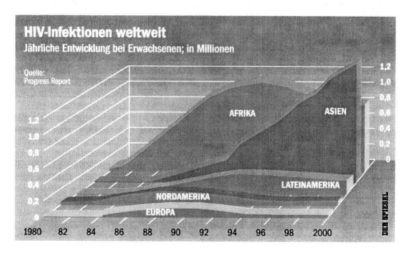

Figure 8.7   (© *Der Spiegel*, July 10, 1995, 168).

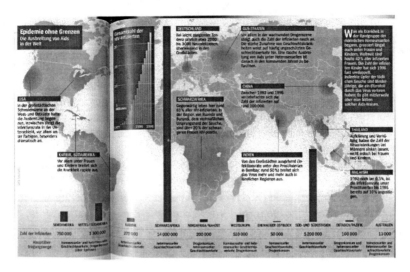

Figure 8.8   (© *Der Spiegel*, January 16, 1997, 122–23).

people, which represents infected "homosexuals." Depending on the viewer's choice, the cloud can either be decoded as a ghost or as poison smog, or even as a figurative symbol of the threat of tidal waves. The threat is visualized as a cloud that "endangers" the "heterosexual society."

In an additional illustration, a graph, printed in *Time Magazine* on February 12, 2001, portrays a historical chronology of the AIDS epidemic. This chronology is positioned in the lower section of the page. The upper section contains the article written in text. Into this chronology, the assumed performance of a red frequency curve of infected cases of HIV is inserted. This red curve dramatically exceeds the framework of the historical chronology. The curve leaves the sections of the AIDS chronology at the bottom of the page and extends beyond the uppermost scale of measurement and continues through the textual part of the page. The numeric logic of the curve transforms into a red track that runs beyond the limits, even over the linguistic sections of the article, the text. The picture appears as if the linguistic knowledge—the text—is crossed out wit h a red marker, that is, the curve. Textual logic is confronted with iconic logic, indicating the unpredictability of pandemic threats.

CONCLUDING REMARKS

In this study of the case of AIDS in public media, the analysis of AIDS-related isotypes shows how these visualizations mark the threshold of probability and uncertainty. The visual presentations of AIDS infection rates indicate the cultural impact of uncertainty. Uncertainty is not fully tamable by risk calculation. As the counterpart to risk, uncertainty maintains its productive power to create imagined future scenarios. Political decisions and public fears refer to these imagined scenes. They can be misused for diverse purposes. Only a strong program of visual sociology can provide insights into these forms of meaning production.

Neurath's concept of isotypes provided a methodological tool to analyze the public power of statistical knowledge. The advantage of isotypes lies in their iconic modality: their meaning is realized by perception and not by understanding. The power to create evidence results from the combination and fusion of different modes of episteme: a numerical rationale is contrasted with iconic imaginations. This iconic fusion of both logics into one visual image alters the meanings of probability and uncertainty. In reference to Boehm's concept of "iconic difference," this contrastive combination of different epistemes has been called elsewhere "isotypic difference" (Rauer 2009).

A strong research program in cultural meaning systems should not prioritize one episteme as a hypersystem, from which cultural meaning can just be deduced. If we had focused on just one isolated episteme alone, we would have missed the crucial interference of rationality and iconicity altogether. It is the combination of linguistic logic and iconic logic that affects and alters the threshold of cultural knowledge and the limits of uncertainty.

NOTES

1. Following is the German original of the translation that is provided in the main text: "Bilder besitzen eine eigene, nur ihnen zugehörige Logik. Unter Logik verstehen wir: die konsistente Erzeugung von Sinn aus *genuin* bildnerischen Mitteln.... Diese Logik ist nicht-prädikativ, das heißt nicht nach dem Muster des Satzes oder anderer Sprachformen gebildet." (Boehm 2004: 28–29).

2. Following is the German original of the translation that is provided in the main text: " Sie wird nicht gesprochen, sie wird wahrnehmend realisiert" (Boehm 2004: 29).

3. Cf. further: Bohn, C. 2001. "Sprache—Schrift—Bild" [Language—writing—picture]. In *Mit dem Auge denken: Strategien der Sichtbarmachung in wissenschaftlichen und virtuellen Welten* [Thinking with the eye: stragegies of making visible in the scientific and virtual worlds], edited by B. Heintz and J. Huber, 321–45. Zurich: Edition Voldemeer.

4. Following is the German original of the translation that is provided in the main text: Durch die "Vieldeutigkeit ihrer Form" (Boehm 1994: 28) legen Bilder "überraschende Synthesen" (ebd.) nahe.

5. A similar relation of foreground and background representation has been identified by Jeffrey C. Alexander's approach to performance (Alexander and Giesen et al. 2006).

6. Following is the German original of the translation that is provided in the main text: "In unserer Wortsprache können wir Gefühlselemente und Argumente viel mehr durcheinanderbringen als in der Isotype-Sprache, die viel 'neutraler' ist als unsere Alltagssprache. Wenn man in unserer Wortsprache so 'neutrale' und 'nüchterne' Aussagen machte wie in einer Isotype-Veranschaulichung, so würden sie oft recht matt und langweilig werden, während man Isotype in jedem Fall reizvoll machen kann" (Neurath 1991: 595).

7. The metaphorical and historical traces of HIV and AIDS have been analyzed in detail by Sontag (1989) and Gilman (1988). Their results cannot be repeated here, because the question is not just to focus on the cultural representations of a disease, but on how images and scientific knowledge are combined. Cf. Fleck (1994).

8. The categories were: Politicians / Activists (n=87); Photos/Graphics of the Virus and Biological Consequences (n=74); Scientists / Medical Experts (n=61); People with HIV / AIDS (n=24); Endangered Healthy People (n=22) ; Cartoons / Drawings

(n=22); Public Campaigns (n=21); Virus Tests / Laboratory / Blood Donations (n=21); Demonstrations (n=16) ; Gay Scene (n=13); Prostitutes (n=13); Funerals (n=13); Medical Hstory of Pandemics (n=12); Immune System (n=11); Monkeys (n=1).

9. Interpreted in narrative terms (cf. Cerulo 1998), these three most frequent categories represent the classic triad of, first, "victims" as patients, second, "heroes" as scientists, and third, the "villain" or "perpetrator" in gestalt of the virus as image or of images illustrating its epidemiological effects. The heroes represent the protection and maintenance of the medical order. However, for the sake of visual studies, I do not want to get further into narrative analyses.

10. Please supplement by visualizing the missing parts of the pages; these parts have not been scanned.

REFERENCES

Alexander, J. C. 2000. "The Strong Program in Cultural Theory: Elements of a Structural Hermeneutics." Paper presented at the Colloquium of the Special Research Program 485 "Norms and Symbols," University of Constance, Constance, Germany, October.

Alexander, J. C., B. Giesen, and J. L. Mast, eds. 2006. *Social Performance: Symbolic Action, Cultural Pragmatics, and Ritual*. Cambridge, UK; New York: Cambridge University Press.

Alexander, J. C., and P. Smith. 1996. "Social Science and Salvation: Risk Society as a Mythic Discourse." *Zeitschrift für Soziologie* 25 (4): 251–62.

Austin, J. L. 1967. *How to Do Things with Words*. Oxford: University Press.

Bauman, Z. 2010. *Liquid Times: Living in an Age of Uncertainty*. Cambridge: Polity Press.

Beck, U. 1992. *Risk Society: Towards a New Modernity*. Theory, culture and society. London: Sage.

Boehm, G. 1994. "Die Wiederkehr der Bilder" [The return of pictures]. In *Was ist ein Bild?* [What is a picture?], 11–38. Munich: Fink.

———. 2004. "Jenseits der Sprache? Zur Logik der Bilder" [Beyond language? On the logic of pictures]. In *Iconic Turn: Die neue Macht der Bilder* [The new power of pictures], edited by C. Maar and H. Burda, 28–43. Cologne: Dumont.

Bonss, W. 1995. *Vom Risiko: Unsicherheit und Ungewissheit in der Moderne* [On risk: insecurity and uncertainty in modern times]. Hamburg: Hamburger Edition.

Burri, R. 2008. "Images as Social Practice: Outline of a Sociology of the Visual." *Zeitschrift für Soziologie* 37 (4): 342–58.

Cerulo, K. A. 1998. *Deciphering Violence: The Cognitive Structure of Right and Wrong*. New York: Routledge.

Daase, C. 2010. "National, Societal, and Human Security: On the Transformation of Political Language." *Historical Social Research* 35 (4): 22–37.

Daase, C., and O. Kessler 2007. "Knowns and Unknowns in the 'War on Terror': Uncertainty and the Political Construction of Danger." *Security Dialogue* 38 (4): 411–34.

Douglas, M. 1992. *Risk and Blame. Essays in Cultural Theory*. London; New York: Routledge.

Fleck, L., L. Schäfer, and T. Schnelle 1994. *Entstehung und Entwicklung einer wissenschaftlichen Tatsache: Einführung in die Lehre vom Denkstil und Denkkollektiv.* [The emergence and development of scientific fact: introduction to the theory of style of thought and collective of thought]. Frankfurt am Main: Suhrkamp.

Foucault, M. 2007. *Security, Territory, Population: Lectures at the College de France 1977–1978*. Palgrave Macmillan.

Geertz, C. 1973. *The Interpretation of Cultures: Selected essays*. New York: Basic Books.

Giesen, B 2004. *Triumph and Trauma*. Boulder, CO: Paradigm.

Gilman, S 1988. *Disease and Representation: Images of Illness from Madness to AIDS*. Ithaca, NY: Cornell University Press.

Goffman, E 1996. *Frame Analysis: An Essay on the Organization of Experience*. Boston: Northeasten University Press.

Guggenheim, M., and J. Potthast. forthcoming. "Symmetrical Twins. On the Relationship between Actor-Network Theory and the Sociology of Critical Capacities." *European Journal of Sociological Theory*.

Hartmann, F. and E. K. Bauer 2002. *Bildersprache: Otto Neurath Visualisierungen* [Picture-Language: Otto Neurath's visualisations]. Vienna: Wiener Universitätsverlag.

Holloway, D. 2008. *9/11 and the War on Terror*. Edinburgh: Edinburgh University Press.

Knieper, T., and M. G. Müller, eds. 2005. *War Visions: Bildkommunikation und Krieg* [War and the communication of pictures]. Cologne: Herbert von Halem Verlag.

Koselleck, R. 1979. *Vergangene Zukunft: Zur Semantik geschichtlicher Zeiten* [Past-future: on the semantics of historical times]. Frankfurt am Main: Suhrkamp.

Leonard, R. J. 1999. "'Seeing Is Believing': Otto Neurath, Graphic Art, and the Social Order." In *Economic Engagements with Art*, edited by N. de Marchi and Goodwin Craufurd D.W., 452–78. Durham, NC; London: Duke University Press.

Neurath, O. 1991. *Gesammelte bildpädagogische Schriften* [Collected picture-pedagogical writings], with R. Haller, vol 3. Vienna: Hölder-Pichler-Tempsky.

Nikolow, S. 2007. "Aufklärung durch und mit Beobachtungstatsachen: Otto Neuraths Bildstatistik als Vehikel zur Verbreitung der wissenschaftlichen Weltauffassung des Wiener Kreises." [Enlightenment by and with facts of observation: Otto Neurath's pictorial statistics as vehicle to propel the scientific worldview of the Vienna Circle]. In *Wissenschaft und Öffentlichkeit als Ressourcen für einander* [Science and the public sphere as resources for each other], edited by S. Nikolow and A, Schirrmacher, 245–72. Frankfurt am Main: Campus.

Nowottny, H. 2005. "The Increase of Complexity and Its Reduction: Emergent Interfaces between the Natural Sciences, Humanities and Social Sciences." *Theory Culture & Society* 22 (5): 15–31.

Panofsky, E. 1962. *Studies in Iconology: Humanistic Themes in the Art of Renaissance*. New York: Harper Torchbooks.

Pierson, P. 2004. *Politics in Time: History Institutions and Social Analysis*. Princeton: Princeton University Press.

Raab, J. 2008. *Visuelle Wissenssoziologie: Theoretische Konzeption und materiale Analysen* [Visual sociology of knowledge: theoretical conceptions and material analyses]. Constance: UVK Verl.-Ges.

Rauer, V. 2006. "Symbols Action: Willy Brandt's Kneefall at the Warsaw Memorial." In *Social Performance: Symbolic Action, Cultural Pragmatics, and Ritual*, edited by J. C. Alexander, B. Giesen, and J. Mast, 257–82. Cambridge, NY: Cambridge University Press.

———. 2009. "Isotypische Differenz: Eine serielle Analyse der symbolischen Formen von öffentlichen HIV-Statistiken" [Isotypical difference: a serial analysis of the symbolic forms of public HIV statistics]. In *Visuelle Stereotype* [Visual stereotypes], edited by T. Petersen and C. Schwender, 124–40. Cologne: Herbert von Halem Verlag.

Reckwitz, A. 2006. *Die Transformation der Kulturtheorien* [The transformation of cultural theories]. Weilerswist: Velbrück Wissenschaft.

Rose, G. C. 2001. *Visual Methodologies: An Introduction to the Interpretation of Visual Materials*. London: Sage.

Sontag, S. 1989. *AIDS and Its Metaphors*. New York: Farrar Straus and Giroux.

Soussloff, C. M. 2007. "Post-Colonial Torture: Rituals of Viewing in Abu Ghraib." In *Ritual and Event*, edited by M. Franko, 159–89. London: Routledge.

Thomas, W. I., and D. S. Thomas 1928. *The Child in America: Behavior Problems and Programs*. New York: Knopf.

CHAPTER 9

HOW TO MAKE AN ICONIC COMMODITY: THE CASE OF PENFOLDS' GRANGE WINE

IAN WOODWARD AND DAVID ELLISON

INTRODUCTION

New approaches to iconicity in cultural sociology link the aesthetic surface of an object with the depths of its cultural meanings. Linking pragmatics and haptics with symbolism and mythology, such innovations offer a way of understanding how the aesthetic surface features of an object or image attract and enroll human interest by way of physical engagements. In addition, these approaches promise cultural analysts new resources to identify how such objects frame, and ultimately concretize in aesthetic form, complex culture structures of myth and narrative. By using the case study of a much-lauded wine, this chapter considers the conditions under which an object assumes iconic form, as well as the uses and understandings made available by this transfigured state. For our purposes, we have selected Penfolds Grange, widely regarded in the popular imagination as Australia's premier wine. Because of its expense, Grange is tasted relatively rarely, and even then it is only engaged directly by a small group. Yet, while it is not widely circulated among the population at large, Grange is nevertheless generally perceived as a landmark Australian wine. More than this, it draws on a cache of national myths and powerful cultural stories that both elevate and continue to authorize its status as an iconic Australian wine. Thus, like any cultural icon, this wine not only stands as an exemplar of the Australian wine industry, but refers to cherished and valued national stories. Therefore—confirming its iconic status—as much as it is valued for being a premier wine, the wine thus also distinguishes and stands for the history of Australia's wine industry while simultaneously drawing on, and giving tangible expression to, archetypes, narratives, and coded symbols of important national myths.

The theoretical positioning of the icon must begin from a wide-ranging perspective. Within the realm of popular culture, characterized by the intensifying speed and volume of cultural flows to which we are exposed and of which we are expected to be competently aware, cultural brokers such as magazines, and other institutions—including national libraries (for example, the U.S. Library of Congress) and media corporations (such as the U.S. media conglomerate Forbes Media)—devote much attention to amateur cultural histories promoting the "superlativization" of experience reflected in the "top ten" lists of people, objects, places, events, and media, from films to albums. Each item on such a list can be taken to be "iconic" of a certain time or place in recent history. Within popular culture, the number of self-proclaimed iconic objects also multiplies quickly, with the interests of brands and corporations clearly served by such proselytizing.

Many consumers enjoy the mobilizing effects of this talk of icons, as it either affirms their choices and thus assuages their consumption anxieties, or alternately offers them a chance for symbolic maneuver by rejecting and rallying against an object's spurious claims to iconicity. Awash in a forest of objects—some in an ascendancy phase of an icon's lifecycle and bound for iconicity, others in an expiration phase and on the path to cultural extinction—we play in and among their surfaces as one way of finding some "depth" (Alexander 2008a). In social theory, at the meeting point of allied areas of research within consumption studies, material culture studies, consumer research studies, and aesthetics, new questions about the nature of iconicity can help to generate richer theories of objectualization and mediation. Bringing the object into any theory of sociality, theories of the icon challenge the empty materialism and productionist quality of much modern thought and invite recognition of the role of object aesthetics in symbolizing and mediating human action (Alexander 2008a).

In this chapter, our analysis of the Grange wine begins with the discursive and narrative construction of the object: the imaginative mapping of the wine experience. Here we differentiate a number of interested groups that contribute to its elevation as a supreme expression of not only a particular type of Australian wine, but *the* one supreme wine: the producers who wish to maintain brand value; the critics and connoisseurs who appraise and adjudicate; and the collectors and consumers whose practices include, but are in no way limited to or necessarily tend towards the drinking of the wine. For example, Penfolds offers clinics that educate owners in how to cellar and conserve the wine, ostensibly promoting wine connoisseurship as a type of craft as well as providing a location dedicated to measuring, amplifying, and exchanging the cultural energy contained in the wine. In addition, we use historical material from the manufacturer, Penfolds, and various other media texts to show how the wine's iconicity draws on a reserve of shared myths of Australian nationhood. Using the wine production categories of "old world" and "new world" as a way of understanding Australia's "youth" as a nation, Grange finds its iconic origins in its capacity to dismiss the techniques and established traditions of wine making. We also draw upon texts by critics such as Robert Parker Jr., analyzing the language used by these critics to describe the wine's aesthetic surface and thus mapping the terrain of vocabularies of iconic engagement. The choice of an iconic wine over an art object allows us to expand the study of iconicity into the intimate realm of sensate consumption, extending visual and semiotic explorations of iconicity to include embodied sensations. Moreover, the example of wine allows us to consider the historical construction of an icon through the myriad discursive and material accretions that ultimately culminate in the realization of its iconic status.

ICONS AND CONTEMPORARY CULTURE

Within theories of materiality, there are two master schemes that direct how theories of the icon as object can be constructed. On the one hand, there is the idea that objects are about prosaic, material engagements; they are opportunities for mundane, embodied modes of experience that reflect modernity's logic of rationalization and de-magicalization. The theoretical bedrock of this view is in Karl Marx's theory of the commodity: any commodity is the same as any other commodity, different only in terms of its market price, the market point at which it can be traded (Alexander 2008b). The second is that objects are cultural categories materialized: they sublate and then make tangible and handleable the moral, emotive, and aesthetic realms. Articulated in Durkheimian terms, in order to express our ideas to others and ourselves, we need to attach those ideas to the material things that we take to symbolize them. Such objects become self-extensions (Belk 1988), opportunities for the subject to externalize its being (Miller 1987).

These theoretical antipodes, which pit an emptied-out, technologized conception of materiality against cultural conceptions, are evident once again in more recent theoretical discourses. In actor-network approaches to objects—new studies of objects as "actants," inspired by ideas of relationality and pragmatics—the "material" element has been the subject of much research and theoretical interest, often at the expense of the "culture" aspects. What comes first are the material interlinkages of person and object, rather than questions of meaning, narrative, and interpretation. Against this recent perspective we have the now consolidated tradition of the "new" material culture studies, best exemplified in the work of Daniel Miller (1987, 2008), Igor Kopytoff (1986), Arjun Appadurai (1986), and its newer proponents (Money 2008; Woodward 2001, 2007). This is a nomenclature term for a variety of disciplinary approaches to objects and materiality that put questions of meaning, manipulation, and symbolization at the center of person–object engagements. Writing objects into a theory of culture, material culture studies points to how material things are integral to doing cultural work, not just pragmatically but via processes of symbolic extension and symbolization, as well as processes whereby cultural categories become realized in material form. It is from this point of understanding—where objects are realized as cultural categories, rather than merely exchangeable objects—that we can begin to consider the nature of iconicity.

Jeffrey C. Alexander (2008b: 782), following Sigmund Freud as an entry point into his discussion of iconicity, defines the icon as a "symbolic condensation," a thing that holds within its material form a cultural, moral meaning. To be iconic, an object must be culturally ascendant within particular communities or cultural networks and, paradoxically, pointing to an icon's taken-for-granted status as both the supreme object of a particular class and as concrete expression of a collective representation, it must be known to be an iconic thing without consciously knowing

(Alexander 2008b: 782). Moreover, an icon must—as Roland Barthes (1957) says of the mythological objects he surveyed—point beyond itself to larger mythologies and widely held, cherished beliefs to the extent that, within various communities, an icon materially symbolizes consensually held, foundational cultural values (Holt 2004). Beyond being a concrete distillation of collective values, icons also have a special performative power: a capacity to stir up and cultivate a type of restlessness, representing and reminding people of desires, anxieties, tensions, and subconscious wishes. Then, almost as if by magic, icons resolve such subconscious currents through breakthrough, ritualized performances—typically, though not always, within media spaces—which both tap into and stimulate these cultural values, anxieties, and desires, and then simultaneously suggest a solution to them (Holt 2004).

One of the features of semiotically and materially saturated late-modern life is that a great range of objects can become iconic. Certainly, an important aspect of iconicity refers to objects widely regarded to be at the pinnacle of any cultural field, but this process of becoming iconic may occur within varied cultural spaces across the cultural spectrum. The capability to confer iconicity does not just reside with powerful or elite cultural groups. It is often quite the opposite, as Douglas Holt (2004) points out: the cultural efficacy that underpins iconicity is borne in populist, everyday texts that are taken to authentically bear out widely held values. As a consequence, we can surmise that iconicity is also a status conferred by a process of consensus-making within a cultural field by various interested actors who form a collective sense of its value. The so-called iconic qualities of an object are the product of meaning and sense-making processes within a cultural group, which by a series of many small acts in conjunction with various integral texts and performances elevate an object as a supreme expression of a particular type or class of objects. Furthermore, icons must have influence outside their immediate cultural sphere—an icon must be appreciated by connoisseurs and amateurs alike. Thus, in the case of the wine considered here, it is not only serious wine drinkers who know about Grange but Australians generally. Thus the icon does not need to be directly, materially experienced, and is only occasionally sighted and rarely touched. Yet it is known not just within particular groups, but across the cultural spectrum as preeminent, a material container of cultural power, authenticity, and authority.

THEORIZING THE ICON: TRAJECTORIES OF ASCENDANCY AND EXPIRATION, NARRATIVE, AND PRAGMATIC MODES

Attention to the processes of making iconicity allow us to track the fate of particular objects through cultural space. The fragmented, pluralized and excessive nature of contemporary culture is "post-postmodern," yet it is still saturated by opportunities for cultural distinction, self-construction, and play. Seen in the context of such cultural changes, the idea of the icon as a universal symbol needs some revision. Studying the iconic allows us to explore the ways in which some objects attract continuously high levels of praise or esteem within culture over time, and become elevated within culture to symbolize a broader community value. At the same time, the opposite process can occur—objects can descend back into the mass of cultural goods, lose their cultural efficacy, become anachronistic, and eventually be just plain ignored. There is a definite life cycle of the icon, involving movement from the edges to the center of culture and eventually back out again, with phases of emergence, ascendancy, primacy, and then a downward part of the cycle involving descendancy and expiration. All icons must have such a life cycle, though the cycles vary in duration and velocity. An object that seems to be at the absolute core of a culture's values will not seem that way forever; there is always a turn toward anachronism and irrelevance. So, in relation to iconic status, objects are always in process, and such processes reflect the apportionment of cultural value. This tells us how iconic objects attach to larger myths or create new ones. The icon needs a story to be told on its behalf and to then represent that story, entangling itself with other cultural events, ideas, or things and drawing on their power, but then proselytizing on behalf of these other myths and indeed adding to their stories (Holt 2004).

One of the basic insights of recent conceptualizations of material culture has been the idea that objects have "social lives" (Appadurai 1986) or "biographies" (Kopytoff 1986). In modern culture, where the meanings and interpretations attached to images are relatively flexible and fluid across social spaces, objects have careers or trajectories whereby their meanings for consumers change over time and space. Object icons thus have an inherently mobile and mutable quality, and are constructed not just by their materiality but by stories, narratives, and myths. Some objects ascend to higher status and are thrust along the path to iconicism, and others move toward marginality or mere usefulness—or indeed disappear completely from not just the cultural space but the production line. Kopytoff (1986) has been the pioneer of this emphasis on the cultural mobility of objects. He points out this may involve objects shifting in and out of commodity status. That is, at some stage of their lives objects are defined primarily by their relation to a monetary or exchange value, which establishes them as "commodities," while at other times—generally some time after an economic exchange has taken place—they become "de-commodified" as they are incorporated—or "subjectified" (Miller 1987) and "singularized" (Kopytoff 1986)—by people according to personal meanings, relationships, or rituals. Yet the trajectories and biographies of objects are not just related to their commodity status, but to more complex meanings and interpretations given to them by individuals, restricted taste communities (such as those who appreciate the avant-garde, or fans of a particular pop group or television show), and larger social groups. The underlying assumption of this argument is that, in complex, differentiated, pluralistic societies inhabited by omnivorous, voracious, knowledgeable, and flexible consumers, the rules or criteria for discriminating and classifying the worth of material culture are diffuse and variable. As Kopytoff (1986) states:

> the public culture offers discriminating classifications here no less than it does in small-scale societies. But these must constantly compete with classifications by individuals and by small networks, whose members also belong to other networks expounding yet other value systems. The discriminating criteria that each individual or network can bring to the task of classification are extremely varied. Not only is

every individual's or network's version of exchange spheres idiosyncratic and different from those of others, but it also shifts contextually and biographically as the originators perspectives, affiliations and interests shift. The result is a debate not only between people and groups, but within each person as well. (178–79)

Dick Hebdige's (1988) essay on the networks, or production and consumption meanings and discourses, that construct the life of the Italian scooter is a seminal illustration of how commodities have such trajectories. The first scooters were the Vespa, manufactured by Piaggio in 1946, and the Lambretta, produced by Innocenti in 1947. The scooters were originally targeted to European women and to youths in general, who were the new, emergent consumers of the era. The scooters offered mobility and freedom, and were marketed as an object that contained possible "emancipatory" powers for young women. In 1950s Britain, the scooter acquired a strong association with notions of "Italianness," and continental style and sophistication, which for design- and aesthetics-conscious British consumers symbolized "everything that was chic and modern" (Hebdige 1988: 106). The 1953 romantic comedy film *Roman Holiday*, starring Audrey Hepburn and Gregory Peck, became an important visual representation of the scooter's cultural cachet. In a famous scene, which promises to cement the romantic interests of the unlikely royal and commoner pairing, Peck and Hepburn travel gaily and stylishly through the iconic urban scenery of Rome on their Vespa scooter. Immersed within the idealized images of Rome, the Italian scooter becomes a symbol of freedom, romance, and elegance. In the late 1950s and 1960s, the scooter was appropriated by mod youth as an identity marker, which flexibly fitted with their sartorial and musical preferences and aspirations. Within this subculture, customization and accessorization of the scooter followed, as did the establishment of sartorial rules for scooter wear and an associated correct way of riding the scooter. Turning to more recent phases in the biography of the scooter, scooters remain associated with youth—particularly inner-city consumers—due to their economy, size, and mobility. The scooter example demonstrates that icons need not cling to the same story or narrative for their long-term survival and symbolic efficacy. In fact, the longevity of an icon comes in part from its ability to endure cultural changes and generate evolving meanings across multiple cultural times and spaces—an icon has the capacity to write over and stamp culture with its own imperatives. We can see this in the sphere of popular music through a well-known example. The pop music singer Madonna is considered to be an iconic performer in part because she performs multiple symbolic self-reinventions that apparently maintain a core identity, but freshen up and modify stylistic elements that suggest both her endurance and up-to-dateness. Interestingly, Madonna's apparent displacement by more powerful and culturally relevant pop icons confirms the centrality of her core identity in that they effectively pursue symbolic self-reinvention on her behalf. Thus, one measure of iconicity may be read in the various ways in which Britney Spears, Shakira, Christina Aguilera, and most recently Lady Gaga recapitulate phases of Madonna's career. In this way, we can see how cycles of decline and ascendancy nevertheless maintain certain continuities necessary to the maintenance of the category of, in this instance, pop iconicity.

DISCURSIVE AND NONDISCURSIVE THEORIES OF THE ICON

How are objects made into icons? There are two broad schools of thought on this. The first focuses on the role of narrative, event, and performance in constructing the meaning of an object, along the way building and affirming its iconic status. Objects acquire cultural meaning and power in the context of stories or narratives that locate, value, and render them visible and important. Without such narrative storylines and events that performatively crystallize meanings—be they accounts spoken by individuals or those that hold more general sway within a population, such as a discourse—an object is rendered less powerful within a culture. The way objects acquire their cultural meaning is partly a matter of their material form and its affordances, but an object's meaning is also created within local settings, where participants construct a social life for an object through offering active, creative narratives. Likewise, an object's power is also partly acquired through the culture-wide stories or myths it incarnates. Thus, an important starting principle is that stories and narratives hold an object together, giving it cultural meaning. Rom Harré (2002) proposes a number of principles for theorizing objects, which put narrative at the center of meaning creation. Two of these are that:

1. An object is transformed from a piece of stuff definable independently of any story line into a social object by its embedment in a narrative.
2. Material things have magic powers only in the contexts of the narratives in which they are embedded (25).

Thus there is a relational quality to the entanglement of social action with things and words, which is also summed up nicely by Dick Pels, Kevin Hetherington, and Frédéric Vandenberghe (2002): "Objects need symbolic framings, storylines and human spokespersons in order to acquire social lives; social relationships and practices in turn need to be materially grounded in order to gain temporal and spatial endurance" (11). Against this model, which suggests it is story lines that elevate objects within cultural space, Alexander (2008a, 2008b) urges us to go back to the sensuous physicality or materiality of the object to look for the sources of its iconicity. He states: "The sensuous surface of things seems more important than simply a means to the end of meaning. Is it not the sensuous surface of stuff that allows us to see, hear, and touch their narrative bindings?" (2008b: 784). Alexander's (2008a) theory of iconicity models the exchanges between social actors and objects. He shows how objects afford movement from their surfaces to their moral depth via a form of "immersion." Immersion involves a dual process: one called "subjectification," where people are seemingly able to draw an object into themselves, transforming it from object to subject, and allowing it to take on a life whereby one no longer sees the object itself, but "oneself, one's projections, one's convictions and beliefs" (7). Simultaneously, through a process called "materialization," a person is drawn into an object, effectively becoming it, or that for which it is seen to stand. Via immersion, what exists is not an object, nor a person, but a oneness of material and human, united by a material-affective—rather than merely mechanical or pragmatic—connection. Such connections with consumed, material objects are the basis for the

performance and learning of norms and ideals and—through the use of typifications and iconic representations—the foundation for our social life. At the heart of
these dynamics of immersion is the *aesthetic surface* of an object—rather than any
narrative constructing it—attracting us and then affording us the opportunity to
look for, attach, and even construct moral meanings in its materiality.

THE SURFACE OF THE OBJECT

Alexander (2008) argues that it is in coming into contact with an object—either
physically or visually—that we have the possibility of being drawn most strongly
into its depth, to its symbolic dimensions. Notwithstanding the fact that, as Colin
Campbell (1987) points out, much object engagement is actually imaginative and
anticipatory—involving the preparatory stimulation of mental faculties of arousal
and interest manifested in daydreaming or fantasizing through various scripts and
scenes pertaining to consumption objects—it is in direct engagements that we can
concretely test our ideas about the value and status of an object. For example, in
seeing the red Ferrari before us, we can hear the deep hum of its engine, admire the
striking finish of its paint and the form and detail of its design, and observe how
it sits on the road. We get information about its driver, we see it speed away—such
engagements confirm our ideas about a red Ferrari, or its driver. In standing before
Leonardo da Vinci's *Mona Lisa*, we might feel underwhelmed, or deeply touched.
The nature of our reactions is somewhat irrelevant—presumably being a product of
our own cultural location involving quotients of knowledge and attitudes, as well
as aspects of touristic context. The point is that in coming into proximity with an
object, possibly directly touching an object, or at least visually playing within its
surfaces at close range, we are drawn closer to an object's aura and thus reminded
directly of its power.

The idea that we find the meaning and purpose of consumption in direct material engagements has also become an important theme in recent theories of consumption. The point is that it is not so much about having, or desiring to have, but
through various peformativities of "doing" that we encounter the most powerful
capacities of consumption to engage us via the materialized networks in which we
participate. We find meaning through coordinated pragmatic, physical, and haptic engagements with objects, and it is through such embodied engagements that
we both find and construct the meanings of consumption. With wine—like any
drink—the case for such a pragmatics of materiality is clear. We encounter a drink's
odor or perfume in our nostrils, its texture is experienced, its color is discerned, and
we feel all of these aspects of the drink on our palates as it passes our lips. Our reaction to the range of drinks we encounter is shaped by our conditioned—although
educable—palates, our previous experiences, and the cultural context of drinking.
For many drinks that we experience routinely—water and milk, for example—we
notice only when our expectations for flavor or quality are breached. For wine,
we enter a different realm of engagement shaped entirely by the way in which the
consumption of wine is culturally and aesthetically fashioned. Wine is possibly the
drink that is most mysterious to many people, but at the same time it is overdetermined by mythical qualities of the type identified by Barthes (1957), and thus also

demands evidence of knowledge and connoisseurship. It is to this set of problems that we turn through our consideration of the case of Grange, an iconic Australian wine.

Penfolds' Grange: History, Narrative, Myth

In this section of the chapter, we explore three aspects of Grange as an iconic object. First, we look at the way the experience of Grange has been imaginatively mapped by its producer, Penfolds, as well as by critics and by consumers. Second, we use historical material from Penfolds, together with various other media texts, to show how iconicity draws on a reserve of shared myths of Australian nationhood and plays up against established categories of the "old world" and the "new world." We also draw upon texts by critics such as Robert Parker Jr., analyzing the language used by these critics to describe the wine's aesthetic surface and allowing us to map the vocabularies of iconic engagement. We argue in this chapter for a practical, material, and discursive theory of the icon, which is sensitive to the ways in which engagements between people and objects are bought into being by institutions, practices, and narratives. Though it is popularly understood as a magical object, the icon is an accretion of cultural meanings reliant on materialized sets of practices, powered by discourses and narratives, and united with corporate interests and other powerful cultural figures; the icon is an apotheosis of aestheticized capitalism.

Australian wine finds its origins in religious observance, with the first colonial grape plantings yielding fruit destined for the communion goblet. By 1844, Dr. Christopher Rawson Penfolds began making curative wines for his patients from French vine cuttings planted on the outskirts of Adelaide. The accepted practice at this time, and for nearly a century thereafter, was to focus production on brandy and fortified wines such as sherry and port. So-called dry table wines were not considered commercially significant, and played a minor role in Australian viniculture up to 1945. The foundation story of Penfolds' Grange Hermitage occurs against this backdrop of protracted solecism, of a narrowly conceived wine industry servicing the needs of an immature and untutored national palate. Max Schubert breaks this frame. The story of Schubert that we have gleaned from Penfolds' documentation and various popular wine histories bears out the narrative frames used to understand his career and the wine he made famous. The first thread of this narrative emphasizes Schubert's long personal history with the company, and his rise through the ranks from lowly assistant to ascendant, serious winemaker. Originally hired as a messenger boy at Penfolds in the 1930s, Schubert had by the early 1950s assumed a position of considerable influence as one of the company's chief winemakers. In 1950, he toured the Bordeaux region, taking note of techniques he might employ on his return to his Magill Estate. It was here that he produced the first experimental vintage of Grange Hermitage, a Shiraz modeled after the long-lived wines of the Rhone Valley. When making the wine, Schubert not only relied on what he had learned in Bordeaux, but also drew on Porto methods of multiple estate sourcing, thus placing him in the unusual professional position of apparently honoring French winemaking practice while simultaneously ignoring concerns for *terroir*, a French word referring to the local characteristics of the soil, terrain, and climate which are held to contribute to the unique characteristics of a wine. However, it was subsequently revealed that much of what Schubert had observed in Bordeaux was far from typical, and in some aspects represented spontaneous innovations following an unexpectedly large vintage. Each component of this narrative—from the studied indifference to market tastes, through to the mix of deliberate and accidental rejection of old-world methods—contributes to the emerging understanding of Grange as a profoundly novel wine borne from iconoclasm. In broad terms, Schubert's preliminary work set the pattern for the ongoing production: batch sourcing superior grapes from old, low-yield vines; blending Shiraz with small amounts of Cabernet Sauvignon (if required) to lend structure; and aging in new American, as opposed to French, oak. Here, with the suggestion of Schubert's strong personality and nonconformist vision, the elements of winemaker as maverick begin to cement.

The first release of Schubert's Grange blend was poorly received for reasons that seem obvious in retrospect: the wine not only flew in the face of prevailing tastes, but also required further bottle aging in order to suggest its potential. Most damning of all, the wine's intensity of flavor was perceived as a kind of rogue "dry port." In the face of the negative critical response, Penfolds' management ordered Schubert to abandon the project. Legendarily—and here we must frankly acknowledge that this narrative assumes the pleasing shape of myth—Schubert ignored this edict from above and continued work on the wine in secret, going so far as to store his labors behind false walls until such time as the maturing bottles had begun to reveal their true promise. When these wines finally started to receive their due recognition from critics, Penfolds directed Schubert to resume work, at which point—coup de théâtre—he revealed the fruits of his underground labors. This foundation narrative of Grange—which seldom fails to appear in some form in introductory, evaluative, or summative writings about the wine—bears the traces, albeit gracefully, of considerable effort: national myth, chronologies, and other cultural materials have been shaped towards literary ends—the revelation of gratifying ironies, dramatic reversals, and heroic triumph. Whether icons can exist or be perceived outside of these discursive networks is an important question; we only observe that in this example they rarely do (cf. D. J. De Pree's visit to the millwright's widow—now part of Herman Miller lore and as expressive in its design ethos as the lines of an Eames chair).

The narrative inextricability of Schubert's status as a nonconformist and visionary winemaker from that of Grange as an object introduces an element of what might be termed *"bio-terroir,"* where the wine object expresses not the soil and microclimates of individual vineyards, but the man who labored to produce it—as Penfolds' marketing imagery vividly testifies. One of many images of the near-ubiquitous Schubert shows him with the outline of grapes watermarked over his head in a condensed image that seems to borrow equally from myths of Bacchus, god of the grape, and Zeus, who delivered life directly from his head. In the construction of Grange as a new-world contender, the narrative of Schubert's *bio-terroir* neatly supplements the lack of traditional *terroir*, resolves the institutional paradox of a rare wine emerging from what is now the vast multinational Southcorp corporation, and makes a virtue of improvisatory youthfulness (on both the personal and national stage), unhampered by the burdens and strictures of old-world viniculture.

From 1957 onwards, Grange (the word "Hermitage" was dropped following French legal action in the 1970s) received a string of national and international awards. It is now routinely, although not incontestably, viewed as Australia's finest wine: supreme, quintessential, indispensable, and iconic. As such, its symbolic reach is much wider than the expected circuits of wine trade, collection, and appreciation. Grange appears as a center of eventfulness; it is a thing that spawns other things. In the media, Grange may appear as a symbol of wealth and lifestyle rather than as an expensive wine with desirable features. The popular Australian newspapers' deployment of the stereotypical working-class Australian places Grange far outside the reach of the represented audience, and accordingly it is shown as a symbol of the "other-half's" outrageous and decadent lifestyle. This is in contrast to previous decades, when the myth seemed to revolve more around the wine itself as a symbol of Australian winemaking expertise. While media accounts of the wine certainly acknowledge the newsworthiness of vintage releases as well as speculate on market values over time, they also consider iconoclastic treatment of the wine as a means of understanding the dubious lifestyle choices of sports stars, corrupt politicians, and business people. There is a rich vein of material devoted to the misuses of the wine, sometimes referred to in ways that comically expose the pollution of its iconic status. By referring to its expense, these stories frequently associate it with a rich playboy culture of businessmen, politicians, and sports stars. For example, coverage of the recent high-profile divorce proceedings between a millionaire tuna fisherman and his second wife lingered over the revelation that bottles of Grange were either punitively or unknowingly emptied into a humble Bolognese sauce.

Aside from superior pasta and the deep pleasures of schadenfreude, what does the wine afford? What does it mean to possess something that apotheosizes an entire category of sensual experience? Broadly speaking, iconic wine collection permits a kind of temporal luxuriance, an attenuated form of consumption of an object that logically would exist only in one of two states—consumed and unconsumed. The iconic wine exists in a hinterland between these two poles. When the bottle is finished, the wine enters into a canon of superlative experience against which all other wines are to be judged. This suggests an intriguing form of gustatory extension. While the wine has long departed from the palate, much less the body, its trace is secured in an archival sensorium of wine criticism, in defiance of the evanescent qualities of the body's sense organs. Wine writing serves an important function in this regard, as a supplementary transcription of ephemeral sensory experience. This is also where the deeper metaphysical claims of the wine find articulate voice, as well being considered in a comparative and adjudicative light.

THE REBIRTH OF THE CLINIC: TECHNOLOGIES OF CARING FOR GRANGE

Yet this capacity to meaningfully retain the postconsumed icon in the form of evaluative wine writing has a more literal counterpart in Grange culture. The investor or collector who purchases a bottle may meet other like-minded people at one of the regular "Grange Clinics."

An important aspect of consuming Grange is the way ownership offers access to an exclusive club—the "Grange Clinic"—which periodically assesses the quality and health of aged Granges. At these clinics, those who purchase a bottle can subject it to a range of technical and cultural evaluations, and extend their consumption experience. Under carefully controlled conditions, a small amount of the wine is extracted and sampled by an expert as well as by the owner. The missing portion is refilled with the current release vintage, the bottle is recorked, gassed, and sealed, and the owner receives a score report on the health of the wine and its future aging potential. Wines that have not fared well are stripped of their identity as Grange, and issued with plain labels and corks. The purpose of this ritual is twofold. First, it gives important feedback to the owner about the health of his or her individual bottle. In doing so, it gives a report of confidence that the wine is of good and pristine condition, effectively conferring upon it "blue chip" long-term investment status. It thus involves a constant revisioning of the value (health) of the object at hand. Both the owner and the object are evaluated in a process overseen by technical experts. The process has implications for both the object and the consumer—are both judged? If the wine is faulty, is the fault yours? The result is that if bottles are judged inferior, and thus they are unlikely to last long into the future, the owner of the bottle may choose to "drink now." This move is not just part of Penfolds' customer care relations, but performs the important function of protecting the economic integrity of the Grange second-ary and investment market. More than this, it protects the Penfolds brand, given that Grange is the best-known symbol of a brand that houses a family of related Penfolds brands across a range of price points, down to as little as AUD$10.00. At the other end of the consumption process, owners of Grange are brought into elaborate systems of craft and care for their purchase. Though the clinic represents a stage of technical evaluation, where both the object and its owner are subjected to scrutiny, both before and after the clinic, the owner must make appropriate, practical attempts to protect the future drinkability and salability of his or her purchase. This encourages various types of tending and practical care—a type of craft of care—which constitute an important aspect of the consumption experi-ence for wine enthusiasts and collectors alike, who can find elaborate ways to store their collection and extend their wine storage experience by taking wine out into the world. The silent duration of cellarage is interrupted and enlivened by purposeful and communal activity.

MATERIALITY AND DESCRIPTIONS OF THE IMMATERIAL

Most wines are drunk within a few hours of their purchase, and it is sufficient in most circles to remark generally on the wine in terms of approval and disapproval, possibly with a few rhetorical embellishments. With Grange, we have a further complication, however: despite the fact that relatively few Australians have tasted Grange (we do not have any statistical evidence here, but are quite sure it is a tiny minority), what is "known" is that it is a famous Australian wine, the benchmark for the Shiraz style in Australia, and an object that points to the whole Australian wine industry. We know this in part by its mythical qualities, which we elaborated earlier in this chapter, but we also may know it by other material signals. The first is the aesthetic dimensions of Penfolds' branding, directly communicated by the Bordeaux-style label and its distinctive fancy, cursive font, written in a claret-red color on creamy white paper in a style that has remained since the original vintage. Understood today as conservative, and even "antidesign" and "unhip," the label draws its power principally from its longevity, but it also has a retro styling that some would see as attractive. The label cites and acknowledges Grange's original winemaker, Max Schubert, not only suggesting the history of the brand, but also referring to the myths associated with Schubert. The bottle shape is important too—the Bordeaux-style shape refers to the famous French wine-producing region, and once again highlights Grange's Old World heritage. The label, however, tells us a different story, reinforcing the maverick status of the wine by reciting the story of Schubert, the "creator" of Grange, referring to his time spent in Europe learning old-world winemaking techniques, but also reinforcing his fierce independence and innovation as a serious maker of Australian wines.

Critics must play an important role in communicating the qualities of wines. In the case of Grange, they offer a coded language for understanding the nature of the wine, but they also make it available to consumers well before it is ready to drink. In effect, wine critics make a predictive reading of the wine, projecting its qualities during phases of maturation. Moreover, in the case of Grange, their scoring is not seen as evidence of its greatness, but rather as one additional evaluation of a vintage that justifies the wine's inclusion in the canon of "great" wines. In the case of wine criticism, it is the nose and palate of the taster critic that serious drinkers must learn to know, interpret, and trust, for this becomes a proxy for the wine itself. In lieu of being able to drink it themselves, consumers cede adjudicative experience to experts, who look into the future on the basis of what they find now. To understand the structures of wine critics' appreciation of Grange, we undertook an analysis of the words, codes, and conventions used by the world's most fêted and influential wine critic, Robert M. Parker Jr., to describe various Grange vintages. Initially, we note an obvious aspect of Parker Jr.'s tasting notes—his typical progression through facts about the wine's blend of grapes, its vintage, aspects of harvesting, and any related personal notes, to dimensions of wine color and flavors, the degree of tannins, and finally a "drinking recommendation." In relation to Grange, the recurring adjectives used by Parker Jr. across all tastings are "blackberries," "cherries," "earth," "camphor," "crème de cassis," and "chocolate."

To explore the communicative capacities of critics a little further, we took a sample of the widely perceived "classic" vintages of Grange, which receive high tasting scores, and also the acknowledged "poor" vintages, which receive relatively lower scores. Taking this basket of vintages, we then performed a basic textual analysis of Parker Jr.'s descriptions of each Grange vintage, looking for key discursive and conceptual markers. Interestingly, Parker Jr.'s notes on Grange articulate an element of the binary aesthetic relationship of surface and depth (Alexander 2008a). On the one hand, the high-scoring classic Grange vintages are noted by Parker Jr. for being "massive" and having "huge structure and massive concentration," while at the same time they are often described as having qualities of being "nuanced," "open-knit," "seductive," and "voluptuous." Such descriptions play on a binary of scale and sheer mass in conjunction with notions of finesse, nuance, quality, and tenor. These schemes resemble the elemental structuring features of iconic engagement, described by Alexander (2008a) as the interplay of surface and depth within aesthetic objects. According to this scheme, a key feature of iconicity is this affordance of movement between an object's aesthetic surfaces and its depths of meaning, which is a product of its aesthetic form. Grange's surface features are described as granite-like, massive, and huge, but at the same time they are not seen as monolithic; rather, these strong surfaces are capable of being penetrated and found by the wine's tasters to be nuanced, open-knit, and seductive. When we come to consider the Grange vintages that receive poor scores from Parker Jr., they are described in ways that resist this capacity to delve into the intimate depths of the wine. Thus the relatively poorer Grange vintages are described as "closed down," "unforthcoming," "attenuated," and having a "very hard, angular, austere style." These are all phrases that suggest consumers of these relatively inferior vintages of the wine will find it difficult to penetrate the wine's depths, as it is "built" in such a way as to resist the drinker's desire to intimately find the "depths" of the wine. The best examples of Grange thus successfully fuse might, scale, and size with an inviting subtlety and exquisite form, a feature discovered and confirmed by the cultural critic Parker Jr., deemed to have the necessary qualifications to make such an assessment.

CONCLUSION

Our case study suggests that iconic objects emerge historically, performatively, materially, and discursively. The wine we have discussed is the result of countless accretions of events, images, and actions. The icon we take to be an historical accretion, a type of assemblage. We have also suggested that the icon wine emerges from performances that are both mundane and significant. It rests within frames of symbolic action that are visible and witnessed, and that provide evidence of status. The icon is also sensed materially, through senses of touch, sight, taste, and smell, providing direct feedback of an icon's quality. Even when it cannot be directly touched or tasted by many, as in the case of a very expensive wine such as Grange, an icon is recognized nonetheless. Once an icon, it can effectively perform its iconicity from a distance—such is its power. Finally, the icon is constructed discursively. The narrative it creates draws from and then recirculates the particular myths from which it draws strength. The icon is thus at the center of myth: it draws upon the powerful cultural storylines it needs for its existence and meaning, then in turn engages and gives material expression and form to these myths. Without such myths, the icon may just be another object within a particular series. What allows it to rise from the serial object is its relationship to the productive center of myth. The cyclical rise and fall of given icons in turn allows for the continual renewal of cultural myths without appearing subject to the historically contingent vagaries of fashion or taste. Thus icons may ascend or descend over time, but myths apparently remain unchanged.

In summary, we suggest that the iconic wine emerges within a mutually constitutive constellation of activities, behaviors, and narrative forms. In this light, the iconic wine always exceeds the restricted range of meanings it might express as a less exalted bottle. Thus the exchange of Grange as a gift (itself a supreme index of generosity) can bear the symbolic weight of significant life transitions—birth, graduation, marriage, retirement, and so on. In other contexts, Grange's public use and misuse, as recounted in the media and elsewhere, abbreviate forms of social knowledge about affluence from the gaucheries of sporting figures to the routinization of luxury associated with celebrity lifestyles. Yet, for those with an interest in Grange as wine, a range of technical, historical, and evaluative meanings from other sources—notably the wine producer and critics—comes into play. Whether in concert or dispute, these engaged meditations contribute to the excavation, description, and mapping of the wine's metaphysical depths. Cumulatively, and at different intensities of influence and persistence, these disparate elements of myth, narrative, sense impression, and representation constitute what we understand to be iconic.

REFERENCES

Alexander, J. C. 2008a. "Iconic Consciousness: The Material Feeling of Meaning." *Environment and Planning D: Society and Space* 26: 782–94.
———. 2008b. "Iconic Experience in Art and Life: Surface/Depth Beginning with Giacometti's *Standing Woman.*" *Theory, Culture and Society* 25 (5): 1–19.
Appadurai, A. 1986. "Introduction: Commodities and the Politics of Value." In *The Social Life of Things: Commodities in Cultural Perspective*, edited by A. Appadurai, 3–63. Melbourne: Cambridge University Press.
Barthes, R. 1957. *Mythologies.* Translated by Annette Lavers. London: Vintage.
Belk, R. W. 1988. "Possessions and the Extended Self." *The Journal of Consumer Research* 15: 139–65.
Campbell, C. 1987. *The Romantic Ethic and the Spirit of Modern Consumerism.* New York: Blackwell.
Harré, R. 2002. "Material Objects in Social Worlds." *Theory, Culture and Society* 19 (5/6): 23–33.
Hebdige, D. 1988. *Hiding in the Light: On Images and Things.* New York: Routledge,.
Holt, D. 2004. *How Brands Become Icons: The Principles of Cultural Branding.* Boston: Harvard Business School Press.
Kopytoff, I. 1986. "The Cultural Biography of Things: Commoditization as Process." In *The Social Life of Things: Commodities in Cultural Perspective*, edited by A. Appadurai, 64–94. Cambridge, UK: Cambridge University Press.
Miller, D. 1987. *Material Culture and Mass Consumption.* Oxford: Blackwell.
———. 2008. *The Comfort of Things.* London: Polity Press.
Money, A. 2008. "Material Culture and the Living Room: The Appropriation and Use of Goods in Everyday Life." *Journal of Consumer Culture* 7 (3): 355–77.
Pels, D., K. Hetherington, and F. Vandenberghe. 2002. "The Status of the Object: Performances, Mediations, and Techniques." *Theory, Culture and Society* 19 (5/6): 1–21.
Woodward, I. 2001. "Domestic Objects and the Taste Epiphany: A Resource for Consumption Methodology." *Journal of Material Culture* 6 (2): 115–36.
———. 2007. *Understanding Material Culture.* London: Sage.

CHAPTER 10

BECOMING ICONIC: THE CASES OF WOODSTOCK AND BAYREUTH

PHILIP SMITH

INTRODUCTION

In his *Elementary Forms of Religious Life* (1912), Émile Durkheim reflects at length on the role of ritual. Its purpose, he says, is to renew social bonds. This is achieved through the manipulation and invocation of sacred and profane symbols in situations involving intense, rhythmical, embodied actions such as music and dance. A current dispute in Durkheimian sociology concerns a matter of analytic primacy, in effect weighting either the first or the second part of the sentence you have just read. Scholarly attention was traditionally given to symbol content. Ritual is said to "work" because of tightly held, deeply meaningful beliefs. It is the close encounter with sacred icons, texts, and myths that generates ritual behaviors. These might in turn drive broader social outcomes such as solidarity, collective identity, and coordinated political action. More recently, critics have suggested that action comes before meaning. The argument here is that the content of symbolic belief systems is vague or contradictory, and whatever significance is present is not fully shared. Yet embodied ritual actions can still have effects. They generate emotional energy in the absence of meaning through the experience of bodily copresence and rhythmic alignment (Bellah 2005; Collins 2005). From unpromising beginnings arise those very same sociological outcomes of solidarity, identity, and action. Meanings exist, to be sure, but as the outcome of proximate activity. They emerge, it is said, from the interaction process. This argument against a strongly semiotic or hermeneutic version of the cultural turn is in essence a pragmatistic one. It goes back to William James and his claim that action produces affect, and that emotions are responses to physiological states. The position, to be sure, is ingenious as a counterintuitive and sociologically imaginative way of explaining ritual's force. Yet it does not quite do justice to a curious fact. Some ritual encounters become themselves highly charged symbols. They expand beyond their initial context to exert influence at distant points in space and time. These condensed clusters of meaning carry ritual effects with them through generations and over national borders. They intersect with other charged semiotic systems. People who have *never been present* at the ritual point of origin feel emotions, form their identities and shape their actions not from proximate engagement but rather with reference to second-hand but deeply meaningful generalized symbolic representations of the ritual act.

What we have just described is an arc from event to iconicity. Only a few embodied ritual encounters attain this status. One thinks, for example, of the Last Supper (a ritual meal that for the sake of argument we will assume really took place) or of Adolf Hitler's Nuremberg rallies (mass political rituals). The iconicity of such events, however, lies in more than just a field of stock visual representations, such as those of Leonardo da Vinci or Leni Riefenstahl. It is also, perhaps mostly, in the ability of these events to compress and express whole fields of myth and meaning, then to connect these to other discursive webs. Each of the famous images, be it on the wall in Santa Maria delle Grazie or the film stock of *Triumph of the Will*, offers merely a further fixing of an already condensed yet expansive cultural system. We might think of two types of iconicity at play in this process. These match the two principal dimensions we find in the *Oxford English Dictionary*. First, the icon can be "an image, figure or portrait." We might refer to this as "type one iconicity." It is the kind of iconicity that this edited volume is trying to theorize as an important aspect of cultural life. An iconic ritual might be expected to generate a fair number of these striking images that impact upon the visual field. Second, an icon can be "a person or thing regarded as a representative symbol, especially of a culture or movement." We can call this "type two iconicity." It is more strongly connected to myth and narrative, to language rather than to visual representation or mimesis. One might very loosely think of these two dictionary-defined modes of iconicity as those theorized by Charles Peirce and Roland Barthes, resemblance and metaphoric field respectively. Iconic power is magnified to the extent that these two dimensions, aesthetic or sensory surface and deep background representations, are understood as in alignment (Alexander 2008). The total iconicity of the ritual event is underwritten by the stability of the pact. This is between the foreground that is the immediate synchronic experience of "sensing" type one representations and a more epistemic, discursive, diachronic, myth-driven background of type two representations. The latter directs "perception" towards "meaning," and thence leads to interpretation rather than simply recognition.

In this chapter I would like to examine this theme with reference to a defined empirical domain—the music festival. I chose two contrasting cases, Woodstock and Bayreuth. Woodstock involved popular music, was a one-time event, and found itself somewhat unexpectedly iconic. Bayreuth by contrast is a "traditional" festival that runs every year. It is elitist and was fully intended by its myth-inspired founder, Richard Wagner, to be a sacred node in the wider national and aesthetic spheres. We will see that the cultural impact and social influence of neither festival can be explained simply with pragmatist theories about face-to-face encounters. Rather, to understand their force we need to explore a generalized iconic process.

WOODSTOCK

Woodstock remains today the single most iconic rock festival ever. It has been described by the leading music sociologist Andy Bennett as "the defining and last great moment of the 1960s" (Bennett 2004a: xiv). This status was due not only to what "really" happened but also to a process of narration and mythologization (Bennett 2004b). First, some reasonably uncontroversial facts to give a context: the event was held over four days in August 1969, and it featured many of the most important rock, blues, and folk music artists of its day; the venue was a rural area in upstate New York; between 300 thousand and half a million people attended; the weather was often rainy; there were problems with sanitation and transport; the crowd was mostly good natured; there was some nudity, drug taking, and public sex; most or many attending had a negative attitude towards the war in Vietnam. Another fact is that Woodstock was originally a business venture. It only became a free festival after the perimeter fence was cut and those without tickets flooded in.

How can we explain Woodstock's iconicity? The scale of the event and the number and quality of the performers and their performances were no doubt important. These are perhaps necessary but not sufficient for explaining: why Woodstock is in the *Dictionary of Cultural Literacy*; why the U.S. Postal Service issued a Woodstock stamp; why there is now a museum related to the event and a proliferation of Web sites; why other festivals copy the Woodstock model or try to make use of the name; and perhaps most important of all, why many of those who were not there wish so ardently that they had been.

For Woodstock to emerge as iconic, as a pivotal symbol in a cultural landscape, there had to be a complex narrative sifting and sorting of Woodstock's raw material. There are many possible Woodstocks that could be told. There were millions of positive and negative face-to-face encounters, ambivalent episodes, and idiosyncratic individual impressions. Inverting the logic of the pragmatists as they assault myth-based explanation, we might argue that it is these microdetails that are truly incoherent and without pattern. Unlike an anthill, we cannot build a myth from the simple accumulation or piling up of those grains of infinite variety. The experiences of half a million people must be variously ordered, aligned, rejected, and amplified. Only with the help of a cultural system can Woodstock come to have a structure of meaning, can Woodstock the event become "Woodstock" the iconic referent as we know it (for a parallel treatment of this theme, see Alexander 2002).

Put simply, we might think of Woodstock as the outcome of storytelling. Following the literary critic Northrop Frye, we can say that stories are shaped by genre logics. Each genre has certain properties with regard to plot and character. To radically simplify, in the case of Woodstock there was a rapid move out of low mimesis towards romantic myth. Low mimesis is the genre of "business as usual." Nothing much is at stake, humans are motivated by the ordinary range of material and ideal interests, powers of action are limited. In the mythic romance, however, events are epochal, action motivations are strongly idealized, and agents can bring about immense change. In romance, there is also often a movement away from disaster, problem, social disorganization, or fragmentation and towards solidarity and harmony. One can get a sense of this by thinking a little on the contrast between the British kitchen sink drama of the 1950s and a Barbara Cartland novel. At the end of the former, life goes on, usually in some compromised way. At the end of the latter, the idealist wins out—and we have a royal wedding. Woodstock the event became Woodstock the myth due to such a romantic scripting. Mundane realities of budget and squalor were forgotten, transcended, or written out of the story, even before images (type one iconicity) were circulating.

We can trace the early stages of this apotheosis in the work of the junior *New York Times* reporter Barnard Collier. Amazingly enough, he was the only journalist present in the initial hours of the event. The paper's expectations, clearly, had been for just a routine festival. The editorial staff pressured Collier for stories on logistical problems relating to traffic and for details of petty crime such as drug taking. Collier might also have been expected to comment on the music—this after all was an artistic event involving noted figures. Yet his reports soon came to indicate another possible interpretation—that this was a gathering of a very special kind. In his copy of August 14, we read first that "security officials reported at least two deaths and 4,000 people treated for injuries, illness and adverse drug reactions"; a little later that there was a "threat of bronchial disease and influenza," and further that "the state police said they had about 150 men on duty to help deal with the traffic in a 20-mile radius." So far, so bad. Yet Collier at the same time conjured an upward movement toward romance. He remarked the Arcadian image of camp-fires "that flickered around the hillside" in the natural amphitheatre. He quoted a youth who had experienced "an incredible unification." Respectable sources back this up. We find Dr. William Abruzzi, the chief medical officer of the festival, saying, "There has been no violence whatsoever, which is remarkable for a crowd of this size. These people really are beautiful." Likewise, Collier quoted a salt-of-the-earth bus driver. He had been impressed by the civility of the Woodstock youth whom he had driven back to Manhattan's Port Authority terminal. "I'll haul kids any day rather than commuters," he declared (Collier 1969). Here, then, we see an uneasy tension between low mimesis and romance, with conventional journalistic norms just winning out. News, for the most part, is about disorder, or potential disorder, and much reporting at the time focused on this (Warner 2004). Yet the big story that was to emerge from Woodstock in the days and weeks that followed was of a form of order that just looked like disorder. As *Rolling Stone Magazine* put it years later, this was "the decade's most famous and successful experiment in peace and community" ("Woodstock in 1989" 2004), one where solidarity and self-organization had prevailed in an unlikely set of circumstances. In this transformation, the people and not the star performers were the true heroic protagonists of Woodstock. The festival became a material embodiment or totem of an abstract, sacred, and somewhat hard-to-grasp idea, the democratic power of the social. *Time Magazine*, America's national myth engine, began moving things forward very rapidly:

> The baffling history of mankind is full of obvious turning points and significant events: battles won, treaties signed, rulers elected or disposed, and now seemingly, planets conquered. Equally important are the great groundswells of popular movements that affect the minds and values of a generation or more, not all of which can be neatly tied to a time or place. Looking back upon the America of the '60s, future historians may well search for the meaning of one such movement. It drew the public's notice on the days and nights of Aug. 15 through 17, 1969, on the 600-acre farm of Max Yasgur in Bethel, N.Y. ("The Message of History's Biggest Happening" 1969)

In time, Woodstock-the-icon came to represent a utopian moment, perhaps never to be repeated. Importantly, the indicators of hardship, which might have denoted incompetence or bodily pollution, served to mark out the magnitude of the achievement. Peace had been maintained in a situation that some might have seen as stressful: the recipe of narcotics, mud, rain, poor sanitation, free riders who had not paid for tickets, traffic snarls, and so forth was not propitious for peace.

Returning to the concerns of ritual theory, we should acknowledge that the embodied actions of the physically present crowd play a role in Woodstock's mythical apotheosis. Yet they do so not so much as the source of direct emotional energy from intense interpersonal exchange (only [some of] those present would have had this experience), but rather as an observable performance for onlookers that could be easily captured in type one iconic representations. As the 1960s wore on, young people had been increasingly associated with confrontation, irrationality and disorder, this arising from selective and trope-laden media reporting on anti-war protests and campus sit-ins. Ronald Reagan had famously vowed to "clean up the mess" at Berkeley in his successful 1966 run for governor of California. In contrast to network news footage of disorder, the images from Woodstock seemed to indicate another path was possible, one in which a spirit of peace could unite young strangers.

Cultural products, such as films, books, and Web sites have for the most part continued to fix the dominant meaning of Woodstock. They back up eyewitness testimony. They stand as seemingly authentic representations of an event and serve as the basis for an ongoing cult of Woodstock nostalgia (Bennett 2004c). For example, the repertoire of Woodstock images of type one iconicity (crowds, mud, hippies, which can be instantly typified by any American using common-sense knowledge) provides evidence for Woodstock's type two iconicity. The myth in its turn strongly overcodes visual interpretation and aesthetic experience. Mud is seen as sublime or sensual, not as disgusting. Pivotal to the ascent of Arcadian reverie from primeval ooze was the role of the Academy Award-winning documentary film *Woodstock* (Wadleigh 1970). Extraordinarily popular on campuses, this was to become an evidentiary tool, a forum for the indirect witnessing of communion. Crucially, a decision was made by director Michael Wadleigh even before shooting to focus on the ordinary concertgoers as much as on the musical acts, and to include interviews looking at their values, beliefs, and collective experiences. Roving crews had people speak to the camera, or the simply shot what they saw. In the cutting room, Martin Scorsese and Thelma Schoonmaker had hours of material with which to construct the idyll, like all editors eliminating the less interesting, pithy or spectacular, pushing into the background the more contradictory or ironic. Now the more fundamental symbolic concept of the "Woodstock Nation" could be born. The title of hippie activist Abbie Hoffman's (1969) somewhat experimental book recounting his utopian experiences, this term refers in its narrow sense to those present at the event. Yet a process of symbolic extension and generalization saw the label applied generically to all left- and counterculture-leaning individuals of a particular generation. Woodstock condensed a particular set of representations, visual, textual and sonic, drawing these into a coherent pattern. Then it exploded them outwards. Simplification, condensation, expansion: these are the hallmarks of iconic process. Woodstock mythology simplified a complex and multifaceted set of events, characteristics, and individual experiences, condensed a free-floating structure of feeling that emerged in the 1960s into a single event symbol, then pushed this back out into the public sphere as a shared iconic referent and representation.

It should be added that Woodstock's symbolic importance was underlined not simply by active if sometimes inadvertent myth formation but also by other more structural forces in the rock music industry. Over a few years, the opportunity space for such a mass happening shrunk and then disappeared. This was to leave Woodstock without subsequent challenge as the sine qua non, or icon of a positive countercultural experience. In part as a response to Woodstock's lessons about crowd control, provisioning, financial viability and safety, many of the most important youth culture events moved to stadiums. Now access, security, and ticketing could be better regulated. Stadium seating removed many chances for spontaneous fraternal interaction. These future events usually took only one or two days or did not have a camping option. Ticket prices increased so as to offer better weather protection and sanitation than had been available at Woodstock, but such amenities reduced the possibilities for solidarity through suffering. Bands demanded higher fees, making Woodstock-style, all-star, cross-genre lineups unaffordable and risky. Consequently, the mass mobilization of fans was less likely. The insurance industry imposed standards. Local authorities, especially in rural areas, were more wary of the promises of promoters and refused licenses for open-air events (Doyle 2001). It is notable that the elected official who had approved the Bethel gathering was voted out. There was no real upside to allowing such an event in one's own backyard.

Assisting myth consolidation, there was also the symbolically fortuitous emergence of a counter-Woodstock icon, the Altamont Free Concert of December in the same year. This violent event is sometimes seen as marking the end of the 1960s. If now less well known than Woodstock, it assisted the sedimentation of the Woodstock dream among younger people at the time. A stage only four feet off the ground, combined with beer drinking and aggressive Hells Angel Security guards was a recipe for disaster. There was one homicide, three accidental deaths, and a tense atmosphere. Altamont's dystopian narration as a tragic event leading to the disintegration of the social was itself reinforced itself through the images of type one iconicity, and in particular the documentary film *Gimme Shelter* (1970). Now Altamont could only be contrasted with the romantic apotheosis of Woodstock as a gathering of self-organizing love. Later festivals bearing the Woodstock moniker would further sanctify the original by virtue of their perceived failings relative to the myth. Woodstock '99, for example, was an event where there were four rapes reported. Riots broke out that saw speaker towers toppled, trucks burned, and ATM machines looted. The event was condemned for commercialism, price gouging, crowd violence, and misogyny, and all by means of easy contrasts with the mythical Woodstock '69. The word "Woodstock" had been "blasphemed," according to one veteran of the original ("Sounds of '69" 1999). A letter to the editor is sufficient for our purposes to illustrate this process of binary coding:

> It is not surprising that Woodstock '99 ended in riots. Alcohol, drugs and bored young people are a volatile combination. The Vietnam War and its activism brought the youth of 1969 together in search of peace, tolerance and an end to a frightening era of bloodshed. The only crises facing the young people of today are who will pay the next credit-card bill and whose house to live in until they're 40, mom's or dad's.
>
> The young people at Woodstock of 1969 may have wanted to trash the Government, but they were not out to victimize each other. The differences between 1969 and 1999 are just another indication of the isolation of today's young people not only from the establishment but also from their peers. (Miller 1999)

If many believe the myth and recite it, the enduring iconic significance of Woodstock has also been underwritten by a series of challenges. Like other iconic events in the collective memory, it is seen as a cultural node, or some high ground that needs to be fought over and reclaimed. For opponents of Woodstock, the challenge is to debunk the myth. For right-wingers, the ambition has been to drag Woodstock back down the genre gamut, from romance to satire. From the Aristotelian perspective on drama, this involves attributing confused or base motivations to action and establishing an epistemological advantage of spectators over participants. "If there is any significance to Woodstock…it is the symbolic irony of it," writes one right-wing critic in a Web posting. Far from being an egalitarian gathering of the people, Woodstock was "not for the poor." The only people who could afford to attend were "enlightened and compassionate liberals" from wealthy backgrounds. The money spent on tickets could have fed many hungry families. Yet these people were so greedy "they crashed the gate." Far from being an autonomous and self-sufficient community, they were incompetent and disorganized: "when Woodstock's well-to-do audience could not feed themselves…the hippies called on the very people they spurned to feed them: the National Guard" (Cincinatus's Wife 2004).

Woodstock has always been inserted in a specifically national narrative. Many of the performers made verbal mention of their opposition to the war in Vietnam, most notably Country Joe, with his "Fixin' to Die." The topic also arises in moments of vox populi from the Woodstock movie. Famously there is Jimi Hendrix's critically acclaimed reworking of "The Star Spangled Banner," widely considered to be both an expressive, analogical critique of the war and a symbolic effort to redefine a nation. So it is hardly surprising that Woodstock continues to be exhibited along with the Roe v. Wade decision as a strategic site in the culture wars. Satirical deflation again: looking to Woodstock, we can find "young fools" who went "to get stoned and to have an orgy." These people were "addled by a haze of drugs and sex" into a rejection not just of America but also a "lurid and brazen renunciation of Western culture and values" (Hutchinson 2008). Myth is replaced with countermyth. Such a denunciation of type two iconicity allows in turn a re-description of more basic sensory experience that is type one iconicity. Woodstock's music was not sublime, but an abomination—especially for the Christian Right and the moral majority. Writes one Web intellectual:

> It should come as no surprise that Woodstock, the most morally and visually squalid event in American history, was accompanied by the ugliest music ever heard by human ears. A return to barbarism includes a preference for the music of primitivism. Woodstock's version of primitivism included the screams of the damned. Janis Joplin and Jimmy Hendrix hysterically screamed into the microphones at Woodstock as though they were being tortured. Joplin was addicted to heroin and Hendrix was addicted to LSD, a hallucinogenic drug. (Hutchinson 2008)

Somewhat more low-key, but still drawing in an implicit way upon such counterrepresentations, was presidential hopeful John McCain's mobilization of Woodstock during the 2007–08 presidential race. In an effort to connect with the Republican base of "values voters" espousing these sorts of views, he lampooned Democratic Senator Hillary Clinton's request for $1 million for a Woodstock Museum. This was "a cultural and pharmaceutical event" that could be juxtaposed to his military service in Vietnam. Television ads showed images of Woodstock hippies having fun. Then they cut to pictures of McCain talking with Reagan and interacting with veterans (Baldwin 2007). The implicit contrast behind the images is of irresponsible, unpatriotic, and selfish youth with civic virtue. This was a binary cultural structure that had already been cemented by conservative commentator Pat Buchanan. During the 1990s, he had pointedly identified President Bill Clinton with "Woodstock values"—a selfish realm where "one chooses one's moral code to suit one's personality and lifestyle" (1998).

The irony is that such disputes have been beneficial for Woodstock's ongoing iconicity. They retain its place in the attention space of popular culture. They confirm it as a pivotal moment in the identity politics of the United States and as something worth fighting over. Whether narrated as a sacred moment for the people or as a profane and irresponsible bacchanal, Woodstock remains a point of reference.

THE BAYREUTHER FESTSPIELE

Our second and somewhat briefer case study of iconicity, Bayreuth, raises many points of structural contrast. It comes from the world of high culture rather than popular culture. The audience is somewhat older, more conservative, and represents "the establishment." It is an annual event. Nevertheless the culture structures at play are broadly similar to those at Woodstock.

First, some facts. The Bayreuther Festspiele (Bayreuth Festival) was established by the composer Richard Wagner in the 1870s. It takes place every summer and remains devoted to his works. Fans must make futile applications by letter year after year until they finally reach the top of the pile. Demand for tickets exceeds supply by a factor of seven to one. Friedrich Nietzsche came to the Festspiele. So did Hitler. Nietzsche came to see the event as symptomatic of Germany's bourgeois decadence. Hitler saw it as an expression of the German spirit.

It is at this point that I can stop and point to our first similarity with Woodstock. Both festivals participate in wider narrative struggles over national identity and culture. Wagner saw his works as expressions of Germanic themes, and further he wrote some political tracts including horrible works of anti-Semitism. These were the seeds for the later emergence of a nationalistic and fully anti-Semitic festival, the process driven by Wagner's widow Cosima and the subsequent "sect-like" Bayreuth Circle. Thanks to the ideological efforts of the British-born H. S. Chamberlain and others, this Bayreuth Circle converted Wagner's somewhat incoherent but arguably at times universalistic artistic philosophy into something far more exclusionary. It did so by "maneuvering his ideas into a Germanic-Christian gospel of salvation" (Rosefield 1998). Next, there emerged a mutually rewarding relationship with National Socialism. Hitler found heavy-hitting intellectual support for his personal revelation, which could now be seen as part of a great tradition. Bayreuth enjoyed political patronage and protection. Hitler wrote in *Mein Kampf* of how he had been deeply inspired by Wagner's work at a young age. He came every summer in the mid- and late-1930s to the festival and established close personal ties with Winifred Wagner, the controller of Wagner's artistic legacy. The Nazis used Wagner and Bayreuth for propagandistic purposes. Driven by type two iconicity, the visible and performative surface of the stage productions pointedly showcased nationalist themes. Widely distributed visual representations sustained this exclusionary myth. Posters showed paintings of Hitler in armor as the heroic Parsifal or Lohengrin (see Figure 1). A particularly notorious photograph shows him greeting Winifred, a uniformed SS soldier standing guard in the background. Here type one and type two iconicities are even more tightly fused: the Wagner bloodline, National Socialism, and the evils of Nazi militarism combine in one image.

So for National Socialism, Bayreuth was a shrine to the national spirit. Efforts at a purge of this myth complex began after World War Two. Until 1951, no Wagner operas were performed. During the 1950s and 1960s, Wieland Wagner directed productions that were minimalist. This has been generally interpreted as an effort to eliminate nationalistic referents, to purify both Wagner's opus and the festival by highlighting connections to universal rather than German themes. Or put another way, to offer a visual aesthetic surface (or type one iconicity) that was resistant to nationalist coding and that could in turn redirect or blunt the enduring type two iconicity of the Bayreuther Festspiele. Wieland's efforts have often been considered too dry and boring to be truly effective. More recently, another visually iconic strategy has been tried. Katharina Wagner's widely despised production of *Die Meistersinger* tried to ridicule the luminaries of German culture like Johann Wolfgang von Goethe and Friedrich Schiller. Characters on stage wore grotesque rubber heads that caricatured these revered ancestors. All this was an effort to establish distance from the nationalistic praise of Germanic art expressed in the rousing and sensual but in retrospect somewhat sinister final moments of Hitler's favorite opera (Riding 2007). Such innovations have been undercut by the howling of traditionalists, for whom the sacred duty is to perform the operas as

Wagner intended. Further, these type one (visual) initiatives have been limited in their impact by the regular recurrence of scandal in type two (discursive) iconicity. This kind of controversy, unlike those relating to stage direction and costuming, gains attention outside of the aesthetic public sphere. For example, an interview by Winifred Wagner in the late 1970s rekindled all the old concerns. Perhaps unaware that she was being tape recorded, she spoke of her love for the *Führer* and said she would greet him as an old friend if he walked through the door. Wieland Wagner, the once great antifascist, was more recently discovered to have constructed anti-Semitic puppet shows as a child and later to have been the controller of a labor camp (Hamann 2006).

This charismatic power of the Festspiele that makes it worth thinking and fighting over was not simply the result of such posthumous developments. Even in his day, Wagner encouraged a cult-like deference as he spun his own iconic myth. Nietzsche was for a while caught up in this and captures its spirit in his *Untimely Meditations*. He writes here portentously of Wagner laying the foundation stone of his opera house "amid pouring rain and under a darkened sky" and sees him as a prophetic figure burdened with a nearly superhuman "moral and spiritual maturity." Hence for the Nietzsche of this period, "Bayreuth signifies the morning consecration of the day of battle" in which a bold new vision would confront its critics and sceptics (1876). This myth-driven charismatic power has been passed down, albeit in attenuated form, through the blood generations. Family control of the Festspiele has been consecrated by a tie at once biological, biographical, and mythical. Hence descendents of Wagner have had a privileged role in the activities of the festival, even though formally outnumbered in the Wagner Foundation that controls the Festspielhaus and much of the event (Riding 2007).

Today, the iconic power of Bayreuth is perhaps more under threat than that of Woodstock. The founding myth has been contaminated by Nazism, yet the alternative surfaces of iconicity and experience that have been put forward seem banal. Attacks often mirror Nietzsche's (1888) understanding in his essay entitled "The Case of Richard Wagner" that was written following his split with the composer. For this later-Nietzsche, Bayreuth's ritual congress was characterized by decadence rather than a quest for transcendence. Likewise audiences today are often represented as shallow and materialistic, the incursion of the profane generating a failed ritual experience.

> Wagner might be alarmed to find how near to his citadel of purity the coarseness of the world has encroached. The high street leading to his house, Wahnfried, is a merchandiser's gantlet of cheap-looking clothes, fast food and expensive watches.
>
> Vulgarity has even made its way up the hill. The opening night audience, with only a smattering of foreigners, preened itself with displays of elegance and material good fortune. And inside Wagner's plain but dignified Festspielhaus were intermittent hacks, coughs and unidentified bumps and bangs, intruding on this temple of silence. (Holland 2000)

In a more satiric mode, tabloid and "quality" newspapers today frequently report on the infighting among family members. They are invariably described as a "clan,"

Katharina Wagner as a tall and photogenic blonde, and the disputes over control of the Festspiele as soap opera-like spats worthy of *Dallas* or *Dynasty*. Richard Wagner himself is generally read as ambiguous: On the one hand he is the possessor of God-given talent, on the other a nasty anti-Semite. Visits from Hitler are commonly invoked en passant to ground the problematic status of the Festspiele. Yet although this is a place in its twilight where demonic powers have walked, other German chancellors have felt the obligation to continue to visit. In 1997, for example, Angela Merkel held her party summit in the impractical country town and was called "die Meistersängerin" (Schmidt 2007). Clearly some element of the nation is enacted and contested here.

CONSTRUCTING ICONICITY

Rituals energize those who participate. This is the fundamental claim of the symbolic interactionist reading of Durkheim, with its insistence on embodied action and physical proximity as the driver of passions and the carrier of ritual effects. Woodstock and Bayreuth suggest a limit to this perspective. Some ritual events become deeply meaningful and motivational not as activities but as symbols. Such iconic events influence at a distance and over time due to the sustained proliferation of representations, both textual- and image-based, perhaps even acoustic. These generate somewhat ritualized interpretative disputes over the nature of the social. As they do so, they recharge, rework, and energize social life even if these arguments never quite come to resolution.

What are the culture structures that might be associated with iconic events? Put more pragmatically, what can cultural entrepreneurs do to capture distant audiences and attain amplified symbolic power? Looking to our two examples, we can extract some possibilities. First, and perhaps by definition, the event must be about more than the arts, aesthetics, or business. There is a symbolic resonance with wider and more powerful symbolic struggles over the very definition of a nation, an era, or a people. These take place in a wider public sphere, not in the world of artists, critics, and audiences with appropriate cultural capital. Second, the festival should be seen as controversial. It must be variously interpretable as sacred or profane, thus representing the triumph or the degradation of the social. Emotive disputes over the "true" meaning of the festival continually renew the charismatic energy of the event. They give it a ritual charge. Third, this iconicity cannot be easily manufactured by event entrepreneurs. It seems to depend more on visible audiences than on artists and directors: Hitler, Nietzsche, the Woodstock Nation—all have played their part in the process through which an event comes to carry an augmented symbolic load. Fourth, there seems to be a strong past-orientation in such iconic events. Contemporary candidates never quite measure up to mythical originals. Indeed this might be impossible. Woodstock was a one-off, a spontaneous happening whose very sign value lies in its unanticipated and unplanned qualities. Efforts to produce another Woodstock have seemed shallow, inauthentic, manufactured, or manipulated. Bayreuth's halcyon days lie even further back in the nineteenth century with the work of the charismatic genius Wagner. No current iteration can compete. Finally, a developed iconic surface of sensory and aesthetic experience of type one needs to come into play to support the iconic status of the event qua metaphorical or metonymic symbol, generating concrete referents against which myth can be built or reconfigured. Striking visual compressions of complex narratives can work to anchor particular meanings of myth systems.

All this raises interesting challenges for festival sponsors, directors, and cities, all of which are working in an increasingly crowded space. The traditional approach to building a festival's reputation has been to strive for artistic excellence, for example by hiring the best directors and artists. Controversial rather than simply talent-rich productions have also been used as a way of trying to gain attention. Next, we can have photos of unorthodox stage presentations, or the hair of Peter Sellars. Such producer-centered strategies can only take one so far. That is to say, they count towards status in the field of festivals and gain attention on the arts pages. It is not clear how any of this activity might allow a festival to break out of the festival genre and become a signifier in bigger and more important cultural fields—to become truly iconic. What is needed is some kind of circuit breaker that connects the festival to broader vital concerns—the involvement of a polluted politician, an ambiguous heritage, the emergence of unplanned activities, a mythmaking film, a culture war. Existing templates for building festivals might need to be rethought if iconicity rather than just aesthetic excellence is the goal. Further, this might be a no pain, no gain situation. The European Union and other sponsoring bodies tend to promote festivals as sources of ritual social integration, as a somewhat utopian arena for building mutual understanding and cosmopolitan communication. If our festivals can reach out beyond their immediate audience and gain iconic or at least highly visible status in the wider public sphere, so much the better, one might think. The lessons from Bayreuth and Woodstock suggest something else. The cultural trajectories of building bridges and building iconicity might at the end of the day be asymptotic.

REFERENCES

Alexander, J. C. 2002. "On the Social Construction of Moral Universals: The Holocaust from Mass Murder to Trauma Drama." *European Journal of Social Theory* 5 (1): 5–86.
———. 2008. "Iconic Experience in Art and Life: Beginning with Giacometti's 'Standing Woman.'" *Theory, Culture and Society* 25 (5): 1–19.
Baldwin, T. 2007. "Clinton, McCain and the Ripples from Woodstock," *The Times* (London), November 17, Overseas News sec., 52.
Bellah, R. N. 2005. "Durkheim and Ritual." In *The Cambridge Companion to Durkheim*, edited by J. Alexander and P. Smith, 183–209. Cambridge: Cambridge University Press.
Bennett, A. 2004a. Introduction. In *Remembering Woodstock*, edited by A. Bennett, xiv–xxi. Aldershot, UK: Ashgate.
———. 2004b. *Remembering Woodstock*. Aldershot, UK: Ashgate.
———. 2004c. "'Everybody's Happy, Everybody's Free': Representation and Nostalgia in the Woodstock Film." In *Remembering Woodstock*, edited by A. Bennett, 43–54. Aldershot, UK: Ashgate.
Cincinatus' Wife. 2004. "The Woodstock Myth," *Front Page Magazine*, August, http://www.freerepublic.com/focus/f-news/1192335/posts.
Collier, B. 1969. "Tired Rock Fans Begin Exodus." *New York Times*, August 18, A1.

Collins, R. 2005. *Interaction Ritual Chains*. Princeton: Princeton University Press.

Doyle, M. 2001. "Statement on the Historical and Cultural Significance of the Woodstock Festival Site." Woodstock-Preservation Archives. http://www.woodstockpreservation.org/SignificanceStatement.htm.

Gimme Shelter. 1970. Documentary feature film directed by D. Maysles, A. Maysles, and C. Zwerin. New York: Maysles Films.

Hamann, B. 2006. *Winifred Wagner: A Life at the Heart of Hitler's Bayreuth*. New York: Harcourt.

Hoffman, A. 1969. *Woodstock Nation: A Talk-Rock Book*. New York: Random House.

Holland, B. 2000. "The Citadel Wagner Built, Inside and Out." *New York Times*, July 27, E1.

Hutchinson, F. 2008. "The Early Culture War (1967–1973)." Renew America. http://www.renewamerica.us/columns/hutchison/080728.

"The Message of History's Biggest Happening." 1969. *Time Magazine*, 29 August, 32–33.

Miller, M. 1999. "Not Another Woodstock." Letter to Editor. *New York Times*, July 30, A18.

Nietzsche, F. 1876. *Untimely Meditations: Fourth Part, Richard Wagner in Bayreuth*. http://www.geocities.com/thenietzschechannel/rwbay.htm.

———. 1888. "The Case of Richard Wagner: A Musician's Problem." http://www.geocities.com/thenietzschechannel/wagner.htm.

Riding, A. 2007. "A Bayreuth Drama Worthy of, Well, Wagner." *New York Times*, July 31.

Rosefield, J. 1998. "Wagner's Influence on Hitler—and Hitler's on Wagner." *History Review* December 1, 23.

Schmidt, T. von. 2007. "Die Meistersängerin." *Die Zeit*, July 26. http://www.zeit.de/2007/31/Bayreuth-Gipfel. "Sounds of '69 Return to Woodstock Site." 1999. *New York Times*, August 16, B 4.

Warner, S. 2004. "Reporting Woodstock." *Remembering Woodstock*, edited by A. Bennett, 55–74. Aldershot, UK: Ashgate.

Woodstock. 1970. Documentary feature film directed by M. Wadleigh. USA. Warner Brothers.

"Mud, Nudity, Rock and Roll: Woodstock in 1969." 2004. *Rolling Stone Magazine*, June 24, 122–23.

PART IV

CHAPTER 11

BODY AND IMAGE

HANS BELTING

BODIES AS MEDIA

The discourses of media and body are usually separate, but media and bodies themselves unite in the experience of images. This anthropological constellation of image, medium, and body is expanded with a fourth factor when we introduce the concept of the gaze. Images emerge only in the act of looking. But then we have to understand looking as the carrier of our entire knowledge about images (*Bildwissen*). Gazes are the accomplices of bodies that engage with old and new visual media. They are as active as the gazing subject itself. We are used to thinking of gaze and image as separate, and therefore we speak of *looking at* an image. The present paper, however, develops the idea that images form *in adapting the gaze.* The complicity between body and gaze leads to the image. This is the reason why the "gaze" is such a frequent topic of many visual media. According to the iconology of the gaze (Belting 2005a: 50–58), the act of looking is not only attracted by images but is also displayed in them, as if images had a faculty of looking themselves or could reciprocate our looks.

In the "gaze" the social field of visual practice opens itself up. At their roots, media are products and instruments of social action. Media use strategies of novelty, selection, and seduction to exercise power in social history through images. And media can trigger violence against images in the same way. Thereby media steer our bodies, socializing those that are not already socialized. The present paper is thus not about "essentialized bodies," as some have argued (Bachmann-Medick 2006: 341). Instead it is about bodies as sites of images in contrast to the geographical and public sites that are often discussed. Our bodies interact with the social environment, and both succumb to historical change. Our bodies are often caught by images in a political sense. But they often respond to images in a gender-specific way, which is why images attract the masculine or feminine gaze. Thus in the present study, "body" is just a general term that can then only be defined by its concrete temporal and social situation.

Many media theories distance themselves from the body, and this practice of distantiation provokes contradiction. Since Marshall McLuhan, it has been part of general knowledge that media function as extensions, prosthetic devices of the insufficient body. But this rigid dualism between the competence of media and the incompetence of bodies misrepresents the matter. Naturally, bodies need media as tools, and they improve their perception with media. But bodies also cooperate with media to produce images. Opposing internal (mental) to external (media) images obstructs access to the processes of perception and imagination (Belting 2005b: 303). "The German language ignores the difference between picture and image, which though it seems to be a lack of distinction, nicely connects mental images and physical artifacts to one another." As carrier of its own images and as censor, the gaze participates in the history of images as actor of our bodies. "Internal representations," to use a neuroscientific term, have fluid boundaries with "external representations" because internal representations are products of our bodies, while our bodies themselves are shaped by the external representations of visual media. *Représentation* is used in French as a common term for imagination (*Vorstellung*) and presentation (*Darstellung*). Each generation establishes a new balance between mental and physical images. The imaginary of a given society develops in the "symbiosis" between what Marc Augé called official "icons" and private "dreams" (1997). Thus in each case, the actual universe of images constitutes a unique environment that predisposes us to symbolize the world in collective images.

Our inclination to symbolize can be labeled "image belief." This belief relies on a symbolic act that we call "animation." Unfortunately, the term "animation" is misleading: it is occupied by thoughts about "primitive" magic (animism) and also about electronic simulation technology. However, animation is an innate (and learnable) ability of our bodies to discover life in inanimate images. And it is we who endow images with life. This ritual is practiced by every generation anew. And this is the way in which images gain the power of living creatures. This is also how I understand Tom Mitchell's rhetorical question "What do pictures want?" (2005). It is we who want pictures to also want something. We create a fiction in which visual media are partners of our gazes and glances. Archaic societies identified two separate acts in the metamorphosis from artifacts to images. The Egyptian consecration of images (*Mundöffnung*) was a priestly ritual that followed the hand-made production of artifacts of stone and wood. Mere objects turned into images only through this ritual of animation (Belting 2001: 160). Even later in Christianity there were myths and legends attached to "living pictures" that healed or punished (Belting 2005c). These pictures assume a secret life that allows them to transgress a devotedly protected boundary. The belief in images escalates when images claim a life of their own with which they subjugate us.

Media history is typically understood as the domain of evolution driven by invention. Yet media history has also been inspired by the disappointment that given media have never been able to sustain the attraction of images for a long time. Therefore we feel an ongoing need for new and updated media. This constant process of invention thrives on media's capabilities of being converted into each other. Through such acts of conversion, images suddenly appear as unused and fresh. But media are only convertible into other media, not images. And precisely for this reason, images tenaciously remain alive as they wander from one medium to the other. Images serve the perpetually endangered belief in representation. They represent everything that matters in society. What is important appears in the image. Everything else, including secret knowledge, is excluded. The presence of images is measured today by the frequency with which they appear. In contrast, in historical times the presence of images was physically connected to actual places in the public sphere, where images with their actual media and spectators with their bodies were present.

Images were proxies for absent bodies. Nowadays we use images even when the depicted bodies themselves are present at public meetings. Speakers are multiplied by means of image technology when they meet audiences that desire proximity. In this manner *bodily presence* is exchanged for *media presence*. The video technology of closed circuits allows, for the first time, the simultaneous presence of body and image. The image zooms in on a body and authenticates it. An exchange of media takes place when the audience no longer sees the speaker face to face, "body to body," but on the screen. Nevertheless, screen images rely on the authority of bodies. Without bodies, these images would be empty. The speaker is doubly present, in the withdrawing body and the approaching image, i.e., corporeally as well as virtually with image (screen) and voice (microphone).

The concept of media has a different meaning when it comes to images. The body of an image is its medium. The constellation of *image, body, and medium* always readjusts itself anew. We cannot ignore the relation of bodies and media to images. There is a *place for images* in our bodies. A fitting symbol of this is the blank screen in Hiroshi Sugimoto's famous photographs of empty cinema rooms (Belting 2000). The empty screen symbolizes our "inner screen" on which we constantly project images—our own images and images from the outside world. In the photographs of Sugimoto, only a trace of light remains from the movie images, while the screen already awaits a new film. This is like our own media experience. The body is a location for the projection and the reception of images. The body's existing repertoire of images becomes most evident in dreams, but even while the body is awake, images are more than products of passive reception. Images from outside interact with the accumulated and internally stored images that constantly interfere with what we see.

The concept of bodies as living media can be illustrated and illuminated by a curious example. It is known that the term "medium" was used in the nineteenth century mostly for spiritual sessions at which specific persons lent their voices to ghosts. According to these beliefs, ghosts occupy a living body in order to have a "medium" through which they can speak, and therefore this concept of medium remains very suitable today. In this context, we as Westerners are as close as ever to the topos of "possession" found in other cultures. But in the present context we have something different in mind, namely the imagination of a stranger speaking in a body and of the body as medium. This distinction can be applied to images because images also take possession of the body, and our dream visions are the most well-known examples. In this sense the body is again a living medium, not for ghosts but for images that have been seen, remembered, and finally dreamed. In this case the body does not lend its voice to someone else in the state of unconsciousness. Instead it uses its pictorial memory and imagination as a tool of conscious and unconscious guidance.

Many theories of vision ignore that we experience perception with the whole body and that we use it as a medium with all our senses. We can celebrate or criticize the sense of vision as a "sense of distance" that effortlessly and independently detaches itself from the body, or is even capable of acting against it. However, if we consider the sense of hearing, it immediately undermines this one-sided view and suggests that we need to find our way back to an integral understanding of the body as a medium. Reinhart Meyer-Kalkus rightly emphasizes that there should be no strict separation between the "auditive dimension" and the visual perception. The sense of hearing can even dominate our experience of images without us being conscious of it (Meyer-Kalkus 2001: 451). We do not experience natural or built spaces only through our eyes. Instead, we perceive them with our whole bodies. We connect the sound and the acoustic waves that form within these spaces with our visual impressions of them. It is the very moment in which our strides begin to reverberate upon entering a room that makes us so enchanted by an acoustic experience that we are no longer able to distinguish between the visual and specific auditory impressions.

Bernhard Leitner, who devoted his artistic work to the interaction between sound and space, speaks about a triangular relation of sound, space, and body. By doing so, he provides a useful analogy to the triangular relation between *image, medium, and body. Sound* is analogous to *image, space* to *medium*, and the body remains unchanged. Leitner understands the body as an integral "sensorium" of hearing. Hearing is constituted not only by the ear but also by the entire anatomy of the body with its zones of resonance and the conduits of bones and skin. We hear with our whole bodies and not only with our ears (1998: 86). In a similar way, we see with our whole bodies, not just with our eyes. The interplay of the senses, among which the sense of touch should not be neglected, governs our perception of the world in ways that are hard to discern. Even in our innate ability of symbolization, all the senses are employed. We symbolize what we perceive with the eye as well as with the ear. For example, when we stand in a big crowd, the celebratory or aggressive sounds we hear complement our interpretation of what we see. The mediality of the body becomes apparent only when we look at all the senses.

MIRROR IMAGES AND SHADOWS

The experience of the self in which we discover our own body as a medium for images begins when the child runs into her own shadows or mirror images. In this case we can talk about natural pictorial phenomena or depictions produced by the body itself in the sunlight and in water. Shadows and reflections in the water are *images of the body* that can only emerge with the participation of the body. In one case the body produces its shadow in the sunlight. In the other case it doubles itself in the mirror of water, which we metaphorically call "reflection." In both cases we deal with images. The specificity of those images hinges not only on the fact that the body sees itself as image, but that it observes itself producing this image. In Dante's *Divine Comedy*, the dead recognize Dante's living body because it casts a sharp shadow. As mere shadows and images, the dead have lost the power of mediation, because without bodies they do not possess a medium by which to create images of themselves (Belting 2001: 189).

One can hardly object to the fact that, when it comes to shadows and reflections, sunlight and water serve as media themselves. Just as water and sunlight are media, so is the body in its own way because it interacts with light and water. The pictorial experience of the body is mostly understood as a problem of emergence or loss of the ego. However, we are dealing here with something different, namely with the experience that one's body acts as both medium and image. This distinction is necessary in order to further develop the argument. It is a strange experience for a little child when she wants to relate the shadow or the mirror reflection to herself. Is that my own body "there"? Am I "here" only an image? Narcissus fails in this situation because he takes his own reflection for a body, and specifically for the body of someone else. For Ovid, this is reason enough to deplore the illusion in the relation between body and image. However, this assumes that the distinction between image and body is a real question (Frontisi-Ducroux 1997: 200; Kruse 2003: 307).

But in the present case, the question of Narcissus does not come to the fore. Instead, we deal with the fact that humans had experienced with their own bodies how images pattern it before they began to artificially create pictures. Perhaps one can go even further and assert that humans understood *what images are* through shadows and water reflections and that this experience triggered the drive not only to turn themselves into images but also to produce similar images. Therefore the similarity would not be between the body itself and its image. It would rather be between one image and the other: between the image that arises out of itself in water and light, and the other image that humans fabricate with their pictorial techniques through which they emulate nature. In other words, the production of images can only succeed if we invent media for it that do not exist in nature. It also requires the transposition of an earlier experience of body on such media, since this experience was the first media experience. The body might be primarily the medium for inner images and a medium for the perception of the world. However, at this point I would like to introduce the physical body as medium. The body is medium by nature, as it generates images through shadows and mirror reflections that originally must have elicited dread and amazement.

As soon as we put artificial media to use as pictorial artifacts, the constants we encounter in nature no longer exist. In the course of its *media history*, the mirror has changed in the same way as the look in the mirror has changed in the course of *cultural history*. It is not always granted that a newly emerged medium generates a new perception. As the exhibit "Before Photography" demonstrated, the photographic gaze preceded the photographic technique because it was already present in painting. The mirror built by humans has dramatically and repeatedly changed its appearance during its long history. Ancient Greeks had to settle for the mirror made of polished metal that reflected them as shadows without bodies. The beholders wanted to see more and see something different than what they saw on the surface of the mirror. Thereby the physical reflection (*Reflektion*) as a mechanism of the mirror is transformed into a mental reflection (*Reflexion*) of the image and the boundaries of the medium (Frontisi-Ducroux 1997: 53). Perhaps the interplay of look and medium is best expressed in the term "Reflexion."

Two parallel procedures by which the pictorial experience of mirror and shadow was grafted onto a media production already existed in ancient Greek culture. In the case of the mirror, this transmission of experience riveted only limited attention. The transmission took place first in the handmade production of metal mirrors carried by female caryatids six hundred years before Christ. Later, the portable painting *(Pinax)* was invented along with a similar carrier. The mirror image thus lost its elusiveness and transience, and assumed fixed durable form (Frontisi-Ducroux 1997: 182).

In this context, the Plinius legend of the creation of graphic arts by shadow yields a new sense. In ancient Corinth, a girl tried to preserve her lover's shadow shape on a wall, and in doing so she allegedly invented fine art. The black figures painted on early Greek vases that depict people as dark shadows may have inspired this legend. However, the legend also uses a metaphor. The discovery of the body's shadow was an early *pictorial experience* that was transposed on an analog *image production* in a durable sense. Only a silhouette was needed to separate the wandering shadow that a living body cast from the body. However, as the silhouette ceased to be a shadow that vanished as the lover left, it turned into an image that stayed on the wall and represented the absent body (Kruse 2003: 74). Body and wall both participated in this invention of an image: the body in its short presence and the wall in its endurance, the body in its absence and the wall picture in its iconic presence. The concept of the shadow painting *(skiagraphia)* underwent manifold semantic changes in the Greek writings. However, the analogy of artifact and shadow can be drawn from this concept no less than the human intervention that creates the new shadow or its new image in the act of drawing *(graphein)* or writing.

The *photography* (light drawing) that was for some time even more aptly grasped by the traditional concept of "skiagraphy" (shadow drawing) (Belting 2001: 180) depicts a shadow that becomes an independent image when it is printed on glass or paper and therefore "captured" forever. It is not the light drawing but rather its *fixing* on a carrier medium that extracts the image out of the flow of time and the sensomotoric rhythm of looking. Again, we can speak here about a change of media. By means of a physical pictorial object that can be stored, given or exchanged, the mental image is immobilized.[1] But the connection between photography and body remains irrefutable, because the photograph reminds us when and how we have seen the body. Nowadays we want to free ourselves from the dependence on the body and on our past bodily looks by means of digital photos that we can rework and delete as we please and at any time. Digital photos also repudiate the memory of corporeal materiality. Photography as an index of body became unsurpassable leading to the limits of reproduction. All that was left was the contradiction that detaches us from our own bodies as referents.

Photography had its popular predecessor in silhouettes of Johann Wolfgang von Goethe's time, for their production already stemmed from the indexical impulse to preserve the real trace of the body. The Plinius legend was a close reference when one wanted to freeze the shadow that the body itself casts unaided by another person. However, influenced by physiognomic fashion, the face became the target of all efforts. The silhouette, the name for a profile that was coined after a French aristocrat, preserved the character in one single line. This line, however, is first of all, the index of a body. The line continued the body's presence in its absence with an outline of its shadow. The whole body seemed to be expressed in the profile as a pars pro toto. It became a kind of fetishism to study others with willing eyes in the outline of their shadows. But the shadow does not become its own image here (it is already an image). Rather, it transforms a body into an image that reveals the body's individuality. The change of media does not take us, in a literal sense, out of the shadow of the body (Stoichite 1997: 53).

The proximity of shadow and photography was topical for ethnologists. "The Stolen Shadow," as Thomas Theye calls the topos, was a problem in cultures in which the body's shadow was understood to be the carrier and the image of the soul. When the camera captured one's own image like a shadow, one was afraid of losing a living and bodyless image of oneself that was not supposed to fall into foreign hands (cf. Theye 1989). It seemed that the material and anonymous visibility of a photo threatened the intimate substantial connection between one's own body and its disembodied shadow. Therefore, in some Native American languages, photographers were called "shadow catchers." But one could also think of a mirror whose images were equally elusive and equally connected to the presence of bodies. Therefore, the Native Americans called the photograph "hard water," which meant a congealed and reified water mirror (Mary 1993: 69).[2] This example should not only be taken for "primitive" thinking, because such a metaphoric phrasing recalls an old media history. It was not without reason that during the first years of photography it was seen as "natural magic" and as a "mirror with memory"—a mirror that retains the memory of one's image (Holmes 1859: 739).

SURFACES OF THE MEDIA: THE IMAGE AS SYNTHESIS

Two observers approach an "image" so closely with a magnifying glass that they cannot perceive it as a whole. What are they looking for here? Bernhard Berenson, the legendary American art historian, searches for Albrecht Dürer's brush strokes on the canvas of one of the master's portraits. The reporter in Michelangelo Antonioni's 1966 film "Blow Up" searches in his own picture for the traces of a crime that he perhaps captured without knowing it (Belting 2005d: 52). Berenson investigates painting as a historical medium without paying attention to the portrait as image. The reporter, however, scrutinizes the surface of a photographic print on which he captured a park. Both seem to do the same thing. But in the first case, the attention is directed towards the surface of a medium, and in the second towards the contingency within the surface. One is about art, and the other about a casual snapshot of the everyday world. But this is not the main point here. Berenson investigates Dürer's painting technique, a feature of a medium, on a faded surface. The reporter searches for a dead body that was registered by his medium. In both cases we have to know what they do, in order to evaluate their activities.

With their surfaces that attract our gazes, the media function as an opaque screen that places itself in front of the world. But images come into existence in our glance, in the *here and now* of the medium. They can be found neither "there," on the canvas or photograph, nor "here," in the mind of the beholder. The look creates the images in the interval between "here" and "there." Whenever we do not pay attention to this interaction, we start to complain that we cannot see anything over "there," and the images do not become ours because they appear to be delusions. Then we do not want to see anything else "there" than a mere medium. Between a body's gaze and the carrier medium, be it a painting or a photo, a zone of uncertainty is generated. We see an observer, but we do not see what he sees there. We are unable to reconstruct his gaze because we are observers of observers and outside the context in which their images emerge. As external observers we cannot penetrate their track of looking.

So what and where is the image actually? On the carrier or within the observer? Painters have thematized this confusion on the deceiving surfaces of their art. They went so far in this respect as to paint the mere canvas to simulate it as an image, for instance when they depicted the back side of an image carrier and thus cornered the observers. Around 1670, the Dutch painter C. N. Gijsbrecht created such a trompe l'oeil for a private collector who liked it. The painting that represented and turned a mere collector's item into an image shows on its front side a back side and even contains a slip of paper with the number 36 (the item's number in the collection). The number was apparently placed there by the collector. However, in fact it is also a painted fiction. At that time this confusion was connected to the idea of "nothingness" that victimized the eye. Yet the "nothing" is also a "something," because Gijsbrecht painted the carrier object or medium of any painting. In other words, the painted paper with the collector's number made the medium of the painting visible (canvas, colors, etc.) (Stoichita 1990: 308).

The young Parmigianino created a perfect maneuver of delusion in a self-portrait now held in Vienna with which he introduced himself to an audience in 1524 in Rome. It makes the viewer believe that he is looking at *a real mirror*, not a *painted portrait*. But there he does not see his own face but rather the face of the painter who sat in front of the mirror. It was a convex mirror, and the illusion is so great that even the wood of the canvas has a convex surface, and still the "real illusion" is only painted. Within this artistic fiction, Parmigianino converted a painting into a mirror, a painted surface into a surface of glass, and a portrait into a mirror reflection. This conversion plays with various media. The mirror served the production of a painting that cannot reflect but that has a semblance of being a mirror (Ferino-Pagden and Schianchi 2003: 43). Already Giorgio Vasari praised the technique of illusion of the convex "barber mirror" which contains a quip against the problems of self-portrayal using a mirror. Do we see a mirror image or a portrait? The work summarizes the ambivalence of image and medium. A mirror reflects our own image. A mirror image depends on our presence in front of the mirror. But here we meet a painter who produced his own portrait in front of the mirror. His gaze and the mirror are accomplices. His checking gaze is not directed at us but apparently still towards the mirror glass. His body underwent an anamorphosis on this glass, which was at the same time a mechanical effect of the medium. He could have corrected this effect easily, but then he would have lost the reference to the glass. We often talk about the so-called *intermedial* strategies, yet forget that they are always dependent on the media competence of the observer. What is citation and reference on the part of the media (media of various origins in a multiple "exposed" media carrier), is memory and comparison on the part of the observer. In the case of Parmigianino, we are confronted with the ambivalence of mirror and image in a sense that in its time, the painting reminded one of a mirror without being a mirror. Memory and comparison allow us to evaluate the work as multiple medium. Today, the observer is in a different situation (he knows other mirrors, etc.) and must therefore reconstruct what, at that time, was the effect. However, we have astonishingly maintained the competence to deal with historical media and translate visual impressions. Our images anyway come to existence in a double act of *analysis* and *synthesis*. We analyze the media in which we search for images before we form our own images in an act of synthesis (Stiegler 1996: 165). This process succeeds only because we remember *medium A* in contact with *medium B*, and because we can simultaneously coordinate and perceive both. This is possible because we have the ability to perceive the coexistence of different media within just one medium.

The painter Sigmar Polke has played a subversive game with the material of old and new media. He first reduces the old image prints that he portrays to mere matrix points. Matrices are the distinguishing mark of print media that mostly reproduce already existing images. In contrast to that, Polke uses a reverse procedure to turn reproductions into images and transpose the print matrices into paintings, for example, in the painting *Ziegenwagen* from 1992 (Polke 1992: 120). Through this reversal, media suddenly end up in a "nowhere," where they suspiciously appear to be without media. In Polke's work, images sometimes emerge as zones of disturbance, like hallucinations, within the handmade monotonous print matrix. In one large-format matrix image from 1994, the look searches for a "Marian apparition" based on the title of the image—even though there is nothing to see and everything is imagination (Belting 1997: 140–42). Also, when the painter only analyzes other media, she magically creates images out of our readiness to synthesize. Thereby the synthesis that we call image becomes a mystery of the gaze.

In film, image and medium have an opaque relation to one another. The impact of film depends on the moving reel whose images induce the illusion of the present time. The photographic image is fixed because of the temporal jump from its creation (then) and reception (now), whereas the movie creates a fictitious synchrony of event (now) and image (now). We believe that we see the real thing, whereas it is in fact only the recorded image. We can only detach ourselves from this autosuggestion under special circumstances, for instance, when we watch movies that are produced in an old-fashioned way. Other examples are movies of the Nouvelle Vague, like Alain Resnais's *Last Year in Marienbad,* whose paradoxical slowness stimulates our dreams instead of turning us into observers. The more up-to-date the production of the movie, the more invisible the medium becomes. The more the movie corresponds with our viewing habits, the less we notice the cinematographic technique and the medium, and the more we surrender to images as if they were forming "here and now" in our looking at them. We experience these images in the temporal rhythm of the cinema, and yet we inadvertently embody them in our own imagination. We can even imagine movies that only exist as screenplays just by knowing the director. The screenplay of the unfilmed movie *Hoffmaniana* by Andrei Tarkovsky (1988) has inspired all who are familiar with Tarkovsky's work to imagine it in their own ways.

Artistic videos that are not attached to any linear film plot simulate our own image repertoire below the threshold of consciousness. The artists suggest here the image flow in our mind through electronic processing (free editing and recycling of video material as memory material that was often previously produced by themselves). The world of images that lives in the body seems to be transformed into an external medium. In his playful text about "input time" and "output time," Nam June Paik derives from our imagination the compression or the stretching of time that is staged in his videos: "The meticulous process of cutting is nothing else but a simulation of our brain function. Video art imitates nature not in its appearance or substance" but in its time structure in which we avoid the "irreversibility," for example, of getting old. The irreversibility is thus transformed into the content of imagination. "A certain input time (an actual experience) can be consciously stretched or compressed in output time. And this metamorphosis constitutes the function of our brain" (Paik 1976: 98).

GLANCES

Nothing proves the complicity between bodies and media better than our habit of exchanging glances with inanimate media. This "exchange," of course, can only be fictitious. But we have gotten used to this fiction, or we have learned to ignore it. Because the bodily glance is alive and real, it imagines that the dead or fictitious gaze confronting it is equally alive and real. When the observer is a living medium, she uses artificial media as if they possessed bodily qualities even though it is she herself who attributes these qualities to the media. In this way, a functional analogy between body and media is formed. When bodies behave like media, the media gain bodily qualities. This refers first of all to the look.

Thus far we have talked about this analogy with other concepts. The well-known topos of the "glance out of the image" replaces the concept of "medium" with the concept of "image" in art history, as if the "image" and the work of art were united in one place while the observer stands in another place passively looking at the image. Thereby the interaction that occurs here gets "out of sight" (*aus dem Blick*). When the image is so objectified that it exists only "out there" as work, then the dynamic that produces the image inside the body in the first place is lost. "The glance out of the image" is similar—like a mirror image—to the previously discussed "looking at an image." Two lines of looking meet each other at this moment, one painted and one living. But our glance can only be implicit, and therefore cannot become directly visible "there."

The "exchange of glance" that became a topic of art is not mere play with concepts. Thus we can use the concepts of *body* and *medium* to refer to the partnership between *observer* and *image*. In this way, the concept of image releases itself from its medial objectification and incorporates our glance. Visual media seem to "glance," i.e., they behave like bodies, while bodies react as media and exchange "glances" with other media. Thereby the symmetry between body and medium becomes evident.

However, the asymmetry is likewise evident. Media reify glances because they are themselves technical objects. Reifying means also representing, whereas the elusive, ever active glances in the living body withdraw from each lasting representation. Therefore, it makes sense to speak of an "iconology of the glance" in a sense of a pictorialization of the glance that sees itself coming into the image. Western visual media display the entire spectrum of our gazes, occupying the image in a way that reflects our practice of looking in everyday life. In this complicity the media beckon our glance or reject it and lead it to confusion, that is, it behaves as a body vis-à-vis other bodies. In contact with such media, our glance feels "accompanied." Visual media also attract our viewing when they do not simulate a reciprocal looking but instead stimulate us with an enchanting motif of longing. It can be a thing that we want to possess at least by looking at it. The empty spaces in images are also appealing to us because in this case, our viewing wants to see more than it can and thereby is thrown back on itself.

The primary glancing practice of the body that takes place between subjects is transposed on a secondary glancing practice in Western cultures that we perform in contact with artifacts and media. The exchange of glances with images that actually cannot "glance" by themselves is an achievement of the imagination. The imagination enables us to reciprocate represented glances as if we were exchanging glances with living humans. Also, in front of the images we can experience the awakening of our glance when it meets another glance. In such an exchange of glances, we forget the medium of representation and transfer our glancing onto a fictitious Other or a fictitious object. Even windows and mirrors enable us to perceive our own way of glancing. The mirror reflects the glance that we direct towards the mirror. The window frames our glance and provides a viewpoint.

We deal with visual media in a similar way. Prostheses of bodies are not so much images themselves but rather the media with which we create images. Images that emerge within the body become visible only in suitable media. These are the *milieu of the images* in which they enter the outside world. The fantasy that the image is looking at us (variant one) is similar to the longing to discover one's own glance in the image (variant two). They both depend on premises that must be renegotiated anew in every culture and every era. Historical change is based on the fact that in the repertoire of looking, new media are incessantly invented. Image (media history) and gaze (social history) are not tightly connected to each other. However, they always form alliances with each other.

The so-called "glance out of the image," as Alfred Neumeyer (1964) called his book, comes close to the breach of a taboo in a window image of Bartolomé Murillo (Stoichita 1990: 114). At an open window, two women attract boldly the glances of men as if they wanted to transgress the boundary between reality (body) and fiction (painting). One conceals her smile with her veil, withdrawing behind the window frame. And the other who presents herself openly also allures the observer to cross the boundary of the image that the window represents. The lust of the eyes is amplified by the barely concealed display of bodily lust. Here we have two things, an epitome of the gendered glance in which both genders become active, a central domain of the act of looking. However, the "playing with fire" remains a fiction since the painter cannot fulfill such an offer when two glances (one painted and one responding real) penetrate each another. We only see the painted glance and not the reciprocation. Paradoxically, the real glance remains always invisible, whereas the fictitious glance remains forever image and representation. The interaction of body and medium, which could be called "dialogic" if it were not determined by attraction and violence, is paradigmatically expressed in the asymmetry of the two looks.

The exchange of glances between the body of the viewer and the images has a special meaning when somebody looks at us from an image who claims the authorship of the image. It means that we see everything through only the glance of the person who conceptualized the image. With this gesture, Peter Paul Rubens appears in an early work that unites him with his brother Philip, who was studying at the time in Italy, and with his deceased great mentor, Justus Lipsius (Mai 1987: 40). In the foreground, the painter turns his head over his shoulder towards us so emphatically that we immerse ourselves in his glance before we notice the other people in the image. The daylight that is as fictitious as the meeting of the group illuminates his face so brightly that it appears as if it came from the real room of the observer. But does Rubens look at us at all? At first, he exchanged looks with his own reflection. After that, the exchange of glances was intended for the recipient of the image, perhaps his brother. Today, we relate the glance to us because it has always had an unspecified address. The I-pose (of the person and the painter Rubens) creates the fiction of another look crossing the boundary between the corporeal world and the media world.

Only the glance suggests the real encounter of body and painting. As Jean-Luc Nancy writes, "in the painted look the image itself is turned into look." He calls the look "something that goes out" (*qui sort*), following Ludwig Wittgenstein, who sees the gaze as coming out of the eye (Nancy 2000: 81). If we deal here with a corporeal process, then the look in the young Rubens's group portrait is only imitated and feigned. From a factual point of view, nothing comes out of the painting. Yet we are under the same impression that we have in bodily encounters. We transfer this impression in the act of animation that we have practiced on the medium of painting. Only at this moment (*Augenblick*), the desired fiction emerges.

BODY AND TEXT

Bodies are living media in a double sense. On the one hand, they perceive images of the world through the senses. On the other hand, they are perceived as carriers of images through performance, clothing, and expression. In this double mediality, the looking and the looked at body have already awakened in the course of history the wish to establish a double, which as a represented or pictorial body (*Bildkörper*) has the appearance of the living body. In another way, three-dimensional images have also aimed for this similarity with their corporeal volume, just like the sound image uses the facsimile of voice to simulate the imagination of life today. But this transposition of life is a necessary fiction of these doubles. This sounds perhaps too platonic, but Plato pursued in his media theory precisely the goal of distinguishing image and body in the same way as he did with text and (living) language. However, he was not able to successfully convey his dictum that images and writing were the empty imitations of the living, because he did not consider the cult of the dead, where other laws applied and where life was already lost anyway. As a symbolic act, the dead were equipped with a new pictorial body that lent them presence and took them back to the life of the community. We are still open to such rituals when we temporarily bring back deceased public figures in the form of archival images.

Let us return one more time to Plato and his analogy between image and writing. When we consider this analogy, the similarity of body and image becomes even more apparent in contrast to the separation of body and writing. But if we see in writing an "image" of the spoken, corporeal language, then the pictorial paradigm is overburdened: the spoken language cannot be depicted. Instead it can only be coded in a system of signs that is alien to the body. The medium "writing" separates itself from the medium "image" in an abstraction in which similarity and emulation disappear. Writing is based on agreement and is dependent on learning through reading. Not even a vocalized alphabet, of which the ancient Greeks were so proud, is capable of making a pictorial offer to empathy or body analogy. Signs replace the sensual, affective features of images. We still talk about a writing image (*Schriftbild*); however, this is only a metaphor. The complicity of body and image disappears in writing that does not even reproduce a bodily speech act because writing needs to be read out loud in order to reconnect language with the body. Writing is not an image of the body but a medium of language whose reference to bodies is beyond the scope of this paper.

Rather, we deal here solely with the *difference* between writing and body. When writing first appeared in ancient Mesopotamian culture, it was used on the surface of the already existing cult statues. This was done to turn the observers into readers and to collectively guide their exposure to images. In this sense, the first legal texts were not images but instructions, even if they were promulgated festively (Belting 2001: 143–89). Plato's analogy between writing and image is valid only in the sense that the text lacks the life of the language in the same way that images lack the life of the body. Neither writing nor image, as it is put in his famous quote, "can defend themselves by argument." Only speaking and living bodies can do so. In Plato's critique, mimetic media are deficient when they are confronted with real life. For Plato, this is the only analogy between image and writing (Belting 2001).

Graphology has acknowledged the pictorial features of handwriting in which the writer expresses himself without knowledge and intention. He leaves in his "handwriting" a trace of his personality. However, this finding shares only one quality of the image, namely that it is a trace of the body that has formed in the contact with the body and has been left behind by it. Georges Didi-Huberman has dealt with this genealogy of the image extensively in a catalog of the Centre Pompidou entitled "L'Empreinte" (1997). Even here, the difference is that in an image, a body or a body part "inscribes" itself pictorially on an inanimate surface. In contrast, writing does not even represent the writing hand but executes a bodily act. East Asian writing has developed an analogy to images when a painter and a writer expresses her self (and herself) in a spontaneous writing that approximates an image. However, this concordance cannot be generalized. It is determined by the "trace" that is left by a working hand. The signature of the East Asian writing artist expresses him. It makes a bodily gesture and is a performance, not an image of the body.

In Peter Greenaway's film *The Pillow Book*, the asymmetry between writing and body leads to a drama with a deadly ending. The film pits the body against writing (Greenaway 1996; Kremer 2000: 22). Writing cannot depict a body, and a body cannot transform itself into text. Book and book page are noncorporeal media and not compatible with the living body. The texts that Nagiko writes on the body of her lover can only become a book through his death. The old publisher ordered that the skin of the corpse should be flayed and transformed into a book for him to use as a pillow. In the writing on the skin, the couple is paradoxically united in death. In the movie there are scenes in which the publisher lies, eyes closed, at the text-covered breast of his lover, while in other scenes he sorrowfully reads a writing scroll made of skin (Greenaway 1996: 26–27). The flayed skin, a kind of human parchment, has lost all its bodily life. The writing cannot form a pictorial bond with the face, whereas the mask succeeds in doing so effortlessly. Between sign and image, between writing and body closed zones emerge. When Nagiko was still a child, her father wrote on her face a birthday wish that included the remark that God painted "the eyes, the lips, the sex and the names" on the first human beings. However, the name falls out of this category of body marks. Eyes, lips, and sex lead to the body as images. But names, when they are written down, lead away from the body through writing.

POSTSCRIPTUM: *Q'U'EST-CE QU'UN CORPS?*

An exhibition of the newly opened Musée du Quai Branly in Paris, the successor to Musée de l'Homme, was organized around the question "What is a body?" (cf. Breton 2006). To her surprise, the question makes the visitor aware of how much all the pictorial works from West Africa and Oceania are fixated on the body and make the body indeed the sole content of fantasy and imagery. Human bodies of both sexes that are transformed in the embodiments of roles (*Rollenkörper*) and become the symbolic carriers of demons, gods, and ancestors. As such they enact collective hopes and anxieties. Bodies are prepared like actors who stage the cosmic myth for the purpose of the intervention of other entities taking possession of the myth. Suddenly one recognizes that everything that was expressed by these cultures in pictorial works was also practiced with living bodies that were in this way turned into images. These objects were either destined to be masks for dancers that assumed life when attached to the body or were doubles of the bodies: not in a sense that they would depict a body but rather that they doubled its performative tasks. With an almost obsessive insistence, these objects force the body to go beyond its boundaries and accomplish in images what bodies alone cannot do. These transitions "body—image—body" remain, however, fluid. It is not possible to separate the image of the body and the body as image.

The exhibit goes a step beyond what we are used to: it includes even "Western Europe" as a further province in the list of image cultures fixated on the body. It does not shun the taboo of the West that associates the body with a place of self-distancing. The European part of the exhibition was entitled "The flesh is image." Incarnation, in a theological sense, leads to images that could otherwise not be depicted and would have to remain invisible, like ideas that resist being written down. The question "What is a body?" turns out to be a Western question that necessarily leads to uncertainty as soon as one asks it. "It takes a Melanesian look to discover that the European topic was not soul or spirit, as people would like to

believe, but rather body" (Breton 2006: 59). This is proven not only by the obsti-
nate attempt to historize the body against all reason, but also by the contemporary
genetic utopia to emancipate ourselves from the body. The old game of confronting
the body as a natural condition with its own images awakens the new temptation.
It is the temptation to intervene in the body in order to claim it as a resource for a
posthuman pictorial self-realization (*Bildwerdung*).

Translated by Dominik Bartmański and Julia Sonnevend

NOTES

1. See the PhD dissertation of Ilka Brändle, "Rituale der Fotografie" (University of
   Karlsruhe 2006).
2. I would like to thank Brändle for this reference.

REFERENCES

Augé, M. 1997. *La guerre des reves: Exercises d'ethno-fiction*. Paris: Editions du Seuil. Translated
   by L. Heran as *The War of Dreams: Exercises in Ethno-Fiction* (London; Sterling, VA:
   Pluto Press, 1999).
Bachmann-Medick, D. 2006. *Cultural Turns: Neuorientierungen in den Kulturwissenschaften*
   [New orientations in the cultural sciences]. Reinbek: Rowohlt Taschenbuch Verlag,
   Enzyklopädie Series.
Belting, H. 1997. "Über Lügen und andere Wahrheiten der Malerei" [About lies and
   other truths of painting]. In *Sigmar Polke: Die drei Lügen der Malerei* [Sigmar Polke:
   the three lies of painting], edited by Kunst- und Ausstellungshalle der Bundesrepublik
   Deutschland, 140–42. Berlin: Cantz.
———. 2000. "The Theatre of Illusion." In *Theaters*, edited by H. Sugimoto, 1–7. New
   York: Sonnabend Sundell Editions:.
———. 2001. *Bild-Anthropologie: Entwürfe für eine Bildwissenschaft* [Anthropology of the
   image: essays for a science of images]. 160. Munich: W. Fink.
———. 2005a. "Zur Ikonologie des Blicks" [Iconology of the glance]. In *Ikonologie des
   Performativen* [Iconology of the performative], edited by C. Wulf and J. Zilfas, 50–58.
   Munich: Fink.
———. 2005b. "Image, Medium, Body: A New Approach to Iconology." *Critical Inquiry*
   31: 302–19.
———. 2005c. *Das echte Bild: Bildfragen als Glaubensfragen* [The authentic image:
   image-questions as questions of faith]. Munich: Beck.
———. 2005d. "Toward an Anthropology of the Image." In *Anthropologies of Art*, edited by
   M. Westermann, 41–58. Williamstown, MA: Sterling and Francine Clark Art Institute.
Breton, S., ed. 2006. *Qu'est-ce qu'un corps?* [What is a body?]. Paris: Musée de Quai Branly.
Didi-Huberman, G. 1997. *L'Empreinte* [The imprint]. Paris: Centre Georges Pompidou
   Service Commercial.
Ferino-Pagden, S., and L. Fornari Schianchi, eds. 2003. *Parmigianino und der europäische
   Manierismus* [Parmigianino and European mannerism]. Vienna: Kunsthistorisches
   Museum/Silvana Editoriale. Exhibition catalog.
Frontisi-Ducroux, F. 1997. "Narcisse et ses doubles" [Narcissus and his doubles]. In *Dans
   l'oeil du miroir* [In the eye of the mirror], edited by F. Frontisi-Ducroux and J.-P. Vernant.
   Paris: O. Jacob.

Greenaway, P. 1996. *The Pillow Book*. Paris: Dis Voir.

Holmes, O.W. 1859. "The Stereoscope and the Stereograph." *The Atlantic Monthly*, June, 738-48.

Kremer, D. 2000. "Der Film als Bibliothek" [The movie as library]. *Büchner: Monatszeitschrift für Kunst und Kultur* 6: 20–27.

Kruse, C. 2003. *Wozu Menschen malen: Historische Begründungen eines Bildmediums* [For what reasons humans paint: foundations of an image medium]. Munich: Wilhelm Fink Verlag.

Leitner, B. 1998. *Sound: Space. (Conversation with Wolfgang Pehnt)*. Ostfildern: Cantz.

Mai, E., ed. 1987. *Flämische Malerei von 1550 bis 1650* [Flemish painting from 1550 to 1650]. Cologne: Wallraf-Richartz-Museum, Bildhefte zur Sammlung.

Mary, B. 1993. *La Photo sur la cheminée: Naissance d'un culte modern* [The photograph on the chimney: the birth of a modern cult]. Paris: Diffusion Seuil.

Meyer-Kalkus, R. 2001. *Stimme und Sprechkünste im 20. Jahrhundert.* [Voice and Arts of Speech in the Twentieth Century]. Berlin: Akademie-Verlag.

Mitchell, W. J. T. 2005. *What Do Pictures Want?: The Lives and Loves of Images*. Chicago: University of Chicago Press.

Nancy, J.-L. 2000. *Le regard du portrait* [The gaze of the portrait]. Paris: Galilée.

Neumeyer, A. 1964. *Der Blick aus dem Bilde* [The look out of the image]. Berlin: Gebr. Mann.

Paik, N. J. 1976. "Input Time and Output Time." In *Video Art: An Anthology*, edited by I. Schneider and B. Korot, 98–99. New York: Harcourt Brace Jovanovich.

Stedelijk Museum, ed. 1992. *Sigmar Polke: Schilderijen*. Translated by Ruth Koenig. Amsterdam: Stedelijk Museum. Exhibition catalog.

Stiegler, B. 1996. "L'image discrete" [The discrete image]. In *Echographies de la télévision: entretiens filmés* Echographies of the television: filmed interviews], edited by J. Derrida and B. Stiegler, 160-83. P aris: Galilée: Institut national de l'autovisuel.

Stoichita, V. I. 1997. *A Short History of the Shadow*. London: Reaktion Books.

———. 1990. "Der Quijote-Effekt" [The Quijote effect]. In *Die Trauben des Zeuxis: Formen künstlerischer Wirklichkeitsaneignung* [The grapes of Zeuxis: forms of artistic appropriation of reality], edited by H. Körner. Hildesheim and New York: G. Olms Verlag.

Tarkovsky, A. 1988. *Hoffmaniana: Scénario pour un film non realize*. Munich: Schirmer/ Mosel.

Theye, T. 1989. *Der geraubte Schatten: Photographie als ethnographisches Dokument* [The stolen shadow: photography as ethnographic document]. Munich: Münchner Stadtmuseum.

CHAPTER 12

ICONIC DIFFERENCE AND SEDUCTION

BERNHARD GIESEN

In the following essay, we will argue that the image is a medium of seduction and that seduction, in its turn, is a paradigm for the constitution of sociality on a par with contract and domination. In contrast to many studies of visual sociology that deal mainly with images in popular culture (Mitchell 1994; 2005), we will illustrate our thesis with art, in particular with renaissance paintings.[1] These paintings tell not only mythical stories of seduction such as those of Eve and Adam, Samson and Delilah, John the Baptist and Salome, Mars and Diana, Judith and Holofernes, but they, by their very iconic mode of representation, invite the viewer to look at them and to embark into a realm of ambivalence as the classical figure of seduction does. They attract the viewer's gaze, stimulate his or her imagination, and promise unspecified sensations if we indulge in the visual lure and surrender to the imagined world. Thereby they link the official cultural imagery of the period to the private and secluded dreams of the viewer. A very special effect is caused by the use of three-dimensional perspective in renaissance painting. It not only opens up an illusionary space behind the canvas, but it also presupposes an ideal standpoint of the viewer, thus taking the viewer into account. In addition to these general invitations to the viewer, renaissance portraits present the depicted person already as an autonomous self (Boehm 1985) without a religious or political context, and they show nudity without a religious pretext.

Images show something that is absent, but they also have a material presence as a painted canvas, a wooden relief, or a stone statue. Using a term coined by Gottfried Boehm (2006), we call this difference between material presence and imagined representation "iconic difference."[2] Iconic difference generates a basic ambivalence in every image, and this ambivalence is stronger than the one we can find in other forms of representation (cf. Mitchell 1987). Because images resist argumentative modes of weakening the link between signifier and signified reference much more than texts do, or phrased differently, because the meaning of images resists any attempt to turn it into a metadiscourse,[3] images also provide a more robust foundation for sociality, in particular for collective identity.

But, by their ambivalence, seduction as well as images also open up a space for social communication. Thus both may also shed a new light on the transition between the state of nature and sociality, a transition that is commonly dealt with by notions like "contract" or "domination" (see Baudrillard 1990). Both seduction as well as images disrupt the taken-for-granted everyday world, both transcend the flow of givenness generated by the natural attitude: images show something that is actually absent or invisible, and seduction promises future erotic pleasures but has to avoid specifying these promises or hopes (Bataille 1962)—seduction stimulates the imagination as images seduce the viewer to accept the presence of the absent or invisible.

Because seduction is highly ambivalent, it is the opposite of sexual abuse. It contrasts also to explicitness and unequivocality and, hence, it is as far from the contract between two partners as it is from the use of violence. In seduction there are no certainties and binding agreements. It is all about in-betweenness and equivocality, about hints and lures, about playful gestures and withdrawal. The seducer can always withdraw by pointing to a misunderstanding of his or her intentions, and the person who is to be seduced can always justify his or her resistance by saying that he or she failed to understand the invitation. If the seductive invitation would be unequivocal, at least the refusal to accept the invitation would be offensive and insulting for the seducer.[4]

But even the seemingly clear resistance to seduction cannot escape ambivalence and ambiguity. The male seducer can reinterpret the refusal of the lady he attempts to seduce by reinterpreting her literal resistance as an implicit and indirect invitation not to give up but to double his efforts. With respect to this interpretation, he might be wrong, but there is no clear rule for assessing the true intentions of a lady who, smilingly, tells the seducer that she does not want to give in. The very nature of seduction excludes violence, but everything else is open to future moves of the participants. Thus, seduction opens up a space of freedom and contingencies, of uncertainties and fantasies, of conjectures and illusions.

THE ORIGINAL SEDUCTION AND THE BIRTH OF CIVILIZATION

The original mythical seduction concerned not the male seduction of a lady, but the woman's attempt to civilize the raw warrior who achieved his sexual satisfaction by applying brute violence. By luring the warrior away from his wild companions and into her bed, the seducing lady turned him from an unalienated and uninhibited creature into a civilized courtier, a person of manners and discipline. He still was thrusting for sexual satisfaction, but before he could enjoy it he had to perform courtship, engage in artful communication, and display gracious manners. If we take this as a paradigm, we no longer reduce the transition from the state of nature to culture to an explicit and symmetrical contract. Nor do we reduce it to an asymmetrical relation between the violent master and the succumbing slave. Instead, we see its origin in the seducing smile of the lady who invites the warrior to put away his weapons and rest. Thus the narrative of seduction might tell us a new story about the constitution of society: it was Eve who started it all. She seduced Adam into aspiring for divinity by acquiring the forbidden knowledge and, after trespassing God's command, both discovered their nakedness, i.e., their need for veiling and culture. After and by this recognition, they were expelled from the unalienated and naïve paradise and doomed to veil, work, and knowledge.[5]

The female invitation to give up the male commitment to uninhibited violence could, however, fail, as the classical stories of Odysseus and Circe, John the Baptist and Salome, Joseph and the wife of Potiphar, exemplify. Men could, obviously, resist female seduction, and in this resistance they could develop a sense of individual personhood while rejecting external influences (Adorno and Horkheimer 2002). And if successful, seduction engenders risks and dangers for male superiority, even for a man's life: Judith and Holofernes, Samson and Delilah, Paris and Helena are cases in point.[6] Entering the social realm has, evidently, risks of its own: illusion and deception, alienation and pretension. Here again, the contingency and openness of seduction come to the fore: danger and fulfillment, risk and hope are siblings of seduction. Nothing in seduction has an unequivocal meaning, every gesture allows for ambivalent interpretations, and never should all sidesteps and exit routes be cut off.

This restraint of communication is generated by blunt and straightforward nakedness. Total nakedness is the opposite of ambivalence: there is no playful hinting at possible future pleasures, no play of contingencies, no in-betweenness—just unequivocal and evident, blunt and brute presence—a paradise in which the mind has not acquired independence from natural bodily perceptions[7]. By contrast, partial nakedness, which may also be understood as unintentional negligence, is much more seductive than the frontal presentation of the completely nude body—partial nudity promises the possibility of a further unveiling and an increase in sensual lust. After our exit from the original paradise, we long to unveil the original nakedness, but we are disappointed if we have to face it: there is, indeed, no way back to the original paradise after we have, like Adam and Eve, discovered our nakedness. We need the veil, but we are also driven by a secret longing for the unalienated, unveiled state of nature.

The play between veiling and unveiling is also at the core of the iconic difference (cf. Didi-Huberman 2006). Pictorial art unveils, in the flow of everyday life, something that attracts our attention; it hints at something that represents an absent or fictional reality in the form of a present material object. This imagined reality is a breach, a rupture, a transcendence in the flow of our familiar everyday world. It needs, therefore, a frame that mediates between this extraordinary imagined reality and the immediate environment at hand.

But this pictorial unveiling of an imagined and transcendent reality is only a partial one. Every image is restrained in its presentation and, hence, needs the imagination of the viewer in order to complete the representation. For example, it does not show the backside of the depicted objects, it freezes movements, it skips the past of the imagined persons, and above all, it does not show the pictorial alternatives excluded by the presentation of the image. Thus the image unveils only parts of the represented reality, but by this partial unveiling it lures the viewer into imagining the non-represented parts—as a partial unveiling of the body stimulates erotic fantasies in seduction (Sigmund Freud).

THE LONGING FOR NAKEDNESS AND THE RAW PRESENCE OF THINGS

As veiling a body or an image causes a longing to unveil the whole bare body, civilization, too, generates a longing for the original paradise in which everything had a natural presence and an unveiled immediacy. Returning from civilization to this lost paradise, however, engenders new risks: facing the raw reality unveiled by any imaginary textures would be almost unbearable—a shocking experience beyond and before communication, a frightening dark void beyond description. Like the Apprentice of Sais in Friedrich Schiller's poem (cf. Assmann 1990), we would be left mute if we dared to face the raw magma of the world. Therefore, as seduction can be conceived of as a metaphor for sociality, veiling, too, can be seen as a paradigm for perception and experience. Only the veiling, only the layer of imaginary textures in-between the raw reality and its handling in social interaction allows to represent the world by images.

This encounter of raw reality, of the state of nature, of bodies untouched by communication is reflected in the original gender relations: before seduction came in, gender relations were governed by raw bodily presence. The shielded presence of two persons in a location, the presentation of the naked body, the contact between bodies could trigger off unmediated and blunt sexual behavior. This prelinguistic behavior had not yet left the realm of nature, instinct, and bodily drives. It located humans in the realm of animals.

We can observe this power of presence also in the world of things. When we take a natural attitude towards the things at hand, we take them for granted, as obvious, and plain. Whoever questions them is treated as a fool (or as an overly critical intellectual). The social and semantic operations by which we construct profane objects are disregarded, and only by disregarding them are we able to continue with practical action. Empirical science translates this positivism of natural presence into a widely respected epistemology. The scientific quest for naked truth, for empirical facts, for objective reality aims at a raw world, and it uses the mild shock of presence as a foundation of its epistemology: no reasonable person may question the facts.

But raw presence is not only a matter of profane facticity. We can encounter it also in sacred things. Objects that are seen as endowed with magical powers display a presentational power that does not yet represent or signify something absent. In magical objects like relics or protective amulets, in sacred places and sacred animals there is no iconic difference between the factual material object and the imagined reference in it. The power of the magical object does not rely on its symbolic meaning but on its auratic presence, its contagious permeating qualities or its creative force. This auratic power does not yet require communication, interpretation, or convention. It relies on the immediacy of presence. Here, sacredness is not represented or hinted at, but, instead, it is just there: a sheer, raw, and unveiled presence that commands respect and awe on the part of those who face it.

This immediacy is dissolved as soon as objects and images cease to be sacred and become mere representations or symbolizations of an invisible and absent sacred.

Now the fusion between the sacred and the objects of this world is replaced by the questionable link between signs and symbols on the one hand and the signified reference on the other. What was indistinguishable before can now, in principle, be subjected to debates, doubts, and deliberations. The gap of representation opens up; the representation is no longer coextensive with the reference. Deception and illusion, arbitrariness and fantasy enter the relationship between them. But this indeterminacy between symbol and signified reference also gives way for the exodus of social processes from the realm of nature. Social communication takes off from natural immediacy and equivocality. This exit from raw presence and the state of nature is reflected by seduction and images: images are not just plain material objects, and seduction is not just a plain bodily operation of sexuality.

REPRESENTING THE INVISIBLE:
THE POWER OF SYMBOLIC IMAGES

But, of course, there have been transitions and stages in between this natural immediacy and the free-floating arbitrariness of representations. Images mark such a transitory stage between natural presence and the sheer conventional links between signifier and reference. This reference is not necessarily restricted to profane reality. It can also consist of the sacred items of a particular community: totems, gods, demons, historical or religious events and stories, rulers and other icons of collective identity. This reference to collective identity is at the core of symbolic images. Symbolic images in this sense range from so called "primitive art" (e.g., African masks, heraldic signs, totems), via religious and mythological art (e.g., statues and pictures of gods and saints, of heroes and mythical events, of allegorical and metaphorical representations), monuments and representations of major historical events (e.g., portraits of rulers, representations of battles, triumphant victories or tragic defeats) to the representation of beauty according to conventional taste: sunset, mountains, flowers, pets, nudes, kids. Because images represent the invisible sacred, that is, the core of the social community, presenting these images to the community is a performance of its collective identity.

In symbolic images, the artist or the artful execution of the piece matters less than the topic represented. The artist's creative intention, too, is largely irrelevant for understanding the meaning of symbolic art. He or she can even be unknown, as in the case of "primitive" art, early religious art, or commercial art for home decoration (kitsch). Whoever has carved the crucifix or painted the sunset on the ocean does not matter. The value of symbolic images is not set by craftsmanship, novelty or rarity, but by the identity-inspiring power of the symbols within the respective community.

Symbolic images are embedded in the familiar symbolic universe of a social community—every member of the respective community is able to understand its language, the narrative is obvious and plain, and the emotional impact is clear.

But in spite of this familiarity, symbolic images, too, are based on ambivalence. This ambivalence is not only produced by the difference between a sign and its reference but also by the oppositional perspectives they generate from inside and outside of the community. Symbolic art establishes a boundary between insiders who are familiar with the symbolic image and outsiders who do not understand it and are occasionally even appalled by it. For them, it has it an enigmatic quality. They will ask questions, and they will start to collect it as an "exotic" item and carry it home as a souvenir. Because of this clear distinction between inside and outside, it is difficult to conceive of symbolic images as seductive: symbolic images do not invite outsiders to become insiders and join the respective community. To the contrary, they mark the boundary between inside and outside; their presentation occasionally even infuriates outsiders who try to humiliate the respective community by degrading their symbolic images. For insiders, by contrast, seeing the symbolic image is attractive, uplifting, and fascinating. It strengthens the commitment to the community and even generates a liminal effervescence for its members, but for this very reason it lacks the ambivalence of seduction. Symbolic images are closer to violence than to seduction: they require commitment, and they overwhelm and dissolve any in-betweenness—you surrender without reservation, or you defy it.

In addition to this social ambivalence, symbolic images also engender an ambivalence with respect to the sacredness of the image itself. There is, of course, an iconic difference between the material carrier of the image and the represented reference: the sacred, the source of identity and creativity. In symbolic images the sacredness of the reference is, however, partially transferred to its representation. The symbolic image exudes an auratic power, although we know that it is just a representation, not the real thing. Pictorial representations of Christ, Buddha or Shiva, statues of the princely ruler, or photos of one's children are neither profane nor exchangeable representations, nor full-fledged embodiments of the sacred. Their presence commands respect, and their material substance is exempted from profane use and transformations: faithful Catholics cannot use the wooden statue of the crucified Christ as firewood.

This spillover of sacredness from the image to its material carrier allows for dominating as well as for invigorating the adherents of the community. Presenting the image of the sacralized person instills charismatic effervescence among them, although it is only a representation. Thus iconic representations create stronger emotional bonds and convey a stronger sense of presence than linguistic representations do.

A weird and highly ambivalent sense of presence also underlies the oppositional attitude towards images: iconoclasm attacks images not because they symbolize the collective identity of another community. Iconoclasm attack images mainly because they pretend a faked presence of what in fact is absent and what, for principled reasons, cannot be represented visually in a material object. But it also is driven by the suspicion that this faked embodied presence is still powerful—images are not just ridiculous errors but evils that have to be banned. Without this suspicion of a powerful presence, iconoclastic zeal and vigor would hardly make sense. Fighting pagan magic and burning the statues of pagan cults, toppling the monuments of defeated rulers and banning their images are driven by the same iconoclastic suspicion that the demons are still present in their pictorial representations and that they can still perform their magical powers. Mentioning the names of the demons seems not to invoke their presence, but their faces seem to.

A demonic inversion of symbolic images occurs as well when art uses traditional symbols and rituals deliberately in an alienating, desacralizing and subversive mode. Since medieval times, witchcraft and black magic have been accused of using Christian rituals and symbols in a perverted way. But this perversion or subversion of official imaginary is not only a matter of a remote past. In the 1960s, the Viennese artist Hermann Nitsch slaughtered lambs on stage, dispersed the bloody entrails on the naked bodies of actors, and performed sexual acts on the corpses; old sacrificial blood rituals and elements of Catholic liturgy were merged into a frightening new performance that, however, turned the conventional symbolic elements upside down. Antonin Artaud's Theater of Cruelty, too, used elements of torture and of Catholic liturgy. Joseph Beuys, in one of his most striking performances, "How to Explain Paintings to a Dead Hare" (1965), carried a dead hare in his arms in order to hint at Albrecht Dürer's famous etching, the mass reproduction of which has been turned into standard decoration in German homes. This performative art subverts or even perverts symbolic traditions, runs counter to the conventional interpretation of symbols, shocks the spectators (at least the unprepared ones), and aims at the destruction of everything that is fixed, established, and well accepted. This shocking disclosure of the hidden demonic nature in familiar symbols and rituals relies on their strongly ambivalent nature: what—like the Crucifixion of Christ—from an inside perspective warrants identity and salvation, may, from an outside point of view, appear as horrible, cruel, and disgusting. Although they are double-sided, symbolic images do not display the dynamics of seduction: they attract and promise, or they appall and horrify, but they can never be equivocal or ambivalent. The point of view—inside or outside—determines the response. The image, by separating the insiders from the outsiders, constructs a boundary. Unequivocality reigns.

ILLUSIONARY ART AND SEDUCTION

An entirely different relation between iconic representation and its reference was established by illusionary art as it emerged in classical antiquity (Pheidias and Praxiteles in sculpture, Roman painting) and as it was rediscovered in early-modern times (fifteenth century) in Europe. Illusionary art grounded its pictorial ambition less on the symbolic content than on the sensual refinement and accuracy of representing reality. There have been, of course, transitions and transformations between purely symbolic and purely illusionary images, and to cope with this coexistence, it might be more appropriate to speak of the symbolic and the illusionary dimension of an image. For a long period, renaissance art continued to depict religious subjects in standardized ways, but the accuracy of representation received increasing attention. Georgio Vasari reconstructed the art of the Renaissance as a gradual approximation to a perfect representation of reality (1568). At the end of this process, in the seventeenth century, the pictorial arts aimed at the perfect illusion even of symbolically unimportant or ugly parts of reality. The *natura morta* (still life) of the seventeenth century represents this turn towards illusion probably in its purest form: the reality represented consists of unimportant things of everyday life, fruits and flowers, glass and pottery, meat and fish. What matters in illusionary art is the representation of three-dimensionality and perspective, of details and color, and later on of texture and surface. At the end, light itself became the major concern and ambition of painting. The summit of illusionary art is marked by the trompe l'oeil in which we cannot distinguish—at least from a normal distance—whether we see a two-dimensional painting or a three-dimensional sculpture, a representation or the real thing. Ideally even the artist should surrender to the illusion and take it for true reality. In the end he, like Pygmalion, could fall in love with his own creation.

The seductive power of illusionary images is obvious: they invite the viewer to surrender to the illusion, they promise to invoke an absent reality, and they seduce the viewer to forget his cautiousness and indulge in the pleasures of the unveiled representation. Occasionally, this pictorial seduction is turned into a subject of the image itself: the Elders watching Susanna bathing was a famous subject of renaissance painting. It presents the viewer as unnoticed by the unveiled naked reality. The image, too, does not know yet that it is being gazed at. The viewers remain still in the darkness. Later on, however, the seductive persons in the image return this gaze: they smile at the viewer, and the light reflected in their eyes hints at the fact that the viewer is standing in the light. The gazing Elders are discovered, an embarrassing experience for them.

Sandro Botticelli was the first artist to turn the face of the portrayed person to look at the viewer. Lucas Cranach's Venus, Titian's Venus of Urbino, Michelangelo Caravaggio's depiction of Amor and Cupido, Francisco Goya's Maya, Jean Ingres's Odalique, and Édouard Manet's Olympia are only the most famous examples of this inviting gaze of the imagined persons. Adult men, the subjects of many renaissance portraits, do not smile at the viewer. Instead, they show a skeptical gaze, and they have weapons, scholarly instruments, or letters in their hands that hint at their earnest occupation.

An indirect mode of referring to the viewer in the image consists of mirrors that, as in Jan van Eyck's *Arnolfini* painting or Diego Velázquez's *Las Meninas*, show the viewer in the painting.[8] Like the represented reality, the viewer, too, is imagined in the painting, although, in reality, he or she is not there. Here, art plays not only with the iconic difference and its inescapable ambivalence but also with the process of looking at it. A similar effect is generated by the use of three-dimensional perspective that presupposes an ideal standpoint of the viewer in front of the painting or, as in the case of distorted perspectives, from a slanted angle aside.[9] The image exerts power with respect to the viewer: it forces him or her into a fixed position.

As in seduction, the viewing of images, too, should not be governed by blunt sexual immediacy and brute instinct. Instead, it should be attracted by the illusion, but also withdraw from surrendering to it immediately. It should be fascinated by the refined pictorial representation but should avoid getting immersed in it without reservation and confusing it with reality. The viewing of illusionary images, too, is a matter of ambivalence and in-betweenness, of playful hints and vague horizons that are not exhausted by the forms and colors visible on the material carrier of the image.

Vagueness and ambivalence are even reflected in the pictorial mode of illusionary images. In order to attract the attention of viewers, the illusionary image has to hide the fact that it is just an illusion. It has to rule out suspicion and doubts, and, paradoxically, these doubts are increased by perfecting the representation. If the surface is too perfect and too polished, the suspicion of deceptive illusion rises, at least for the experienced spectator. In contrast, the veiling or the visual covering of the surface seduces the viewer into assuming a hidden reality behind it as is achieved in erotic seduction. Therefore, sometimes the intentionally blurred rendition of contours and the darkening of colors can be used to conceal the illusion and to heighten the sense of realness at which illusionary art aims. The sfumato of Leonardo da Vinci, Andrea del Sarto, or Moroni at the beginning of the sixteenth century, or the somber and fuzzy manner of Gustave Courbet and other tenebrists in the second half of the nineteenth century worked in this direction.

Similar modes of tricking the suspicious eye can be found in modern photography. The out-of-focus photo conveys more sense of the real event than the ultrasharp one (see, for example, Gerhard Richter's series of paintings showing photos of the Baader-Meinhof gang), whereas the ultra-accurate rendition of a moment gives it a weird sense of surrealism. The observer assumes something hidden behind the slick and accurately reproduced surface. This effect is thoroughly used by photorealism. Occasionally, modern art uses explicit veiling in order to increase the sense of realism by estranging or erasing familiar images: Christo and Jeanne Claude wrapped famous landmark buildings in white canvas; Arnulf Rainer covers his photo portraits or the paintings of other artists with black paint; Robert Rauschenberg paints over material objects in his paintings and so forth.

As in images so also in seduction are veiling and withdrawal powerful devices to attract attention. We mentioned above already that plain nudity is unequivocal and, hence, the opposite of seduction. The play of ambivalences is gone. Unveiling parts of the body retains the promise of unspecified future pleasures and allows for contingencies, equivocality, and misunderstanding. Veiling is, in the visual mode, the equivalent of a weakened link between signifier and the represented reality. We imagine rather than perceive this reality. This weakening between the visible signifier and the imagined reality corresponds to the decoupling of the intended meaning from the explicit content of the conversation in seduction. Thus, seduction as well as illusionary art come close to the semantic figure that is at the core of irony: what is explicitly said differs from what is actually meant. Both arenas— seduction and illusionary art—allow for an increase in artful refinement, both invite one to surrender to a mostly fictional world, and both are bound to conceal this fictionality. We know that the material image is not the represented reality, and we know that the seducer stimulates fantasies, but we also are tempted to surrender and to forget, if only just for a moment, the iconic difference and the seductive difference.

Having outlined the correspondences between seduction and illusionary images and presented seduction as an alternative paradigm for the transition between nature and culture, we should point to a major change that was generated by the success of the female seduction of the male warrior. It occurred in early modern times when, paradoxically, many paintings, from Paolo Veronese's *Diana and Mars* to Peter Paul Rubens's famous *Consequences of War* focus still on the failed female attempt to seduce the male warrior.[10]

At this very period, however, the change from warriors to courtiers was already completed. The rise of the early-modern princely states and the attraction of the courts had turned the once ferocious and independent warriors into courteous *gentilhommes* who used their weapons just for tournament and ornament. Instead of engaging in agonal male violence, they tried to excel in elegant conversation and gracious dances, controlling their bodies, civilizing their emotions, and transforming their sexual drives into sublimated seduction (Elias 2000; but see also Duerr 1988).

This transformation changed the gendered direction of seduction. In early-modern court society, the gentlemen took over the position of the seducer while the lady tried to resist. Reversing the gender positions affected also the meaning of seduction. Famous seducers such as Casanova and the Duc de Lauzon or their mythological embodiments, for example, Don Giovanni, regarded seduction not as a matter of civilization but as one of sportive domination, the success of which could be counted, compared, and narrated in a similar way as the warriors or the hunters deeds could before (e.g., the famous catalog aria of Leporello, Don Giovanni's servant in Mozart's opera). In certain respects, male seduction compensated for the decline of male violence.

The rise of seduction as a male preoccupation was not, however, only a matter of domination. It also civilized the copresence of both genders at the princely court: dances, *le ballet de cour* (court ballet, Claude-Francois Menestrier 1660) allowed for close bodily proximity without risking the triggering of brute sexuality. Gracious courtship was an integral part of these dances.

EXPRESSIVE IMAGES, LOVE AS PASSION, AND THE RISE OF INDIVIDUAL SUBJECTIVITY

When, in seduction, erotic attraction was no longer immediately turned into genital activities, but rather civilized and controlled by bodily discipline and gracious manners, this change affected also the idea of individual personhood. Previously, it was mainly conceived of as a screen that mirrored immediately external influences, while later it was seen as an enclosed container that developed an internal life of its own. The separation between the inner space of emotions and the external behavior engendered a new problem: invisible inner feelings had to be properly expressed by external looks, speech and movements, and these, in their turn, had to be interpreted as indicating internal states of mind. If the link between external behavior and inner emotions is weakened, the inner realm of emotions acquires autonomy of its own. All of the sudden and with no predictable necessity or reason, love could strike a person, as the famous novel *La princesse de Cleves* by Madame de Lafayette showed for the first time at the end of the seventeenth century. This autonomous love could not only inspire and enchant but also destroy and darken those who were struck by it.

Crossing the boundary between inner emotions and outer behavior also generated a new kind of ambivalence: the suspicion that the display of passion, longing, and torment communicated to the loved person was a faked expression. With respect to this basic ambivalence between visible sign and invisible state of mind, seduction strongly resembles religious salvation. Both must cope with a basic uncertainty about future fulfillment, both are driven by the quest for visible signs indicating this fulfillment, and both pursue this quest as internal dialogue in the privacy of the self who is talking to herself. Personal diaries reported the religious and the emotional as well as the religious life, and this internal life took, with respect to satisfaction and salvation, the position that the focus on external bodily behavior had before.

In early modern court society, special rules and codes as described by authors like Gracian, Castiglione, and Machiavelli still allowed to cope with the uncertainty about the inner emotions by observing social rules that substituted the weakened religious control of behavior as sinful or salvatory. Instead of rooting social control in God's will, it was grounded in autonomous rules of prudence and courtship. Every move generated a countermove, every advance a withdrawal, every confession a surrender; it was a *ballet de cour* (court ballet, Claude-Francois Menstrier 1660) in which the display of emotions mated well with the control of movements.

This certainty about the rule governing the expression of inner emotions eroded gradually in the eighteenth century. New and unknown people entered the stage, and nobody could rely on the old rules anymore. The inner space of other persons became unreadable and impenetrable. At the end of the century, seduction was increasingly treated as a superficial theatricality, as illusion and deception in which nobody could know about the true feelings of the other any more: Pierre Choderlos de Laclos's *Les liasons dangereuses* marks this radical decoupling of the seductive gesture from the hidden inner emotion. This decoupling of the visible mask from the invisible true identity is at the core of the discourse in the eighteenth century. It was driven by the general suspicion that the public appearance was incongruent with a hidden private identity: stories of false priests, of rulers meeting their people incognito, of spies and masks, of hidden crimes and private vices abound, and it is always the inner private realm that constitutes true identity and a stronger reality, as contrasted with the fake and treacherous surface.

This autonomy of the inner emotions not only put a dubious light on seduction but it also liberated love from its behavioral complement. Instead of being a state of fulfillment, it was increasingly seen as an infinite longing for the presence of the other. The longing for immediacy and presence was even intensified by distance and separation, and mirrored by a new form of erotic communication: the love letter. Love letters gave rise to a purified in-betweenness: they were driven by the longing for a presence that was irredeemably lost by entering civilization and, consequently, love engendered ultimate suffering (Johann Wolfgang von Goethe's Werther). In the black Romanticism of Novalis, Percy Bysshe Shelley, and William Wordsworth, love was no longer seen as a rule-governed dance of exaltation, but as an infinite longing, as a dark abyss, as a madness that was beyond control, as a suffering that ended up in death and that could find fulfillment only in death. Passion overwhelmed and disrupted the playful exchange of gestures. Love was seen as the opposite of rule-governed behavior. The time of seduction was over.

This autonomy of private emotional life and the problem of expressing it also had an impact on the visual arts, although in a belated way. At the beginning of the nineteenth century, romanticism still centered the representation of extraordinary emotions by collectively shared gestures and events, mostly negative ones like solitude or suffering, mourning or despair; there was still a valid code of gestures and a common perspective on emotions. Even if this common perspective was questioned, there was some hope that it could be restored, and this hope drove the quest for a new mythology. The nineteenth century witnessed an increasing interest in mythical, pagan, and primitive foundations of our perception of the world, and romanticism, symbolism, and neoarchaic painting tried to respond to this demand (Richard Wagner, Friedrich Nietzsche, Arnold Böcklin, Dante Gabriel Rossetti).

The hope of rediscovering a link between inner space and visible bodily attributes fostered as well the attempt of new scientific disciplines like phrenology or physiognomy to infer from the shape of the face and skull an individual's personal character and moral righteousness (Johann Caspar Lavater, Cesare Lombroso, Franz Joseph Gall). It can even be discovered in the rise of racism that, after the demise of the classical hierarchy of being, tried to explore the racial foundations of character and personality (Arthur de Gobineau).

At the end of the nineteenth century, however, pictorial art replaced collectively shared emotions with individual and subjective experiences: painting represented what was invisible—the inner space of emotions—as an individual distortion in the perception of the visible world. The viewers of an image did not at look at a collectively generated emotional setting and its embodied expression, but, instead, they saw the environment through the eyes of the emotionally moved person: fear, anguish, and nightmares became the themes of an expressive art. The inner space of subjectivity affected even the pictorial means. Color and form were decoupled from the illusion of reality and submitted directly to the thrust of crossing the boundary between inside and outside (Vincent Van Gogh, Paul Gauguin, Ernst Ludwig Kirchner).

This modern move towards subjective consciousness is, of course, not only a matter of images. It also transformed the novel (James Joyce, Marcel Proust, Robert Musil), it produced a new philosophy of consciousness (Edmund Husserl), and it had an impact on the scholarly investigation of dreams and fantasies as representations of the unconscious that drive our behavior without our knowing it (Sigmund Freud).

Later on, in surrealism, the inner realm of fantasies, dreams and obsessions was no longer just hinted at by its traces in perceiving the external world, but instead its content was presented in a direct and literal form (René Magritte, Max Ernst, Salvador Dalí). The world as depicted in surrealism claimed to be a stronger one than the blunt objective reality as presented by science. Surrealism continued a line that began with William Blake and Alfred Kubin.

Finally, in abstract expressionism and in *peinture informelle* (informal painting), form and color even ceased to be deliberately chosen for expressing an emotional event, and they were instead used just to spontaneously generate traces of emotional events on the canvas (Hans Hartung, Jackson Pollock, Cy Twombly, Yves Klein), corresponding to the traces that the light produces on photographic film. Here, art completes its quest for autonomy. It is decoupled from the illusionary representation of reality as well as from traditional imaginations of collective identity. These standardized representations of the sacred were replaced by a new idea of it: the inner realm of the individual person, her consciousness, emotions, memories, and dreams. This is even mirrored in the social perspective on the artist: in the nineteenth century the artist become an icon of heightened subjectivity. The creative genius set apart from profane social relations was divinized as was the prince before.

THE DECLINE OF SEDUCTION AND
THE RETURN OF IMMEDIATE PRESENCE

A similar thrust for autonomy occurs in the field of modern gender relations. In the twentieth century, the art of seduction continued its decline. There were still mythological accounts of seduction in film and literature that reiterated the original seduction and its risks (the femme fatale), but the actual practice of gender relations was increasingly based on presentations of the naked body devoid of oral or literal communication. The dance floor and the nightly *promenade à deux* ceased to be the foremost places for erotic relations. They were largely replaced by the beach. On the modern beach, unveiled bodies are presented to the gaze of others who, however, try to conceal their gazing from being noticed by others (Kaufmann). Oral communication is restricted, as are bodily movements. For the most part, people on the beach do not move but rather rest and expose their bodies to the sun. In a feeling of heightened presence, bodies talk to bodies, but this bodily communication is without narration or irony.

A similar blunt gaze at naked bodies drives pornography. Pornography presupposes the communicative barrier between the viewer and the bodies that he or she is lusting for. Like the Elders watching Susanna bathing, the consumer of pornography can assume that he will remain unnoticed by others. He is a voyeur. Pornography reduces gender relations to the display of naked bodies and to the operation of genitals. It is unequivocal, without any ambivalence or irony, autonomous sexuality without any further meaning or mediation.

We have mentioned before that the "seductive difference" collapses as soon as the unveiled naked body is frontally presented: playful seduction, ambiguity, and multilayered meaning are replaced by immediate and blunt natural givenness, and this givenness is the sister of violence.[11] Both suspend the realm of ambivalence, both introduce inescapable directness, both appear, in their awkwardness, as monstrous as well as ridiculous if they are noticed by outside observers. Face to face with the unveiled naked body as well as the plain unveiled reality, we are shocked and speechless. Communication breaks down, profane immediacy, and corporeal presence reign. There is neither past nor future to which meaning could refer when it reaches out to something absent.

Although located at the opposite end of the field between sacred and profane, this brute and meaningless presence returns in nonrepresentational minimalist art of the twentieth century: "a rose is a rose is a rose" (Gertrude Stein), a black canvas is a black canvas (Kazimir Malevich), a rectangular cube is a rectangular cube (Donald Judd) and nothing else. Barnett Newman's famous slogan "The sublime is now" refers exactly to this presentism and concreteness of nonrepresentational painting. A piece of art no longer shows something that is actually absent, but it is the object itself and nothing but this object. In a weird twist, the return of presentism and concreteness in nonrepresentational art produces a new revelation of the sacred: the sacred is here and now, unveiled, raw, and frightening. This shocking epiphany of what previously was called the sacred is at the core of nonrepresentational art. Barnett Newman titled one of his most famous paintings "Who Is Afraid of Red, Yellow and Blue?"—it is just color, why are you shocked? And the biblical Yahweh told Moses: "I am who I am"—the sacred does not represent something else; it is the insurmountable ultimate reality, a reality, however, that is disclosed only in epiphanic moments. After the demise of the personal God, art steps in to fill the vacancy of pure and ultimate presence revealed only in epiphanic encounters.

It is important, however, to note that this new aesthetics of presence as the sudden disclosure of the sacred differs strongly from traditional symbolic art. It is insensitive to social bonding and social boundaries. It has no meaning; it does not represent anything; it is just there; and this insurmountable presence commands a shocking awe. We can find this meaningless but overwhelming presence not only in minimalist painting and sculpture, but also in op art or in *arte povera* ("poor art," Mario Merz, Joseph Beuys, Richard Long) that displays ordinary materials (felt, earth, broken glass, rusty iron) as pieces of art. Here, utterly enigmatic stuff is endowed with a sacral presence that we encountered already in the original embodiment of the sacred in nature.

As in other areas of society, too, the modern thrust for functional autonomy and *Eigenlogik* (logic of its own) has generated a draining out of ambivalence and equivocal communication in the field of sexuality and as well as in visual art. Rationalization drives a seemingly inescapable trend from multilayered ironical communication towards decontextualized and abbreviated codings with respect to one functional reference. Money has no use except as a medium for exchange; political power has no meaning except for symbolizing support for collective action. In a similar way, nonrepresentational art has no meaning except for unveiling the presence of the sacred, just as pornography has no meaning except for presenting utterly profane bodies for corporeal functions and nothing else.[12] Both are situated beyond any semiosis: the seductive difference and the iconic one collapse. Thus we seem to have returned, after a long trajectory through the realm of symbols and images, to the blunt immediacy of presence that reigned before Eve and Adam had to leave paradise, before ambivalence came in, before the dance of signs started.

The rise of nonrepresentational art and the spread of pornography cannot, however, blur the fact that both are, by their very nature, extraordinary and liminal phenomena, shocking exceptions surrounded by an everyday world that is still governed by iconic representations and double-layered communication. And even if we should get accustomed to a piece of art or to a pornographic image, as soon as they become a part of our habitual everyday world, they loose their shocking presence and are turned into ordinary things that can be bought and sold. The profane everyday attitude is invincible, and smiling resists rationalization.

NOTES

1. Our rather swift and superficial reference to these paintings will certainly provoke harsh criticism on the part of professional art historians who insist on a thorough and detailed analysis of each single painting mentioned, but we do not intend to invade their turf and to provide a contribution to art history.

2. See also Boehm in this volume and Jean-Luc Nancy (2006). Jeffrey C. Alexander uses a similar distinction between iconic surface and iconic depth. See Alexander in this volume.

3. An image can hardly question, negate, specify the conditions of its validity or use the subjunctive mode.

4. This was the unfortunate situation for the wife of Potiphar, who tried to seduce Joseph. Salome took a violent response to cope with John's refusal and the insult implied by it.

5. We may speculate about the question of whether it was Eve or the monstrous snake symbolizing the devil that triggered the seduction in Genesis.

6. Monastic chastity was an institutional way of preventing female seduction and its dangers.

7. Hence the pictorial representation of Pothiphar's wife seducing Joseph and of Diana restraining Mars from warfare show them as naked persons: their seductive efforts were in vain.

8. For a famous interpretation of Velázquez's painting, see: Foucault (1970).

9. See Hans Holbein's famous double portrait *The Ambassadors* in the National Gallery, London.

10. There was, however, also some reference to male seduction in art and literature. See Tasso, Jerusaleme with respect to Tancredi; the death of Lucretia, by contrast, refers to male violence instead of seduction.

11. We may explore how far Heidegger's notion of *Dasein* (1993) or Husserl's notion of *Anschauung* come close to this idea of presence.

12. Jeff Koons, however, has got a weird sense of the affinity between art and pornography.

REFERENCES

Adorno, T. W., and M. Horkheimer. 2002. *Dialectic of Enlightenment*. Stanford: Stanford University Press.

Assmann, J. 1990. "Das verschleierte Bild zu Sais: Griechische Neugier und ägyptische Andacht" ["The veiled image at Sais. Greek curiosity and devotion"]. In Geheimnis und Neugierde: *Schleier und Schwelle. Archäologie der literarischen Kommunikation* [Secret and threshold: Archeology of literary communication], vol. 3, edited by A. Assmann and J. Assmann. 45–66. Munich: Fink.

Bacon, F. 2000. *The New Organon*. Cambridge: NY: Cambridge University Press.

Baudrillard, J. 1990. *Seduction,* trans. Brian Singer. New York: St. Martin's.

Bataille, G. 1962. *Death and Sensuality: A Study of Eroticism and the Taboo*. New York: Ballantine Books.

Belting, H. 2006. *Bild-Anthropologie: Entwürfe für eine Bildwissenschaft* [Anthropology of the image. Essays for a science of images]. Munich: Fink.

Benjamin, W. 1982. *Gesammelte Schriften V: Das Passagen-Werk* [Collected Writings V: Arcades Project]. Frankfurt am Main: Suhrkamp.

Boehm, G. 1985. *Bildnis und Individuum: Über den Ursprung der Porträtmalerei in der italienischen Renaissance* [Image and individual: On the origin of portrait painting in the Italian Renaissance]. Munich: Prestel.

———. 2006. *Was ist ein Bild?* [What is an image?] Munich: Fink.

Didi-Huberman, G. (2006). *Venus öffnen: Nacktheit, Traum, Grausamkeit* [Opening Venus: Nudity, dream and cruelty]. Zurich; Berlin: Diaphanes.

Douglas, M. 2007. *Natural Symbols: Explorations in Cosmology*. London: Routledge.

Duerr, H.-P. 1988. Nacktheit und Scham: Der Mythos vom Zivilisationsprozess [Nudity and shame: The myth of the civilizing process]. Frankfurt am Main: Suhrkamp.

Elias, N. 2000. *The Civilizing Process*. Oxford: Blackwell.

Felman, S. 2003. *The Scandal of the Speaking Body: Don Juan with J. L. Austin, or Seduction in Two Languages*. Stanford, CA: Stanford University Press.

Foucault, M. 1970. *The Order of Things: An Archaeology of the Human Sciences*. New York: Random House.

Giesen, B. 2006. "Performance Art." In *Social Performance. Symbolic Action, Cultural Pragmatics and Ritual*, edited by J. C. Alexander, J. L. Mast, and B. Giesen, 315–24, Cambridge: Cambridge University Press.

Heidegger, M. 1993. *Sein und Zeit* [Being and time]. Tübingen: Niemeyer.

Hondrich, K. O. 2002. *Enthüllung und Entrüstung: Eine Phänomenologie des politischen Skandals* [*Disclosure and outrage: A phenomenology of the political scandal*]. Frankfurt am Main: Suhrkamp.

Lasch, C. 1978. *The Culture of Narcissism: American Life in an Age of Diminishing Expectations*. New York: Norton.

Mitchell, W. J. T. 1987. *Iconology: Image, Text, Ideology*. Chicago: University of Chicago Press.

———. 1994. *Picture Theory. Essays on Verbal and Visual Representation*. Chicago: University of Chicago Press.

———. 2005. *What Do Pictures Want? The Lives and Loves of Images*. Chicago: University of Chicago Press.Nancy, J.-L. 2006. *The Ground of the Image: Perspectives in Continental Philosophy*. New York: Fordham University Press.

Panofsky, E. 1970. *Meaning in the Visual Arts*. Harmondsworth: Penguin Books.

Schopenhauer, A. 2008. *The World as Will and Presentation*, trans. Richard E. Aquila in collaboration with David Carus. New York: Longman.Shilling, C. 2003. *The Body and Social Theory*. London: Sage.

Simmel, G. 1996. "Die Koketterie" ["On coquetry"]. In *Georg Simmel Gesamtausgabe. Band 14. Hauptprobleme der Philosophie* [*Collected works of Georg Simmel. Vol. 14. Main problems of philosophy*], edited by O. Rammstedt, 256–77. Frankfurt am Main: Suhrkamp.

CHAPTER 13

ICONIC RITUALS: TOWARDS A SOCIAL THEORY OF ENCOUNTERING IMAGES

JULIA SONNEVEND

INTRODUCTION

Images are fellow travelers in time: they are permanent residents in our lives. We look at images in our homes, we see them on the surfaces of urban environments, and we encounter them in old and new media spheres. When we look at images, we "meet" them and engage in a complex game of distance and closeness. We search for familiarity and for difference; we enjoy the meeting or wish to forget it immediately. We try to understand the image by interpretation, but the encounter is far from being only rational: it also has a mysterious and unpredictable chemistry. Similar to looking at people, we frequently look at images, and on a very few occasions, we fall in love with them.

An image is more than simply a surface, for it has a material presence, a biography, and representational abilities. And our meeting with the image is more than a mere projection of social meanings: it is a complex sensory experience. Still, our sociological theories of objects, which we apply to images, tend to use the simple binary structure of surface and projection as if an image were an empty screen on which we could project arbitrary content. The limited approach of focusing only on "surface" and "projection" also fails to consider that we meet images at a certain moment of life and history, in a particular space and social setting. How we perceive an image is influenced by the space (involving light, noise, smell, and other sensory offerings) where we see it, and by the available interpretations.

Moreover, many sociological theories on objects have a tendency to forget the relevance of personal feelings and assume that an object with the "best" possible surface, presented in the most favorable social and spatial setting will inevitably find its way to people's hearts. Social scientists often imply that "love" toward an object (in this case toward an image) is predictable, can be rationally planned, produced, and interpreted. There is not much magic involved. The feelings of the individual perceiving the image are almost like an embarrassing factor—subjective, nonmeasurable, and idiosyncratic.

In this chapter I will present a social theoretical model of perception that moves beyond the traditional understanding of surface and projection *and* identifies individual feelings involved in the encounter. As I will show in subsequent parts of the chapter, this understanding is already present in visual studies and art history (and in some forms in anthropology, history, and science and technology studies). The aim of the chapter is to develop a model that brings together related achievements of various disciplines and can be applied to sociology. The theoretical model is based on what I call the "image encounter" and the "iconic ritual." I mean "image" in the broadest sense, including every visual representation.

The image encounter is our regular meeting with images, in which we come in contact with the image and negotiate our relationship with it. The image encounter is never exclusively visual, but rather a diffuse sensory experience that also includes our perception of and interaction with the spatial and social environment. Our image encounters are diverse: most of the time we pass by images rather quickly, they are only part of the visual background, and during the course of our usual day they rarely become focal. In some cases the image encounter is emotionally intense and intellectually focused, the image is in the center of our attention, and we cannot imagine being indifferent to it. Many sensory experiences and interpretational practices influence our encounters with images. I will elaborate on four in this chapter: the intrinsic qualities of the image, the spatial setting where the encounter takes place, the practices of "old-fashioned" projection, and the unpredictable "chemistry" of the meeting. This is not an exhaustive list of factors involved in the encounter, but these paradigmatic elements influence most image encounters.

Within the larger category of the image encounter, the iconic ritual is a potential and exceptional outcome of our regular encounters with images; it is the unique case when we strongly feel toward an image and develop a deep emotional bond. Here we register its iconic significance. The iconic ritual is an extraordinary performance, the exception when the image as window opens up a larger "world" to us and contributes to our personal and collective identity-formation. The image stands out from the large pool of images; we fuse with the image and feel like keeping it in our memories forever. We remember the image because it presents a significant event or scene in a visually meaningful way; it freezes a moment of life and gives us continued access to joyful or traumatic moments. In most cases these arresting images do not resemble a moment or period of time in its entirety. They do not show us all of the relevant details. Iconic images, rather, create a channel to access something, and show us a powerful and memorable scene that attracts attention and refers to something much larger, be it an event or some other central aspect of life. Iconic images can also connect us to imagined and real communities: groups where we want to or happen to belong. They often contribute to strong social solidarity but also to painful alienation from others.

Some iconic rituals are less personal than mechanical. For instance, photojournalists, image editors, art curators, and public relations agents have a daily work routine of choosing certain images over others. They have not only their own preferences, but also try to predict the reactions of others. While participating in image encounters, these broadcasters, printers, and distributors also hope to understand others' encounters with images. They sit at coffee tables where people open the newspapers, walk around with visitors in art museums, and intend to predict what kind of images will likely be popular in online media. They desire personal iconic rituals, but their job is to extend this desire beyond personal preferences. These professionals hope for and try to plan the iconic rituals of many individuals. They hope and plan, again hope and plan, and still often fail. A more complex sociological understanding of our meetings with images can potentially help us interpret these failures as well.

Encounters with images thus take place in many social settings and with diverse motivations, and out of these various encounters a few encounters become iconic rituals. When the image triggers iconic rituals in many individuals, social groups, and societies over a long period of time, the image might turn into a widely remembered iconic image.

I will start the chapter by briefly specifying what I mean by "iconic." Iconic is a broadly applied, perhaps even overused term, and this problem has to be addressed first. In the second part of the chapter, I will present the social theoretical model of the "image encounter" and its exceptional case, "the iconic ritual." And in the final part of the chapter, I will sketch out the social-historical conditions that have contributed to the increased frequency of image encounters in the last two centuries. Although image encounters and iconic rituals happened well before the nineteenth century, the continuous, almost uninterrupted meeting with visual representations on every surface is a modern experience. Industrialization, urbanization, and capitalism also altered the conditions under which we encounter sacred images. While traditional societies tended to present sacred images in sacred places, the modern viewer can meet them on every possible surface, at every minute, and without any preparation for the experience. The last part of the chapter is therefore dedicated to the argument that the iconic ritual is a dominantly modern ritual.

THE IMAGE ENCOUNTER

"ICON": DEFINITIONS AND FEELINGS

"Icon" is as confusing as only an iconic word can be. We rarely struggle to identify individual icons, but "icon" and "iconic" pose definitional challenges. Being both confusing and popular at the same time, "icon" and especially "iconic" have recently received immense creative criticism for being meaningless and overused. "Iconic" was one of the most nominated words for the Lake Superior State University's 34th Annual List of Words to be Banished from the Queen's English for Misuse, Overuse and General Uselessness in 2009 (Johnston 2009). Journalists, who tend to be particularly sensitive to recent changes in how we use words, have called it "the most tedious word at the moment," and "the most dismal of vogue words." The latter comment came from a journalist who published a long list of nouns and compound nouns prefixed by iconic, ranging from "iconic albino" and "iconic assassin" to "iconic hanging laundry" and "iconic zip hoodie" (Meades 2009). It seems like almost everything can become iconic, and as a result of the extension of its meaning and appropriation, the legitimacy of the word is often questioned.

Even if we limit our considerations to image icons, which I will do in this chapter, there are still images of icons (like photographs of the *Eames Lounge Chair* or images of the *Christ the Redeemer* statue in Rio de Janeiro), iconic images (such as Henri Cartier-Bresson's *Behind the Gare St. Lazare,* Walker Evans's photograph of Allie Mae Burroughs or Johannes Vermeer's *The Milkmaid*), and a combination of the two: when we have an iconic image of an icon (such as Farrah Fawcett's famous swimsuit poster or the popular "Hope" Obama campaign image by Shepard Fairey).

Moreover, even in connection with one single image icon, we often experience overlapping iconic layers. For instance, 9/11 has multiple interrelated icons: although Ground Zero came into being as a result of the physical destruction of the Twin Towers, both are engraved in our visual memory (Mitchell 2008: 186). Ground Zero as an iconic place has materially replaced the iconic Twin Towers, but it has not replaced the towers in our imagination and imagery. The attacks on the World Trade Center have added new icons to already existing ones. Some of the new icons have been ephemeral in their physical presence, but have still become unforgettable through images, such as the iconic grey cloud around the skyscrapers of Manhattan. And the dust that did not become an "iconic" cloud but "remained" on the ground was handled as sacred in official ceremonies represented in many images, even ritually placed in urns for the families of the victims. The dust itself has become an icon, inspiring the interpretation that "it is perhaps in the dust of Ground Zero that the meanings of this site are most complexly embodied" (Sturken 2007: 166). It seems like 9/11 is a meeting point of intertwined old and new icons, and we evoke all of them when we remember that day. Furthermore,, there are also cases when we recall collections of images in connection with an event rather than one single image icon; visual memory is often constructed with the help of sequences of images. This is especially true for recent events, which have a strong digital presence and are represented in hundreds of competing images.

Icons also continuously trigger questions about their symbolic boundaries. When we discuss whether to build a Muslim community center close to Ground Zero, we must consider where to draw the symbolic boundaries of an iconic place. Where does an icon ultimately begin and end? Where is its sacred center? Some icons are also unconventional or even controversial, and we might end up questioning whether we can call a particular object an icon at all. A recent *New York Times* article about the reconstruction of the exhibition at the Auschwitz-Birkenau State Museum pointed out that the proposed new exhibition "occupying some of the same barracks or blocks, will retain the piled hair and other remains, which by now have become icons, as inextricable from Auschwitz as the crematoria and railway tracks" (Kimmelman 2011). Articles like these raise questions about the moral limitations of iconicity; we again and again ask whether in fact *everything* could be called "iconic" or whether there are any absolute exceptions. Where we draw the symbolic boundaries of an icon influences what kinds of images are selected as iconic representations. And the reverse is also true; the available images shape the symbolic boundaries of icons.

Due to variations in the substance of icons (they can be persons, objects, ideas, places, events, and even material evidences of mass murder) and their complex inter-relations (icons can overlap, merge, and dissolve), it is arguably impossible to precisely define and use "icon" for sociological purposes. But for the general concept of the "image encounter" and the "iconic ritual," these variations of iconic substance are not particularly relevant.

This theory on the "image encounter" and the "iconic ritual" is focused on the practice we all seem to actualize in our lives: seeing images, getting to know them, and ultimately feeling them. The theory is focused only on images, which can be iconic images or iconic images of icons (based on the categorization above). We might develop a uniquely strong connection to a particular image that appears as the most essential representation of somebody we love. We might select an image, because it seems to capture a decisive moment. We may form an emotional bond with an image due to its exceptional expressive capabilities. But, ultimately, what matters is that these images stand out as reference points for us. We select them from multiple competing images and assign special significance to them in representing a memorable moment of life.

In the center of this theory is the encounter among images, viewers, and spatial and social settings. The images can have personal and/or public relevance. The theoretical model covers both cases because it gives a phenomenological account of the meeting with the image independently from the image's potential public (after) life. This model notes the relevance of the industrial and instrumental selection of icons (for example, by photo editors of newspapers), but focuses on personal and subjective encounters with images. The theory has the potential to be extended to nonimage icons, as well, and it can also lead to subtheories, which are interested in certain types of iconic images. But here I intend to provide a broad and flexible general conceptual framework for the ways in which we ritualistically register the iconic significance of images in social and spatial settings.

THE ELEMENTS OF THE IMAGE ENCOUNTER

The Intrinsic Qualities of the Image: Materiality, Biography, and the Represented

The intrinsic qualities of the image constitute the first element of the image encounter. Bruno Latour (1993: 52) famously wrote that at least since Émile Durkheim "the price of entry to the sociological profession" was the assumption that the inner properties of objects do not count, and Gods, money, fashion, and art are simply surfaces on which we can project our social needs and interests. But how can we understand the experience of "meeting" an image, if we do not consider its intrinsic qualities? Out of the many possible intrinsic qualities, I will highlight three: the materiality of the image, the biography of the image, and the image's representational qualities.

When we look at the image, we experience its materiality and the meanings attached to that particular material presence. Materiality matters. In certain cases we find the material presence of the image particularly attractive. We admire the surface of a Velázquez self-portrait, with its strong and time-bridging presence. We see the small marks of time on the canvas and enjoy how the lights of the museum reveal and hide "moments" of the painting's visual landscape. There are also reproductions of the paintings, which we send as postcards or use as posters on our walls. All these surfaces have a material presence, which reflects the passing of time, but still preserves something from the essence of the particular material. For us to understand the intrinsic qualities of images, we must consider their material presence.

The strong art historical tradition of focusing on the materiality (and "heaviness") of images, however, invites the social thinker to relate her theory exclusively to the material surface of the image. But materiality is often considered insubstantial, and the image still attracts attention. We might not admire the materiality of the image, but we still accept the power of the image. For instance, by the beginning of the twentieth century, photography received intense, though contested, criticism for lacking texture. The German-Hungarian art critic Ernő Kállai wrote in 1927 (1989: 96), "photography produces marvelously clear and distinct reproductions of reality," but "the material substrate of this rich illusion is exceedingly poor and insubstantial." Remarkably, at the time of the invention of digital photography, many have feared the *loss* of authenticity and texture, "features they believed were inherent in old image technologies and missing in the 'cold inhuman perfection' of the digital" (Murray 2008: 160).

Both early photography and digital photography have produced anxiety among those who see materiality and texture as the most important intrinsic quality of aesthetically powerful images. While during the invention of photography this anxiety was related to the strong reality effect of the image and its "simplistic" surface, by the time of digital photography the fears about surface were mainly related to the authenticity of the image deeply rooted in its material substance. Both types of anxiety provide a warning sign for attempts to produce social theories of encountering images with an exclusive focus on the excellence of materiality.

Moreover, materiality can even completely change, and the image still remain powerful. Just to mention one example, digital technologies enable images to travel in a second from a digital camera to a laptop and from a cell phone to a popular social networking site, and during the travel the materiality of the image gets altered. When we meet a digital image on a screen, we see its momentary surface and can then quickly engage in an affair with a completely different image on the very same surface just by clicking "next." Materiality is relevant for the image encounter, but it is also an issue.

Moreover, materiality is only one among the many intrinsic qualities of images. Images also have a history, a specific story of how they have reached us and what they have "done" beforehand. This trajectory is influenced by meanings inscribed in the objects' forms, and the trajectory itself also adds new intrinsic meanings to the objects (Appadurai 1986: 5). Understanding these embedded historical meanings requires an interpreting human being, but the interpreter does not enjoy absolute freedom from the historical narratives and facts of the objects and the social practices attached to those narratives and facts. When images become commodities, these embedded values become especially apparent. When we look at images, we try to place them in a certain historical moment and social context. When we project meanings on the image, we do that by connecting to the embedded historical and social knowledge of the image. The image communicates its history and biography, and just as with people, we hope to understand that life story.

A third intrinsic quality of the image is its ability to represent something. Whether we like it or not, our interpretational practices are constrained by the image's representational qualities. Our projection cannot be absolutely independent and arbitrary; it is somewhat limited by what we see on the surface. The practice of looking is not a one-directional activity between a human capable of expressing social meanings and a speechless object. Although an image cannot formulate verbal responses to our questions, it can convey social meanings. Some of these social meanings are clearly universal, deeply rooted in the icon. For instance, the visible fear of the Vietnamese girl running from a napalm attack toward the camera in the "accidental napalm" image provides widely and immediately accessible meaning (Harriman and Lucaites 2007: 171–208). Images also use social and aesthetic conventions, which we often decode automatically, but frequently struggle to understand (Sturken and Cartwright 2001: 26–27). While our interpretations are certainly creative, we also must pay attention to what the image offers to us as interpretation: what the image itself allows us to say.

The Space Where We Meet the Image: Architecture,
Design, Noise, Light, and Smell

The second element of the image encounter is the space where we negotiate our relationship with the intrinsic qualities of the image. We might encounter the image in the spectacular halls of the Metropolitan Museum of Art, in a shanty town in Rio de Janeiro, or in an airport terminal in Berlin. We may sit in a self-assembled Ikea armchair, on the couches of the Yale Center for British Art, or on the floor of a large university lecture hall. The place can be noisy or characterized by deep silence. The building might have large windows that let the sunshine in, or possess the most effective artificial lighting, or be in half or complete darkness. The places where we meet the image also smell differently, even if we do not consciously realize the difference. Our experience of meeting the image is influenced by these (and other) mundane aspects of spatiality. As Georges Didi-Huberman writes about his encounter with Fra Angelico's Renaissance fresco in a small cell in the monastery of San Marco in Florence:

> [n]ext to the fresco is a small window, facing east, that provides enough light to envelop our faces, to veil in advance the anticipated spectacle. Deliberately painted "against" this light, Angelico's fresco obscures the obvious fact of its own presence. It creates a vague impression that there isn't much to see. After one's eyes are adjusted to the light, this impression is oddly persistent: the fresco "comes clear" only to revert to the white of the wall, for it consists only of two or three strains of attenuated color placed against a slightly shaded background of the same whitewash. Thus where natural light besieged our gaze—and almost blinded us—there is henceforth white, the pigmentary white of the background, which comes to possess us. (2005: 11)

Didi-Huberman presents an encounter with an image, in which the interplay between spatiality and materiality strongly influences our impressions of the image. Even when we are focusing on an image, our visual field always includes a broader space. Every space, just as every object, has a history and embedded social relations, our built and natural environments are shaped by human intentions and symbolic meanings (Lefebvre 1991). In addition to the influences of the physical space, in the case of digital images the interfaces of our laptops, cell phones, digital cameras, and other devices also orchestrate our shaping perception. Social values built into these technological designs alter our communication with images (Flanagen, Howe, and Nissenbaum 2008: 322).

The space in which we meet the image can also limit our experience with the image and prevent the image encounters from becoming ritualized. Just as with the materiality of the image, space is also an issue and can elicit various effects as well. Beyond the physical limitations a space can present to the image (it might hide the image literally), indirect, symbolic spatial limitations are just as important to note. For instance, any image presented at symbolic places carries the weight of the place. Images displayed in symbolically powerful places like sites of memory immediately enter the complex and sensitive symbolic sphere of the place and are judged accordingly. Similarly, images entering different regions and cultures might not find a home and understanding audiences, and can face ignorance or even vehement rejection. Space might enrich our perception of the image, but it can also block our communication with it.

How We Interpret the Image: Practices of Old-Fashioned Projection

The third element of the image encounter is the interpretation of the image. In the various social spaces where we meet images, we encounter not only objects but also other beholders, who provide us with ideas. Sentiments of fellow viewers can restructure our impressions or contribute to the formulation of new feelings and meanings. We can also connect to imagined communities by virtue of looking at their relevant images. Texts, especially ideological ones, can also frame our understanding of images and help recycle the images in new contexts. The available interpretations thus situate the image in a certain social context.

We rely not only on these external meaning-making processes but also on our own cognitive and emotional process of producing and projecting social meanings (Alexander 2003: 3). We construct these meanings within the diffuse sensory experience of the image encounter. We look at the surface of the image in a spatial and social setting and try to interpret it. The projection on the surface provides us with feelings of power and control in two distinct ways. First, we feel like we gain control over the image by interpretation: we regulate its powers by keeping its meanings within certain boundaries. We try to make sure that images serve the purposes we intend them to serve. Second, projecting meanings on the surface of the image is also a powerful way of differentiating our "modern" societies from "traditional" societies. Social science explained to us that while "naïve" societies have strong beliefs in sacred objects, we "moderns" even if we have fetishes, *know* that the sacredness of these objects is a product of social construction (Latour 1993). We learned that we only pretend to forget our rational interpretations for moments, when we admire favorite objects and practices, but somewhere deep inside we are aware that this is nothing other than projection.

However, social science also emphasized to us that we do not act as free, independent, and powerful individuals, when we seemingly exert interpretational power over images. We are subject to larger societal powers like political economy, social domination, and social inequality (Latour 2004: 163). The power of projection is taken away from the hands of the interpreting and feeling individual and is placed in the hands of society. While we might feel powerful when we project meanings, we also learned that this is an imagined power. While social science seemingly accepts the power of individuals to interpret, it also makes sure that this individual power is under social control.

The conscious practice of projecting social meanings on the image and the related "modern" beliefs are therefore important constitutive elements of the image encounter; but, they are not the only ones.

How We "Feel" the Image: Chemistry

Finally, during our meetings with images, we also experience something that is beyond the rational elements I have presented so far. There is an uncertain, unpredictable, and often uncanny aspect to the encounter. This "something" that resists linguistic appropriation is an elusive concept for social science. Many disciplines, however, have already started to conceptualize the presence of objects in contrast to traditional understandings that considered them only as representations. The steps of change occurred in various, often noncommunicating disciplines and in the triangular French, German and Anglo-American discourses. In his paper on the historiography of the iconic turn in art history/visual studies, Keith Moxey presents recent conceptualizations of the presence-effect of images and places these theories within the broader movement to understand the "other" side of experiences: "what comes to us, rather than what we bring to the encounter" (2008: 133). According to Moxey, this broader movement has its exponents, for instance, in the disciplines of history (Frank Ankersmit speaking about "sublime historical experience"), philosophy (Gilles Deleuze, Felix Guattari, Alain Badiou resisting homogenizing linguistic representational efforts related to the human experience), science studies (Lorraine Daston, Peter Galison, Bruno Latour blurring the subject/object, human/nonhuman distinctions), and social-cultural anthropology (Alfred Gell and Arjun Appadurai writing about the social life of things and lives and families of images). Within art history and visual studies, French (Didi-Huberman), German (Hans Belting, Gottfried Boehm, and Horst Bredekamp) and American (James Elkins, W. J. T. Mitchell, and Nicholas Mirzoeff) scholars have advocated for the inclusion of nonartistic images in the study of images and for moving beyond the linguistic model of understanding media (Moxey 2008: 133–37).

Social science is often suspicious of the "magical," especially when it comes to contemporary objects. We easily accept that the encounter of two people is an experiment with unpredictable outcomes; even if they have similar social backgrounds and agree on everything, nobody—beyond hopeful parents—expects them to fall in love. But we tend to see objects differently than people. We think that if an object fulfills certain functional and aesthetic requirements, it will inevitably seduce people. But anybody who has ever produced an image-based advertisement, sent multiple digital photographs to friends, or put together a family album knows that predicting the popularity and "sacredness" of an image is close to magic. We can help the image provoke feelings, but whether the *individual* viewer will actually develop an emotional bond to the image (and how and why she will do so) still remains a mystery, as nowadays many posters say in New York: "Chamber Music, It's Not What You Think, It's What You Feel." Acknowledging this mystery, the theoretical model of the image encounter regards chemistry between image and viewer as a central part of the encounter.

The Iconic Ritual: Registering Iconic Significance

In the complex game of the image encounter, the viewer experiences the intrinsic qualities of the image, and in the momentary spatial setting in which the experience takes place, she perceives and constructs social and individual meanings, and experiences the unpredictable chemistry of the encounter. Not all encounters include all these players, but most of them do. And while experiencing the sensory offerings of the image encounter, the viewer may or may not register the iconic significance of the image. That is, the image encounter may or may not turn into an iconic ritual.

During the image encounter, we might ignore or forget the image. This practice is dominant; the iconic ritual is the exception. Sometimes we remember the image, and in a very few cases we strongly feel, either during the first image encounter or after a process of repeated meetings with the image, that the image is exceptional: we register its iconic significance. In these cases, instead of participating in a routine image encounter, we experience the extraordinary performance of the iconic ritual. Instead of feeling mere indifference, we form an emotional bond with the image. Instead of simply meeting the image, we access its sacred center and connect with communities.

After registering iconic significance, we can express our appreciation to the selected image in many distinct ways. For instance, we can choose the image as a desktop background on our laptops, put it into our wallets, send the image to friends, post the image to photo sharing sites, or display it in our homes. These decisions reflect conscious efforts to remember the iconic significance of the image and to communicate this significance to others. These cases are also similar to the industrialized processes of image selection. The history of photojournalism and mass media has many stories of explicit iconic selection. For instance, on September 11, 2001, the Associated Press (AP) photographer Richard Drew shot multiple sequences of photographs of people who jumped from the towers of the World Trade Center. When Drew returned to his office and looked at the images, he instantly found the right photograph: "[y]ou have to recognize it. That picture just jumped off the screen because of its verticality and symmetry. It just had that look" (Junod 2003). On the next day, the *New York Times* printed *The Falling Man* photograph and then hundreds of newspapers republished it all around the world. In most U.S. newspapers it ran only once, but still remained—partly with the help online publications—in the public consciousness. People like Drew are the kingmakers of images, who have a deep and professional understanding of the power of visuals.

In contrast to the professional selections of iconic images, registering iconic significance in personal contexts is often not a conscious, visible, and productive cognitive act. It can be a long process or a "decision" we reach after a considerable amount of time, and later we might even alter our point of view given the changing circumstances. The process of registering iconic significance is often invisible, effectively resisting efforts to measure the "effects" of visuals. The theory of iconic ritual has to accept and accommodate these immeasurable aspects of iconic selection.

WHY DO WE NEED THE ICONIC RITUAL? THE SOCIAL-HISTORICAL CONDITIONS OF THE AMPLIFICATION OF THE IMAGE ENCOUNTER

The iconic ritual is a personal and subjective experience. But once many people in a society fuse with the image and continue to feel so over a long period of time, the image gains iconic status and enters a small elite group of iconic images. Iconic images are results of the accumulation of iconic rituals in societies. This accumulation of iconic rituals was supported by certain social and historical conditions. While there had been numerous processes of image selection well before the nineteenth century, the industrialized production and distribution of images and visual effects exposed the viewer to more images than ever before. Moreover, viewers experienced the proliferation of images along with other new visual and spatial impressions.

The social surface of the nineteenth century was widely altered by the ever-growing capitalistic circulation of people, goods, signs, values, and desires. These changes shaped the identity, concept, and practices of the observer (Crary 1992, 2001, 2002). When it comes to the visual sphere of the viewer, modernization meant many new forces of disorientation. Modernization destabilized familiar urban spaces and produced the urban culture of "transparent" modern cities (Crary 2001: 83). Train travel also altered the previously seemingly stable relationships between distance and closeness. Where they existed, railways brought places that were earlier perceived as far away suddenly closer, and the seemingly close places such as the nearby cities became almost incomprehensibly close. The railway both diminished and expanded space (Schivelbusch 1987: 35–37). Many felt disoriented because of the novel experience of traveling fast and looking at moving images of landscapes without directly and physically experiencing the spatial surroundings.

Technological inventions, and especially the rhetoric of modernization supporting them, provided the viewer not only with feelings of disorientation but also a feeling of power over space and over *looking* at spaces. As Mahatma Gandhi wrote to a close friend in 1900: "[i]t is not the British people who are ruling India, but it is modern civilization, through its railways, telegraphs, telephones, and almost every invention which has been claimed to be a triumph of civilization" (2003: 130). Among these inventions, the telegraph became a particularly strong symbol of progress and had a profound impact on everyday sensory experiences in relation to spatial distance. The telegraph separated the practice of communication from the physical transportation of the message (Carey 1992: 203).

Changes in the culture of spreading the news also added to the amplification of the image encounter. The commercial revolution in the American press meant a move from a reliance on the annual subscription of mercantile and political elites as readership to a much cheaper penny press sold by newsboys in the streets each day and read by larger and more diverse audiences. In 1830, the country had

650 weeklies, 65 dailies, and total daily circulation of 78,000; by 1840 this increased to 1,141 weeklies, 138 dailies, and total daily circulation of 300,000. (Schudson 1978: 13–17). The intense competition for readers inspired news publications to use more and larger illustrations, and also simpler language and larger headlines (Schudson 2008: 44). A new culture of urban commuting also contributed to people's changing habits of encountering images in newspapers. Many, and not only the wealthy, started to ride omnibuses and railways on a daily basis; during these regular commutes, they read their papers and looked out the window to view the spectacles of the city (Schudson 1978: 102–06).

During the twentieth century, the rise of nationally circulated photo magazines also increased our encounters with images. The most famous example is the success story of *Life*, the first all-photography magazine in the United States. During the planning stage of *Life* in August 1936, the circulation projection was around a modest 200,000 copies. Later in the same year, *Life* already had 235,000 charter submissions. And by early 1937, the magazine reached a readership of one million (Tagg 2003: 5). Popular photo magazines selected particular images for large audiences, directing the image encounters in certain directions, contributing to many personal iconic rituals and, through the accumulation of these iconic rituals, to the selection of iconic photographs that were accepted nationally.

Modernity also altered the ways in which we present "sacred" images. The modern viewer can meet iconic images on every possible surface, while being influenced by diverse sensory experiences. The viewer is no longer always prepared for the experience: she does not need to enter a sacred place in order to meet the sacred image. Recognizing the iconic image in modern settings requires extra attention and also acts of blocking out other sensory offerings. The image might be available for only a second and might be presented as a regular image without any interpretations offering praise. The modern viewer gets curatorial help in selecting her exceptional images, but she is just as often left alone with the decision. The sacred images of modernity gained independence from the sacred spaces and elites that presented them as such.

Many of these shifts already occurred in the nineteenth century, and then the twentieth century provided the viewer with an ever-growing availability of still and moving images, and finally, the early twenty-first century experienced the arrival of the global digital image and sound flow. In this proliferation of imagery, the viewer needs moments of visual stability and safety. Looking at images on all surfaces, the viewer experiences the regular image encounter, and, in a very few moments the exceptional and memorable iconic ritual. During our many regular image encounters, we frequently look at images, try to find the emotional and cognitive connection between "us" and "them," and are drawn to certain images in spatial and social settings characterized by the multiplicity of sensory experiences and forces of disorientation. In the case of a very few image encounters, the image surprises us with its power and charm, and we move out from the sphere of indifference to the sphere of strong feelings. We fuse with the image and have the extraordinary experience of the iconic ritual (Alexander 2006: 55). We also need commonly accepted images for our imagined communities. When many personal iconic rituals come together in agreement over an image, societies gain much-needed common visual references.

CONCLUSION: THE IMAGE ENCOUNTER AND THE ICONIC RITUAL AS ICON-SORTING PRACTICES

The social theoretical model I presented in this chapter highlights that when we see images, we do much more than simply project meaning, and we are much less free in projecting arbitrary content onto the image than we think. We do not deal with an empty surface, and we do not experience images in spaces without sensory offerings and already available interpretations. The model also emphasizes that we navigate our relationships to images in spheres filled with sensory spectacles, and we often "navigate" by feeling nothing more than indifference to the image. We make selections based on the intrinsic qualities of the image, on individual and social interpretations and feelings while being present in specific social and spatial settings.

Acknowledging that we forget most of the images we meet in our lives, the social theoretical model of the "image encounter" and the "iconic ritual" also helps us see how the act of registering iconic significance is placed in the experience of getting continuous, multiple, and dense social and spatial impressions. When we select particular images, we leave other images behind. When we choose certain images, we abandon other ones. The image encounter is our effectively repeated personal and social icon-sorting practice to deal with modernity's unstoppable flow of potential icons: we forget in order to have a chance to remember.

NOTE

The chapter has benefited from comments by Colin Agur, Jeffrey C. Alexander, László Darvasi, Ron Eyerman, Bernhard Giesen, Todd Gitlin, Ri Pierce-Grove, Péter György, Richard R. John, Michael Schudson, and from Jonathan Crary's *Origins of Modern Visual Culture* lecture and Keith Moxey's *Iconic Turn* seminar at Columbia University.

REFERENCES

Alexander, J. C. 2003. *The Meanings of Social Life*. New York: Oxford University Press.
———. 2006. "Cultural Pragmatics: Social Performance Between Ritual and Strategy." In *Social Performance: Symbolic Action, Cultural Pragmatics, and Ritual*, edited by J. C. Alexander, B. Giesen, and J. L. Mast, 29–91. Cambridge, UK: Cambridge University Press.
Appadurai, A. 1986. *The Social Life of Things: Commodities in a Cultural Perspective*. Cambridge, UK: Cambridge University Press.
Barthes, R. 1981. *Camera Lucida: Reflections on Photography*. Translated by Richard Howard. New York: Hill and Wang.
Carey, J. W. 1992. *Communication as Culture: Essays on Media and Society*. New York: Routledge.
Crary, J. 1992. *Techniques of the Observer: On Vision and Modernity in the 19th Century*. Cambridge, MA: MIT Press.
———. 2001. *Suspensions of Perception: Attention, Spectacle and Modern Culture*. Cambridge, MA: MIT Press.
———. 2002. "Géricault, the Panorama and Sites of Reality in the Early Nineteenth Century." *Grey Room* 9: 5–25.

Didi-Huberman, G. 2005. *Confronting Images: Questioning the Ends of a Certain History of Art*. University Park, PA: Pennsylvania State University Press.

Flanagen, M., D. C. Howe, and H. Nissenbaum. 2008. "Embodying Values in Technology: Theory and Practice." In *Information Technology and Moral Philosophy*, edited by J. van den Hoven and J Weckert. 322–53. Cambridge: Cambridge University Press.

Gandhi, M. K. 2003. *Hind Swaraj and Other Writings*, edited by A. Parel. Cambridge: Cambridge University Press.

Goffman, E. 1967. *Interaction Ritual: Essays on Face-To-Face Behavior*. New York: Pantheon Books.

Hariman, R., and J. L. Lucaites. 2007. *No Caption Needed: Iconic Photographs, Public Culture, and Liberal Democracy*. Chicago: University of Chicago Press.

Holly, M. A. 2007. "Interventions: The Melancholy Art." *The Art Bulletin* 89: 7–18.

Johnston, I. 2009. "Why 2009 Is No Time to Be Iconic." *The Independent*, January 2.

Junod, T. 2003. "The Falling Man." *Esquire*, September, http://www.esquire.com/features/ESQ0903-SEP_FALLINGMAN.

Kállai, E. 1989. "Painting and Photography" [excerpts with responses from Willi Baumeister, Adolf Behne, and Laszlo Moholy-Nagy, 1927]. In *Photography in the Modern Era: European Documents and Critical Writings, 1913-1940*, edited by C. Phillips, 94–104. New York: The Metropolitan Museum of Art / Aperture.

Kimmelman, M. 2011. "Auschwitz Shifts From Memorializing to Teaching," *New York Times*, February 18, http://www.nytimes.com/2011/02/19/arts/19auschwitz.html?_r=2.

Latour, B. 1993. *We Have Never Been Modern*. Cambridge, MA: Harvard University Press.

———. 2004. "Why Has Critique Run Out of Steam? From Matters of Fact to Matters of Concern." In *Things*, edited by B. Brown, 151–74. Chicago: University of Chicago Press Journals.

Lefebvre, H. 1991. *The Production of Space*. Translated by D. Nicholson-Smith. Oxford: Blackwell.

Meades, J. 2009. "Enough Already." *Weekend Australian*, April 18..

Mitchell, W. J. T. 2008. "Cloning Terror: The War of Images 2001–04." In *The Life and Death of Images*, edited by D. Costello and D. D.Willsdon, 179–208. Ithaca, NY: Cornell University Press..

Moxey, K. 2008. "Visual Studies and the Iconic Turn." *Journal of Visual Culture* 7: 131–46.

Murray, S. 2008. "Digital Images, Photo-Sharing, and Our Shifting Notions of Everyday Aesthetics." *Journal of Visual Culture* 7: 147–63.

Schivelbusch, W. 1987. *The Railway Journey: The Industrialization and Perception of Time and Space*. Berkeley: University of California Press.

Schudson, M. 1978. *Discovering the News: A Social History of American Newspapers*. New York: Basic Books.

———. 2008. *Why Democracies Need an Unlovable Press*. Cambridge/Malden: Polity Press.

Sturken, M. 2007. *Tourists of History: Memory, Kitsch, and Consumerism from Oklahoma City to Ground Zero*. Durham; London: Duke University Press.

Sturken, M., and L. Cartwright. 2001. *Practices of Looking: An Introduction to Visual Culture*. Oxford; New York: Oxford University Press.

Tagg, J. 2003. "Melancholy Realism: Walker Evans's Resistance to Meaning." *Narrative* 11: 3–77.

Zelizer, B. 1998. *Remembering to Forget: Holocaust Memory Through the Camera's Eye*. Chicago; London: University of Chicago Press.

CHAPTER 14

VISIBLE MEANINGS

PIOTR SZTOMPKA

> The human eye has a unique sociological function.
> (Georg Simmel [1908] 1921: 358)

MEANINGS DISPLAYED

At least since the time of Max Weber, we have known that social life is meaning-ful. Typically we believe that meanings are deeply hidden, underlying empirical, observable reality and not directly perceivable. Some are hidden in human minds, as psychological meanings: motivations, intentions, reasons, aspirations, dreams. Other are hidden in social facts in the Durkheimian sense, as cultural meanings: values, rules, norms, ideologies, shared beliefs, creeds, utopias.

But it was already Weber who gave a hint that there is some level of meaning which can be directly perceivable, and which is amenable to direct understanding (*aktuelles Verstehen*). He gave an example: we see a man with a rifle in the woods. It is obvious that he is hunting. The meaning of the action is immediately and directly revealed. But, Weber continued, this is only a part of the story, as we do not know who the man is and why he is hunting: is he following some custom of his social class—is it a lifestyle, a snobbish aristocratic leisure, or is he a poor peasant hunting for food? Such questions demand deeper, explanatory understanding (*erklärendes Verstehen*) (Weber [1922] 1979: 3–4).

Since the time of Weber, human society has changed dramatically. Our era is unique, whether labeled as "high modernity," "late modernity" (Giddens 1990), or "postmodernity" (Bauman 1991). Among the insane, nihilistic and, fortunately, already abandoned claims of some philosophical postmodernists, there are inspiring observations of those who identify new phenomena and new trends and tenden-cies in the society of our time. For our purposes, the works of Jean Baudrillard (1994), Roland Barthes (1983), and Susan Sontag (1978) are particularly important. They were among those who noticed that a striking feature of contemporary, "late modern" society is the saturation with images, the tremendous enrichment of the directly observable outer layers of social life, of the social iconosphere. We live in

Figure 14.1   Eye image.
Photo courtesy of the author Piotr Sztompka.

an *exhibitionist society*, and as its obvious counterpart, in a *voyeuristic society* (I owe this term to Dominik Bartmański). We use images to convey meanings, because there are others ready to read images and discover meanings. These new traits of our society are manifested in four ways.

First, we live in the *society of the spectacle*. Many of the collective situations in which people find themselves are orchestrated according to certain scenarios and occur in carefully designed settings. The rich visuality of social situations and social scenes is intended to impress, to convey directly visible, obvious meanings. The Goffmanian "presentation of self" (Goffman 1959) has become extended from persons to collective actions and even to institutions. In an earlier time, rich, colorful visuality was found in the domain of the "sacred" (in the Durkheimian sense ([1912] 1915), whereas the "profane" remained dull and drab. Visual abundance has usually been typical for the religious domain, with its impressive rituals, colorful robes, and the opulent interiors of churches. It could be found at monarchical courts, and more generally in the everyday life of the elites (Chartier 1985; Perrot 1986; Prost and Vincent 1986). It has also been typical of the army with their uniforms, drills and parades, and the judiciary with its wigs, chains, and robes. Now the visual spectacles have become democratized, entered the realm of the "profane," and they play an important part in the everyday experiences of common people. In the domain of leisure, just think of the rock concerts where music no longer dominates, and the lights, costumes, hairdos, choreography, fireworks, mist, and smoke are central elements of the performance. Or consider carnivals, celebrations of the New Year, sporting events (the inaugurations of the Olympics, or the World Cup in soccer, or the Rose Parade in Pasadena), film festivals, prize-giving ceremonies (Oscar or Nobel Prize presentations). In the domain of the economy, just remind yourself of the shopping galleries or malls designed like Baroque churches or royal palaces, shop windows arranged like theater stages, or opera settings, Christmas markets, bank halls that are like museums, executive offices with huge mahogany desks and carefully arranged family portraits. In the domain of politics just look at the party conventions, presidential inaugurations, parliamentary rituals, patriotic parades, mass rallies, protest gatherings, and street riots. No wonder that on most such collective occasions we see hordes of press photographers. It is easier to grasp the meaning of these situations in pictures than in words.

Second, we live in the *society of the display*. The presentation of the individual, autonomous self, the universal human tendency so aptly demonstrated by Erving Goffman (1959) has found much more extensive and enriched manifestations. The syndrome of Thorstein Veblen's "conspicuous consumption" ([1899] 1953), which in the old days was a way of life of the elites, the nouveau riche or celebrities, has become universal. The external, observable requisites: the cars we drive, the houses we live in, the clothing and shoes we wear, the watches on our wrists, the jewelry on our necks, the pens we write with, the leather briefcases in which we carry office papers—are the symbols of status and the building blocks with which we construct our identity, to be admired and envied by others. The celebrities whose lifestyles have become more accessible than ever through tabloids, inquisitive paparazzi, and snobbish magazines, are serving as role models to be imitated. Famous brands have become democratized through franchising; they are much cheaper and more accessible than before. And for those who still cannot afford Rolex, Omega, Louis Vuitton, or Dolce & Gabana, there are cheap fakes from Asia that are easily available. Quite often the symbolic, visually displayed value of products, gadgets, or toys for grown-ups has become more important than their actual use value or function. In extreme cases, the social identity is constructed exclusively on such grounds: there are communities of taste, of style, of trends and fashions, there fans of sport cars, motorcycles, or boats, and there are devotees of certain brands (demonstrating forms of solidarity formerly reserved to the believers in the same God).

Third, we live in the *society of the design*. The attention devoted to the packaging, shape, and color of various products (just think of cars, boats, mobile phones, computers, skis, dresses, and ties), the furniture of apartments, the architecture of houses, the urban planning of streets, parks, stadiums, and airports is incomparable to any time before. Experts in design are everywhere and in great demand; it is their time. The everyday life of consumer society is saturated with tremendous diversity and a variety of intentionally created visual impressions: of colors, forms, styles, and fashions. This tendency is driven by the logic of the commercial competitive market and the need for novelty and originality, and for standing out, drawing attention and even shocking the consumer.

Fourth, we live in the *society of the icons*. We are surrounded with lots of intentionally created pictures: billboards, commercials, advertisements, banners, flags, coats of arms, color magazines, television programs, the Internet, multimedia presentations. The press is more colorful and full of pictures than ever. Not only in tabloids but also in serious journals or even daily newspapers, photographs appear together with written texts. Interestingly, the photo editors are also influenced by the Windows style, and instead of full-page photos as in the old days of *Life, Look,*

Paris Match, and *The Illustrated London News*, we now have a large number of small images resembling another Web page on the Internet. The icons in all their variety are representations of something, but their main function is not to describe but to communicate some meanings, convey a message, "make a statement" of some sort, and they have been created for that purpose. Their connotation is more important than their denotation.

As a result of all four features of our society, the meanings have become more transparent, directly observable; they have crawled to the surface. In our time of exhibitionism *much of the invisible has become visible,* and hence—observable.

CONSEQUENCES FOR SOCIOLOGY

This existential situation opens new opportunities for sociological research. There are two types of methodological consequences. The weak implication is the creation of a new subfield of *visual sociology* and the emergence of a new tribe of visual sociologists. The strong implication is the revival of observational methods and the need for *visual imagination* as the competence of every sociologist.

The impressive career of visual sociology is parallel, and perhaps related, to the wider theoretical and methodological tendency (Sztompka 2006). At the level of a subject matter, we observe the turn from the abstractions of system theories, functionalisms, and structuralisms toward the concreteness of the *sociology of everyday life* (Sztompka 2008). And at the level of research methods, there is a revival of *qualitative methodologies* after a long domination of quantitative procedures. And it is precisely at the level of everyday life that social phenomena and processes become directly observable, and that the observational methods with their extension through the technologies of recording images become useful. Another reason for the ascendance of visual sociology may be related to the technological revolution in photography that made of a popular digital camera an extremely simple gadget that may be used successfully without any special competence. Everybody seems to own some camera now and to take snapshots of everything. This creates an abundant, new research resource for sociologists: private collections, photo Web pages, and photo blogs on the Internet, supplementing the more traditional resource: press photography and the photo essay. And the popularity of the latter has grown tremendously, also partly because of the technological advancements in image making and image processing. It is easier to be a press photographer than an old-style journalist.

Visual sociology (sometimes still labeled "visual anthropology," or "visual ethnography," as these fields were the first to use visual methods) has established itself as a distinct sociological subdiscipline since the last decades of the twentieth century, and acquired institutional recognition. It has its own journals, textbooks, conferences, university departments, professional associations (see: Collier and Collier 1986; Emmison and Smith 2000; Rose 2001; El Guindi 2004; Wright 2008). It attempts to use technologies of recording images—photography, video, film, digitalization—for the purposes of sociological research. It treats the pictures as a new type of research resource: either the pictures collected by the researcher from the surrounding iconosphere, or those taken by the researcher him- or herself. Most often the visual techniques are treated as a supplement and extension of more traditional qualitative methods: aiding observation (including participant observation when cameras are put in the hands of the research subjects for spontaneous picture-taking that reveals the insider perspective), eliciting photos in interviews or focus groups, inserting photographs in questionnaires to evoke spontaneous reactions (as in Rorschach ink blots in psychology), using private collections of photographs as new type of personal documents, and carrying out content analysis of pictures in addition to the scrutiny of texts.

But the need for new methods is not limited to the visual sociologists. It has become a useful skill for every sociologist. I am concerned in this article with the strong implication of the turn of our society toward a society of the spectacle, of the design, of the display, and of the icons. Namely, I treat the visual imagination as a necessary competence for every sociologist, and the developing *visual imagination* as a crucial aspect of sociological education.

It was Georg Simmel who observed that the eye is for the sociologist the most important of the five senses ([1908] 1921: 358). And a century later, I have been listening to the eminent German sociologist Erwin Scheuch telling me over breakfast at a conference in Amalfi: "if I want truly to understand Italian society I go to the piazza or the corner cafe and I *just look around*" (private communication).

But the eye can perform two completely different operations: *seeing,* which means passively recording visual impressions that float in immense numbers and variety in front of us, and *looking* which means actively, intentionally searching for meaningful visual experiences. And an especial variety of looking may be labeled a *sociological gaze*: actively, intentionally searching for social meanings in the spectacles, designs, displays, and iconosphere of social life.

And here enters photography as a helpful tool for training and practicing visual imagination and the sociological gaze. In the remaining part of the article, I will be concerned with *sociological photography:* the grasping of social events and their meanings with the help of a photo camera. In other words: decoding photographs with the help of the conceptual and theoretical apparatus of sociology. This is an area in which I feel competent as a professional sociologist and a semiprofessional photographer. But several arguments and conclusions may perhaps be applicable mutatis mutandis also to other techniques of video or film recording.

Sociological Photography

Two different types of practices are involved in sociological photography. The first, which does not require photographic skills, is simply *using existing photographic images* as a sociological resource: interpreting photographs as recordings or representations of social life, unraveling and unpacking meanings that are encoded in them. The second is more ambitious, as it requires at least basic photographic skills: *taking pictures oneself* as a research activity with the intention of revealing meanings in social situations or scenes. The latter is also more fruitful, as it provides double, deeper understanding.

Thus, first, it requires recognizing, discerning, identifying what is significant and carries important meanings among the visual chaos of social life. Going out in the field with the camera at hand immediately creates a different attitude and intentionality: it encourages looking and not just seeing. The photographic technique itself is very helpful as it immediately enforces four necessary decisions: selecting the crucial aspects of the social situation or scene by *focusing*, bracketing unimportant aspects or parts of the setting by *framing*, distinguishing the hierarchy of significance, that is, the primary and secondary components of the situation, separating the front and the background by employing *depth of vision*, and finally selecting the significant moment in the flow of incessant movement and change by using the *shutter*.

But this is only the beginning. Now comes the second benefit: the opportunity of interpreting and reinterpreting pictures taken by oneself, which multiplies the original visual experience. We have a chance not only to look at the social world, but to look critically at our own visual representations of the social world. Thus we are interacting with the visual surface of social life twice. We are involved in the "double observation": with visual reality while taking the photograph, and with the visual image, the representation of that reality, frozen, recorded and preserved, while critically studying photographs.

When we have taken just one, single photograph, the use is mostly descriptive. By scrutinizing a picture, we may systematically list the important features of the situation, and sometimes discover new traits that have been missed in the hurried direct observation. I call the letter a "blow up effect" after the famous movie by Michelangelo Antonioni, in which a photographer, after enlarging a picture in the laboratory, discovers a mysterious hand carrying a gun sticking out from the shrubbery, and that starts the whole storyline.

With multiple pictures, there is a possibility of discovering not only traits but also regularities. Here, taking photographs acquires theoretical and not only descriptive importance. Comparing similar situations or scenes in different cultural or civilizational contexts helps us to answer two kinds of theoretical questions. The first, why do the same, universal types of human activity or its products take such different shapes in different cultural or civilizational settings? A good visual illustration of this query is the photographic chronicle of the pilgrimages of Pope John Paul II (Giansanti 1996), which shows a tremendous diversity of audiences and their looks and behavior in over one hundred countries the pope visited. The second theoretical question is why, in spite of the diversity of cultures or civilizations, some types of human activity or its products are so strikingly similar. Here, an impressive evidence of the commonalities of our human race is presented in the famous photo exhibition in the New York Museum of Modern Art titled tellingly "The Family of Man" (Steichen 1955). In the earlier case, we search for cultural and civilizational diversity, in the latter for cultural or civilizational universals. This provides proofs for cultural localism (relativism), or for cultural homogenization (universalism). Another opportunity is open when we compare the similar situations or scenes (settings) in various moments of time, taking sequences of photographs in shorter or longer time intervals. Then we can discover temporal regularities, changes, trends, developments. For example, it is immensely enlightening to study the photo albums from the period of communist rule in order to grasp the meaning of the postcommunist transformations in Eastern Europe and the incredible scope of the change (Niedenthal 2004).

In both types of research practices: whether we use existing photographs or take photographs ourselves, we follow certain strategies of interpretation, get involved with what Barthes calls the "studium" (Barthes 1983). It is important that those strategies were consciously recognized and critically applied. In using existing photographs, the interpretative strategies suggest possible directions of their deconstruction, unpacking and unraveling meanings. In taking our own photographs, the interpretative strategies indicate possible directions in the search for meanings. They provide an intentional frame of mind with which the sociologist-photographer goes into the field, attempting to orient him- or herself in the flow of chaotic social life.

We shall introduce an analytical typology of such strategies, remembering that they may be used in various combinations. Some social situations are singular in meaning, and one strategy may be sufficient; others are complex and pluralistic, requiring multiple strategies. The following typology of interpretative strategies is informed by a specific approach to social life, a theoretical and methodological orientation that must be revealed beforehand. I call it the theory of *social existence,* which is complementary to the theory of *social becoming* that I proposed earlier (Sztompka 1991). There is a strong (and of course contestable) ontological assumption behind such an orientation, namely that what is "really real," what is ontologically prior and fundamentally constitutive of a society is neither an organic, holistic system or structure, nor an individual action, but a multidimensional existence of human beings in the environment of other human beings. The qualifier "social" indicates that for the human species the central dimension of existence is "togetherness": living with others, for the sake of others, side by side with others, against others—but never alone. Therefore the ultimate, constitutive components of society are interpersonal, *situated events* bringing together two or more individuals mutually related in many ways. The social world is nothing else but an interpersonal field filled with encounters, interactions, relationships, social bonds, ties, ligatures, links with others, covering the whole spectrum from love and intimacy to interests and contracts, from cooperation to competition, from peace to conflict, from consensus to quarrel. Society, as the Polish poet Stanislaw J. Lec put it, is an "*inter-human space*" (1966: 111). And the embeddedness of human beings in the net of relationships with other human beings occurs nowhere else but in our everyday experiences. It is the central, social aspect of our existence as humans. All other aspects of society—macrostructures, macroprocesses, cultures, civilizations, technological systems, organizations, institutions—in fact exist not somewhere outside, but inside of social existence, permeate from within the simplest everyday events in which we routinely participate. Society is not somewhere outside of ourselves but *within us and between us.* And sociology is about what happens between and among the people.

This kind of ontological perspective is a mark of what I call "the third sociology" (Sztompka 2009). The first sociology of Auguste Comte, Herbert Spencer, and Karl Marx looked at societies as integrated wholes: social organisms, socioeconomic formations, social systems. And the subject of what they discussed as social or historical change was humanity as a whole. The second sociology of Weber, Vilfredo Pareto, and Florian Znaniecki focused on actions: the meaningful conduct of individuals. The third sociology centers on social events, episodes actually occurring in a society in particular situations, and incorporating both the *agential input* of individuals carrying out certain practices, and the *situational constraints* of structures, cultures, ecologies, and so forth. Through a set of concepts the "third sociology" identifies various dimensions of social existence. Apart from events, episodes, and their surrounding situations, it indicates typical "sites" where events take place—the home, the street, the pub, the church, the football stadium, the hospital, the school. It singles out typical, more complex "occasions," congeries of events—the wedding, shopping, the sports game, the mass, the lecture. Apart from actual behavior or "practices," it looks for standardized or ritualized conduct—"performances." It takes into account the flow of time, linking events in sequences: "chains," "careers," and ultimately—"biographies." And from the bird's eye perspective it sees society as a dynamic, fluid "socio-individual field" of events, in the course of incessant "social becoming": the production and reproduction of society by society. The interhuman space in the incessant dynamics of social becoming is constituted of *social events*. There are two aspects to any social event: agential (the input of acting people), depending on their agential endowment, and structural (the frames, constraints, and limitations provided ultimately by other people, living or dead). At both levels, meanings enter: psychological meanings (in the minds of acting people) and cultural meanings (from the surrounding—constraining or facilitating—structures). In each social event we may discover at least seven layers of meaning: contextual or situational meaning, intentional or personal meaning, and four types of structural meaning—interactional meaning, normative meaning, ideal meaning and distributional meaning. Therefore, the interpretation of meaning embedded in social events must take seven steps. And this applies to interpretation of photographs that capture social events.

STRATEGIES OF VISUAL INTERPRETATION

Contextual (or situational) interpretation: recognizes the context of a photographically depicted social event and the typical site (the social scene, the social setting) where the social event is occurring. This is the primary guideline for the search for meaning, because the meanings found in various contexts are typically different. People look different, dress differently, talk differently, behave differently, and even think differently—depending on the context that they enter and leave, often during one day, or a week, or a month, and certainly during the whole biographical span. Without pretensions for completeness, I suggest the distinctions among the following contexts and corresponding sites: family and intimacy (home), education (school), work (office, factory), consumption (street, shopping mall), transportation (train station or airport), tourism (beaches or mountains), leisure (parks, gyms), art (museums, theaters, concert halls), sports (stadiums, tennis courts), public participation (election booth, convention halls), health (hospital), religion (the church), and death (cemetery).

When we study existing photographs, we first have to specify the context and the site, as a key to further deconstruction and the search for meanings. When we take photographs ourselves, we may have a specific interest in a given context, and therefore choose a relevant site: for example, recording the forms and expressions of religion—by entering the church, or manifestations of consumption—by shooting in the shopping mall, or the functioning of the health care system—by entering the hospital, and so forth.

Hermeneutical (or intentional) interpretation is the search for motivations, intentions, and reasons why people are participating in the event (actors on the social stage), for their unique configuration of thoughts and emotions. "To understand human action is to grasp meaning which has been injected by the intention of the actor" (Bauman 1978: 12). There are several cues to motivations, intentions, reasons that are visible, observable—and hence also available for photography. They include: (a) face, physiognomy, and looks, (b) appearance indicative of age, gender, race, (c) gestures and body language, (d) objects and gadgets serving as status symbols: cars, watches, mobile phones, jewelry, (e) situational context: home, street, office, shopping mall, and (f) uniforms, dresses, ornamentation signifying professional attitudes and orientations.

A special situation in our society of pervasive icons arises when we have to interpret images within images: those intentionally created by somebody to convey meanings, for example, billboards, advertisements, banners, and so forth grasped in photographs that are also taken by somebody (or by us) with some intentions, for some purposes that are usually different from the author of the original picture. Then there are two levels of hermeneutical interpretation: the meanings infused by the advertising agencies, marketing experts, media editors, and so on into the picture grasped in the photograph, and the motivations, intentions, reasons of the photographer.

Semiological (or symbolic) interpretation is the search for the visual elements that serve in a given society as signs and symbols and are displayed in the social event. They are historically coded in the practices of a given society (Barthes 1983: 206), injected by the culture. In our own culture, they are accessible by participation, acquire a taken-for-granted quality. In alien cultures, they require critical knowledge about the local codes. It is useful to distinguish—after Charles Peirce—three types of signs (1955). Iconic signs are similar in shape (form) to the signified. Examples include reindeer on a Swedish road sign, a crossed dog meaning "no dogs" on a lawn, a fishing rod on a prohibition to fish, or an airplane indicating the direction to the gates. Another type of signs, called indexes, is linked with the signified by some social (or even natural) regularities, or normative regulations. For example: the crowd of people on the beach indicates summer, the highway with no trucks and only passenger cars indicates the weekend, and a farmer harvesting indicates autumn. The third type of signs and symbols is entirely conventional and limited to a certain community that recognizes the common meaning, for example: the flag, the cross, the Star of David, the Red Cross, the coat-of-arms, the medal of merit, ceremonial uniforms. Symbols are observable and available for photography when they are displayed on the stage of action or in environments of action.

The next four types are the *varieties of structural interpretation*. It is assumed that social life (events, practices) reflects some underlying structures, frames, or figures, which constrain or facilitate it, curbing arbitrariness. Not everything is equally possible or probable in society, due to the existence of such structures. I distinguish four types of structures (the INID scheme), depending on the types of elements they integrate: interactions-norms-ideas-distributions of life chances. Therefore, there are four types of structures: interactional, normative, ideal, and distributional (Sztompka 1991). Unraveling them through the interpretation of photographs may proceed in four directions.

Interactional interpretation focuses on the form the event takes, the shape of "inter-human space'" or the "interpersonal field," and the "geometry of social relations" within which the event occurs. There are visible configurations of people in the inter-human space, which may be ordered along the axis of individualism versus commu-nity: solitude, loneliness, encounters, interactions, social relationships, social bonds, and social identities (defined by "we" feelings). There is also the visible impact of such configurations on the intensiveness of relations and their "vectors"—positive or negative (cooperation or conflict, friendliness or hostility, solidarity or exclusion, etc).

The *normative (axiological) interpretation* seeks to determine which rules, values, norms, socially defined roles, fashions, or binding lifestyles are manifest, and how people relate to them along the axis of conformity versus deviance. Sometimes we may visually observe the norms themselves: permissions, prescriptions, proscrip-tions, preferences—the famous Robert K. Merton's "4 P's" (1996: 133). For exam-ple, lines as opposed to chaotic crowds reflect a rule: first come, first served, whereas the military drill indicates a focus on orderliness and unreflecting obedience. More often, we may clearly see the reactions of people to the violence of norms (the acts of deviance) by means of various social sanctions. We may also observe social reactions to exemplary, conformist conduct. The indicators of norms and values may also be found in the visible standardization, routinization, or ritualization of behavior (e.g., greetings, table manners, street behavior, religious rites, forms of applause).

Ideal (cognitive) interpretation seeks to unravel what kinds of cognitive beliefs, creeds, doctrines, or ideologies are manifest or displayed by the people participat-ing in the event, and how people embrace or reject such beliefs along the axis of acceptance versus contestation. Sometimes the content of ideas is visibly displayed: on posters, billboards of social campaigns, car stickers, or T-shirt inscriptions. Sometimes the appeal and popularity of some beliefs may be grasped by observing their followers: crowds of believers in churches, masses of participants at a political rally or protest march, or the reverse—few employees on a street picket line or on strike, or a single protester against experiments on animals.

Distributional (status) interpretation tries to determine who are the people depicted in the photograph in terms of social status and hierarchies of inequality: of wealth, power, prestige, education, cultural tastes, lifestyles, life chances. Where are they located in the distributional structure along the axis of egalitarianism versus elitism? Many aspects of such social divisions and distributions are observable: visible afflu-ence or poverty, visible marks of power, visible celebrity status or fame, visible life-styles of the rich and famous, visible marginality or exclusion, visible homelessness, unemployment, degradation.

THE FUNCTIONS OF VISUAL INTERPRETATION

What is the use and effect of all those interpretative strategies—analyzing pictures in these terms or taking pictures with such interpretative intentions—in sociological practice and the training of sociologists?

Some functions are obvious and have a long tradition: they appear in the *context of the dissemination* of sociological knowledge. Photographs provide a shorthand; they are persuasive illustrations useful in sociological education or in the popularizing of sociological concepts, theories, and research results. Anchoring written texts in photographic images is particularly important for a young generation who is now accustomed to visual discourse in communication, work, and recreation (MMSes in mobile phones, face pictures in interactions via Skype, the computer style of Windows and iconic interfaces, computer games). The photographs may be useful in illustrating sociological concepts by bringing them down to earth and proving that they are ultimately represented in everyday human actions, the events of everyday life. The association of a concept with an image endows a concept with concreteness and flesh. The images may also illustrate sociological descriptive diagnoses of traits as well as sociological regularities (comparisons across space and sequential series of pictures along the axis of time).

Some other functions are more ambitious and appear in the *context of justification* or verification of sociological claims. Which claims? For example, those concerning the typical, dominant quality of phenomena that can be substantiated by a large number of pictures can be considered as representative. A famous case is the volume by Goffman on *Gender Advertisements* (1979) that grasps in several hundred images the typical cultural definitions of femininity and masculinity. The claims of social tendencies in civilizational developments or modernizing processes may be justified by temporally arranged pictures of the same community, the same city or region, or the same house or apartment over several years. Gregory Bateson and Margaret Mead, in their impressive project on the *Balinese Character* (1942), grasped the tendencies in the upbringing and socialization of children by taking more than twenty thousand pictures in the local community on the Pacific island.

But for me, the most important function is heuristic, realized in the *context of discovery*. Studying pictures and taking pictures enhances and multiplies the engagement with social life. It mobilizes our attention and makes us more sensitive to salient features of social events and situations. It helps us to understand social life better, paves the road *to the level of invisible meanings by studying visible meanings*. And it helps to ask the right questions about social life by defining our ignorance. Sometimes it also provides serendipities and surprises, shocks and bolts of conscience: those most important stimuli for scientific investigations that mobilize creativity. This may be particularly true of the pictures rich in "punctum," as opposed to "studium" in Barthes's terminology (1983). How can the horrors of war be depicted better than in that famous picture showing naked Vietnamese children fleeing from approaching soldiers and the wall of napalm fires in the background? How can the meaning of political resistance and contestation be grasped better than in the picture of a lonely Chinese student facing the cavalcade of approaching tanks at Tiananmen Square? And how can the meaning of the accession to the European Union (EU) be rendered better than in the picture of a smiling, beautiful woman waving an EU flag from the desolate window of an industrial slum in Polish Silesia?

To realize the heuristic function—preparation and training is necessary. Hence the role of *visual education* as a part of sociological education. Training is needed to develop the inclination to look around rather than only to see, to actively perceive and pursue social life as it flows around us. Training allows us to develop the ability to translate abstract concepts and theories into their concrete, miniscule manifestations in everyday life, "grounding" them in social events. It also helps to discern empty concepts, pure abstractions devoid of empirical reference, not "grounded" in the experiences of people.

In short: taking pictures of social life and interpreting pictures of social life helps one to develop the habit of looking at social life, to acquire a *sociological gaze or a visual imagination*. In other words, it allows us to read the invisible meanings of social events from their visible manifestations. In my view, this is the fundamental skill for a sociologist.

ENDING ON A PERSONAL NOTE

I have been taking photographs as a hobby for several decades. Their themes were typical for amateur photography: mostly beautiful landscapes and striking architecture, flowers, and animals, especially in exotic places. The criterion of selection was mainly aesthetic. People and social situations appeared in my pictures only occasionally, as a background rather than a foreground. But then I discovered that the effects of that hobby were not only hundreds of pictures depicting the beauty of the natural world or material civilization, but also personal enrichment, the development of a particularly strong sensitivity to the beauty of nature as well as to the elegance and design of human creations.

And that realization led me to visual sociology. I started taking photographs of social situations, people in their contexts of everyday life, reversing the earlier focus: now the landscapes and architecture became the background, and people emerged in the foreground. And the same effect occurred: I became much more sensitive, discerning, and focused on the social life and all its dimensions. Now wherever I am, with or without a camera, I look around (as Erwin Scheuch advised me on that hotel balcony at Amalfi) with a sociological gaze. And I have begun *to see* abstract sociological concepts and sociological theories in the concrete chaotic flow of human activity. I feel photography has enriched my sociological grasp of society.

Thus when I teach a class in visual sociology, I do not attempt to make my students into professional photographers. Of course, it is good if they have photographic skills. But this is not the main point. Instead, I want to make them sensitive to the rich visual evidence of social phenomena and processes. And for that purpose, a photographic camera appears to be a most useful tool. In the hands of a visually sensitive sociologist, the camera lens becomes a *sociological lens* through which the social world appears in bold relief.

REFERENCES

Barthes, R. 1984. *Camera Lucida: Reflections on Photography*. Translated by Richard Howard. London:Flamingo.

Bateson, G., and M. Mead. 1942. *Balinese Character. A Photographic Analysis*. New York: New York Academy of Sciences.

Baudrillard, J. 1994. *Simulacra and Simulation*. Ann Arbor: University of Michigan Press.

Bauman, Z. 1978. *Hermeneutics and Social Science*. London: Hutchison.

———. 1991, *Modernity and Ambivalence*. Cambridge, UK: Polity Press.

Chartier, R., ed. 1985. *Histoire de la vie privée: De la Renaissance aux Lumières* [The history of private life: from the Renaissance to the Enlightenment]s. Paris: Editions du Seuil.

Collier, J., and M. Collier. 1986. *Visual Anthropology Photography as a Research Method*. Albuquerque: University of New Mexico Press.

Durkheim, É. (1912) 1995. *The Elementary Forms of Religious Life*. Translated by Karen E. Fields. New York: Free Press.

El Guindi, F. 2004. *Visual Anthropology*. Walnut Creek, CA: Altamira Press.

Emmison, M., and P. Smith. 2000. *Researching the Visual*. London: Sage.

Giansanti, G. 1996. *John Paul II*. Vercelli: White Star Publishers.

Giddens, A. 1990. The *Consequences of Modernity*. Cambridge, UK: Polity Press.

Goffman, E. 1959. *Presentation of Self in Everyday Life*. New York: Doubleday.

———. 1979. *Gender Advertisements*. London: Macmillan.

Lec, S. J. 1966. *Mysli nieuczesane nowe* [The new disorderly thoughts]. Cracow: Wydawnictwo Literackie.

Merton, R. K. 1996. *On Social Structure and Science*. Edited by Piotr Sztompka. Chicago: University of Chicago Press.

Niedenthal, C. 2004. *Polska Rzeczpospolita Ludowa: Rekwizyty* [The Polish Peoples Republic: Props]. Warsaw: Bosz Publishers.

Peirce, C. S. 1955. *Philosophical Writings*. Edited by Justus Buchler. New York: Dover Press.

Perrot, M., ed. 1986. *Histoire de la vie privée: De la Révolution à la Grande Guerre* [The history of private life: from the Revolution to the Great War]. Paris: Editions du Seuil.

Prost, A., and G. Vincent, eds. 1986. *Histoire de la vie privée: De la Première Guerre mondiale à nos jours* [The history of private life: from the First World War to our time]. Paris: Editions du Seuil.

Rose, G. 2001. *Visual Methodologies*. London: Sage.

Simmel, G. (1908) 1921. "Sociology of the Senses: Visual Interaction." In: *Introduction to the Science of Sociology*, edited by R. Park and E. Burgess. Chicago: University of Chicago Press.

Sontag, S. 1978. *On Photography,* New York: Farrar, Strauss and Giroux.

Steichen, E., curator and ed. 1955. *The Family of* Man. New York: Museum of Modern Art.

Sztompka, P. 1991. *Society in Action: The Theory of Social Becoming*. Cambridge, UK: Polity Press.

———. 2006. *Socjologia wizualna: fotografia jako metoda badawcza* [Visual sociology: photography as a research method]. Warszawa: Wydawnictwo PWN [also published in Russian, Czech and Hungarian].

———. 2008. "The Focus on Everyday Life: A New Turn in Sociology." *European Review* 16 (1): 23–38.

———. 2009. "Przestrzeń życia codziennego" [The space of everyday life]. In *Barwy codziennosci* [The colors of the everyday], edited by M. Bogunia-Borowska, 29–50. Warsaw: Scholar Publishers.

Veblen, T. (1899) 1953. *The Theory of the Leisure Class,* New York: A Mentor Book.

Weber, M. (1922) 1979. *Economy and Society: An Outline of Interpretive Sociology*. Edited by G. Roth and C. Wittich. Berkeley: University of California Press.

Wright, T. 2008. *Visual Impact*. Oxford: Berg.

Afterword

Bernhard Giesen

In their introduction to this volume, Dominik Bartmański and Jeffrey C. Alexander announce a new paradigm that not only continues the line of cultural sociology, but also covers the impact that material things, images, and events exert on collective emotions and the emergence of community. The key notion is iconicity. "Iconicity" refers to the mobilizing power of objects, images, and events. Icons convey, for those who look at them as icons, an unequivocality, straightforwardness, and immediacy that run counter to the enigmatic ambivalence that is the hallmark of pictorial art. Icons are immediately understood even if their meaning is diffuse and vague. They stir up and trigger off a strong emotional response—be it attractive or repulsive, traumatic or triumphant. Sometimes icons split their audiences into those who gather around them as the embodiment of their collective identity and those for whom the same icons represent a demonic and dangerous threat to their communities. The face of Osama bin Laden, for example, stands for leadership and saviordom among Islamist radicals as well as for a devilish assault on Western civilization among the defenders of liberal democracy. To use a Durkheimian phrasing: icons exude the redemptive aura of the sacred and the destructive aura of the demonic. They hint at triumphant events that occurred against all odds as well as at shocking moments when destructive powers were suddenly disclosed.

Icons do have a referential meaning, and this meaning is unequivocal. Their message seems to be straightforward and simple, and it is only because of this apparent lack of complexity that they are able to trigger off strong emotions, split audiences, and mobilize people. Icons do not just refer to an external object or event, but they fuse this reference with emotions and communality. Their fundamental reference is social, but they hide this reference by embedding it in a cultural universe— entangled in stories and oppositions, linked to recollections and aspirations, fears and hopes. This is one aspect of Alexander's "depth" dimension of images.

The depth dimension distinguishes also between icons and visual everyday signs and images. Everyday objects carry, orient, and direct social communication because they escape our attention—they are the background of interaction that is taken for granted; they do not enter the arena of attention; we do not talk about them; they remain almost invisible. Icons, by contrast, attract and focus the attention and heighten the level of awareness. Showing them highlights the flow of communication and triggers off emotions. In contrast to controversial issues of conversation that are also attentively and consciously dealt with, but that generate divisive communication, icons produce an integrating liminality, an unequivocal orientation, a moment of collective effervescence, a charismatic transcendence of everyday life. Icons are extraordinary. They have an aura. Perceiving them and showing them uplifts the ordinary flow of time and marks an event that can be recalled and renarrated.

If we conceive of icons in this way as extraordinary imaginative references of communication, we have to cease treating regular emblems or signs such as the stop or start signs on our computer screens as "icons." They are, instead, visual devices of ordinary everyday technologies. When we use them habitually, they escape our attention, and we follow their message without noticing it.

Many of the American contributions to this volume focus and center this depth dimension of icons as extraordinary references. As important, even as constitutive as this search for something behind the obvious content of icons is in order to decode its cultural meaning, it still falls short of Erwin Panofsky's famous distinction between "iconography" and "iconology" (1955: 19). Iconography aims at the historical context and the range of pictorial and symbolic means (allegories, metaphors, predecessors) available for representing the respective content at the respective period. Iconology, by distinction, tries to relate the image to the "underlying principles which reveal the basic attitude of a nation, a period, a class, a religious or philosophical persuasion—qualified by one personality and condensed in one work" (Panofsky 1955: 30). If we distinguish just between surface and depth, we risk plunging immediately to the iconological dimension without accounting for the different symbolic and pictorial varieties available in a particular historical situation.

It is no surprise that not all texts in this volume match the idea of iconicity equally well. Gottfried Boehm's and Hans Belting's contributions to this volume, for example, address questions of producing and viewing images from an ambitious though very general perspective. Boehm aims at a phenomenology of viewing images by investigating the relationship between the material presence of images and the represented, but in fact absent, imagined reality. This "iconic difference" becomes the key notion of many essays in this volume (Boehm, Werner Binder, Bernhard Giesen, Valentin Rauer, Daniel Šuber, and others), rivaling the concept of iconicity that is at the core of many other texts. This difference mirrors the stronger leaning of some contributions towards theoretical issues of pictorial representation and the formal logic of images, while other essays—although not disregarding these issues—seem to be more interested in the mobilizing power of icons and in the conditions that foster the rise to iconic power. They are, in a way, more sociological than their theory-heavy counterparts. Forcing all contributions into the bed of Procrustes of a single concept would, however, suffocate a vivid debate and turn the colorful diversity of current thinking about icons into the pale and dead systemacity of a uniform account. We will, therefore, not conceal that—despite large areas of agreement and a long history of common ideas—there is still some disagreement among the contributors.

As strongly as we agree on the extraordinariness of icons, we may disagree as to whether the fuzziness that surrounds the everyday meaning of "iconic" should be clarified or kept in its colorful multifariousness: if we follow the everyday use of the terms, "icons," "iconicity," or "iconic power" may be understood just as the socially eminent status of an object or an event. In this case, a vineyard or a festival of music can, indeed, be called "iconic." What we can achieve within the confines of this everyday meaning of the term is a range of colorful stories about the rise of an "icon" to fame and its impact on collective identity. Some of the contributions of this volume present such vivid and insightful histories of icons. They build on the new attention that contemporary social theory pays to objects as stabilizing anchors of the volatility of social communication.

What we risk losing by broadening the meaning of the term to include everything socially important is, however, the strong link between social extraordinariness and its visual representation. Icons, we may argue, are visual media, and they partake in the nature of visuality as distinct from acoustic or olfactorial signs. [1]

Visuality is not to be mixed up with materiality—and here the title of the introduction is slightly misleading: the sound of voices and the smell of burned rubber are material signs, too. Visual representations presuppose material carriers, and they are somehow limited by the carrier medium, but they can, certainly, not be reduced to them, since, for example, one image can be represented by various material carriers—fresco painting, oil and canvas painting, photography, and so forth. [2]

Visuality has one distinctive feature: it allows for presenting colors, forms, and sizes that escape even a fine-grained linguistic description. We can, at best, refer metaphorically to a particular kind of red ("cherry red"), while presenting it visually is easy. But there are also some drawbacks implied by visual media: for example, they can represent temporal sequences only in a very indirect way. Visuality is bound to a certain simultaneity of presentation. The gaze of the viewer might wander across the surface of an image, but the temporal mode of the image is coexistence and simultaneity. [3] There are, obviously, limits to intermediality, and it is the task of studies in intermediality to investigate these limits.

Much more than texts, images exude an unconditional claim of validity: while we can negate or conditionalize, affirm or criticize texts by speech acts or by other texts, we cannot do the same with images. Arguing in the way in which philosophy does is not the domain of images. Philosophy is bound to language, whereas the image is more apt to convey a sense of presence to the sacred that is beyond any doubt for the viewer. Arguments and images engender quite different ritual or habitual responses: it is hard to imagine somebody kneeling in front of a philosophical argument, or looking at a thesis in the way we are used to looking at photos of our loved ones. Images can easily stimulate emotions, while philosophical discourse has to exclude these very emotions and so forth. This strong and unconditional impact of images is certainly related to the simultaneity of representation that we mentioned above. Images shrink the temporal sequence to one single moment, intensify it, and thus continue the moment forever.

If we accept visuality as a defining element of icons, we can no longer include pop songs within the class of icons. Even musical events become iconic only and insofar as they are presented by images. Without widely recognized representations in images, an event might be epochal, but it can hardly become iconic. Globally known music lines, famous football teams, the taste of a special food, or the name of commercial brands can be surrounded by a strong charismatic aura, they can inspire a liminal *communitas* for the respective adherents, and hey can even mobilize collective action—but they become iconic only via images. If we can reduce without remainder the meaning of "iconic" to "auratic" or "charismatic," why do we need the term?

This brings us to explore the logic of images. Some essays in this volume treat icons mainly as emblems of collective identity or as purified embodiments of the sacred in a world that sees itself as disenchanted or ratiocinated. Others claim that icons partake, even if they are largely unequivocal, in the ability of images to generate a heightened sense of reality. This claim rejects Plato's despising attitude towards images as a second-rate reality, as imitation, as illusion and deception. The reality of the image is, as Boehm has shown, "stronger" than the represented reality: it links the presence of the image to the absence of the represented reality, it selects and freezes a volatile moment, and most importantly, it shows occasionally something that the viewer did not expect or foresee. Following Georges Didi-Hubermann (1999), we may even assume that images are "actants" that look at us and communicate with us.[4]

In the act of gazing at an image, we may discover something new. Images of art may contain and disclose, by their material surface, meaning that exceeds the represented reality. Discovering this unexpected and surprising meaning in the material surface of the painting may even produce an uncanny frisson on the part of the viewer. Boehm had this in mind when he spoke of the "iconic difference" between the represented content and the form that "discloses itself" or "shows itself" (German: *es zeigt sich*) without being intended by the painter or being expected by the viewer.

But there may also be some doubts raised against the universality of the iconic difference: some radically minimalist paintings or sculptures (Marcel Duchamp, Robert Ryman, Lucio Fontana, Frank Stella, Donald Judd, Sol LeWitt) try to escape the iconic difference by presenting themselves as sheer surface, as plain materiality and objectness: a white painting is just a canvas covered with white paint (Gertrude Stein: "A rose is a rose is a rose..."). It does not represent anything except itself, it has no referential meaning, and it has no iconic depth in Alexander's sense of the term. If there is a reference at all in minimalist painting, it consists of reflecting analytically about the means of painting: pure materiality devoid of any relationship to an absent reality. Occasionally, the remaining traces of representation are even deliberately wiped out or painted over (e.g., Robert Ryman's white or Frank Stella's black "allover" paintings).

But in a weird twist, this sheer and raw reality that seems to be devoid of any cultural meaning acquires a transcendental quality: its void attracts and fascinates, it stimulates almost religious feelings, and its purity is venerated by the connoisseur of modern art. There is definitely an iconographical and an iconological dimension for these voids that a weird modern iconoclasm creates. Despite all efforts to purge representation and to enforce radical self-reference, the sacred survives all attempts to destroy its embodiments. It reemerges ever more strongly in empty spaces from which the representing image has been expelled. Thus, even the nonimage becomes an image. We cannot escape its power.

Konstanz
January 2011
Bernhard Giesen

NOTES

1. There might be even a certain coexistence of sensory perceptions in different dimensions, as Belting points out in his essay, but this does not dispense us from investigating the special logic of different media.
2. Visuality also does not distinguish texts from images. Texts can be represented visually by writing and acoustically by speaking. Exploring the meaning of icons, we may even use spoken language—the requirement to remain within the domain of visual media when investigating them is awkward and nonsensical.
3. Boehm disagrees, however, on this issue. He argues that images can represent temporal differences by showing, for example, different scenes of a life and guiding the viewer's gaze through this sequence.
4. Didi-Hubermann was, however, not the first to raise this claim. Martin Heidegger noted already in 1935 in his "Der Ursprung des Kunstwerks" (1977 10f.) that an "object may look at us" and that Vincent Van Gogh's painting "talked" to us. A piece of art constructs a meaningful world around it, and this world is not just the arbitrary invention of the viewer, but a world of objects that claim "truth." This truth is not, of course, a uniform one, but it varies according to its object source. We can find similar observations in Jacques Lacan (1973: 89). Lacan (1973: 71) claims that "in the theatre of the world we are beings who are gazed at [que nous sommes des etres regardees, dans le spectacle du monde]." All these turn-taking shifts between images and viewers are—hardly surprising—related to attempts to deconstruct the traditional distinction between subject and object.

REFERENCES

Alexander, J. C. 2008. "Iconic Experience in Art and Life: Surface/Depth Beginning with Giacometti's 'Standing Woman.'" *Theory, Culture & Society* 25 (5): 1–19.

Didi-Hubermann, G. 1999. *Ouvrir Venus*. Paris: Gallimard.

Heidegger, M. 1977. *Holzwege*. Frankfurt am Main: Klostermann.

Lacan, J. 1973. *Les quatre concepts fondamentaux de la psychanalyse*. Paris: Seuil.

Panofsky, E. 1955. *Meaning in the Visual Arts: Papers in and on Art History*. Garden City: Doubleday.

CONTRIBUTORS

Jeffrey C. Alexander is the Lillian Chavenson Saden Professor of Sociology at Yale University, and he works in the areas of theory, culture and politics, developing a meaning-centered approach to the tensions and possibilities of modern social life. He is Director of the Center for Cultural Sociology, also at Yale. His recent publications include: *Understanding the Holocaust: A Debate* (2009); *A Contemporary Introduction to Sociology: Culture and Society in Transition* (with Thompson) (2008); *Social Performances: Symbolic Action, Cultural Pragmatics, and Ritual* (with Giesen and Mast) (2006); *Cultural Trauma and Collective Identity* (with Eyerman, Giesen, Sztompka, and Smelser) (2004); and *The Meanings of Social Life: A Cultural Sociology* (2003). In his major work, *The Civil Sphere* (2006), Alexander developed a new cultural-sociological theory of democracy, a perspective that provides the foundation for his newest volume, *The Performance of Politics: Obama's Victory and the Democratic Struggle for Power* (2010).

Dominik Bartmański earned his PhD in Sociology at Yale University. His dissertation thematizes the iconic turn as a new epistemological framework for sociological research and examines iconicity in the context of the transitional urban landscapes of Berlin and Warsaw after 1989. He works in the areas of cultural sociology and social theory. His interests include visuality, public design, urban studies, sociology of knowledge, and symbolic anthropology. He has been connecting these sociological domains to the ongoing preoccupation with aesthetics, travel, and photography since beginning his work as a researcher at the New York City–based Photo Library Peter Arnold Inc. in 2003. Among his recent articles are: "Successful Icons of Failed Time: Rethinking Post-Communist Nostalgia" (*Acta Sociologica*, 2011), and "How to Become an Iconic Social Thinker: The Intellectual Pursuits of Malinowski and Foucault" (*European Journal of Social Theory*, 2011).

Hans Belting is Professor Emeritus at the Institute for Art History and Media Theory at the School of Design in Karlsruhe, Germany. He studied art history, archaeology, and history at the University of Mainz and earned his PhD there. He taught at the Universities of Hamburg, Heidelberg, and Munich before coming to Karlsruhe. He has held visiting appointments at Harvard University, Columbia University, and the Collège de France. Among his numerous books are: *Likeness and Presence: A History of the Image Before the Era of Art* (1984); *The End of the History of Art* (1987); *The Germans and Their Art: A Troublesome Relationship* (1998); *The Invisible Masterpiece: The Modern Myths of Art* (2001); and *Hieronymus Bosch: The Garden of Earthly Delights* (2002).

Werner Binder studied sociology, philosophy, and literature in Mannheim, Potsdam, and Berlin, Germany. He earned his MA in sociology with a study on Turkish immigrants in Germany. Currently, he is junior lecturer and research assistant at the University of Konstanz, Germany. The subject of his ongoing dissertation project is the Abu Ghraib scandal. His other fields of interest include classical sociological theory, qualitative methodology, visual sociology, sociology of violence, and morality and civil society.

Gottfried Boehm is Professor at the University of Basel, Switzerland. He earned his PhD in philosophy at Heidelberg, and subsequently taught art history in Bochum and Giessen in Germany. He is currently Director of the Swiss national research project Eikones/NCCR Iconic Criticism. His works lay a foundation for the "iconic turn" in the human sciences. Among his numerous books and edited volumes that have advanced new theories of perception and image are: *Was ist ein Bild?* (1994); *Homo Pictor* (2001); *Was Bilder Sinn erzuegen: Die Macht des Zeigens* (2007); *Ikonologie der Gegenwart* (with Bredekamp, 2008).

Wendy Bowler is Lecturer in Journalism in the Media & Cinema Studies Program of La Trobe University in Melbourne, Australia, and a former daily newspaper and magazine journalist and editor. Her doctoral thesis, *From Terror to Tragedy* (La Trobe University library, 2007), is a review and interpretation of the 9/11 visual news narrative from a sociology of culture perspective, using largely Friedrich Nietzsche's theory of tragedy. She is working on a book manuscript based on her PhD research.

David Ellison has a PhD in English Literature from Princeton University. He teaches in the School of Humanities at Griffith University, Brisbane, Australia, in the areas of Literary Studies and Cultural History. He is Reviews Editor for the *Journal of Australasian Victorian Studies*, and on the Editorial Committee of *Cultural Studies Review*. He has research interests in Victorian literature and culture, domesticity, technology, architecture, and bioethics. His current book project challenges accounts of domestic comfort's progressive triumph over the Victorian home, focusing instead on discomfort's curious dispersion into the improvisatory and everyday practices that shape modern life.

Bernhard Giesen is Professor of Sociology at the University of Konstanz, Germany. He is Research Director of the DFG Research Centre "Norm & Symbol" as well as a member of the Executive Board of the Center of Excellence 16 "Cultural Foundations of Social Integration" at the University of Konstanz. His latest books are: *Social Performance: Symbolic Action, Cultural Pragmatics and Ritual* (ed. with Alexander and Mast, 2006); *Religion and Politics: Cultural Perspectives* (2005); *Cultural Trauma and Collective Identity* (with Alexander, Eyerman, Smelser, and Sztompka); *Triumph and Trauma* (2004); *European Citizenship: Between National Legacies and Postnational Projects* (ed. with Eder, 2001).

Slobodan Karamanić is Research Associate at the Center of Excellence 16 "Cultural Foundations of Integration" (University of Konstanz) and a doctoral candidate at the Ljubljana Graduate School of the Humanities in Slovenia. He has also been a research fellow at the School for History and Theory of Images, Belgrade (2000–01), the University of Tromsø (2002), and The New School for Social Research (2003). His main research interests are social and political theory, theories of subjectivity, visual studies, and the political and cultural history of Yugoslavia and the Balkans. He was a founder and coeditor of *Prelom [Break]— Journal for Images and Politics*, Belgrade (2001–06).

Fuyuki Kurasawa is Associate Professor of Sociology and Social and Political Thought at York University in Toronto, Canada. He is Co-President of the International Sociological Association's Research Committee on Sociological Theory. He works in areas of social theory, cultural sociology, cinema, and human rights. Among his recent publications are *The Ethnological Imagination: A Cross-Cultural Critique of Modernity* (2004) and *The Work of Global Justice: Human Rights as Practices* (2007).

Valentin Rauer studied Social Sciences and Medicine in Freiburg and Berlin, Germany, and worked at the University of Konstanz, Germany, within the Cluster of Excellence "Cultural Foundations of Integration." Currently, he is a researcher at the Goethe-University in Frankfurt am Main, Germany. His research fields include: cultures of memory, media, the public sphere, and migration and human security. Among his publications are: "Symbols in Action: Willy Brandt's Kneefall at the Warsaw Memorial (in J. C. Alexander, B. Giesen, and J. Mast, *Social Performance: Symbolic Action, Cultural Pragmatics, and Ritual* [2006]); "Transversale Spuren von Generation und Nation" (in Özkan Ezli, *Kultur als Ereignis: Fatih Akins Film "Auf der anderen Seite" als transkulturelle Narration*, forthcoming).

Philip Smith is Professor of Sociology at Yale University and Co-Director of the Center for Cultural Sociology there. He earned his BA in Anthropology at University of Edinburgh and PhD in Sociology at UCLA. He subsequently taught for a decade in Australia prior to his arrival at Yale. Among his recent books are: *Incivility: The Rude Stranger in Everyday Life* (with Philips and King, 2010); *Punishment and Culture* (2008); and *Why War? The Cultural Logic of Iraq, The Gulf War and Suez* (2005). The book he coauthored with Michael Emmison, *Researching the Visual* (2000), has become one of the standard introductions to visual sociology, and its revised 2nd edition will be published in 2012. His manifold interests include criminology and social theory.

Julia Sonnevend is Doctoral Candidate in Communications at Columbia University. Her dissertation examines news icons of social movements focusing on the role of journalistic narratives in the construction of icons. Bringing together sociology, media studies, art history and literary theory, she aims to construct a theoretical framework for revolutionary icons that can be applied to diverse national and journalistic contexts. Her research interests include social remembrance, media events, theories of performance, space and design, trauma studies, and the intellectual history of media and communication research. She studied law, aesthetics, and German literature in Budapest, Berlin, and New Haven.

Daniel Šuber is Assistant Professor at the University of Luzern, Switzerland, and he taught sociology from 2000–10 at the University of Konstanz, Germany, from which he received his PhD in Sociology in 2006. Since 2007, he has been a research member of the Konstanz Center of Excellence 16 "The Cultural Foundations of Integration." He specialized in the field of social and cultural theory, visual sociology, and sociology of religion. He is coeditor of *Religion and Politics: Cultural Perspectives* (2005) and *Erleben, Erleiden, Erfahren: Zur Konstitution sozialen Sinns jenseits instrumenteller Vernunft* (2008) (in German). He has contributed book chapters on the sociology of knowledge, phenomenological theory, visual sociology in the Balkans, and the history of sociology.

Piotr Sztompka is Professor of Theoretical Sociology at Jagiellonian University in Kraków, Poland. He has taught at numerous universities in the United States, Europe, Latin America and Australia, and held fellowships at Oxford University, SCASSS Uppsala, Wissenschaftskolleg zu Berlin, NIAS at Wassenaar, and Stanford Center for Advanced Study in the Behavioral Sciences. In the years 2002–06 he served as an elected President of the International Sociological Association (ISA). Among his books are: *Society in Action* (1991); *The Sociology of Social Change* (1993); *Trust: a Sociological Theory* (1999); and *Cultural Trauma and Collective Identity* (with Alexander, Eyerman, Giesen, and Smelser (2004). In Poland, his book *Sociology: Analysis of Society* (2005) (in Polish) has become a nationwide bestseller, selling 45,000 copies.

Ian Woodward is Senior Lecturer in cultural sociology in the School of Humanities, and Deputy Director, Griffith Centre for Cultural Research, at Griffith University, Brisbane, Australia. He has research interests in the sociology of consumption, aesthetics and material culture, and in the cultural dimensions of cosmopolitanism. He has published research papers in leading journals such as *Theory, Culture and Society, The British Journal of Sociology, The Sociological Review, Journal of Material Culture*, and *Poetics*. His critical survey of the field of material culture studies, *Understanding Material Culture*, was published by Sage in 2007. With Gavin Kendall and Zlatko Skrbis, he is coauthor of *The Sociology of Cosmopolitanism* (Palgrave, 2009). He is currently an editor of the *Journal of Sociology*.

INDEX